Helping Without Hurting in Africa

FACILITATOR MANUAL

Jonny Kabiswa Kyazze ***and*** **Anthony Sytsma**
with **Brian Fikkert**

Helping Without Hurting in Africa

ISBN 13: 978-1-59452-769-2

ISBN: 1-59452-769-5

Published by Oasis International Ltd, in partnership with The Chalmers Center. To find out more about The Chalmers Center, visit www.chalmers.org.

Oasis International is a ministry devoted to growing discipleship through publishing African voices.

- We ***engage*** Africa's most influential, most relevant, and best communicators for the sake of the gospel.
- We ***cultivate*** local and global partnerships in order to publish and distribute high-quality books and Bibles.
- We ***create*** contextual content that meets the specific needs of Africa, has the power to transform individuals and societies, and gives the church in Africa a global voice.

Oasis is: *Satisfying Africa's Thirst for God's Word*. For more information, go to oasisinternational.com.

Edited by Lisa Brown and Justin Lonas, The Chalmers Center
Cover design: Derek Gyssels
Interior design: Lisa Brown and Justin Lonas, The Chalmers Center

All websites and phone numbers listed herein are accurate at the time of publication, but may change in the future or cease to exist. The listing of website references and resources does not imply publisher endorsement of the site's entire contents. Groups and organizations are listed for informational purposes, and listing does not imply publisher endorsement of their activities.

In consideration of our primary audience, this work uses British English spellings throughout.

We hope you find this resource from The Chalmers Center helpful. Our vision is for local churches to declare and demonstrate to people who are poor that Jesus Christ is making all things new. Our mission is to equip churches to walk alongside people who are poor, breaking the spiritual, social, and material bonds of poverty.

Printed in India.

23 24 25 26 27 BPI 10 9 8 7 6 5 4 3

Helping Without Hurting in Africa

Facilitator Manual

Table of Contents

Helping Without Hurting in Africa

Facilitator Manual

About This Training

About This Training

Welcome to *Helping Without Hurting in Africa*!

As a facilitator of this training, you are preparing to embark on a journey that could change your life, your church, your family, your community, and your country as well. Are you ready?

In this section, you will find:

- An overview and background of the training.
- An introduction to the methods and tools you will use for facilitation.

1. Overview

Helping Without Hurting in Africa is designed to inspire churches, pastors, community leaders, missionaries, development workers, NGOs, government institutions, and donors to foster transformation in their communities. This training teaches a holistic approach, explaining how to preach the gospel through word and deed. It aims at changing people's mind-set and helping them apply biblical principles to care wisely and compassionately for poor people without unintentionally hurting them. Most Christians have a *heart* for poor people, but this training seeks to help Christians also have a *mind* for poor people.[1]

1.1 Background

By God's grace alone, the book *When Helping Hurts* is changing the paradigm of many North American Christians about the most effective ways to alleviate poverty. There is a need for a similar resource for Africa for four reasons:

- **First**, as churches in Africa and other development organisations try to help the poor, we often make the same mistakes as North American churches. We try to solve what is fundamentally a relational problem through the provision of material resources alone—a quick fix approach. We need to understand the true nature of poverty and be equipped with practical tools to alleviate poverty more effectively.

- **Second**, there is great need to work against the inferiority and dependency mind-set among many Christians in Africa with respect to North Americans. When North American missionaries, development workers, and donors come to Africa with feelings of superiority and material definitions of poverty, it results in the pursuit of strategies that undermine local dignity and resource use, thereby contributing to an ongoing cycle of poverty and dependency. Africa could be the wealthiest continent in the world, and people on the African continent need to be empowered to reflect on the blessings, gifts, and abilities that God has given to us. This will stop us from looking only to other countries to solve our problems and help us to challenge foreigners when we see them using unwise methods of fighting poverty.

- **Third**, many North American Christians who have been impacted by *When Helping Hurts* are looking for ways to share this message with us, their brothers and sisters in Africa, and redefine their relationships.

- **Fourth**, Christian leaders in Africa, pastors, and development workers have been looking for materials to use to train their churches and communities, opening them up to new understanding, helping them to see the resources that God has given them, and empowering them to develop their communities on their own without waiting for aid.

This training, *Helping without Hurting in Africa*, produced by the Chalmers Center in the United States, but written by a Ugandan (Jonny) and an American missionary in East Africa (Anthony), is our attempt to help respond to the needs and requests outlined above. Many of us want to help the poor. But we don't always know what to do. This calls for prayer, seeking the guidance of the Holy Spirit, and studying God's word, as well as learning from other Christians. This training will teach important principles about how to help the poor wisely. The content is accumulated from Scripture and Christians throughout history as they have learned and shared what works and what doesn't. We felt a call from God to take what we had learned from so many others, people who have faithfully cared for and worked with the poor over many years, and put it in an accessible format that can be easily reproduced so that this knowledge can spread throughout our beloved continent of Africa.

We have been inspired by the words of Kenyan environmental activist, Wangari Maathai. Her words here help to further make clear the urgent need for this training:

> Africa has been on her knees for too long, whether during the dehumanizing slave trade, under the colonial yoke, begging for aid from the international community, paying now-illegitimate debts, or praying for miracles. At both the top and the bottom, all people on the African continent must change the mind-set that affects many colonized peoples everywhere. They must believe in themselves again; that they are capable of clearing their own path and forging their own identity; that they have a right to be governed with justice, accountability, and transparency; that they can honour and practise their cultures and make them relevant to today's needs; and that they no longer need to be indebted—financially, intellectually, and spiritually—to those who once governed them. They must rise up and walk....[2]
>
> It cannot be overemphasized: people on the African continent must decide to manage their natural resources responsibly and accountably, agree to share them more equitably, and use them for the good of fellow Africans. Otherwise, they will continue to allow outside forces to seduce or bully their governments into arrangements that allow those resources to be removed from the continent for a pittance. It is for the people on the African continent to determine whether they will work hard to build up their own talents and abilities, strengthen their democracies and institutions of governance, and foster their peoples's creativity and industry. Or, instead, whether they will continue to nurture a culture of dependency.[3]

We believe that what Maathai was passionately calling for can only be accomplished by our

Lord Jesus Christ, who not only saves people from their sins, but is right now working out his good rule and kingdom in this world. Only in Jesus can we hope for people on the African continent to know God personally and experience his love and eternal life. Only through the work of Jesus can we hope that the people of Africa will realise that they have been made in the image of God and have been given skills, resources, and creativity by God that they can use to develop themselves and their communities without feeling inferior and helpless. Only through the work of Jesus can we hope for success in our struggles against war, corruption, environmental degradation, and the many other challenges that Africa is facing today. This training will help churches and leaders embrace their calling to preach the gospel and live as citizens of Jesus's kingdom in this broken world.

1.2 Two Resources

Two Manuals have been published as part of this training: The **Facilitator Manual** and the **Participant Manual**.

The Facilitator Manual can be ordered directly from Amazon's website but is also available at various bookstores and Bible societies in Africa. The price is relatively low to enable more people to access it.

The Participant Manual is for participants attending the training. They will be able to follow along with the lectures and activities and will write down their answers to discussion questions in the manual. In addition, there will be specific activities and Bible studies in each lesson that the participants will take home and implement within their own congregations, communities, or teams.

To ensure that the manual gets into the hands of as many leaders as possible without people being hindered by financial constraints, the Participant Manual can be freely downloaded and printed/photocopied from the Chalmers Center—visit **www.chalmers.org/HWHAfrica**.

As a facilitator, you can download the Participant Manual and print the number of copies you need for your participants, and staple or bind the manuals as you see fit. We encourage you to have each participant pay for the photocopies. This is an important step and part of the mind-set change the training aims for. It helps the participants to realise that they are made in the image of God, that they can do something to help themselves, that God has given them resources, and that they can pay something to participate in the training. In this way, the payment for the training can be done in partnership; the facilitator provides for his or her own expenses and a Facilitator Manual for him or herself, but participants can pay a very small fee for the paper and photocopies they are being given. They will then feel ownership of their manual and their own learning and development, and are therefore much more likely to utilise and value what they learn from the training. In certain extreme circumstances, a facilitator could pay for the photocopies himself or herself, but then the participants should still be encouraged to pay for something themselves, such as their own food and accommodation. In all cases, however, **we strongly discourage the practice of paying participants a "sitting fee"** for being willing to attend the training. This practice goes against the principles we are trying to teach. If participants are not willing to take part in the training without a sitting fee, then it is probably better to spend your time training others who are willing. Once people become aware of the impact of the training, some people might change their expectation and come to the training without needing a sitting fee.

- It is recommended that the facilitator keeps one copy of the Participant Manual for him or herself. This way the facilitator can keep both the Facilitator Manual and the Participant Manual open and out during the training so that he can see what notes are included in the Participant Manual, and guide participants to the page they should be on.

- Also, the facilitator should notice that all text in the lessons with a lightly shaded background, like this paragraph, is intended to be communicated or lectured to the participants in the training. **This text does not have to be read word for word. The facilitator is allowed and encouraged to paraphrase the content in his or her own words.** The facilitator should have the material internalised so that he or she is speaking from the heart and from his or her understanding, rather than simply standing and reading from the manual. Other text in a lesson without this shaded background is instruction only for the facilitator about what he or she should be doing.

1.3 Training Objectives

The goal of this training is to transform the mind-sets of Christian leaders in Africa and equip them to wisely help materially poor people in their churches and communities. This is not an easy task, but the result will benefit the rest of society. As Nelson Mandela, former president of South Africa, said: "One of the most difficult things is not to change society but to change yourself."[4]

We believe that as leaders in Africa begin by changing their own mind-sets and behaviour in the ways they try to help the poor, this will in turn begin to change the rest of African societies as they lead by example, and as they lead their organisations and church ministries in a more effective way.

Expected Outcomes of the Training

As a result of walking through this course, we hope participants will:

- Grow in their relationships with God, others, self, and the rest of creation.
- Gain a new focus on the Kingdom of God in their ministries.
- Renew their love and compassion for the materially poor.
- Obtain knowledge about how to help the materially poor and materially poor communities wisely.
- Be equipped to go and teach these development principles to their churches and communities.
- Go home after the training is over, and put into practise the "Take-Home" activities of each lesson.

- Begin working on their own development with their churches and communities, using their own resources, even before receiving help from missionaries, foreign donors, or NGOs (non-government organisations).

The training should allow fruitful networking and collaboration among pastors, churches, and organisations in their work of fighting poverty, through discussion and interaction during the training. Hopefully, a few participants, having been trained, will go out and facilitate more *Helping Without Hurting in Africa* trainings to benefit other leaders and communities.

1.4 Target Audience

Workshop participants will come from a wide range of institutions with different experiences. The primary audience of this training guide is Christian leaders in Africa including pastors, church leaders, missionaries, government workers, NGO workers, politicians, community leaders, business owners and any other interested groups. Foreign missionaries could also be welcomed as participants. Some of the most engaging discussions in the training come when there is a mixture of people from African nations and foreigners discussing these principles together.

There are already many very effective biblically-based curricula that target the materially poor in Africa, and help them to identify their resources and develop. Many of these are simple enough to be of great help even to those who are uneducated. This training is different. This material seeks to equip leaders who are trying to help the materially poor. The hope is that these leaders can change the way their ministries run to become more effective in helping the poor in their communities according to biblical principles. The last lesson of the Facilitator Manual includes references to biblically-based curricula that these leaders can use to train materially poor people.

Participants should have a knowledge of English in order to make use of the Participant Manual. However, in cases where there is a skilled facilitator who knows English and also the local language, the facilitator could attempt to train others in the local language. Though this is not ideal, it would be possible in cases where the participants do not know English. This would mean doing the training without Participant Manuals, and the facilitator would have to translate and write down all the discussion questions and many of the notes, so that the participants could write down notes and questions in their own notebooks throughout the training. It is our desire that, in the future, God may raise up others to translate these manuals into their native tongues, in partnership with the Chalmers Center.

Though we hope that as many people as possible will encounter this material, we recognise that not every leader who completes this training will actually have the ability or opportunity to facilitate another *Helping Without Hurting in Africa* training themselves. Most participants who get trained will not become facilitators, and that is okay. However, every participant will have a chance to go home and teach certain principles and activities to their churches, teams, and families through the take-home activities.

The ideal facilitator is an African who has already completed the full *Helping Without*

Hurting in Africa training, and received the certificate of completion (see section 2.1 for more information on certification). Because there is so much emphasis on the local church in the training, the most fitting facilitators might be pastors, church leaders, or church-based development workers. Besides having completed the training themselves, facilitators should also have a good understanding of the information and principles in the curriculum, good knowledge of English, and some past experience in working with the materially poor. Most importantly, facilitators should be people who practise what they preach. They should be people who love and care for the poor, and who are caring for the materially poor in wise ways according to the principles of this curriculum.

Christian missionaries from countries outside Africa could also make good facilitators. We emphasize caution here, however. Foreign missionaries should have read and carefully studied the entire book *When Helping Hurts*, or they should have completed the *Helping without Hurting in Africa* training themselves and received the certificate. They should have at least a little experience working with materially poor people in their own country and also in the African country in which they want to facilitate. They should be familiar with the host culture and, hopefully, have lived for some years on the African continent. For short-term missionaries, we emphasize even more caution. They should have the above qualifications and, in addition, have a long-term relationship with the people they plan to train.

Having foreigners as facilitators can at times unintentionally support the notion that foreigners are superior to people from Africa, or that the people of Africa always need to be dependent on foreigners for facilitation and training. These are false ideas that this curriculum seeks to change. Foreign missionaries should not assume they are capable of facilitating just because they are missionaries. In addition, foreign missionaries or foreign development workers would do well to make sure they are trying to work themselves out of a job. A missionary facilitator should do the training together with another leader from Africa if possible. Then, once a training finishes, the facilitator should encourage and help the participants to go and train other groups, rather than doing every one of the trainings him or herself. A foreign facilitator might also help participants gain access to purchase Facilitator Manuals from other countries in case they are not available in local bookstores.

2. Methodology

The methodology used is highly participatory, following effective adult education principles. The training utilises both local knowledge and local resources. The format consists of lecture, large group discussion, small group discussion, and miscellaneous activities. The recommended training group size is around 20-40 people, and then around 5-6 people per group for small group discussions. Large groups of 50-70 people may be accommodated and still be successful, but groups larger than this may not be effective because people will not be able to participate as much.

Participants will follow along in their manuals and take notes. Bible passages will also be read, preferably by volunteer participants, and the facilitator is expected to summarise what the passage says. The facilitator should try to promote discussion, ask questions, receive questions, and ask for participant comments to keep participants stimulated and engaged. The facilitator should allow questions or comments at any time, but if necessary he or she can tell participants that the question will be dealt with more fully in a later lesson, and then keep moving forward through the lesson.

For the large group discussions, the facilitator should monitor the time closely and allow various people to speak, instead of letting certain people monopolise the conversation. Most of the large group discussions will have to be cut short in order to keep the training moving forward. During small group discussions, the groups should try to stay within the same room or area, so that the facilitator can roam freely between the groups and give instructions to all the groups at once as needed. The facilitator should be listening in, guiding the groups, rephrasing the questions in a different way if they are confused, and monitoring the time left that the group has for discussion. It is important that the groups receive enough time to discuss the questions, but it is also important that the facilitator keeps each group moving at a good pace so that each group can finish the questions within the allotted time. If the participants are agreeable to having a longer training, the facilitator can freely increase the length of time for each lesson, going beyond the suggested time allotments outlined in the manual (see section 2.2). But please be sure that spending a long time on certain discussions does not force you to completely skip other content in the lessons.

The facilitator will have to divide people into small groups. The easiest way to do this is to figure out how many groups you will have in total, by looking at the number of participants, remembering that you want 5 or 6 per group. Then you can give each person a number. If there are 6 groups, you give each person a 1, 2, 3, 4, 5, or 6. All the ones go together, all the twos, etc. If you would like, these can be the same people they will meet with the whole day for small group discussion, or you can give them a new group each time you break out into small groups.

The facilitator should have a whiteboard, chalkboard, flip chart, or large sheets of paper to tape on the wall. This way the facilitator can write down key terms, notes, and diagrams to assist the participants in their understanding during lectures. The facilitator has freedom to write down whatever notes they would like, but at times in the Facilitator Manual, there will be specific instructions for what the facilitator should write on the papers or board. The facilitator will also explain the take-home activities at the end of each lesson, encouraging the participants to take those activities seriously and to really try to do them when they get home from the training. Additionally, the facilitator should point out the "Further Reflection" section at the end of most of the lessons, guiding the participants to read and reflect on these pages at home.

The Participant Manual may be photocopied freely by the participants and used in order to share information with others. The Chalmers Center requests that no one should try to facilitate a *Helping Without Hurting in Africa* training without a Facilitator Manual, and that the Facilitator Manual **should not be photocopied**. As a facilitator, be ready to guide your participants on how they could obtain a Facilitator Manual.

This training is most effective when it can be contextualised for the people, location, and culture of your training group. In order to achieve this, you, as the facilitator, should think of stories and examples from your own country and communities that are similar to the stories that are shared in the lessons. In some cases it would be good to substitute a local story of your own instead of the story that is given to you in the manual. This will be more meaningful to the people you are training. Just ensure that your own story illustrates the same principle that the story in the lesson is illustrating.

2.1 Training Timeline

There are 20 lessons in this curriculum. To complete the whole curriculum, we suggest that you will need approximately **39 hours** of class time, which includes both the time for the lectures and the discussions.

However, the first eight lessons teach the most important principles of the curriculum and can be used as a short stand-alone course. Therefore, some training groups may decide to complete only Lessons 1-8, and conclude with testimonies and evaluations at that time. These groups will get important learning, but they will not qualify for the certificate of completion for the entire curriculum. Training groups that complete Lessons 1-8 are also free to choose other specific lessons from the rest of the curriculum to complete as they have time and interest for. While the time length of the lessons will vary from group to group, we recommend that you plan for around **16 hours** total for completing this first section consisting of Lessons 1-8.

We encourage most training groups to finish all 20 lessons in sequence. This will give the participants better understanding and allow them to engage with more advanced principles. The facilitator, together with the participants, can decide how to schedule time to cover all of the lessons. But we recommend choosing from the following options:

1. One Lesson per Week

In this format, the training group comes together once a week for 2-3 hours to complete only one lesson. This works well when the participants already meet together regularly in a school group, Bible study group, or church ministry or when the participants all live nearby each other. The participants and facilitator would meet together on a continuous basis. Though this will mean the curriculum will take a longer time to finish, there are several advantages:

- The participants do not need to take time off their work for the training, and can simply meet during an afternoon or evening each week.
- In many contexts, this format will allow people to save money by not needing accommodation or food during the training event.
- The participants will be able to discuss the questions for as long as they want and take as much time as they need to finish all the lessons. The material may be better learned and digested when the training is not rushed.

2. Multiple Day Training Sessions

In this format, the facilitator and participants come together for several days to complete a number of lessons at one time. This format works best when the participants do not live close to one another, or when the facilitator is coming from another region or country. The number of days and training sessions that will be required will differ from group to group. Some training groups may enjoy a relaxed schedule of several days with many meal and tea breaks. Other groups may decide to meet for long hours each day in order to finish quickly. Please do not try to finish all 20 lessons in a single week as you would have to skip a lot of content and the participants would not absorb the material well. Whether you choose option A or option B below, plan for time at the beginning of each new training session to review what was covered the previous training session, especially if training sessions are divided by several months. Here are two recommended ways to finish the curriculum by doing multiple day training sessions:

A. **Three training sessions of 2 days each.** The three training sessions could be scheduled over three months, or stretched out over six months. You could take longer than the suggested allotments per lesson, but the structure might look like this:

	Training Session 1	
Day 1	Lesson 1 - Lesson 4 (1st half)	7.75 Hours
Day 2	Lesson 4 (2nd half) - Lesson 8	7.75 Hours
	Training Session 2	
Day 1	Lesson 9 - Lesson 11	6.25 Hours
Day 2	Lesson 12 - Lesson 14	6 Hours
	Training Session 3	
Day 1	Lesson 15 - Lesson 17	6 Hours
Day 2	Lesson 18 - Lesson 20	5 Hours

Please note that Lesson 1- Lesson 8 functions as the beginning unit of the course, and so it is best to cover this cohesive section in one training session. However, this first section can take longer than two days for some training groups. You can see that it needs more hours than the other sessions. In order to have plenty of time for breaks throughout your training days, we recommend that you plan two and a half days for the first training session. Then you could plan one and a half days for the second training session, and one and a half days for the third training session.

B. **Two training sessions of 2.5 or 3 days each.** Half of the lessons would be covered in the first training session, and half would be covered in the second training session. You could take longer than the suggested allotments per lesson, but the structure might look like this:

	Training Session 1	
Day 1	Lesson 1 - Lesson 3	6.75 Hours
Day 2	Lesson 4 - Lesson 6	6.25 Hours
Day 3	Lesson 7 - Lesson 9	4.5 Hours

	Training Session 2	
Day 1	Lesson 10 - Lesson 13	8.75 Hours
Day 2	Lesson 14 - Lesson 17	7.5 Hours
Day 3	Lesson 18 - Evaluation	5 Hours

3. College Course

We believe *Helping Without Hurting in Africa* could fulfil the curriculum requirements for some development or ministry courses in universities or colleges. The facilitator could either provide the students with photocopies of the Participant Manual, or have the students pay for photocopying the Participant Manual as their textbook for the course.

Participants are expected to attend and complete all of the 20 lessons to qualify for a certificate at the end of the training. The facilitator will record the names of all the participants that have fully attended all the lessons. The facilitator will submit these names to the Chalmers Center (HWHAfrica@chalmers.org), which will then process the certificates and email them to the facilitator for printing. Certification will ensure quality control of the trainings. The only people facilitating should be people who have been trained and certified themselves. In addition, the certificate is beneficial in many cultures to give evidence of the learning the participant has received, for ministry or work purposes. Last, a certificate is something a participant can be proud of, as it is a reminder of the education they were willing to pay for themselves in order to equip them to better serve others. To take records for certificate purposes, the facilitator should place someone in charge of keeping attendance, including marking if people come very late. The facilitator can show grace and have some flexibility, but people are generally required to attend all lessons, including not coming late, in order to get the certificate.

2.2 Training Outline and Structure

Each lesson is estimated to take about two hours, though lesson lengths and structure vary. A two-hour lesson could look like this:

- Large Group Opening Discussion – 10 minutes
- Interactive Lecture and Activities – 80 minutes
- Small Group Discussion – 30 minutes

Curriculum Outline

Lesson 1: Introduction and Opening Exercise	1.75	hours
Lesson 2: Why did Jesus Come to Earth?	2	hours
Lesson 3: What is Poverty?	3	hours
Lesson 4: Broken Relationships in Africa	2	hours
Lesson 5: Fighting Poverty through Reconciliation	1.75	hours
Lesson 6: Relief, Rehabilitation, and Development	2.5	hours
Lesson 7: Asset-Based Community Development	1.5	hours

Lesson 8: Opening Exercise Evaluation	1	hour
For groups stopping here:		
Feedback, Testimonies, Evaluation and Prayer	(30 minutes)	
Lesson 9: Working for God's Glory	2	hours
Lesson 10: Worldview Transformation	2	hours
Lesson 11: Broken Systems	2.25	hours
Lesson 12: The Prosperity Gospel	2	hours
Lesson 13: African Culture and Money	2.5	hours
Lesson 14: What Causes Change in Someone's Life?	1.5	hours
Lesson 15: Participation of the Community	1.5	hour
Lesson 16: Church Benevolence Ministry	2	hours
Lesson 17: Urban Ministry: Opportunities and Challenges	2.5	hours
Lesson 18: Mission Trips within Africa	1.5	hours
Lesson 19: Foreigners, Missionaries and Sponsors	2	hours
Lesson 20: Seed Projects and Further Resources	1	hour
Feedback, Testimonies, Evaluation and Prayer	30 minutes	
Total =	**38.75**	**hours**

2.3 Workshop Requirements

The following supplies will be required of facilitators for each training:

- **Facilitator Manual.**
- **Photocopied Participant Manual** for each participant.
- **Flip chart stand** and **paper**, **chalkboard**, or **whiteboard** for facilitator.
- **Large sheets of paper** (flip chart size, but can be simple newsprint)—This will be needed for group activities even if the facilitator is using a whiteboard.
- A couple of packs of simple **markers**, in multiple colours, for both the facilitator and for small group activities.
- **Masking tape**.
- **The Bible**.
- **Participant sign-in sheet**. Have the participants write their full name clearly (as they want it to appear on their certificates), the name of their church or organisation, their phone number, and their email address if they have one.
- **Name-tags** for the participants. These are not absolutely necessary, but they are helpful, especially in large trainings where participants are coming from different places and do not know each other already.

Be creative with materials. The authors of this curriculum have even used big sheets of paper taped to trees or to a vehicle. **Do what works for your group and what is within your financial means!**

Participants are expected to come with their own notebooks, pens, and Bible. The participants are expected to pay for their own meals and refreshments. Refreshments such as snacks and tea throughout the day can be taken during the small group discussions to save time. The facilitator should coordinate with the host church or conference hall to figure out how the food will be prepared and how much each participant should pay for it. In local settings, participants could go home for lunch during the meal break and then return to the training in the afternoon.

2.4 Workshop Logistics

It is the facilitator's responsibility to ensure that all logistical arrangements are made for the training. This might involve doing it yourself or confirming that someone else has made the necessary arrangements associated with the training. Always double check all arrangements in advance.

Ensure that the seating arrangement allows for free participation and discussion. A U-shape or a circle is ideal, and with movable chairs. The location should have enough space to allow people to divide into small groups. Groups should be able to be shaded from the hot African sun, and also close enough to each other that the facilitator can roam freely between groups and speak to them all at once if necessary.

We gently want to discourage the idea that you need an expensive hotel or conference hall to run this workshop. Local churches are best, or sitting under a tree, etc. It is important that participants don't get the idea that they cannot go out and teach on their own without a lot of money. **Keep it simple!**

2.5 Tips for Facilitation

The following tips are offered to support you in your role as facilitator:

- **Be flexible**. Plan your lessons in advance but be ready to change or adapt to meet the needs of the group.
- **Arrive early** each day to make sure that everything is prepared. This is also a good time to interact with participants. Arriving early will also set a good example for participants so that together, everyone can learn to avoid being late, and learn to be good stewards of the time that God has given us.
- Consider **beginning each day of training with prayer** or a worship song.
- **Allow time** for meaningful discussions and sharing of ideas because that is the best way for adults to learn.
- **Stop frequently** to ask questions or review to make sure people are following along and understanding. If people don't respond to a question immediately, give them some time to think about it before you speak again.

- At the beginning of each new day of training, it is a good idea to spend 10 minutes **reviewing the main principles** of the previous day.
- Ensure that you **strike a balance** between keeping the training moving along and giving people time to express themselves. It is alright to say, "Okay, I will take one more question" or "Just one more comment before we go on."
- It's important to **have knowledge of the group** and their objectives in advance of the session, including their issues and concerns.
- **Think through the issues** or problems that may arise in the facilitated session and know how you will respond.
- Ensure that all participants have a **common understanding of the purpose** and intended results of the session.
- **An introductory exercise** is often advisable as it breaks the ice and allows you to develop rapport with the group.
- Remember that your job is to keep the process on track, and **not to dominate discussion** or make decisions for the group.
- You can help participants think through issues by simply **asking questions as a neutral party**. If people respond to questions with a simple "yes" or "no" answer, then ask them to explain their answer.
- Consider **gently calling on certain people** to get their opinion if they have been very quiet, even if they did not raise their hand. But give them the option of not speaking if they do not have anything to say. For example, "Peter, we haven't heard anything from you yet, would you like to comment on this?"
- You must **trust that the group will take responsibility** for its own learning and problem-solving. Your role is to provide a structure or support for doing this.
- **Be a good listener**.
- When people have been sitting too long, have people **stand up and do some quick exercise** to get the blood flowing again and to keep people awake.
- It is okay to say, "I don't know" when asked a question. **Poverty is an extremely complex topic**. None of us know everything about it. It is also okay to say, "I'm not really sure, but I guess my opinion would be..."
- **Feedback is important**, so ask for it, listen to it carefully, and see if you can learn from it.
- Please feel free to reach out to the **authors** via email with questions and testimonies. **Jonny**: jonny.kabiswa@chalmers.org **Anthony**: anthony.sytsma@chalmers.org

Helping Without Hurting in Africa

Facilitator Manual

Lesson 1: Introduction

Lesson 1: Introduction

In this lesson, you will find:

- Tools and messages to introduce the training to participants.
- Expected outcomes of the training.
- An outline of the lessons in this curriculum.
- Statistics on poverty and wealth in Africa.
- Opening exercises.

Lesson Objectives:

- To Introduce the training to participants.
- To complete an opening exercise to be reviewed in Lesson 8.

Time Length: 1.75 Hours

As you begin facilitating the lessons in this curriculum, you will be given some suggestions on how to make the lessons flow well.

For this lesson, you as the facilitator should pray or ask one of the participants to pray as you begin the training.

Introductions (10 Minutes)

Start with the facilitators introducing themselves and then move on to the participants.

This can be done by asking participants to say their name, what they do, and where they have come from. Alternatively, the facilitator can tell the participants to pair up with another person they have never met or are not familiar with. While together, they should each answer the following:

- "What is your name?"
- "What work do you do?"
- "Are you ministering to the poor in some way?"
- "What do you expect from this training?"

After everyone has introduced themselves to a partner, you can have each participant stand up and briefly tell their name and where they come from to the whole group. Spend a minute in the large group to hear a few of the expectations that participants shared with their partners.

Workshop Logistics (10 Minutes)

Take attendance, unless you have done so already when the participants arrived.

Discuss fees, payments for manuals and food, location of washrooms, and meal times if you have not done so already. Remind participants to bring pen, paper, and their Bible with them each day.

Decide as a group on other rules and guidelines if you need them. For example, you could discuss arrival times, appointing a time keeper, appointing a person to take attendance, consequences for coming late, cell phones needing to be turned off, respecting others's opinions, etc.

Explain to the group about the two manuals:
The **Participant Manual** can be photocopied for the participants. But the **Facilitator Manual** can only be purchased, and may not be photocopied. You should not try to facilitate this training without the Facilitator Manual. The Facilitator Manual can be purchased through Amazon.com or in select bookstores in Africa. Talk to me after the training for more details on how to get the Facilitator Manual. During the training, follow along in your Participant Manual and take notes throughout the lectures and group discussions.

Each lesson generally consists of large group discussion and lecture, followed by small group discussion. Throughout each lecture, raise your hand whenever you want to give a comment or ask a question. At the end of each lesson, I will number you off into groups of about 5 people so that you can go and discuss the small group questions.

Overview of the Training (5 Minutes)

This training curriculum—*Helping Without Hurting in Africa*—is designed to inspire churches, pastors, and community leaders to foster transformation in their communities. In this training, you will learn the importance of preaching the gospel in both word and deed. Hopefully we will all leave with a changed mind-set, thinking about poverty differently, and learning new skills and biblical principles so that we can all help the poor in our communities effectively, not only with compassion but also with wisdom. Hopefully you already have a heart for the poor, but this training will help you to have a mind for the poor as well.[1]

Read the quotation from Wangari Maathai to the group. It is found on page 7 (section 1.1) of the Facilitator Manual.

Tell the group:
We believe that what Maathai was passionately calling for can only be accomplished by our Lord Jesus Christ, who not only saves people from their sins, but is right now working out his good rule and kingdom in this world. Only in Jesus can we hope for people on the African

continent to know God personally and experience his love and eternal life. Only through the work of Jesus can we hope that the people of Africa will realise that they have been made in the image of God, and have been given skills, resources, and creativity by God that they can use to develop themselves and their communities without feeling inferior and helpless. Only through the work of Jesus can we hope for success in our struggles against war, corruption, environmental degradation, and the many other challenges that Africa is facing today. This training will help churches and leaders to embrace their calling to preach the gospel and live as citizens of Jesus's kingdom in this broken world.

Training Objectives (1 Minute)

The facilitator will present the workshop objectives and relate them to the participants's expectations. The aim is to illustrate how the objectives will meet their expectations. Expectations that will not be covered by this workshop should be pointed out.

The goal of this training is to transform the mind-sets of Christian leaders in Africa, like you, and equip you to wisely help poor people in your churches and communities. This is not an easy task. As Nelson Mandela, former president of South Africa, said, "One of the most difficult things is not to change society but to change yourself."[2]

In most settings, it is suitable to simply and quickly summarise the outcomes and tell the participants that they can read the outcomes for themselves.

Expected Outcomes of the Training

As a result of walking through this course, we hope you will:

- Grow in your relationships with God, others, self, and the rest of creation.
- Gain a new focus on the Kingdom of God in your ministries.
- Renew your love and compassion for the materially poor.
- Obtain knowledge about how to help the materially poor and materially poor communities wisely.
- Be equipped to go and teach these development principles to your churches and communities.
- Go home after the training is over, and put into practise the "Take-Home" activities for each lesson.
- Begin working on your own development with your churches and communities, using your own resources, even before receiving help from missionaries, foreign donors, or NGOs.

Hopefully, a few of you, having been trained, will go out and facilitate more *Helping Without Hurting in Africa* trainings to benefit other leaders and communities. Not everyone will have the capacity to facilitate this training, but every participant will have a chance to go home and teach principles and activities to their churches, teams, and families through the take-home activities.

Course Timeline (5 Minutes)

Explain to the participants that there are a total of 20 lessons in this curriculum. Give them an overview of your training plan including how many lessons you plan to go through together and how many training sessions you will need to complete those lessons. Explain to them that they will receive a certificate from the Chalmers Center for completing this curriculum only if they complete all 20 lessons. Make sure that they understand a certificate is required for anyone who wants to facilitate *Helping Without Hurting in Africa* with another training group.

Tell the participants that they can look over the curriculum outline of all the lessons. Read to the participants only the lesson titles. They can read the descriptions of the lessons themselves briefly, or study them more carefully at home or during a break.

Lesson 1: Introduction **1.75 hours**

Lesson 2: Why did Jesus Come to Earth? **2 hours**
This lesson will give us a biblical and theological foundation for how to think about the role of the church in development and fighting poverty.

Lesson 3: What is Poverty? **3 hours**
This lesson will take us deeper into understanding what poverty really is, and we will learn about different types of poverty.

Lesson 4: Broken Relationships in Africa **2 hours**
In this lesson, we will look at how the different types of poverty are present in Africa and how they are challenging our communities today.

Lesson 5:Fighting Poverty through Reconciliation **1.75 hours**
This lesson will look at what success means in fighting poverty, what we are aiming for. We will begin to see what we should be doing to fight poverty.

Lesson 6: Relief, Rehabilitation, and Development **2.5 hours**
This lesson will look at the different types of responses we should give to different types of needs. Especially, we will learn when to give money and when not to give.

Lesson 7: Asset-Based Community Development **1.5 hours**
In this lesson, we will learn how to encourage people to see the resources and abilities that God has given to them.

Lesson 8: Opening Exercise Evaluation **1 hour**
This lesson will review the exercise that we are about to do here in the introduction.

Feedback, Testimonies, Evaluation, and Prayer **30 minutes**
(Evaluation and Testimonies—For groups stopping here)

Lesson 9: Working for God's Glory **2 hours**
This lesson will look at the importance of work and business in overcoming poverty.

Lesson 10: Worldview Transformation **2 hours**
This lesson will examine the importance of our beliefs and attitudes in overcoming poverty.

Lesson 11: Broken Systems **2.25 hours**
In this lesson, we will discuss how to change broken systems that keep people trapped in poverty.

Lesson 12: The Prosperity Gospel **2 hours**
This lesson will explain why the prosperity gospel is false and how it harms materially poor people.

Lesson 13: African Culture and Money **2.5 hours**
In this lesson, we will compare the way our cultures view and handle money with the principles we have learning in this curriculum.

Lesson 14: What Causes Change in Someone's Life **1.5 hours**
This lesson will examine what causes someone to make a change in their life. We will also study Bible passages and determine if it is ever right to withhold money from someone who asks.

Lesson 15: Participation of the Community **1.5 hours**
This lesson will explain the importance of community participation in the process of development.

Lesson 16: Church Benevolence Ministry **2 hours**
In this lesson, we will learn how to set up a benevolence ministry at our churches, and what policies we should put in place to respond to poor people in our church and community.

Lesson 17: Urban Ministry: Opportunities and Challenges **2.5 hours**
In this lesson, we will look at the current urbanisation in Africa and the opportunities and challenges it brings to our church ministries.

Lesson 18: Mission Trips within Africa **1.5 hours**
This lesson will examine how to help without hurting as our churches send teams on trips to other communities in order to preach the gospel and/or respond to the needs of the poor.

Lesson 19: Foreigners, Missionaries and Sponsors **2 hours**

In this lesson, we will discuss the complexities and misunderstandings involved in our relationships to foreigners in Africa, especially foreigners acting as donors to our governments, NGOs, or churches.

Lesson 20: Seed Projects and Further Resources **1 hour**

This last lesson will encourage us to take practical action to apply what we have learned from this curriculum in our communities. Possible next steps and programs will be suggested.

Feedback, Testimonies, Evaluation, and Prayer **30 minutes**

Total = 38.5 hours

Statistics about Poverty in Africa (10 Minutes)

Participants are able to read these statistics themselves, so you do not have to read every one out loud. Read a few of them of your choice. If you read all of them, participants will become bored and it will take too long. Alternatively, you can give the participants 30 seconds to read a few of them silently to themselves or you can appoint volunteers to read a few of them aloud to the group. Any statistics the participants do not read during Lesson 1 can be read during a break or at home.

Listen to these statistics about poverty in Africa today. First, there is actually some good news. God has been working through his people and changes have been taking place. According to the World Bank report from 2016,[3] it was noted that there was a decline of people in extreme poverty in Africa, from 57 percent in 1990 to 43 percent in 2012. This is an amazing improvement! Specifically, we can see:

- GDP in Africa is increasing at nearly 4% a year, higher than the world average of about 3% per year.[4]
- Life expectancy has increased in Africa. In 2013 compared to 2000, life expectancy increased by 6.2 years per person on average.[5]
- Between 1995 and 2012, adult literacy rates in Africa increased by 4 percent.[6]
- We can all see the ways people on the African continent are utilising the new technologies of the Internet and cell phones for education, communication, and development.
- Despite all of these good changes, however, poverty in Africa persists. Sub-Saharan Africa remains the poorest region in the world.[7] It is unacceptable that 43% of the entire population lives in extreme poverty, which is measured as living on less than $1.90 USD per person per day.[8]

- It is also discouraging that this poverty remains despite over $1 trillion USD in development aid having been transferred to the African continent from rich countries in the last fifty years.[9] While this aid has helped a lot in certain cases, it has not always been given wisely nor used wisely.

- Only 25% of people in Africa have access to an improved water source.[10]

- There is great inequality in Africa. The 10 richest individuals in Africa possess wealth equivalent to the wealth of the poorest half of the population.[11]

- HIV remains a serious problem in Africa. In 2012, 1.1 million people in the region died of AIDS—almost four times as many as in the rest of world combined (about 300,000).[12]

- Malaria is another serious problem. The U.N. Millennium Project has calculated that a child in Africa dies from malaria every 30 seconds, or about 3,000 each day.[13]

- Since 2010, violence has been on the rise in Africa, due to civil war, terrorism, and political unrest. There are four times more violent events currently than in the 1990s.[14]

- Unfortunately, all this violence and war has not been helped much by aid from other countries. About 40 percent of Africa's military spending is financed by misused aid.[15]

- Many nations in Africa are also suffering because of huge debt burdens that they owe to rich nations. Because of debt interest, and in some cases because of corrupt rulers, many African nations find it impossible to pay off these loans.

- In the last 50 years, there has been real change in Africa. By certain measures, there has been a decrease in poverty. But many challenges still remain. There is still a lot more work to do, and we need to do the work in better and more effective ways than we have done in the past.

Tell the participants to stay in their place but to pair up with one person seated next to them. Tell them to discuss these questions with each other for three to five minutes.

1. **We have looked at statistics from Africa as a continent, but what good things are happening in your community? How are people developing or overcoming poverty?**

2. **What challenges of poverty remain in your community?**

3. **Do you think you and your church are doing enough to help poor people in your church and community?**

After the discussion, conclude this section with these ideas:

Clearly God has been working in Africa and good things are happening, but many challenges remain. We put our hope in Christ, that he will keep working in this world, building his kingdom, and he will work through us to make a difference in the lives of the people of our churches and communities.

Opening Exercise—Small Groups (40 Minutes)

Explain to the participants that this small group opening exercise is a way for us to learn from our mistakes as we try to help the poor. The participants will go into groups, and each group will make a plan to help people in a specific situation. In Lesson 8, the plan will be reviewed and analysed. It will be very helpful for learning and applying the principles of the course, as participants will be able to see what they did well in their plan, and what they did not do well. It is a helpful way to learn from our mistakes, without actually hurting real people through those mistakes.

As a facilitator, choose one of these scenarios that you think fits your group's context. Only choose one that you think would be the most helpful. The Participant Manual includes the various scenarios, so the participants can simply circle the one you choose. The questions that the participants need to answer are the same for every scenario. All the participants should discuss the same scenario that you have chosen, as having different groups discussing different scenarios will make things very complicated when it comes to reviewing this exercise.

- **Scenario 1**—You must plan how to help the **beggars** in your city. One of the pastors in your city recently preached about giving to the poor, and many people in the church were convicted and wanted to do more to help the poor. Particularly, members of your church have felt a burden to help the beggars who they always see in the market. Up to this point, the church members have mostly ignored the beggars and avoided them, but a few church members sometimes give them some coins. The beggars beg for food while sitting on the ground. Some have physical disabilities while others seem healthy. Many of them are old. Your church really wants to give generously and help them.

- **Scenario 2**—You must plan how to help the **widows** in your village community. A church member recently announced her opinion that your church should be doing more to assist the widows in the church. The other church members agreed, and added that the church should also at least do something small for the widows in the wider community who don't belong to the church. Many of the widows in the community are struggling, even though the cultural expectation is that their children and relatives are supposed to be taking care of them. Some very elderly widows are struggling, and some widows with small children lost their husbands at a young age.

- **Scenario 3**—You must plan how to help **street children** in your city. Street children have been spending their time near your church. On Sunday, as people are coming to church, they beg for money and food from church members as they walk and drive to church. This annoys the church members very much. At times, the street children have even written graffiti on the church building. All the church members have agreed that the street children have become a problem, so something must be done. The church leaders have suggested that the church tries to love and care for them rather than calling for the police to intervene. The church members agreed to try.

The questions in the box below will guide the participants while working on the scenario you have chosen. Note that they are already in the Participant Manual. Before you have the groups begin to discuss and work, read through these questions and make sure everyone understands them. A group of five people may have people from five different churches or cities. They should try to come up with answers that are general enough to work for all of them. It is a hypothetical scenario and the participants should imagine that they are all making a ministry plan together from one church.

1. **How will you *plan and prepare*, before making a final decision on what to do?**
2. **What *money or resources* will you give away?**
3. **Besides giving resources away, *what other things will you do* as part of this ministry?**
4. **Which *people* from your church will take part in this ministry?**
5. ***How* will you put your ministry plans into action?**

The participants will be divided into small groups of 4-6 people and informed that they do not need to elect a group leader or secretary. This is unnecessary and consumes time. Don't give the groups any answers, even if you see them writing down ideas that you think are mistaken. You'll have a chance Lesson 8 to review this exercise and help people learn from their mistakes. Move around to each group often during their work time so you can get an idea of what things they are discussing and writing down.

Each group should write down their answers to the questions on large sheets of paper using markers. At the end, if there is time, these sheets can be hung up around the room so participants can read what other groups wrote, or the groups can take turns presenting briefly what they wrote. However, in most cases there will not be time to share answers with the other groups, and it is okay to simply move on and tell the groups they will get to hear each other's answers during the review in Lesson 8. The facilitator should ask the participants if it's okay to move on or if they want to discuss what has been written by different groups.

The facilitator will collect and keep the written documents until the end of Lesson 8, when they will be evaluated for learning. The group members should write their names on the papers. This is very important because the people in each small group will likely change many times throughout the training. People will forget who was in their original group. At the end of the exercise, thank the participants for their good work. As you go throughout the lessons, you should be able to refer back to the exercise and mention what some of the groups wrote down, both things they did well and things they forgot to include. Tell the participants to keep what they wrote in their minds as they go through the lessons, so that they can begin to evaluate their plan, even before the final review of the exercise during Lesson 8.

Introducing the Course Content and Title (15 Minutes)

Let's get down to business. The reason we are all here is because we care about the poor and we want to know how to help them effectively. Unfortunately, as the title to this workshop suggests, wanting to help the poor is not always enough. Sometimes we try to help and nothing changes. Even worse, sometimes we try to help and the situation of the person or the community seems to get worse. Or sometimes after trying so long to help someone without seeing a change, we get angry, frustrated and even bitter. Maybe this has happened to you.

Jonny's Story

Listen to what happened to one of the authors of this curriculum, Jonny, when he tried to help someone. **In his words:**

> My name is Jonny. Some years back, before being introduced to the principles in this curriculum, I tried to help my elder brother. My brother lost his job many years ago and decided to go and stay in our village home. While in the village, he could not afford to look after his family and himself.
>
> As a way of helping him, I approached him and suggested he start farming as his source of income, to which he agreed. I was excited to start helping and I began by sending him money to clear the ground and buy the seedlings. To my surprise, no work was done and instead he used the money to buy himself alcohol. After some time, I decided not to send money again, but instead I bought the seedlings directly, hoping that he couldn't sell them for local brew or alcohol. Unfortunately, he did exchange the seedlings for alcohol.
>
> All my efforts to try to help him made him worse—to the extent that he would get drunk and fall by the roadside. Village mates would have to call his children and wife almost every day to take him home. This led to his separation with his wife and disrespect from his children. I later realised that my good intentions of helping were causing more harm to him, his family and myself; dependence, alcoholism, poverty, self-shame, broken relationships, and sin were now taking a centre stage.
>
> I was disappointed with him and myself because I thought my helping was going to improve his family's well-being. My helping only made him go deeper in his sin, and it hurt the relationship between us. Later in this curriculum, you will hear how I changed my approach after this and helped my brother in a better, more fruitful, way.

Helping Without Hurting in Africa

Think about the title—*Helping Without Hurting in Africa*. This training will help us to stop making such mistakes when helping the materially poor. We will have more success in fighting poverty. We want to help the poor without hurting them or ourselves. We will learn how to do things in a better and more godly way. By the end of this training, you should feel better equipped to help without hurting in your ministry here in Africa.

After the story, lead a **large group discussion** (with all the participants) over the following question. Allow people to briefly share their stories.

Share a time you or your church tried to help a poor person or community, but later found out that you made their situation worse.

This training is based on the principles in the book *When Helping Hurts*. This curriculum will show you the complicated nature of addressing poverty and you will see the many ways we can accidentally harm people while trying to help. One possible response to this training is that some people may stop trying to help the poor at all, because they are afraid of doing things wrong. This is exactly what happened to one of the authors, Anthony. When he first read *When Helping Hurts*, he was so worried about doing things the right way that he felt frozen and stopped caring for the poor for a while. But he repents of that. This curriculum should instead encourage us to do more—serving more and giving more generously of our time and resources. We just have to do so wisely. After taking this training, try to help the poor. Give generously. Repent where you fail and make mistakes, study this material again, and then try to help again. But don't give up trying to help the poor just because it is complicated and easy to make mistakes. We are called to do it. God will help us. He will use us, even in our imperfections, to transform the lives of others.

Helping Without Hurting in Africa

FACILITATOR MANUAL

LESSON 2: WHY DID JESUS COME TO EARTH?

Lesson 2:
Why Did Jesus Come to Earth?

In this section, you will find:

- A biblical and theological foundation for how to think about the role of the church in development and fighting poverty.

Lesson Objectives:

- To understand fully the ministry of Jesus.
- To understand the Kingdom of God and the role of the church.
- To call Christians to compassion and generosity to the poor.

Time Length: 2 Hours

Notes to the Facilitator

Please refer back to pp. 11-18 for full facilitator guidelines, but some particular tips for this lesson include:

- Ensure that long notes, quotations, and group questions are prepared in advance and written on flip chart paper.

- Unless otherwise noted, all Scripture passages in **bold** should be read out loud by a participant for the whole group.

- When the participants read the selected Bible passages throughout the lesson, make brief summaries of what each Bible passage is about and what it means.

- There is a lot of theology in Lesson 2. Make sure that participants understand each concept before moving forward. Take time for questions before moving on, especially questions concerning confusing theological concepts.

- When talking about justification by faith and salvation, if you sense that participants lack a good understanding of these concepts, take extra time to discuss so that they really understand the good news of the gospel. This is more important than rushing to get to the next lessons!

- At the end of the lesson, explain the take home activities clearly to participants and encourage them to ask questions to make sure everyone understands what they are to do before going home.

- At the end of the lesson, if there is time, consider asking participants questions to review the key points made during the lesson.

Opening Discussion (5 Minutes)

Ask the participants the following question and take note of their responses on a flip chart. Ask them to give short simple answers of one sentence each.

> **How would your church members at home respond if you asked them this question:**
>
> **Why did Jesus come to earth?**

You don't have to discuss this question for too long because you will be giving the correct answer in the lesson. Most participants will answer: "Jesus came to save us from our sins." This is fine, as you will give them the more complete answer concerning God's kingdom during the lecture.

Facilitator Lecture (40 Minutes)
Jesus's Ministry and Justification by Faith

- Most Christians can quickly answer that question. But, there are actually small differences in the way some Christians answer and think about this question. And our different responses to that question might have a connection to the way that we each respond differently to the poor.

- Many Christians say that Jesus came to die on the cross and save us from our sins so that we can go to Heaven. That is correct! But it is not complete because it leaves out other things Jesus came to do. **A more complete answer is that Jesus came to bring his kingdom**. He came to bring healing and redemption to the entire universe.

- Let's look at what Jesus himself said about why he came. Approximately 600 years before Jesus was born, the prophet Isaiah foretold that a King was coming who would create a wonderful kingdom. This kingdom would increase without end and bring healing and restoration from all the effects of sin. Someone please read **Luke 4:16-21**. Jesus read this prophecy from the book of Isaiah and was applying the prophecy to himself. He was really the true King and Saviour that they were waiting for. And Jesus practised what he preached. He really did the things in the prophecy. We can read about this in **Luke 7:18-23**. John the Baptist was wondering if Jesus was really the King they were waiting for, and the evidence Jesus gave was that he was doing these good works of his kingdom such as caring for the poor and healing the sick. Jesus preached the good news of the Kingdom of God, and showed the good news of the Kingdom of God through his actions. Jesus preached the good news of God's love and salvation to those who were poor in spirit, and gave hope to those who were physically poor as well.

- It is important to note, however, that Jesus did not fully usher in his kingdom. He did not actually release all people from prisons, he did not heal everyone, and he did not take away all of their poverty. Taking away all danger, sicknesses, and poverty was not to be completed in Jesus's first coming. We wait for those things to happen fully when Jesus comes again. In Jesus's first coming, he announces his kingdom and gives glimpses of what it will look like when the kingdom comes in its fullness at his second coming. Jesus really does reign over all things right now, and from time to time he uses his power to make things better right now. But he has chosen to delay the full benefits of his reign until he comes again.

- It's difficult to give a short answer to the question of why Jesus came. Jesus came to do so many things. He came to show love to the poor and to the sick. He came to defeat the devil and destroy his work. He came to live a perfect life without sin so we could be saved from our sins. He came to die on the cross to take our punishment. He came to conquer death itself through his resurrection. He came to show us the goodness of his kingdom. Jesus came to do many things, but how do we summarise what he came to do?

- In **Luke 4:43** Jesus summarised his ministry for us. So we can see that if we want to summarise all those things that Jesus came to do, under one title, we could say, "Jesus came to earth to preach the good news of the Kingdom of God." And all of Jesus's words and deeds were designed to demonstrate the nature of that kingdom and to call people to enter into that kingdom through faith and repentance. We can only enter the kingdom because of Jesus's death on the cross through which we have forgiveness of sins.

- **Jesus's death and resurrection** are the most important events in God's plan to bring about his kingdom, so it is right for us to primarily emphasize those events. The cross and the resurrection are the good news of the gospel, but if we don't have a full kingdom perspective, we might get the idea that Jesus only cares about forgiving our sins and bringing our souls to Heaven. But Jesus reigns as our King right now and he wants to work in our lives and communities right now to demonstrate that kingdom by bringing healing and change! As he works through us, we cannot expect to completely get rid of all the problems in the world right now, but God will use us to declare his kingdom and to call people to join that kingdom through faith and repentance.

- **Jesus came to preach the good news of his kingdom**. This means that Jesus, as the King of kings, is using his power to fix everything in this world that our sin has ruined. He did not come just to save our souls, but to heal our diseases, bring peace, establish his kingdom, and make us new. He started this work during his first coming and will complete it later in his second coming.

- You can see why our answer to this question of why Jesus came will determine how we respond to the poor. If we think Jesus only came to bring our souls to Heaven, we will only try to save souls. But if we have a kingdom perspective, we will live as citizens of the kingdom, people who preach the gospel and show love and care to others in their daily lives. We will fulfil the church's mission of preaching the good news, but while doing that, as citizens of the Kingdom, we will also heal the sick, care for the poor, counsel the broken, give justice to the oppressed, and give hope to the hopeless.

- **Questions?**

Justification by Faith

This section is about how we are able to enter into God's kingdom as a gift of grace, and not by works. This section might seem out of place, but it is important to understand that the gospel is not only concerned with following Jesus's example in doing good deeds for others. And the gospel is not just about going to Heaven. This section will explain how we are saved from our sins through justification by faith in Jesus. It is through that salvation that we become citizens of God's kingdom and begin to take part in the work of the kingdom. Before we can think about taking part in God's kingdom work, we need to make sure that we truly know how it is that we can become part of the kingdom.

Most participants will probably know how to be saved in Christ and already know Jesus personally. However, in some groups, there may be people who have this chance to hear the good news of the gospel for the first time. There may also be people in your group who have gone to church for many years and believe that Jesus is God, but they still think of salvation as something achieved by doing good works. Many people in our churches live in fear of death, wondering if they've been "good enough" to go to Heaven. This section will help your participants to understand the good news of salvation, to know that we are saved by grace and not by our good works!

- We will discuss more deeply about the Kingdom of God in a moment. But first, we need to make sure we all understand how it is that a person can become a part of the Kingdom of God. Let's make sure we all have the same understanding about what it means to "be saved". All Christians agree that it is through the life, death, and resurrection of Christ that we can receive salvation. Once we receive salvation and are born again, we become adopted as God's children. We become citizens of God's kingdom, enjoying the blessings of the kingdom and taking part in Jesus's kingdom work. But again, we need to know how it is that we are able to be reconciled to God, and to become a part of his kingdom. How does the life, death, and resurrection of Jesus actually save us?

Ask the participants these questions, but only take a few minutes to receive various answers. Don't write down their answers on the flipchart.

How does Jesus save us? How are we able to join his kingdom?

- First, let's remember that we are not able to save ourselves. We are all sinners who deserve God's judgement. We do not deserve to be a part of his kingdom. **Romans 3:10-12, 23**. To save ourselves from God's judgement, we would have to be perfect, never having sinned even once in our lives. But none of us can be good enough to save ourselves. We cannot be saved by doing good things or being a good person.

- To avoid punishment from God for our sins and to receive salvation and eternal life we must be perfect. We must be **justified** in God's sight. Think of justification as a term that would be used by the judges and the court. If you have committed a crime, the judge will pronounce you guilty, and you will be put in prison. But if the judge justifies you, or acquits you, by calling you innocent, then you are free to go your way. We all have sinned before God and will be judged. In the courtroom with God, God the judge will have to declare whether we are innocent and will inherit eternal life, or if we are guilty, and will be sent to Hell.

- On our own, we would all be condemned. But there is good news! The Bible makes clear that we can be justified by faith in Christ. **Ephesians 2:8-9**. **Romans 3:21-24**. All we have to do is have faith in Christ! But if we try to be saved by our good deeds, we will fail and not be able to be saved. Instead, we need to believe and trust in Jesus, that he is our Lord and Saviour. He lived the perfect life we could not live, and he died to take our punishment. He is our representative. When we are united to Christ, we are justified in God's sight. He looks at us as people who have already been punished for our sins, since Christ was punished for us. He looks at us as people who are perfectly righteous, since Jesus's perfect righteousness has been given to us as a gift. **Romans 5:17-19**.

- We are saved, not because we live good lives, but because of Christ's perfect life! We do not have to try to be "good enough" in order to make it through Judgement Day. No! We can never be good enough to join his kingdom on our own. But through our faith in Christ, God looks at us as perfect. We are saved by Christ's righteousness and good works, not our own. So we don't need to live in fear of death or Judgement Day. We are saved, 100%, completely and fully, by faith in Christ, and nothing else. This doctrine is called **justification by faith**, and it is what makes the gospel very *good* news.

- But do we still need to do good works? Yes! We cannot use justification by faith as an excuse to sin. The apostle Paul knew we would wonder about this. **Romans 6:1-2, 15**. We do good works as Christians, not in order to be saved, but in response to our salvation. Back in Ephesians, in the same breath that Paul talks about being saved by faith, he talks of the good works that God prepared for us to do. **Ephesians 2:10**. We were saved not just to sit here and wait for God to give us blessings, we were saved to do good and be a blessing to others. Because we are born again, and have received a new heart, we actually want to please God. Good works are not what saves us, but good works are the evidence that we have been truly born again and are truly in Christ. Good works are the evidence that our faith is real. **Matthew 7:17**. **James 2:17-18**. We will struggle with sin until Jesus returns and makes us new, but we will also walk in the light, repent and confess daily, keep on living for Christ, and produce good fruit. **1 John 1:8-10**. We obey God out of love and thanksgiving, not out of fear.

Pause your lecture briefly to ask the participants this discussion question (on the next page):

Do most people in your country become Christians to be justified by faith in Christ and enter into his kingdom, or do they become Christians because they want God to give them food, money, or physical healing?

Explain your answer.

After the discussion, continue with these points:

- God truly does provide for his people, and God does heal the sick. This is part of Jesus's building of his kingdom and bringing restoration to all things. But the central message of the gospel, the good news, is that by faith in Christ, we are justified in God's sight. It is only because of justification by faith in Christ that we can be adopted as God's children and enjoy the blessings of being part of the Kingdom of God. We cannot become a part of Jesus's wonderful kingdom through being a good person, but only through faith in Christ as our full and complete Saviour. In fact, the good news of the kingdom is only good for those who are justified by faith in Christ. For others who don't trust in Christ for salvation, but only want things from God, the Kingdom of God brings judgement and punishment.

- Many Christians in Africa do not focus on justification by faith nor on God's kingdom. Instead, they become Christians for health and prosperity, rather than for forgiveness of sins, a reconciled relationship with God, and becoming a part of the Kingdom of God. If we want to enjoy having God as our loving Father who cares for us as his children by giving us good things, we must first become reconciled to God and have our sins forgiven, through justification by faith in Christ.

- **Questions**?

- Now that we've understood more clearly how it is that Jesus saves us so that we can become a part of his kingdom, let's now look more deeply at the Kingdom of God and what it means to live as citizens of God's kingdom.

The Kingdom of God

Discussion Question (5 minutes)

Ask the following question to the whole group and write the participants's answers down on the flip chart.

We've been talking about the Kingdom of God, but what *is* the Kingdom of God? Is it here right now, or are we still waiting for it?

Explain.

Facilitator Lecture (30 Minutes)
The Kingdom of God and the Role of the Church

As you give participants the definition of the *Kingdom of God*, be sure to write down some basic notes of the definition on the flip chart for participants to see and copy down.

What is the Kingdom of God? It is not so much place as it is the rule of Jesus Christ as the King. It is God's reign over his redeemed people.[1] "The kingdom is the renewal of the whole world through the entrance of supernatural forces. As things are brought back under Christ's rule and authority, they are restored to health, beauty, and freedom."[2] Jesus is the King, and in his kingdom, he wants everything to be perfect, having everything the way it is supposed to be. People should be worshiping God and loving one another.

A beautiful passage about Jesus's kingdom work and what he came to do is **Colossians 1:15-20**. We learn from this passage that Jesus is the Creator, Sustainer, and Reconciler of **EVERYTHING**. Jesus died to save us, but he also died to reconcile all things that he created. This means he wants to put **EVERYTHING** into right relationship with him and each other. Jesus is making all things new!

Ask the participants these questions. You should receive very quick "yes" answers.

- **Does everything include you?**
- **Does everything include our neighbours?**
- **Does everything include our political leaders?**
- **Does everything include the poor in our communities?**
- **Does everything include our bodies?**
- **Does everything include our land?**
- **Does everything include our cattle?**
- **Does everything include mosquitoes?** (Yes, when Jesus returns, even mosquitoes will be transformed and reconciled to God. There will be no malaria and mosquito bites in God's perfect kingdom!)

But this leads to a question. Is the Kingdom of God something we experience right now, or is it something we will experience when Jesus returns? We need to understand that the kingdom is ***already here, but not yet fully here***. God's kingdom that Jesus preached about is ***already*** here. It came for the first time when Jesus came and died and rose again. We are experiencing the blessings of Jesus's kingdom. But it is not yet ***fully*** here. We will experience a new Heaven and a new earth joined together when Jesus comes again and then we will experience his kingdom in its perfection and fullness. **Revelation 21:1-4**.

Because the kingdom is here, we experience the power of the kingdom now. But because the kingdom is not yet fully here, we still suffer and not everything is the way it should be. For example:

- Before Jesus came, people were often in bondage to demons. But when Jesus came with the kingdom, he conquered the power of Satan and gave his people the power to drive out demons. We no longer have to be afraid of Satan. The power of Christ in us is greater than the power of Satan. We can resist demonic schemes with the armour of God. However, the kingdom is not yet fully here, so Satan is still tempting Christians to sin and keeping many non-Christians in fear and bondage. When Jesus returns and his kingdom is complete, the Devil will be thrown into the Lake of Fire and we won't ever be bothered by him again.
- There are more examples of how we experience the kingdom already, but not yet fully, that you can read in the further reflection section at the end of this lesson. But it's important to note that this "already but not yet" quality of God's kingdom affects our work of fighting poverty. **Because the Kingdom of God is already here and the Holy Spirit is at work**, we can be optimistic that God will use us to make change and bring people out of poverty and develop our communities. Jesus came to preach good news to the poor, but **because the Kingdom of God is not yet fully here**, we can be realistic and know that we will always have some poor people and some poverty ourselves until Jesus comes back. Christians who think that we can't make change and help the poor don't understand the reality of the Kingdom of God here and now. And Christians who think that we can make the world a perfect place of happiness right now don't understand that the kingdom will not be complete until Jesus returns.

The Kingdom of God is not fully here, but Jesus is actively at work building his kingdom on earth. That is why we pray for his kingdom to come. **Matthew 6:9–10**. We are praying that God makes his kingdom more complete on earth. We know it won't be complete until he returns, but in the meantime, Jesus uses us for his kingdom work.

This gives us great hope in our work of fighting poverty. Listen to this quotation from Desmond Tutu, former Archbishop in South Africa:

> Dear Child of God, I write these words because we all experience sadness, we all come at times to despair, and we all lose hope that the suffering in our lives and in the world will ever end. I want to share with you my faith and my understanding that this suffering can be transformed and redeemed. There is no such thing as a totally hopeless case. Our God is an expert at dealing with chaos, with brokenness, with all the worst that we can imagine. God created order out of disorder, cosmos out of chaos, and God can do so always, can do so now—in our personal lives and in our lives as nations, globally.... Indeed, God is transforming the world now—through us—because God loves us.[3]

The Kingdom of God not only gives us hope, but it should transform our thinking in every area of life. King Jesus reigns over all things—individuals, creation, cultural systems, and spiritual forces. Some of the missionaries who came to Africa failed to teach this in the past. So some Christians in Africa trusted in Christ for salvation, but still lived in fear of the spirits and ancestors in their traditional religions. We will talk about traditional religions again in a later lesson.

Knowing the power of Christ's kingdom should take away our fear and change every part of our lives. Nothing in our lives will remain the same when we see how everything we do should be done for Christ our King. We are to do our preaching, our daily work, our family duties, and everything else in our life as citizens of the Kingdom of God, and we do these things for God's glory. Jesus saves us for eternal life, but he also saves us for abundant life now, and he wants to transform every area of our lives for his glory.

The Role of the Church

Discussion Question

Are Christians on the African continent taught well about the Kingdom of God and the church's role in Jesus's kingdom?

Explain.

Jesus preached the good news of the kingdom and showed the good news of the kingdom through his actions. The church needs to follow the example of Jesus. The church in Africa must continue preaching the gospel with passion so people can be saved from their sins. But the church in Africa also needs to ask: "What can we do to help people out of the suffering they are experiencing right now?"

There are two common mistakes our churches need to avoid.

- The first mistake is when churches point people to Jesus but ignore their suffering. These churches are worshipping the King, pointing people to the King, but they are not bearing fruit and doing good to others. They have not understood what it means to live as a citizen of Jesus's kingdom.

- The second mistake is when churches care for people's physical needs and help them out of suffering, but they do not tell them how to have their sins forgiven by faith in Christ. These churches are bearing good fruit and in a way they are living as citizens of the kingdom. But they are ignoring the King and not telling people how to be reconciled to the King.

- Our churches need to be worshipping King Jesus, telling others how to be reconciled to King Jesus, and doing good works as citizens of the kingdom.

- We should aim to be more like the Early Church. **Acts 4:32-35**.

Discussion Question

Explain whether Christians in Afrcia today both worship together and care for each other's physical needs as the early Christians did?

Before sending the participants to small groups for discussion, explain to the participants the "Further Reflection" section at the end of this lesson. Encourage the participants to go home and study these extra pages and even discuss them with a friend. Be sure to explain the take-home activities as well.

Take-Home Activities

The take-home activities will include assignments or activities that the participants should carry out in their communities, churches, or place of work, applying the lessons they have learned. The facilitator should provide detailed guidelines and clear instructions on how to go about the take-home activities. For most lessons, there will be two take-home activities for participants to choose from, mainly determined by whether or not the participant is a church leader. Read aloud the two activities and explain that pastors should probably choose #1, and others attending the training should probably choose #2. If the participants are doing only one or two lessons per week, then they could possibly do this activity before they come back for the next lesson. If they are completing multiple lessons over several days, they can do all the take-home activities for those lessons after they go back home from the training.

Take-Home Activities for Lesson 2

1. **Preach a sermon to your church on one of the Bible passages from this lesson about justification by faith or the Kingdom of God. Alternatively, preach on one of the Bible passages in the small group discussion questions.**

2. **Have a conversation with your family, work colleagues, or community group about what you learned in this lesson concerning the Kingdom of God. If they are interested and willing, try to organise a Bible study with them so that you can look at some of the key Bible passages mentioned in this lesson and discuss them together.**

Small Group Discussion (40 Minutes)

Inform the participants that they will be going into small groups to discuss together the questions listed at the end of Lesson 2 in their manual. These questions will help them to review and understand the principles taught in the lesson. Explain to them that the questions will help them to apply and live out these principles in their daily lives. They will discuss some Bible passages and think about how to obey them today.

- Read out loud the questions that they will be answering and make sure they understand them.

- Tell them that they don't need a group leader or a secretary. They also are only writing down notes for themselves. They will not be presenting their answers to anyone. Divide them up into groups of about 5 people (anywhere from 3-6 people per group) and encourage them to begin by sharing their names with each other. After this short introduction, they should begin discussing immediately as they only have 40 minutes to discuss. They should save 10 minutes at the end for question number 2. After 30 minutes has passed, tell them to move on to question number 2 even if they have not finished all of the Bible passages in number 1. It is okay if they do not finish looking at all of the Bible passages. Tell them they can read the other Bible passages that they did not have time to discuss at home.

- If you have organised the whole workshop to take longer than what has been outlined, then feel free to give the participants a longer time for discussion.

- Remember to move around and listen in with the groups as they discuss. Be available to answer their questions. You can give guidance or input if necessary during their discussions, but they have heard you talk a lot, so try to let them do the talking now. If you do say something, one good strategy is to point out interesting things in the Bible passages that they might not have noticed or talked enough about, and encourage them to think about how to apply the principles to their lives and communities. Remind them periodically about how much time remains for their discussion.

Small Group Discussion Questions

1. **Read the following Scripture passages. Discuss together what God teaches us in these passages about how to love and care for the poor. What general principles do these passages teach? What would it look like to try to apply these teachings today in our time and culture?** If you run out of time to discuss all the passages, study the remaining passages at home on your own.

    a. Amos 2:6-7 and Amos 5:21-24

    b. Leviticus 19:9-10

    c. Deuteronomy 14:28-29

    d. Proverbs 19:17

    e. Proverbs 21:13

    f. Isaiah 58:1-10

    g. Luke 12:32-34

    h. James 1:27

    i. 1 John 3:16-18

2. **What can you and your church change to become more focused on Jesus and his kingdom?** After discussing with each other how you will change, pray together as a group asking God to help you change.

Further Reflection

Read this section at home for further learning.

- **Justification By Faith**

African theologian Matthew Michael claims that the doctrine, *justification by faith alone*, is the least preached doctrine in churches in Africa.[4] **Why do you think some pastors in Africa don't preach about this doctrine?** Discuss this with a friend.

Sometimes pastors are afraid that if Christians believe in justification by faith, they will make excuses for their sins. But if people truly understand justification by faith they will not be able to make this kind of excuse for sin. A person who is truly born again has a desire to please God and obey him. A good tree bears good fruit. Good works are evidence of true faith. Someone who has real faith in Christ will not use justification by faith as an excuse to sin. A true Christian will not be perfect, but he or she will not walk in sin. They will keep repenting, confessing, and trying to live for Christ.

Think about these questions and discuss them with others if you are able:

1. ***What could you or your pastor say during a sermon to make sure that people do not misunderstand justification by faith?***

2. ***How would you counsel someone in your church who has been using justification by faith and God's forgiveness of sin as an excuse for disobeying God? What Scripture passages would you share with this person?***

- **The Kingdom of God**

Here are some more examples that illustrate how we already experience being in the Kingdom of God now, but we are not yet experiencing the fullness of the Kingdom of God until Jesus returns. Reflect on these examples.

1. Before Jesus came, people suffered from many sicknesses. After Jesus came with the kingdom, many people were healed of sicknesses and he even heals us today. Because the kingdom is not yet fully here, though, we are not always miraculously healed every time we get sick. In fact, we all die eventually. But when Jesus returns the second time, and the kingdom is complete, there will be no more sickness at all. And there will be no more death. We will live forever with him.

2. When Jesus came he set us free from slavery to sin. So now we have the power to say "no" to sin in our lives, but we still struggle with sin each day. We often do what we do not want to do. When Jesus comes again, he will completely take away our desire and ability to sin.

3. Before Jesus came, people did not experience the intimacy of God's presence as fully as we do now. After Jesus came he sent us the Holy Spirit to be God's presence with us, but we still do not see Jesus face to face, which we will be able to do when he comes again.

Can you think of other examples that illustrate this feature of the Kingdom of God?

- **Inspirational Stories**

Read and reflect on these stories of churches that were taught about the Kingdom of God. With a new mind-set focused on the Kingdom of God, these churches greatly changed the way that they did ministry in their communities. Let us learn from their examples.

1. In 2005, in Rev. Emmanuel's church in central Burundi, the church members began literacy classes. After learning how to read, church members began reading the Bible and applying it to their lives. After learning about the Kingdom of God, and that faith without works is dead, they began to get more involved in ministry and reaching out to

the community. The church was able to teach people not only literacy, but also business skills and how to form community savings groups. Through these outreaches, the church has grown, regularly taking in new members. Their Sunday School program has grown from a few children to over 200 participants every week. The community was surprised when the church started to educate women and train them in financial management, but now their husbands are very grateful because they have seen the benefits of these trainings. Families from their church have new hope and new unity.[5]

2. Nigerian Anglican pastor, Canon Isaac, mobilised his church members as well as community members to undergo a program called Church and Community Transformation (CCT). It transformed the mind-sets of the people, giving them a more holistic view of the church's ministry. They were able to work together to build a simple health centre. Previously, they had to walk 1 hour to access the nearest health centre. They built the new health centre completely with their own resources. The health centre has blessed so many people, especially the 134 pregnant mothers who were able to safely give birth there so far! The church and community were also able to build a school. Because of this wonderful kingdom work, Isaac's church has grown from a few members to 170 members![6]

3. In the year 2000, the leaders of Kampala Pentecostal Church in Uganda went to a conference and were taught a biblical worldview about Jesus's ministry and the Kingdom of God. At the conference, God planted a desire in the leaders to reach out to their community with the love of Christ. The head pastor challenged the church members to identify the needs in their communities and take ownership of their problems. Church members went out and did very loving deeds in the community such as fixing wells, replacing roofs for homes of needy families, and providing food for orphans. At one time the church was looking after 1,200 orphans and built homes for about half of them! In addition, every cell group of the church was asked to look after a family with at least one person in the family having AIDS. The church members regularly go to these families, talk to them, hug them, and pray for them. If the person with AIDS in the family died, the group of church members would hold a worship service with the family. Even the Ugandan government noticed the church and named it one of the country's ten most influential organisations in combating AIDS. Through these ministries the church has grown to nearly 12,000 members.[7]

Helping Without Hurting in Africa

Facilitator Manual

Lesson 3: What Is Poverty?

Lesson 3: What Is Poverty?

In this section, you will find:

- A discussion about the nature and causes of poverty.
- The biblical narrative of Creation, Fall, Redemption, and Consummation.
- Introduction to the Four Key Relationships (God, Self, Others, and the Rest of Creation) and their effect on poverty.

Lesson Objectives:

- To understand the causes of poverty.
- To understand different types of poverty.

Time Length: 3 Hours

Notes to the Facilitator

Please refer back to pages 11-18 for full facilitator guidelines, but some particular tips for this lesson include:

- For some training groups, this lesson may be too long to do in one sitting. If so, you may want to consider handling this lesson over two sessions. You could complete from the beginning through the end of the drama in one session. Then in the next session you would begin from the section on page 55 called, "What does the Bible Teach About Poverty?"

- Review the drama that is in the middle of this lesson. Make sure you are well prepared for it. If possible, during the break between Lessons 2 and 3, find two people who will be willing participants to take part in the drama with you. Otherwise you can ask for volunteers later, as they will not need to prepare themselves much for it.

- Ensure that long notes, quotations, and group questions are prepared in advance and written on a flip chart.

- Unless otherwise noted, all Scripture passages in **bold** should be read out loud by a participant for the whole group.

- When the participants read the selected Bible passages throughout the lesson, make brief summaries of what each Bible passage is about and what it means.

- At the end of the lesson, explain the take home activities clearly to participants.

- If there is time at the end of the lesson, consider asking participants questions to review the key points made during the lesson.

Opening Discussion (10 Minutes)

Ask participants the following questions and take notes of their responses on a flip chart. Ensure that they give short and simple answers, since you are going to give them a deeper understanding of these questions throughout the lesson. For question #1, they do not need to answer out loud unless they would like to. You can tell them to quietly think about the question by themselves, and then write down their answer in their notes. Question #3 should be answered briefly. Participants will give various answers and you can write them down on the flip chart.

1. **Are you a poor person?**
2. **Do you have poor people in your church?**
3. **You would view someone in your church as poor if they ________________? Fill in the blank with your own answers.**

After recording their answers, tell them that many Africans and most Westerners tend to say that someone is poor if they lack money or they lack things. Write this answer down on the flip chart and circle it: "*lacking money or things*". It might actually be a summary of many of their answers. While this answer is incomplete and therefore not fully correct, it will nicely set up the contrast between how many people tend to think of poverty and how the materially poor themselves think of poverty. In the lecture immediately following these questions, you will make this contrast clear, and help the participants to see that poverty is much deeper and more complex than how we usually see it.

When we talk about what it means to be poor, most of us say that being poor means a person lacks money, food, shelter, or other basic needs. If we want to give a definition of poverty, we might say that poverty is "lacking money or things". But how do poor people themselves explain what it means to be poor? How do they define poverty? In the 1990's, the World Bank asked poor people to define poverty in their own words.[1] Listen to what they said. As I read, write down in your notes important words and ideas that you hear about what poverty means to them.

Read these answers from the World Bank survey fairly slowly so that participants have time to really digest them and record some ideas and words:

- A person from **Moldova**: "*For a poor person everything is terrible—illness, humiliation, shame. We are cripples; we are afraid of everything; we depend on everyone. No one needs us. We are like garbage that everyone wants to get rid of.*"[2]
- From **Guinea-Bissau**: "*When I don't have any food, I borrow, mainly from neighbours and friends. I feel ashamed standing before my children when I have nothing to help feed the family. I'm not well when I'm unemployed. It's terrible.*"[3]

- From **Latvia**: "*During the past two years we have not celebrated any holidays with others. We cannot afford to invite anyone to our house and we feel uncomfortable visiting others without bringing a present. The lack of contact leaves one depressed, creates a constant feeling of unhappiness, and a sense of low self-esteem.*"[4]

- From **Uganda**: "*When one is poor, she has no say in public, she feels inferior. She has no food, so there is famine in her house; no clothing, and no progress in her family.*"[5]

- From **Cameroon**: "*The poor have a feeling of powerlessness and an inability to make themselves heard.*"[6]

- From **Vietnam**: "*If you are hungry, you will always be hungry; if you are poor, you will always be poor.*"[7]

- From **Ecuador**: "*The indigenous people's destiny is to be poor.*"[8]

After reading the responses, ask participants the questions below and write their answers on the flip chart. Divide answers clearly, separating these from participants's answers to the opening questions of the lesson. This way, they can easily see on one side of the paper what they themselves said about what it means to be poor, and what the poor people interviewed said about what it means to be poor on the other side.

1. **What words or phrases did you hear that you think are significant?**
2. **What differences are there between how we described poverty at the beginning and how these poor people described their own poverty?**

For the first question, if they mention material things like lacking money or lacking food, do not write them down again, but rather point out that you had already written those down. Take all of their answers first, but if they miss any of the following words and phrases, then tell them to the group yourself and write them along with the answers they gave: (**Illness**, **humiliation**, **shame**, **cripples**, **not valued**, **hopeless**, **fear**, **social isolation**, **unemployment**, **depression**, **unhappiness**, **low self-esteem**, **helpless**, **voiceless**, **feeling inferior**, **powerless**, **no respect**, **dependent**, **fatalism**). You may have to explain that "fatalism" is the idea that you cannot change your life or your circumstances—"If you are poor you will always be poor", "It is our destiny to be poor." Make sure to write these answers on a very good sheet of paper that you will save and keep in a prominent place throughout the training (such as taped to the wall). You will refer back to it during most of the lessons.

Participants should be able to notice that their own answers about what it means to be poor were mostly about material things that are easy to see, such as lacking money or clothing. But the answers of the poor people themselves do not only include material things, but also much deeper emotional, spiritual, and social difficulties that are not so visible. Furthermore, participants should be able to see that these kinds of deeper feelings and problems are much more painful for the poor than the pain of simply lacking money. Quickly summarise these differences before starting the next lecture.

Facilitator Lecture (20 Minutes)
Understanding Poverty[9]

Definitions of poverty vary according to who is doing the measuring, whether it is the World Bank, governments, aid agencies, non-governmental organisations, or people who live in conditions of poverty. We therefore need to carefully listen to the poor and understand their definitions of poverty to be able to support them and work with them to overcome their difficult situations in a more sustainable, cooperative, and helpful way.

As we try to help the poor, a large problem is that we often define poverty very differently from how poor people themselves do. We can see this from the questions we just answered. This happens regularly when foreigners come to Africa to help us. They think they can understand our problems better and get rid of poverty just by giving us money and things, which often does not work. But we also do the same thing when we try to help the poor in our families, churches, and communities. Most of the time we think of poverty much too simply. We think poverty is simply not having enough things or money, but poverty is much more complex than this. The poor themselves describe deeper spiritual, psychological, and social problems in their definitions of poverty. Poverty is not only about lacking money; it is about feeling shame, feeling inferior, and feeling powerless to change your situation.

We need to understand that **the way we define poverty determines the way we try to help people in poverty**. When we think poverty is only lacking money or clean water or medicine, then we will simply give money, clean water, or medicine to people. But will simply giving people those things take away those painful feelings that we just looked at? No. In fact, as we will see, sometimes simply giving people things like this can make them feel even more shame and humiliation. We need to help people, but we need to understand the true nature of poverty in order to help people in the most effective way.

Let me give you an illustration to understand this better.

If you go to a doctor for a health problem, the doctor could make a mistake in one of two ways. The doctor could correctly give you a diagnosis but then prescribe the wrong treatment. He might tell you that you have malaria, but then only give you painkillers for the symptoms of malaria, the headaches. Will you be okay? No. The other mistake a doctor could make is to give you the wrong diagnosis. If he diagnoses you as having malaria and he treats you for malaria, but you really have typhoid, will you be okay? No, your situation might even become worse. So a doctor needs to give both the proper treatment and the proper diagnosis if you are going to get better.

The same is true when we work with poor people. If we prescribe the wrong treatment or make an incorrect diagnosis, we will not be able to help poor people, and might actually make their situation worse. If we diagnose someone's problem with poverty as just a lack of money, then what treatment will we give? We will give them money. But what if that is the wrong diagnosis? As we've seen, poverty is much deeper than simply a lack of money, and in fact, the lack of money is usually just a symptom of a deeper problem, like a headache might be a symptom of malaria. We need to make sure we get a real diagnosis and treat the real problem.

Many foreign governments and organisations who have tried to help African countries have done more harm than good. They have poured a lot of money and resources into Africa as a treatment to a problem that was, in most cases, misdiagnosed or misunderstood. They have often looked at money as a solution to all problems of poverty. Just as it is foolish to suggest that there is only one treatment for all kinds of sickness, it is foolish to say that there is only one treatment for all situations of poverty.[10] We need to learn from the mistakes of these foreigners as well as our own mistakes as we try to help the poor in our communities. We need to understand the true complex nature of poverty and how it is caused.

What we believe about the cause of poverty will determine the treatment we respond with.

- If we think poverty is caused by a lack of material resources, we will give material resources to the poor.
- If we think poverty is caused by a lack of knowledge, we will try to educate the poor.
- If we think it is caused by oppression from powerful people, we will work against corruption.
- If we think people are poor because of their personal sins, we will try to evangelise and disciple the poor.

Causes of Poverty

In fighting poverty, we need the correct diagnosis and correct treatment, so we have to take time to figure out the true cause of poverty before we try to help. When facing someone in need, we need to talk to them and listen well to the person so that we are able to answer this question: what is the cause of this person's poverty?

Discussion Questions

Ask the participants the questions below and record their answers on a flip chart.

1. **What do you think are the main causes of poverty in your country?**
2. **What are the main causes of poverty for poor people in your church and in your community?**

Let's think about a situation that many church leaders might face regularly: *What if a man comes to your church and asks for help paying for school fees for his children? The loving thing to do would be to provide the money, right?*

Allow the participants to briefly answer the question above. Then explain to them that if they said "yes", that is a wrong answer, and if they said "no", that is a wrong answer also. Tell them that the correct answer is, "**it depends**". We must take the time necessary to really find out what is going on in this person's life, and diagnose the cause of his poverty, before we can know whether it is good to give him money or not, and how best to truly help him.

If we talk to him and his family and find out that he has a job and has money for the school fees, but he keeps using all that money on drinking alcohol, then it would be wrong for the church to give him money. That would only encourage him to continue drinking and not really help the children. He might just spend the money on alcohol before he reaches home. Instead, we could counsel the man to repent of his drinking and neglect of his children, and try to help him better care for his family with the church's help and guidance. But imagine a different case. If we talk to the man and find out that he had the money for the school fees, but someone robbed him on the street and took all of it, then the church might decide it's a good idea to pay the school fees for him this one time. We ***MUST*** *get a real diagnosis of the cause of poverty before we can answer whether to give money or not.*

In our African cultures, it is very common to have relatives and acquaintances asking us for money. Most of the time, we feel an obligation to give if we have the money available, or we might truly want to be loving and generous to these relatives. Unfortunately, we most often decide how to help them without carefully listening to them or trying to find out the root causes of their poverty. We must try to get a diagnosis of their situation first. Later, we will have a whole lesson on this cultural issue, so we will discuss it more another time.

When we look at poor people around the world, the symptoms of poor people look mostly the same. They all lack material things. But what is causing the lack of things might be very different for each person. Sometimes the poor person him or herself might even have trouble knowing, or he or she might not be honest with us about it. To figure this out and really get to know the poor person, we need patience. It means we will have to truly befriend the poor person and sacrifice our time to learn about their situation.

Let's read **Isaiah 58:10**. We must *spend ourselves* for the poor. *Spending ourselves* means more than just handing out a few shillings or francs. It means spending our time and our energy to understand and help them. It means working with the poor person to find a right diagnosis and the right solution to the underlying problem. Giving a person a few shillings or francs is easy. But working with someone over many weeks, months, or even years is a much harder process. But as Jesus has patience with us and never gives up on us, we should have patience and work with poor people—even if it takes a lot of time.

So why are people poor? According to the Bible and our observations, there are many reasons a person could be poor. And some people experience several causes of poverty at the same time. Examples of causes of poverty include sinful behaviour—like laziness or sexual immorality, lack of education, being oppressed by people, being oppressed by demonic forces, having false beliefs, disease, lacking opportunities, lacking resources, natural disasters like droughts or floods, social isolation, broken governmental and economic systems, or physical or mental disabilities.

Drama (20 Minutes)

In the drama, you as the facilitator will act as the person who is in need of help. You are acting as if you are a young man who is visiting his aunt and uncle to ask for financial assistance in a time of need. Find two willing participants from the group who can act as aunt and uncle.

They do not need to prepare beforehand. When people come to request financial assistance in real life, they do not have time to prepare either. The point of the drama is to show the participants what it looks like to really take time to diagnose someone's cause of poverty, and seeking for a good solution, rather than simply telling someone "yes" or "no" very quickly concerning giving money.

- Ensure that all the chairs are properly positioned in a circle to allow all the participants to see clearly. Then you and the other two actors would be seated in the centre of the circle. In front of the whole group, instruct the two people acting as a Christian aunt and uncle to do the best they can asking questions, listening well to try to figure out the young man's true cause of poverty and what the right response should be.

- Inform them that this is a practise session so that we can all learn to do better at this in real life. They should try to demonstrate spending our time on behalf of the poor to help them in the best way possible. Encourage them that, even if they as aunt and uncle don't think they should give money to this person, they should still look for ways to truly help the person in the conversation. Tell the actors, in front of the group, that you are their nephew, and that you are newly married with one child.

- In the drama, you are a young man who approaches his aunt and uncle for financial assistance. At the beginning, you should tell them you want money to buy a plow that you will use to cultivate your garden in order to keep supporting your family. But do not say anything more until they ask questions and try to find out more information. The real situation is that the young man's land is very fertile, but at home, his wife is doing almost all the work. The young man is spending all his time in town at sports betting halls. He manages the money for the family but spends almost all of it on sports betting and airtime for his phone as he spends so much time on the Internet. These are the real reasons why they don't have enough money for a plow themselves. The wife is unhappy at home and concerned about how they will be able to care for their child well when the money keeps disappearing. The young man is a Christian and goes to church but is not strong in his spiritual life. In the conversation, don't lie to the aunt and uncle at all, but you don't always have to directly tell them everything quickly either. Make the aunt and uncle work a little bit for the answers. But give them answers easily enough in order to ensure that the drama doesn't take too much time. If the issue of sports betting comes into the conversation, the young man can admit to his relatives that he knows what he is doing is foolish and wrong, but he always feels like he must go back to the betting, hoping that the next time will be the time when he wins a lot of money. He recognises that he is having difficulty quitting the betting. **If you think it would be helpful or if you are a female facilitator, please feel free to adapt the drama to make it more fitting for your cultural context or a female main character.*

- After the drama is finished, reveal to the whole group the truth about the young man. Evaluate together about how well the aunt and uncle did at diagnosing the young man's poverty. If they did not do well, try to help them not feel bad about it; emphasize that it was a learning experience. You could suggest some of the questions they could have asked that would have helped them to get to a better diagnosis.

- **Keep close track of time! Save at least 5 minutes of your 20 minutes to discuss as a group about the drama once it is finished.** While we need to be willing to spend our time on behalf of the poor, you don't have time to do a one hour drama in the training, nor will participants be interested in such a long drama. Keep it short and to the point. Make it clear to the actors that the drama needs to move along quickly so that you finish the drama within the allotted time. Close the drama with the discussion questions for the group below:

1. **Why is it difficult to diagnose someone's true cause of poverty?**
2. **What could the aunt and uncle do to truly help this family?**
3. **Should they give any money or things to the family? Why or why not?**

For these questions, don't spend too much time, because the participants will learn good solutions for how to help in cases like this throughout the rest of the training. For question #2, after taking the participants's responses, you could mention things like:

- Counseling the young man on being a good steward of his money and the foolishness of sports betting.
- Suggesting ways the young man might overcome his addiction with help from others.
- Discipling the young man in his walk with Christ.
- Having the aunt and uncle give marriage counseling to the young couple, or connecting them to the pastor of their church for counselling.
- Asking for the aunt and uncle to loan the young man their plough, or finding a neighbour who could loan it to them while they save money for their own.
- Depending on how they answer question 3, counsel the group against giving cash directly to the young man, as he may spend it all on his addiction to sports betting. Though counter-cultural, the young man could let his wife or uncle hold the family's money for safe-keeping, after he recognises his weakness and addiction.

What Does the Bible Teach about Poverty? (30 Minutes)

Looking at the Bible, we learn that there is actually one root cause of **all** poverty in this world. Why do we experience problems in this world? Why do people lack things that they need? As you can guess, the answer is **sin**. It is because people sinned that this world and our lives are no longer perfect. This doesn't mean that people are only poor because of their personal sins. I am referring to sin in general. When Adam and Eve disobeyed God, sin came into the world, and everything in this world became broken. One major result was poverty. In this lesson and the next few lessons, we will examine the story of the Bible to learn about these deeper problems, as well as what the solution to our sin and poverty is.

Creation, Fall, Redemption, and Consummation

In this section, you will learn some theology. It might seem unrelated to the topic of this course about helping the poor, but you will soon see how very important this theology is in giving us a good understanding of poverty and how to truly help the poor.

The Bible is God's story about this world and God's relationship to it, from beginning to end. The beginning of the story of the Bible is the event of **Creation**. The problem in the story comes in the event we call the Fall. We see the result of the **Fall** into sin throughout the rest of the Bible. The solution to the problem in the story is Jesus at the event we call **Redemption**. The end of the story is a theological term called the **Consummation**, or the final coming of Christ's kingdom.

Ask the participants these questions below in the large group. Just look for very quick answers, as most of these concepts will be already familiar to your participants to some degree. After each event in the biblical story, summarise the important points that the participants have not already said, as given in the facilitator notes. Then move on to the next biblical event. You want to draw the answers out from the group, but it shouldn't be a discussion.

1. ***Creation is the beginning- what do we learn about the very beginning of the story? What happens?***

- God created this world and it was good. God created people to love him, worship him, and enjoy his gifts. He gave Adam and Eve the job of caring for the creation. They were made in God's image and they were supposed to be fruitful and multiply. They were in perfect relationship with God and each other, and even the animals. And we can see that there was abundance in the creation, with no poverty in sight. You can read more about this on your own in Genesis 1–2.

2. ***Fall—What happened at the Fall of Adam and Eve?***

- In the Fall, we see Adam and Eve rebel against God. Sin came into the world. Everything became broken and distorted. God gave the punishment and curse of death, difficult work, and difficult child bearing. Sin affected everything in the world. Things were no longer the way they were supposed to be. We see the effects of the Fall and people's sin in every book of the Bible. You can read more about the Fall on your own in Genesis 3. All our problems and poverty are the result of sin coming into the world.

3. ***Redemption refers to God saving people from their sins and from punishment and death. Where do we see redemption in the Bible?***

- Redemption is not only in the New Testament, but really is throughout the whole Bible. Redemption actually begins in the book of Genesis as God slowly forms a people to be his own. He starts with Abraham and his family, and eventually they become the nation of Israel. God then rescues the Israelites, gives them the Law, protects them, and prepares them for the Saviour who will come. Eventually Jesus comes. He is the redeemer of the world through his life, death, and resurrection. Through him we have forgiveness of sins and eternal life. And we experience already the goodness of his kingdom.

4. *Consummation is the end of the story. Can you guess what events the Consummation refers to?*

- This is when Jesus returns and judges the world and then makes all things new. There will be the resurrection, and we will live with God forever. Heaven and the new earth will be joined together as you can read about on your own in Revelation 21–22. Everything will be perfect. Remember when we said that God's kingdom is already here, but not yet fully here? At the consummation, that is when his kingdom will be fully perfect and complete. We wait eagerly for that day when there will be no more problems nor poverty.

5. *Today, where do we fit into the story?*

- Today we are in between redemption and consummation. We are actually continuing in the time of redemption, as God continues to save people for himself, and uses us to preach the good news of his kingdom to all nations.

Now we need to examine these four events more closely so that we can understand how they relate to poverty. In this lesson and the next, we will only look at the Creation and the Fall. Then in Lesson 5, we will begin to look at Redemption and Consummation.

Creation—The Four Key Relationships (Genesis 1-2)

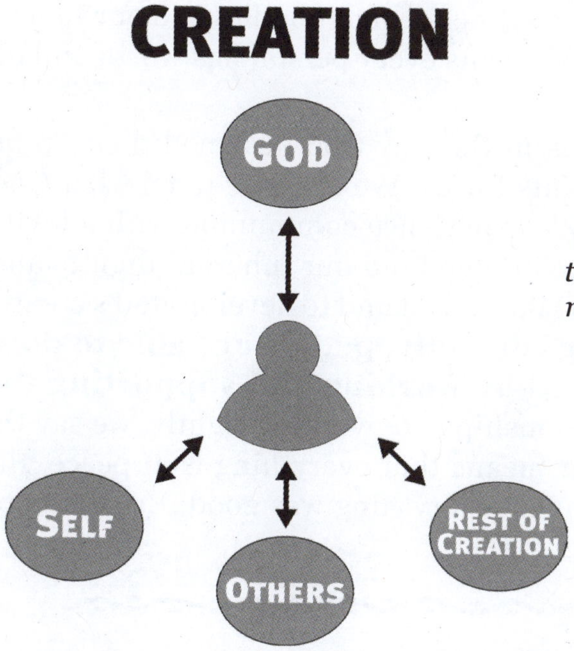

Fig. 2.1
Adapted from Bryant L. Myers, *Walking with the Poor: Principles and Practices of Transformational Development* (Maryknoll, N.Y.: Orbis Books, 1999), 27.

The Bible teaches there is one God who is Triune—**three** persons sharing **one** divine essence. This means that God is a relational God. The Father, Son and Holy Spirit have always been in a perfect relationship of love with one another. Since humans are made in God's image, we were created also to have relationships. We will look at the story of Creation and see four key relationships that God intended humans to have.

1. **Relationship with God.** This is the most important relationship. God created us to worship him. We do this through our actions, thoughts, and words. In the Creation story in Genesis 1–2, we see that Adam and Eve were in perfect relationship with God and they even walked together in the Garden of Eden.

2. **Relationship with Others**. God created us to live in loving relationships with other people. We are not supposed to live apart from others. God made us to know other people, to love other people, and to encourage one another to use the gifts that God has given to each of us. We see that Adam and Eve had a good loving relationship in the story. Adam called Eve, "Bone of my bones and flesh of my flesh", showing how much he valued her.

3. **Relationship with the Rest of Creation.** Read **Genesis 1:28-30**. These verses tell us what people are supposed to do on this earth. We are to be stewards of God's creation. God has given us this world to understand it, to protect it, to rule it, and to manage it. This involves two things. First, we are to care for the creation and preserve the environment by taking care of plants, animals, land, and water. Second, we are to work to develop the creation and its potential. Indeed, our daily work such as plowing a field, or teaching in a school, or selling clothing in the marketplace are all part of our relationship to creation. In the story, we see Adam and Eve in perfect relationship with the creation, taking care of it, being at peace with the animals, and enjoying their work in the garden.

4. **Relationship with Self.** This refers to how we think about ourselves. God created us to be at peace with ourselves and to take care of our bodies and our souls. All people are created in the image of God. This means every person has worth and dignity.

When these four relationships are working in the way God designed them to be, then we as humans have the good life that God wants for us. We are able to be what God wants us to be and to do what God calls us to do. We experience communion with a loving God, we experience fellowship with one another, we understand our inherent dignity and worth as image bearers, and we work responsibly to take care of and to develop God's creation. **When these four relationships are working correctly, people are able to do what God calls them to do. They can glorify God by working and supporting themselves and their families**. When all these relationships are working rightly, we say that there is "**shalom**". Shalom is a Hebrew word that means that everything is at peace, the way it is supposed to be. Before Adam and Eve sinned, everything was good; there was no pain, no problems, no hunger, no disease, and no poverty.

The Fall—The Four Key Relationships (Genesis 3)

Let's now look at what happened during the Fall of Adam and Eve in Genesis 3. We know that Adam and Eve disobeyed God and sin came into the world. Specifically, we can see that all four of their key relationships became broken by sin. We won't read Genesis 3 right now, but you can have your Bibles open there as we answer the next questions.

Ask the participants the questions below in the large group.

1. How was Adam and Eve's relationship with God broken or damaged?

- They lost their intimacy and good fellowship with God through sin. They rebelled and experienced fear of God. They could no longer walk in the Garden with God. They were punished for their sin. Yet God did not destroy them or stop having a relationship with them.

2. How was Adam and Eve's relationship with one another broken or damaged?

- They did not take responsibility for their sin and instead blamed each other. They no longer felt the same towards each other. Adam said to God, *"this woman you put here with me"* instead of seeing Eve as his wife—*"flesh of my flesh"*.

3. How was their relationship with the rest of creation broken or damaged?

- Work became cursed and difficult. The ground did not produce food so easily. Eve was told that childbearing would become painful. The world became a dangerous place. There was death, there were natural disasters, and there was disease. Animals and people were no longer at peace.

4. How was their view of themselves damaged?

- After they sinned, they felt guilt and shame. They had not acted as people made in the image of God should act. They were afraid to be in God's presence.

Thankfully, even though all these relationships were damaged, things were not as bad as they could be. Even after the curse, God continued to give his grace to the world and continued to have a relationship (though no longer perfect and intimate) with Adam and Eve. He provided for them and continued to bless them. In fact, because of God's grace in the world, even non-Christians have provision from God and do some good things. Even non-Christians love and take care of their children. If not for God continuing to give his grace to this world, things would be much worse.

But now we can understand why poverty came into this world. It was the result of the sin of humanity who rebelled against God. We share the guilt with Adam and Eve for that sin, and also for our own sins. Poverty is the result of these four key relationships being broken. And since we all experience broken relationships, we will see that we all have some poverty in our lives.

Five Types of Poverty

On a new sheet of paper from the flip chart, write down these five types of poverty as you teach about them. You will refer back to this page regularly throughout the training.

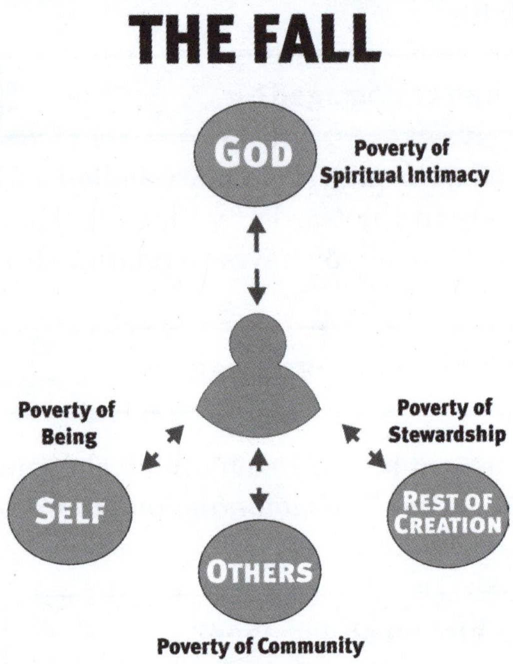

Fig. 2.2
Adapted from Bryant L. Myers, *Walking with the Poor: Principles and Practices of Transformational Development* (Maryknoll, N.Y.: Orbis Books, 1999), 27.

Since poverty is about relationships not working correctly, we begin with four types of poverty based on the four types of broken relationships: our broken relationships with **God**, **self**, **others**, and the **rest of creation**.

1. **Poverty of Spiritual Intimacy.** This is having a broken or damaged relationship with God. Because of our sin, we are under God's wrath and deserving of punishment and Hell. Those who don't believe in God, or who worship spirits and idols, have this type of poverty. Until we come to know Jesus as our Saviour, we have poverty of spiritual intimacy. But even as Christians, we still struggle with sin and with experiencing intimacy with God, so we all continue to have this poverty to some degree until Christ returns.

2. **Poverty of Community.** This is having a broken relationship with other people. We are ultimately self-serving people, which comes at the expense of the greater good and other people. Poverty of community includes abuse, exploitation, discrimination, and violence against one another.

3. **Poverty of Stewardship.** This is having a broken relationship with God's creation. We can have this poverty in two different ways. First, we have poverty of stewardship if we do not care for God's creation as he told us to. If we pollute the creation, beat

our animals, or chop down all the trees, then we are not caring for the creation well. Second, God called us to cultivate the earth and bring forth its fruit through joyful labour. If we refuse to work in God's world, or cannot find work to do, or we have a wrong attitude about our work, then we have poverty of stewardship.

4. **Poverty of Being.** This is having a broken relationship with ourselves. This means that we do not have a true or healthy view of ourselves as made in the image of God. If we don't take care of ourselves, we have poverty of being. If we think of ourselves too highly, or too lowly, we have poverty of being.

So who are the poor? All of us are poor. All people can struggle with one or more of these broken relationships. Apart from God's help, all of us are unable to live out these four relationships in the way God intended.

When we come to know Jesus, we are forgiven for our sins and have peace with God, and begin to recover from our poverty of spiritual intimacy. At that point, Jesus begins to transform our hearts and behaviour so that we hopefully have less poverty in the other three areas: we can have a healthier view of ourselves, a greater love for other people, and a better stewardship of God's creation.

For some people their brokenness in these four relationships results in **material poverty**.

5. **Material Poverty.** This is what people are normally referring to when they use the word "poverty". People have material poverty if they lack money or things that they need to live, such as food, shelter, or healthcare. Material poverty is then the fifth and last type of poverty we will discuss throughout this training. Some material poverty can be directly traced to the Curse pronounced in Genesis 3. We live in a broken world. In this world, we have thorns and weeds that make it difficult to grow crops. We have natural disasters, dangerous animals, disabilities, and disease. But it is very important to note that material poverty is often a symptom of the brokenness in the other four relationships. So in order to address material poverty, we need to work to reconcile the other four relationships as well.

Circle the original answers of the participants about what it means to be poor, where you had originally written—"lacking money or things". Next to the circled answers about lacking food or lacking shelter or lacking money, write a new label—"material poverty". Make it very clear to the participants that from now on, we will refer to lacking money or food as "**material poverty**", while we also discuss the four types of poverty based on broken relationships. This makes a total of **five types of poverty**.

- Some people have material poverty, but they have a good relationship with God and with other people. Other people might be materially rich, but they don't have a good relationship with God or other people. Each person's situation is different. All of us have some poverty because we all have brokenness in these four relationships.

- In the Bible, when God tells us to care for the poor, who is he wanting us to target? He wants us to focus our efforts on caring for materially poor people, which is what this training is about. While it's good to encourage rich people to trust in God and to love other people, in this training we are focusing on materially poor people. But to care for them well, we will have to help them holistically, addressing all of their broken relationships.

Example—The Story of Mary (10 Minutes)

Tell this story to the participants, but read it slowly enough that they can understand it well, so that you can have a discussion about it.

Mary lives in a slum in Kenya and is struggling in poverty. She grew up in a society which informed her that men are superior to women. Her parents did not value her as much as her brothers, so they did not send her to school for very many years. When she was finally married, she was only one of her husband's wives. Her husband beat her regularly until she finally ran away to live on her own. Now she was living with material poverty. She felt so inferior to others that she had no confidence to apply for a job. Instead, in her desperate situation, she decided to become self-employed. She needed a loan to get started.

She got a loan from a local dealer, but he charged her a very unfair 300 percent interest. She started a business of selling homemade charcoal in the local market, but there were hundreds of other people selling charcoal so the prices stayed very low. Mary never even considered doing another more productive kind of work because she felt like she had to do what everyone else was doing. Frustrated by her inability to pay the loan, Mary went to a witch doctor in search of help. The witch doctor said that her problems with poverty were caused by Mary having angered the ancestral spirits. She told Mary to purchase a bull and sacrifice it to them. So Mary used almost all her remaining money from the loan to purchase the bull. At the end, she was even more materially poor than she was at the beginning, and even more frustrated and hopeless.[11]

Have a good group discussion about the questions below. If the participants have trouble getting to the right answers, give them hints to help them. Before proceeding to the next question, make sure you summarise the correct answers as given in the notes below each question. Participants may find it helpful if you write some of the most important answers on the flip chart for them to copy down. But don't try to write down everything; just write some key points in note form.

Discussion Questions

1. What types of poverty did Mary have besides material poverty?

- Mary had poverty of spiritual intimacy in that she was trying to please the spirits rather than God. She did not know Jesus. Mary had poverty of being in that she felt inferior to others, felt she couldn't get a job, felt she could not do something besides what others were doing, and she felt hopeless and powerless to change her situation. Mary had poverty of community, in that she had been mistreated by her parents, abused by her husband, and exploited by the loan dealer. Mary had a poverty of stewardship in that she did not have productive work to do. She thought she had to do the same work as everyone else, instead of realising she can be creative and do something new in God's world.

(Some participants might raise the idea of cutting down trees for charcoal without planting new trees as not caring for God's creation.)

2. How did those other types of poverty contribute to Mary having even worse material poverty?

- Because Mary did not know Jesus as her Saviour, she was afraid of the spirits, and wasted all her money on a bull for a sacrifice. Because Mary had poverty of being, she had no confidence to look for a job instead of starting her own business. Starting her own business was not a bad idea, but, because of her poverty of being, she made unwise decisions about what kind of business to start. Because of Mary's poverty of community, she never got a good education. Because of her husband's abuse, she had no family to help care for her needs. Because of the unfair loan dealer, she had no real chance to start a business and pay back the loan. Because of Mary's poverty of stewardship, she did not try to do some new kind of work different from what others were doing, and she ended up losing money rather than earning more money.

3. If we wanted to help Mary and we simply gave her money, would it help her out of her desperate situation?

- No. In fact, if we gave her money, she might just use it to buy and sell more charcoal, or even worse, she might go purchase another animal sacrifice. Or she might just pay back part of the loan with the money and remain in the same situation.

4. What could we do to truly help Mary, not only with her material poverty, but with all her types of poverty?

- For Mary's **poverty of spiritual intimacy**, we could share with her the gospel of salvation in Christ. After she comes to know Christ, we could teach her that she does not need to fear the spirits or make sacrifices.

- For Mary's **poverty of being**, we could teach her about how she was created in the image of God, that she is equal to men, and not inferior. We would help her to realise that God values her, that God has a plan for her life, and that she can have hope.

- For Mary's **poverty of community**, we could invite Mary to church to give her new friends and a support system. We could try to do marriage counselling between Mary and her husband, and help the husband to repent of his abuse, and see if he is willing to help financially support Mary. We could also visit the loan dealer, especially if we are the pastor of a church in the community, and try to insist that the loan dealer give a more fair interest rate on the loan.

- For Mary's **poverty of stewardship**, we could teach her that she can be creative and do other work in God's world. She doesn't have to do whatever other people are doing. We could encourage her to apply for various jobs, and to have confidence. We could help her identify her gifts and skills. We could give her job skills training, or sponsor her to get some form of education in order to obtain the job she wants.

- To deal with her **material poverty**, we could help Mary to obtain business capital through saving or through loans at more reasonable interest rates. We might decide to help her financially in little ways to make sure she is taken care of as she goes through job training and finding new work to do. The church should also consider paying off Mary's loan to give her a fresh start. If Mary has any money at all, it would be good if she could contribute whatever she can towards this as well.

Conclusion

We need to have a better definition of poverty. Poverty is more than just lacking money. When we realise this, we will be less proud. All people are really on the same level in that we all have poverty of broken relationships, but we each experience this poverty in different ways. **All of us** have broken relationships and we all **equally** need Jesus in our lives to restore our broken relationships.

Take-Home Activities for Lesson 3

The facilitator should provide detailed guidelines and clear instructions on how to go about the take-home activities.

Think of at least one person you know in your church or community in need of help. Try to help this person holistically, in all four of their key relationships. Commit to helping this person over a long period of time. Tell your family about what you plan to do and see if they will commit to helping this person along with you. You might consider beginning by inviting the person to your home for a meal, so that you can build the relationship and get to know one another. Pray for this person every day. Once a month, take time to think about this person and their four key relationships, and review how you've been helping, and what more you could be doing. These are questions you can ask yourself regularly:

- **How have I been helping this person grow in their relationship with God?**
- **How have I been helping this person to have hope, and not feel inferior or worthless?**
- **How have I been helping this person to have a better relationship with his or her family, friends, and neighbours?**
- **How have I been helping this person to get meaningful work to do to support him or herself?**

Small Group Discussion (30 Minutes)

Inform the participants that they will be going into small groups to discuss together the questions listed at the end of Lesson 3 in their manual.

- Read out loud the questions and make sure they understand them.
- Divide them up into groups of 5 people (anywhere from 3-6 people per group). They can be the same groups as before, or you can put them into new groups. They will not be presenting their answers to anyone.
- If you have organised the whole workshop to take longer than what has been outlined, then feel free to give the participants a longer time for discussion.
- Move around and listen in with the groups as they discuss. Be available to answer questions. You can give guidance or input if necessary during their discussions, but they have heard you talk a lot, so try to let them do the talking now. Remind them periodically about how much time remains for their discussion.

Small Group Discussion Questions

1. **Think about your own life. What are some ways in which your relationships with God, self, others, and the rest of creation need healing? What specific things can you do to seek God's healing in these relationships in the next two weeks?**

2. **Have any of the four broken relationships contributed to material poverty in your life or in the life of one of your family members? Which ones?** If you feel comfortable doing so, share your answer with your group members. If the problem is ongoing, discuss together how the broken relationship could be addressed.

3. **a. Briefly, tell your group members a personal story about a time that you helped a poor person.** (Example: I could say, "Last week, I met a beggar in the market and I gave him some groundnuts.") Complete parts a. and b. completely for one story, before the next person shares a story. There will not be time for every person in the group to share a story.

3. **b. Analyse each story that is shared in your group. Critique other people's stories with love and gentleness.**

   - **Did the group member help the poor person to have less material poverty? Explain.**
     - **(Example:** "Yes—I gave the beggar food to provide for his need."**)**
   - **Did they help the poor person to have less poverty of spiritual intimacy? Explain.**
     - **(Example:** "No—I did not help the beggar to grow in his relationship with God."**)**
   - **Did they help the poor person to have less poverty of being? Explain.**
     - **(Example:** "Yes—I shook his hand and talked to him, trying to show him he has dignity and value."**)**
   - **Did they help the poor person to have less poverty of community? Explain.**
     - **(Example:** "No—I did not help him meet new people or get involved at a church."**)**
   - **Did they help the poor person to have less poverty of stewardship?**
     - **(Example:** "No—I did not help him to find meaningful work in God's world."**)**

Helping Without Hurting in Africa

FACILITATOR MANUAL

LESSON 4: BROKEN RELATIONSHIPS IN AFRICA

Lesson 4: Broken Relationships in Africa

In this section, you will find:

- A discussion of how poverty of spiritual intimacy, poverty of stewardship, poverty of community, and poverty of being, play out in peoples's lives and often contribute to material poverty.

Lesson Objectives:

- To better understand the five types of poverty.
- To understand how these types of poverty are manifested in Africa specifically.

Time Length: 2 Hours

Notes to the Facilitator

Please refer back to pages 11-18 for full facilitator guidelines, but some particular tips for this lesson include:

- **It is not possible to cover all of the points and discussion questions in this lesson in only 2 hours.** If you are not pressed for time, you could consider taking 3 hours for this lesson. But if you are following the recommended 2 hour guideline, then you as the facilitator need to choose which points and questions to cover, specifically from among the sections discussing each type of poverty. Poverty of spiritual intimacy, poverty of community, poverty of stewardship, and poverty of being each have around 4-6 questions and corresponding large group discussion questions. We recommend that you choose half of the points and half of the large group questions to discuss under each type of poverty.

  For example, for poverty of spiritual intimacy you could tell the participants: *"Poverty of spiritual intimacy in Africa can include idolatry, pleasing the spirits, witchcraft and charms, hopelessness, materialism, and sin. Looking at our community, it's important for us to talk today about idolatry, hopelessness, and materialism. The other examples can be read and studied more carefully at home."*

  * **For poverty of being try not to skip very much of the lecture material because this type of poverty is one of the hardest for participants to understand.** But you should skip a few of the large group discussion questions within the poverty of being lecture.

  Although there is a lot of material in this lesson, we wanted to present many possible points of discussion in order to allow groups to cover the points and questions that are most relevant to their context and to cover as much as they have time for. The other points that you don't discuss can be read at home.

- Ensure that long notes, quotations, and group questions are prepared in advance and written on a flip chart.
- Unless otherwise noted, all Scripture passages in **bold** should be read out loud by a participant for the whole group.

- When the participants read the selected Bible passages throughout the lesson, make brief summaries of what each Bible passage is about and what it means.
- At the end of the lesson, explain the take-home activities clearly to participants.
- If there is time at the end of the lesson, consider asking participants questions to review the key points made during the lesson.

Opening Discussion (5 Minutes)

Review—First, take two minutes to review the five types of poverty as described in Lesson 3. Have five different people each stand up and try to explain one of the types of poverty. Correct them or summarise if necessary.

Ask the participants the following questions and record all of their responses on a flip chart. Ensure that they give short and simple answers. Tell them you will discuss many of the examples together throughout the rest of the lesson. During this opening discussion, you simply want to list as many examples of each type of poverty as they can come up with. If they have difficulty understanding the questions, you could rephrase them. For example, for question 1 you could say: "Give me some examples of how people can have a broken relationship with God in your church, community, or region."

1. **Share some examples of poverty of spiritual intimacy in your church, community, or region.**
2. **Share some examples of poverty of community in your church, community, or region.**
3. **Share some examples of poverty of stewardship in your church, community, or region.**
4. **Share some examples of poverty of being in your church, community, or region.**

Facilitator Lecture (85 Minutes)

In this lesson, we are going to look at how the different kinds of poverty are present in Africa and how they are affecting our communities today.

Material Poverty

Brokenness in the four relationships results in material poverty for some people. Material poverty is the lack of sufficient income and other basic needs like; food, shelter, clothing, healthcare and even basic education. Think back to the statistics in Lesson 1. We all know that material poverty is a problem in Africa, so we won't spend much time discussing it. Instead, we will focus on the other four types of poverty based on broken relationships, and we will see how each of them contributes to greater material poverty in Africa. The diagram below gives us some common examples of the various types of poverty.

Poverty of Spiritual Intimacy

We have poverty of spiritual intimacy when we have a broken or imperfect relationship with God. Many practices and beliefs keep us from having a good relationship with God. We will look at some specific examples of poverty of spiritual intimacy that we see in Africa, though many of these examples are shared around the world as well.

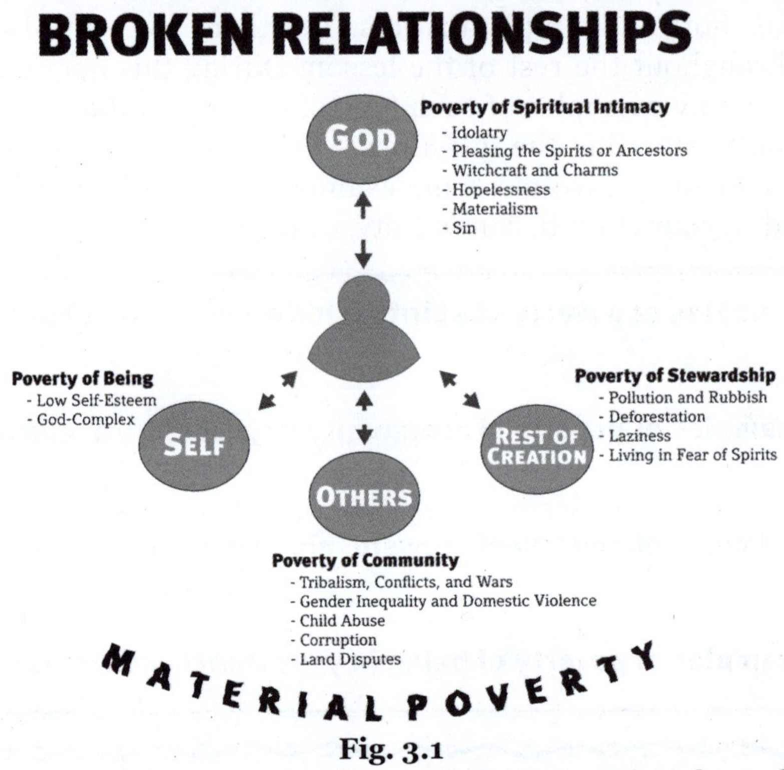

Fig. 3.1

Adapted from Bryant L. Myers, *Walking with the Poor: Principles and Practices of Transformational Development* (Maryknoll, N.Y.: Orbis Books, 1999), 27.

1. **Idolatry**. This is the worshiping of idols. An idol is **anything** that is placed before or above the one true God. It can include worshipping false gods like wood, trees, stones, rivers, mountains, animals, spirits, and statues.

In what way can this type of poverty of spiritual intimacy lead to material poverty?

If participants struggle to answer this, consider asking them about how much money, time, or other resources this kind of false worship requires.

Let's read **Exodus 20:1-6**. Idolatry can also mean taking things that are good, and putting our focus on them instead of on God. If we take anything in our lives and make it more important than God, that is idolatry. Some of us might place earning money as more important than anything else. Some of us might make safety, security, and comfort more important than anything else in our lives. If we take any of the good things God has given us, and make them into our ultimate priority instead of God, then we are giving in to idolatry.

Do we see this type of idolatry in our communities today? In our churches? Explain.

2. **Pleasing the Spirits and Ancestors**. In many places in Africa, people give offerings and sacrifices to please the spirits or ancestors. This is another practice that leads to a broken relationship with God. God wants all of our prayers and sacrifices, and he will not share them with other spirits or other people. It's important to appreciate and respect those who have gone before us, but we are to pray to God alone, not to spirits, not to demons, and not to people who have died. ***Read* Deuteronomy 18:10–11**. We have one mediator in Heaven and that is Jesus; we don't need other mediators. Read **1 Timothy 2:5**. In some of our cultural traditions, people worship or consult the dead, build shrines, sacrifice animals to please the spirits, and in some cases even commit ritual killings of people. It is common to give offerings to the spirits, gods, or ancestors to try to gain spiritual protection, to gain money, to receive healing from disease, or to secure a specific political appointment or job. Unfortunately, the people often doing these practices are the vulnerable and desperate poor who feel like they have nowhere else to turn.

Is ancestor or spirit worship a problem in our communities?

In what ways can this type of poverty of spiritual intimacy lead to material poverty?

If participants struggle to answer this, again, consider asking them about how much money, time, or other resources it takes to try to please the ancestors or spirits.

3. **Witchcraft and Charms**. Other practices that can harm our relationship with God and give us poverty of spiritual intimacy include engaging in witchcraft or using charms. Read **Revelation 21:8**. Using witchcraft and charms is widespread in Africa. In some areas, they are traditional practices. In other areas, they are a desperate search for healing, wealth, protection, or even a way to try to harm other people. These acts include the use of human body parts for medicinal purposes and the belief that human body parts possess supernatural powers that bring prosperity and protection. Through these practices, people are trying to utilise the power of the spirit world to obtain their desires, rather than trusting in God's power alone.

Do Christians need to be afraid of other people using witchcraft or charms against them?

Read **Ephesians 6:10–18 and 1 John 4:4.**

4. **Hopelessness**. Without God, without forgiveness and hope of eternal life, without believing that God has a plan for our lives, people probably do not have hope in the future, and so might do nothing to try to change their situations. Even in the church, there are those who are weak in faith and do not have much hope in God, so they remain full of despair and stuck in their situations of poverty. It is especially common to see youth resorting to alcoholism, drugs, and theft, because they have no hope and no trust in God for their futures. Read **Romans 8:28** and **Philippians 1:4-6**.

Is hopelessness a problem in our communities? How can we give people hope?

5. **Materialism**. Materialism has various definitions, but for this lesson we refer to materialism as valuing material possessions and money as the primary way to find meaning in life and happiness. Normally we associate this problem with Western cultures. But it is becoming a problem in Africa as well. People are becoming greedier for financial gain. They find their meaning in life in what kind of house and vehicle they own rather than in their relationship with God. Our community values are slowly being torn away as everyone only looks to their own financial gain rather than helping others. Even in some churches, the focus is not on glorifying God and thanking him for forgiveness, but rather on worshipping God in order that he gives us more money. Read **Luke 12:15** and **1 Timothy 6:6–10**.

In what way can this type of poverty of spiritual intimacy lead to material poverty?

If participants bring up the prosperity gospel during this discussion, you can very quickly say a few sentences about it, but inform them that there is a whole lesson on the prosperity gospel later in the training, and so you will save the big discussion about it for later.

6. **Sin**. Sin is what separates people from God and all people who have not trusted in Christ as their Saviour will be punished for their sin. But even as Christians we still sin sometimes. We sin every time we don't love our neighbor as ourselves and when we disobey God's commands. If we are truly born again, we will confess our sins and repent and keep fighting against sin. But when we sin, it displeases God, and we also experience natural consequences for living in the foolish way God does not want us to live. So in a way, whenever Christians sin, we experience a little poverty of spiritual intimacy. But the more common example of poverty of spiritual intimacy is non-Christians living in sin. Sin, of course, takes many forms but there are some common examples of sins that not only create poverty of spiritual intimacy, but they also cause material poverty. These include alcoholism, drug addiction, theft, gambling addiction, and sexual immorality. It is largely (though not exclusively) through the sexual sins of adultery and fornication that the epidemic of HIV is spreading throughout Africa.

Are any of these sins causing a lot of material poverty in our communities?

In our churches?

Before moving to the next type of poverty, see if there are any last questions or comments about poverty of spiritual intimacy.

Poverty of Community

Next is poverty of community. We have poverty of community when we have a broken relationship with other people. Let's look at some specific types of poverty of community common in Africa.

1. **Tribalism, Conflicts, and Wars**. Many countries in Africa have a long history of wars, coups, rebel groups, banditry, tribal conflicts, and even genocide. Sometimes these conflicts are because of tribal hatreds or thinking one's culture is superior. At other times they are simply the result of greed. These tribal conflicts and wars have led to millions of deaths, displacement of people from their land, more child-headed families, and increased material poverty throughout Africa. Every day, 9,500 people on average are uprooted from their homes in Africa, mostly due to conflict and violence.[1] At the end of 2015, nearly 12.4 million people in Africa were living as refugees or displaced people.[2] All of this clearly demonstrates poverty of community in Africa, a massive breakdown of relationships.

   Take a moment to reflect on how just one war can destroy all the development work of twenty or thirty years. In many contexts, fighting material poverty through working for peace and reconciliation between people to prevent conflict is far more important than through giving out money or resources. We must not ignore poverty of community.

Is tribalism or conflict a problem in your region?

Is the church speaking out about it?

We need to remember that we are all made in the image of God. God cares about all tribes and wants people of all nations and languages to be included in his kingdom. Read **Revelation 7:9–10**. Thankfully, some leaders in Africa have been speaking out against tribalism and racism in favour of reconciliation, peace, and unity.

> Ellen Johnson Sirlief, president of Liberia, said, "Ethnicity should enrich us; it should make us a unique people in our diversity and not be used to divide us."[3]

> Former Secretary-General of the United Nations, Kofi Annan, writes: "We may have different religions, different languages, different coloured skin, but we all belong to one human race."[4]

2. **Broken Relationships between Men and Women**. Another common type of poverty of community deals with the treatment of men and women generally, and specifically the broken relationships between husbands and wives. Although there can be fault both on the side of men as well as on the side of women, commonly, it is the men who are oppressing the women. In society, this can be manifested by preferring boys to be educated over girls.

In the area of marriage, the broken relationship between a husband and a wife can manifest in rape, polygamy, unfaithfulness, or divorce. Husbands and wives can both abuse one another in marriage through beating, slapping, calling each other names, making threats, or attacking one another's property. Wives can sometimes disrespect their husbands's leadership or try to inflict wounds with their words. In some cultures, it is traditionally accepted for husbands to beat and discipline their wives. About one third of women in Africa report to have experienced domestic violence (physical or sexual), not counting those too afraid to report.[5] Another issue in some marriages in Africa is that some people believe the role of men is to sit while the women do most of the work.

In our churches, do some people think it is acceptable for husbands to beat their wives?

Read **Genesis 1:27**. We must remember that men and women both are equally made in the image of God. Even though created with different bodies and different roles, they were both created to have dignity and value. Women were created to help men with their work, but not to do all the work. Read **Ephesians 5:28–29**. Husbands are to love their wives as their own bodies. To beat one's own body is inhuman. The church must honour both men and women as equally made in the image of God, and try to restore the broken relationships between men and women.

3. **Child Abuse**. Child abuse is another common example of poverty of community in Africa. Many children have been subjected to child labour working as house girls or boys in people's homes, digging in people's gardens. More than 40% of all children aged 5–14 labour for survival in Africa.[6] Excessive beating is often used as a form of punishment by parents. Abuse causes children to grow up in fear and isolation and sometimes react towards others in anger or aggression. It can affect a child's mental and spiritual development as well.

In what ways did you suffer abuse as a child? How did this affect you?

4. **Corruption**. We will have a whole lesson to talk about it later in the course.

5. **Land Disputes**. Land in Africa is never just a commodity or a means of subsistence. It is very much tied to the family and the community, and it is also tied to cultural identity and citizenship. Land disputes occur at all levels and are mainly caused by greed and exploitation, though at times they are also caused by unclear land boundaries and lack of land titles. Examples include arguments between neighbours about field boundaries, arguments between families on issues of inheritance, conflicts between pastoralists and farmers, disputes between the state and indigenous peoples, and arguments between companies and local populations about rights to exploit mineral, water, or other resources. With fast-growing populations in many countries, the competition for scarce land is becoming aggressive.

Are there land disputes in your community? Explain.
What is the church doing to help resolve such disputes?

Before moving to the next type of poverty, see if there are any last questions or comments about poverty of community.

Poverty of Stewardship

We have poverty of stewardship when we have a broken relationship with God's good creation. This could be in the form of improper care of the environment or not working and being productive. If we destroy the environment, or if we fail to do our work well for God's glory, then we are being bad stewards and we have poverty of stewardship. Read **Psalm 8**. We are supposed to rule the creation. Let's look at specific examples of poverty of stewardship that are common in Africa.

1. **Pollution and Rubbish**. One of the consequences of so many countries recently going through the process of industrialisation is pollution. Water, air, and land are being polluted by leaked chemicals, fumes in the air, and plastic rubbish. Many people carelessly throw rubbish on the ground rather than carefully disposing or burning it, or reusing it. The result is unhealthy soil, breeding of pests and disease, and taking away the beauty of God's creation. Because laws are not enforced well, companies regularly dump toxic waste in lakes and rivers and destroy ecosystems, in some places, making it dangerous even to eat the fish from those lakes.

   Farmers often use pesticides, fertilizers, and other chemicals on their soil without reading the instructions, causing great harm to the environment and to their own bodies. Some farmers also overwork the soil by never letting it rest and failing to rotate crops so the land is becoming more infertile. Overgrazing is causing erosion and destruction of the land so that it becomes unsuitable for either pastoralism or farming. When we do not obey God's commands to take care of his creation, we experience the painful natural consequences of our actions.

   Destruction of the environment has also indirectly caused many of the violent conflicts in Africa we talked about earlier. Hear these words from Kenyan Environmental Activist, Wangari Maathai:

   > The challenges facing agricultural communities throughout Kenya are mirrored throughout Africa and many of the poor countries in underdeveloped regions. In these regions, concern for environmental issues is treated as a luxury. But it is not: protecting and restoring ecosystems, and slowing or reversing global warming, are matters of life and death. The equation is simple: whatever we do, we impact the environment; if we destroy it, we will undermine our own ways of life and ultimately kill ourselves. This is why the environment needs to be at the centre of domestic and international policy and practice.[7]

2. **Deforestation.** Deforestation refers to the systematic destruction of trees and forests without replanting the trees. This is another form of poverty of stewardship in Africa. An alarming rate of deforestation in Africa has produced famines, desertification, water

shortages, drought, massive economic and social dislocations, and widespread resource-based conflicts. Unfortunately, material poverty is one of the causes of deforestation while, at the same time, deforestation causes more material poverty. The people who clear forests for firewood and charcoal, for agriculture, pasture, settlement, and building homes are often those who are materially poor and feel like they have no choice. 80% of households in Africa depend on wood or charcoal as their primary energy source.[8] The deforestation rate in Africa is four times the world average.[9] Some places have been hit worse than others. Almost 90% of West Africa's rainforests have been destroyed.[10]

Which of these environmental problems do you see in your community?

Is either the church or the government addressing these issues? Explain.

3. **Laziness**. When we do not work hard or do quality work, this is another example of poverty of stewardship. Laziness is when we have the ability to do good work but we do not do it. It can involve taking shortcuts, not working when the manager is away, showing up late for work, or not completing work within the agreed-upon time frame. It is common, especially for office workers, to report to work but then to spend hours discussing politics, receiving personal calls, shopping, or reading the national dailies. We will talk more about how to work hard for God's glory in a later lesson.

In what ways does this type of poverty of stewardship result in more material poverty in your community?

4. **Living in fear of spirits**. If you think fearing the spirits is actually an example of poverty of spiritual intimacy, you are correct. But it is also an example of poverty of stewardship. There is a common belief among some people that spirits control the land, rivers, or particular forests in Africa. Because of fear, these people refrain from utilising the resources God has given to them. Other people may not do specific jobs or may not work at all, claiming that the spirits would not allow them. These people do not realise that God has given us the power and responsibility of being stewards over the land. The land belongs to God, not to the spirits. We do not need to fear them, and we can utilise the land that God has given to us. While Satan has tried to claim dominion of this world, we do not need to fear him because of Christ's power over him. **Read James 4:7.**

Are there people with this kind of fear in your community?

What can the church do to help them?

Before moving to the next type of poverty, see if there are any last questions or comments about poverty of stewardship.

Poverty of Being

Poverty of being refers to having a broken relationship with ourselves. A person has poverty of being if she or he has an improper view of himself or herself. We will spend longer on poverty of being, because many of the mistakes we make when helping materially poor people are due to ignoring this type of poverty. For this training, we will narrow our discussion to looking at only two types of poverty of being. Basically, people might either 1) think too lowly of themselves and not see their value as people made in the image of God, or 2) they might think too highly of themselves, as more like gods themselves, rather than as servants of God. We could say that people do not have poverty of being if they have a true and healthy view of themselves as people made in the image of God.

Poverty of Being 1: Low Self-Esteem

People have this type of poverty of being when they feel too lowly about themselves. It can include feeling inferior, unworthy, incapable, incompetent, ashamed, fearful, humiliated, voiceless, and dependent. In general, it is having a negative attitude about yourself. Do you notice where we saw these words before? These are words that materially poor people used to define poverty in Lesson 3. It is very common (though not universally true) for materially poor people to have low self-esteem and to feel all of these things.

On the flip chart page from Lesson 3 where you had written the answers concerning the World Bank Survey on poverty, now circle all the answers that relate to poverty of being (shame, voiceless, fear, powerless, etc.). Mark this circled group of phrases and words with a new title—"**Poverty of Being: Low Self-Esteem**".

Many materially poor people struggle with feeling inferior to others because of their poverty. They do not always see themselves as wonderful creations of God blessed with talents and gifts. This can keep them from taking opportunities to improve their situation. They feel hopeless and afraid about making changes to improve their lives. In a way, these feelings are more painful than experiencing hunger or sickness, yet they can also cause more material poverty.

Sometimes people who have this low self-esteem can be Christians like us who know about being made in the image of God. In a fallen world, it is easy for us to forget this truth and start feeling terrible about ourselves. We can think we are not able to do certain tasks and feel like we can't relate well with others who we think are superior to us. We become isolated and lose confidence. We become passive and afraid to voice our opinions. Some of us may even feel so badly about ourselves that we turn to drugs or alcohol to forget our sorrows.

Think about the Israelites after God rescued them from Egypt. They were used to feeling inferior as slaves. In the wilderness, they had God to protect them. But they kept thinking of themselves as slaves and they wanted to go back to their slavery. They didn't want to follow God's commands and conquer the Promised Land. They were so used to feeling inferior that they felt powerless and afraid to change their situation, even with God promising to help them.

Listen to this story from Bryant Myers, an American seminary professor and author. Bryant was sitting at a fire in the Kalahari Desert talking to a woman from a local tribe. He told her that the Son of God had died for her sins. In response to this, she said she could believe that God would let his Son die for a white man, and maybe even a black man, but she could never accept the idea that God would let his Son die for a woman, especially one of her tribe. You can see that she had a poverty of being. Not only can poverty of being contribute to material poverty, but in this case, she felt so worthless and inferior, that she refused to accept even the good news of the gospel. Her poverty of being was also keeping her trapped in poverty of spiritual intimacy. She needed help to recover her identity as a child of God, made in God's image. She needed to be taught that her true role in life is to live and work as a child of God in the world he made for her.[11]

Large Group Discussion Questions:

Ask the participants the questions below and record their answers on a flip chart.

1. **What causes low self-esteem in your family, community, and region?**
2. **How can you counsel materially poor people in your church who feel ashamed and helpless because of their poverty?**

Unfortunately, here in Africa poverty of being is very common. Slavery and colonialism are some of the major causes of people in Africa generally feeling inferior. The incredible evil of the European and American transatlantic slave trade has forever left its mark in Africa. Not only did it cause the enslavement or death of at least twelve million people, but it set Africa back economically for years to come because of all the chaos and disruption.

Colonialism was not much better than the slave trade. When the colonialists came to Africa, they came with a very superior attitude and came to utilise the land and resources of the people of Africa for themselves. They believed their own languages, cultures, and systems of government were better in every way than African ones. Some of these Westerners felt like it was their duty to force Western culture upon the peoples of Africa for their own good. Most of the systems found in Africa were considered inferior, and therefore were either peacefully or (in most cases) forcefully removed. Colonialism was not bad in every aspect. There were missionaries who preached the good news about Christ to the people of Africa. There were those who built schools and hospitals and worked on Bible translation into vernacular languages. Some missionaries and Christian colonialists spoke up against slavery, respected the people of Africa as equals, and tried to protect African people from having their land taken. Even so, the majority of colonialists did not have this attitude, and they stressed the inferiority of the people of Africa through both racism and saying that western culture was superior.

This superiority complex of the colonialists left a mark on the people of Africa that can be seen to this day, even after independence. Through the colonial period, the people in Africa learned to fear westerners, learned to feel shame about their own cultures, and learned to feel submissive and inferior about themselves. To make matters even more complicated, as Africans saw the material wealth and economic development of the other nations, many associated wealth with whiteness and Western culture—and associated poverty with being black and with African culture. To this day, it is not uncommon for Africans to feel inferior to Americans or Europeans, or even to the foreign missionaries or expatriates who live in their countries.

Augustine Musopole, reverend and author from Malawi, said, "This is where the African feels his poverty most: A poverty of being, in which poor Africans have come to believe they are no good and cannot get things right."[12]

We need to learn and preach that Africans are not inferior, that we do not always need to be dependent on foreigners. We as Africans have dignity and value, and we are not inferior to Westerners. We are made in the image of God and God can use us to transform our communities.

Discussion Question

When you see a foreigner in your country, do you feel equal to him in status and value or do you feel inferior?

Why?

Beyond the general low self-esteem many Africans feel, there are certain groups of people in Africa who experience even lower self-esteem. One of these groups is women. In some African cultures, women are not supposed to attend certain functions, be part of a discussion, or even contribute in a meeting. There is a common saying that "A man's or husband's word is final", or "What my husband says is what I say" even when the husband and wife are not in agreement or have not discussed an issue. Women are not supposed to hold any positions of responsibility, according to some cultural and traditional beliefs, and cannot even inherit property of the deceased husband.

Do women in your church and community feel inferior to men or equal in value before God? Explain.

Those with disabilities, whether physical or mental, and also albinos are other groups of people who commonly have low self-esteem. People with albinism in particular are seen as so different, some parents will abort a child with albinism. In some cultures, people with albinism are targets for ritual killings. People with disabilities are seen as inferior and as objects of pity. Many people think there is no use for a disabled person except to be a person who begs, even though many of them can actually do very good meaningful work. Children with disabilities often grow up isolated because some parents keep them secretly tucked away in the home.

Do people with disabilities or albinism in your church feel just as important and valuable to the church ministry as everyone else?

If these people are not in your church, why might that be?

We must preach and we must remember that we are all equally made in the image of God, blessed with talents and gifts, no matter the colour of skin or where we come from. Read **Psalm 139:13-16**.

Poverty of Being 2: God-Complex

The other type of poverty of being people commonly have is called a "**god-complex**". These people think of themselves more highly than they should, as superior to others. We call it a god-complex because these people are putting themselves almost in the position of God. They want to receive glory and honour. They think of themselves as very important. Often, it is those who are materially rich who feel this way.

Many people think they are rich because they are more intelligent, harder working, and better than other people. They may also think they are rich because God is blessing them since they are more righteous than other people. Many of us, even as Christians, can fall into this type of poverty of being. Many of us have this false and unhealthy view of ourselves. Unfortunately, most of us are blind to this problem in ourselves. We accuse other people of seeing themselves as superior, but we never think it of ourselves.

When you walk through town and you see a beggar begging for money, do you feel superior to that person?

Do you feel more important?

One of the times that we most often think of ourselves too highly, with a god-complex, is when we try to help the materially poor. We imagine that we help them out of love, but we must question our motives. Are we helping them in order to be praised as their saviour? Are we helping them for glory and honour? Are we helping them so that we can feel better about ourselves? As we help them, are we blaming them for their poverty, thinking that we are better than them and that they deserve their poverty? Do we think we are more intelligent and have all the best ideas compared to materially poor people? We must ask ourselves the tough question: "Why is it that I want to help the poor?" None of us have 100% pure motives. We are all sinful, but we must keep praying and asking God to heal our hearts, so that we think of ourselves as we ought to, and so that we may help the materially poor out of a true feeling of love and compassion.

Is someone willing to admit their mistakes and share a story about when you yourself had a god-complex when helping materially poor people?

Harming the Poor

The title of this training is *Helping without Hurting in Africa*. We now come to another important principle about how to avoid harming the poor. We will talk about one of the most common ways that people harm the materially poor people they are trying to help, and actually harm themselves in the process too. We call this the equation for harm in fighting poverty:

1. **The rich who are trying to help have a god-complex.**

2. **The materially poor people being helped have low self-esteem.**

1 + 2 = 3

3. **After being helped, the materially poor feel even more ashamed and helpless while remaining in poverty, and the rich feel even more superior. The materially poor and the materially rich who tried to help end up *having bitterness towards one another*.**

You can be almost certain that whenever you see this equation in real life that there is a lot of hurt being caused by the helping. You might see some physical improvement in the lives of people, but they might remain dependent, stuck in their situation, and even more ashamed.

A Case Study

Let me share with you a true story about what this equation looks like in real life.[13] In northern Ghana there is an area of hot and dry land. The local people have to store water in very big pools of water, open dugouts in the ground. Unfortunately, the water gets polluted by animals and becomes very unhealthy to drink. Some years back, many different NGOs and foreigners wanted to help the people in this region with their water problem.

One organisation came to the region and taught about water filtration to groups of women in each village, and helped them to start businesses of water filtration. It was a good project that was self-sustainable because of the profit, and people seemed to appreciate it. Two years into the project, the businesses were thriving, there were many customers, and homes had good clean water in the region. In one village of the region though, the project was failing. Why? The woman with the filtration business in this village had started well, and had many customers when she began. It turns out that the business was failing because of other people who had come in to help, and they had come in with god-complexes.

In the two years since the business began, no less than three other groups came in to the village to do some kind of water filtration project.

First, the government came. Instead of asking people what the people needed, or asking if they already had clean water, the government officials assumed that the people were materially poor, inferior, and that the government knew what was best for them. They distributed water filters (of a new type) to every household in the village. But the government officials never gave the people any training about how to clean the filters. Six months later, all the filters were either clogged or broken.

Second, an American church team came to the village. During a very short trip, they distributed yet another kind of water filter to some—but not all—of the people of the village.

Then they left. Again, they were helping with a god-complex, thinking that they knew what was best for the village and wanted to feel like they were saving poor Ghanaian people. They also did not treat the people of the village with respect, never asking them if they needed filters. The people did not get much training on how to clean these filters either. A few months later, almost all of them were broken or thrown out.

Then an NGO came and gave each person in the village yet another kind of water filter. Again, this NGO came with a god-complex, without talking to the people. Their water filters were useless for the people because they worked so slowly that it would take 22 hours for only 100 households to fill their water containers. Even worse, the filtered water was still contaminated.

What was the end result? All of these groups felt great about themselves for the charity work they did for this village, yet at the end of it all, the first well-planned water project was pushed into failure in this village. The woman who had the original, successful water filter business was forced out of work by competition from the free filters from other "helpers", leaving the entire village without clean water again. Some people who were still using broken filters thought they were getting clean water but actually were not. Children actually got sick and died from this.

We can imagine that the village felt even more hopeless and inferior. Why try to do anything to make change ever again? They had tried four times and only seen failure. Maybe they thought the problem was with themselves. Maybe they thought: "All of these good people tried to help us, but we must be too stupid to know how to use these complicated filters." In the end, we can see that the result was only sickness and hopelessness. In addition, when people with god-complexes try to help like this and do not see the results they want, they often get bitter at the materially poor people they were trying to help.

This is a true story that unfortunately is repeated often throughout Africa in many diverse ways. Sometimes it is foreigners with god-complexes trying to help Africans, but just as often, it is we Africans with god-complexes helping other Africans. **God-complexes of those helping + low self-esteem of those being helped = Hurt to everyone**.

Discussion Questions

1. **What do we learn from this story?**
2. **Does anyone want to share a similar story to illustrate this equation that you have heard or seen? As you share, do not share specific names or organisations.**

So what can we do to avoid making these mistakes when we help people? How can we remove our god-complexes?

First, we need to change our definition of poverty. We need to realise that life is more than having things and money. We must repent of only thinking about money, and understand that there are many types of poverty.

Second, we need to remember that in some ways we all have poverty (in the four important relationships), and so we all need Jesus. This way, we can work to take down our god-complexes. We need to keep remembering our sin and our dependence on Jesus so that we don't think too highly of ourselves.

Third, we need to be humble and keep encouraging the materially poor that they are made in the image of God and are equal to us.

Take-Home Activities for Lesson 4

The facilitator should provide detailed guidelines and clear instructions on how to go about the take-home activities. Read aloud the two activities and explain that pastors should probably choose #1, and others attending the training should probably choose #2.

1. **Plan a worship service centred on the four relationships. Briefly teach the church about them. Consider having a time of repentance and confession, looking at how we have all failed in various ways in our four key relationships. Particularly, take time to confess how we have contributed to making the poor feel low self-esteem. During the service, preach a sermon about how all people are made in God's image, and are worthy of our respect and love.**

2. **Alternative for non-pastors—Teach your family about the four relationships. Then, together as a family, make a plan for how you will try to specifically improve each of the four relationships.**

Small Group Discussion (30 Minutes)

- Inform the participants that they will be going into small groups to discuss together the questions listed at the end of Lesson 4 in their manual.
- Read out loud the questions that they will be answering and make sure they understand them.
- Divide them up into groups of 5 people (or anywhere from 3–6 people per group). They can be the same groups as before, or you can put them into new groups. They will not be presenting their answers to anyone.
- If you have organised the whole workshop to take longer than what has been outlined, then feel free to give the participants a longer time for discussion.
- Remember to move around and listen in with the groups as they discuss. Be available to answer their questions. You can give guidance or input if necessary during their discussions, but they have heard you talk a lot, so try to let them do the talking now. Remind them periodically about how much time remains for their discussion.

Small Group Discussion Questions

1. **Looking at your own relationships with God, self, others, and the rest of creation, what can you do to improve them?**

    - Relationship with God:

    - With self:

    - With others:

    - With the creation:

2. **Read Psalm 19:1–4. The creation is supposed to reveal God's glory. What can your church do to make your community's physical environment a more beautiful and healthier place that better reveals God's glory?**

3. **When we look at materially poor people, do we see them as equals made in the image of God? Explain.**

4. **Read these Bible verses about pride. Discuss how to remove your god-complexes.—Romans 12:3, Romans 12:16, Matthew 23:12, and Proverbs 26:12**

5. **Do you yourself ever feel inferior to those with more money than you? Explain.**

6. **Pray together as a group. Take time to repent, ask for humility, and ask God to transform your relationships with him, self, others, and creation.**

Further Reflection

Read the following pages at home for further learning.

- **Understanding the Image of God**

Read and reflect on Genesis chapters 1-3.

What does being created in the image of God really mean?

On the sixth day of creation, God created his most amazing and unique creatures, human beings. Read **Genesis 1:26–27**. God finished his work of creation with a "personal touch". God formed Adam from the dust and gave him life by sharing his own breath (**Genesis 2:7**). Accordingly, humanity is unique among all God's creations, being made with both a material

body but also an immaterial soul (which we can also call our spirit).
Having the "image" or "likeness" of God means that we were made to resemble God. But we should not think that this resemblance is similar to how we look in a mirror and see an image. Adam did not *physically* look like God. God, in his divine nature, does not have a body; rather he is Spirit. Read **John 4:24**. The Bible talks about God's hands or ears or eyes in a metaphorical way to help us to understand him better. So the image of God must refer to something else besides physical appearance. Throughout church history, Christians have thought deeply about what the image of God means and concluded that being made in the image of God refers to ways that we were created to be like God. And we were created to be like him in many ways:

1. We were created not only as physical beings, but also as spiritual beings, to be like God who is Spirit.
2. We were created to be holy and righteous as God is. This can be called the "moral image of God".
3. We were created differently from the animals to have intelligence, language, emotions, and moral freedom.
4. Our God is a triune God. As the three persons have always been in perfect loving relationship with one another, so also were we created to be in loving relationship with God, ourselves, others, and the rest of creation.
5. God created us to be his stewards and do his work in this world. As God rules the creation, he created us in his image to take part in ruling the creation. Read **Genesis 1:28–30**. We are to manage the creation, lovingly care for it, and work in it to develop it and make it fruitful and beautiful. We will discuss more about this work in the next lesson.

The image of God is something that is shared by all people. Our sin stains the image of God in us, but we are all still people with God's image. Even the evillest people in the world are still made in the image of God. We have to remember that every person is made in the image of God, including non-Christians, including those with physical disabilities, including those who have mental disabilities, including those still in their mothers's wombs—absolutely everyone. This should cause us to have respect for all people, even those who are uneducated and extremely materially poor. Every life is precious. Because we are all made in the image of God, harming another person not only wrongs that person but is a sin against our Almighty God as well. We must treat everyone with honour, dignity, respect, care, and love.

The goal is that we have true and healthy views of ourselves as people made in the image of God. But we can all-too-quickly forget this important truth. Some people have never been taught this at all. When we have an improper view of ourselves, we have poverty of being. We need to avoid both low self-esteem and god-complexes.

- **The Moral Image of God**

It's good to reflect more deeply on the moral image of God (the second meaning of the image of God in the list above). Adam and Eve were created in God's image, but when they rebelled against God, Sin came into the world. Adam was our representative for humanity, so we bear the consequences of his sin together with him **(Romans 5:12)**. Now all people are born with a sinful nature and all people sin against God, just like Adam and Eve did.

Sin has distorted God's image in people. We've used our rationality to think up complicated lies. We've used our relationships to manipulate and use other people. And instead of using our power over the earth to represent the loving rule of God, we've corrupted and ruined much of the creation around us. How do we get out of the mess and destruction that we have caused? We need to have the image of God restored in us. But this is something that we are unable to do on our own. We need a new Adam, a new representative whose image is not stained by sin, someone who perfectly resembles God and perfectly obeys God.

We need Jesus! Jesus is the perfect image of God. He is God himself. Reflect on **2 Corinthians 4:4, Colossians 1:15**, and **Hebrews 1:3**. In the Incarnation, Jesus revealed God to us in the most powerful way. As a human being, he walked and talked with people face to face. And Jesus lived a perfect life of obedience and righteousness. When we have faith in Jesus and become united to him, he restores in us the moral image of God. We are justified by faith and receive the perfect righteousness of Christ as a gift. Now when God looks at us, he sees the perfect moral image of God because he sees Christ in us. Read and reflect on **Colossians 3:9-10, 2 Corinthians 3:18, Ephesians 4:22-24, 1 Corinthians 15:49**, and **Romans 8:28-30** to see how God restores the image of God in us through Christ.

Helping Without Hurting in Africa

Facilitator Manual

Lesson 5: Fighting Poverty Through Reconciliation

Lesson 5: Fighting Poverty through Reconciliation

In this section, you will find:

- An overview of the Bible's teaching on reconciliation and the church's role in the ministry of reconciliation.
- A discussion of what reconciliation might look like in each of the four key relationships.

Lesson Objectives

- To understand how to fight poverty through reconciliation.
- To understand how to reconcile the broken four key relationships.

Time Length: 1.75 hours

Notes to the Facilitator

Please refer back to pp. 11-18 for full facilitator guidelines, but some particular tips for this lesson include:

- Read the concluding stories at the end of the lesson carefully. Choose which one you think will be most beneficial to share with your training group.
- Ensure that long notes, quotations, and group questions are prepared in advance and written on a flip chart.
- Unless otherwise noted, all Scripture passages in **bold** should be read out loud by a participant for the whole group.
- When the participants read the selected Bible passages throughout the lesson, make brief summaries of what each Bible passage is about and what it means.
- At the end of the lesson, explain the take-home activities clearly to participants.
- If there is time at the end of the lesson, consider asking participants questions to review the key points made during the lesson.

Facilitator Lecture: Reconciliation (85 minutes)

Ask the participants the following question and take note of their responses on a flip chart.

What does the word "reconciliation" mean?

Reconciliation means:

- The restoration of a broken relationship.
- Two groups of people who were enemies making peace with each other.

In previous lessons, we looked deeply at the nature of poverty and the four broken relationships. This lesson looks at the solution to those problems of poverty. And the solution is reconciliation.

Think again about the overall story of the Bible. We've already looked at the "Creation" and the "Fall". We saw how God created humans to live in four relationships and looked at the ways those four relationships have become broken. But there is good news! The third part of the biblical story is "**Redemption**". Jesus came to redeem us and this world.

Let's remember again **Colossians 1:19-20**: "*For in him all the fullness of God was pleased to dwell, and through him God was pleased to reconcile to himself all things, whether on earth or in heaven, by making peace through the blood of his cross.*"

Jesus is bringing redemption and reconciliation to the entire universe, to all of our broken relationships. He begins by reconciling us to God. We were enemies of God, but now in Christ we are children of God. Read **Romans 5:10**. After people are reconciled to God, Jesus continues to work in them so that they can be reconciled to other people, to the creation, and to a proper view of themselves.

Of course, we see today that this reconciliation is not yet perfect and complete. Remember this is because the Kingdom of God is already here but not yet fully here. When Jesus returns, he will bring his kingdom fully and he will make a new heaven and a new earth. This is the fourth and last part of the biblical story that we read about in the book of Revelation. We call the end of this biblical story, "**the Consummation**".

The word "consummation" means the end of all things, the fulfilment of God's promises for this world. "The Consummation" refers to when Jesus comes, when every tear will be wiped from our eyes. All our suffering will end. There will be no more poverty. But in the meantime, as we wait for Jesus to come back, Jesus reigns as King in Heaven and continues his ministry of reconciliation in this world. And he uses us in this ministry.

This understanding should affect the way we try to solve the problem of poverty. If we believe that poverty is only about lacking money, we will look to money as the only solution to poverty. But if we believe that poverty is a result of broken relationships, then the only solution to poverty is the power of Jesus's death and resurrection to put everything into right relationship again. In other words, **the solution to poverty is the work of reconciliation**.

The Ministry of Reconciliation

Since reconciliation is the ministry of Jesus, the ministry of the church should be reconciliation as well. We are told about this specifically in **2 Corinthians 5:17-21**. Verse 18 makes clear that we have been given the ministry of reconciliation. Jesus is the one who does the real work of reconciliation, through the power of the Holy Spirit, but we are Jesus's ambassadors, representing his kingdom to a broken world. We preach the gospel so people can be reconciled to God, and we also ask God to use us to bring reconciliation between people as well.

How much progress in the work of reconciliation can we expect?

Is it possible that God will use us to completely eliminate poverty? Explain.

The answer is that it is not likely that we will completely eliminate material poverty until Christ returns and overcomes all of the effects of the Fall. But we can be confident of two very important truths: 1) We will never completely get rid of any of the five types of poverty in this world until Jesus returns. 2) We can expect to see some real reduction in poverty right now, because Jesus is using us for his work through the power of the Holy Spirit in us.
We can be both realistic that we will not solve all of the world's problems this year, and at the same time, go forward in hope and confidence knowing that Jesus is at work. He will use us to bring some restoration to the four broken relationships we see in the world.

Jonny's Story

Let's look at a true story about the power of reconciliation in helping someone who had material poverty. We had a story in Lesson 1 about one of the authors (Jonny) trying to help his brother. Listen now to the rest of the story:

> Remember in the first part of my story, I accidentally caused harm to my brother, his family and myself while trying to help him in my own way. I truly wanted to help him but I only ended up financing his alcohol addiction, which led to more broken relationships. I was really disappointed in him but later on I realised that part of the problem was my approach to helping him. So I prayed about it, and then went to see him again. I apologised for the strong words I had used about my disappointment in him and then reaffirmed my respect for him as my elder brother. He also apologised for letting me and his family down and for the way he conducted himself. We reconciled and had discussions together with his family. Both I and the other family members affirmed his gifts and potential, especially his skill in the area of farming. We also noted the free land in the village which is very fertile for farming. I praised God for this wonderful time of reconciliation and we closed our time together in prayer. Later, I gave him farming tools that he needed. I also continued to encourage him that he can get out of his situation and urged him to pray for guidance and come back to God. After some time, my brother started going around the village looking for work, and was paid for working in other people's gardens. He saved some money and started his own farm and continues in this work up to today.

What did Jonny do well?

What could he have done differently?

Be sure to discuss how the story teaches us the importance of reconciliation in helping those who suffer poverty. Take the participants through the five types of poverty one by one. Ask them if Jonny did anything to help his brother with each type of poverty. If they come up with criticisms of Jonny, or suggestions of what more he could have done, this is okay. No one helps others perfectly, and we are all continually learning together.

Reconciling the Four Relationships

Discussion Questions

Ask the participants the questions below and make a list of their answers on the flip chart for each question. Write down words and phrases, not long paragraphs. For example, for question 3, you might list: marriage counseling, hosting peace events between tribes, preaching on forgiveness, etc.

1. **What can we do to help reconcile people to God?**
2. **What can we do to help people have a healthy view of themselves?**
3. **What can we do to encourage people to reconcile with one another?**
4. **How can we become better stewards of God's creation?**
5. **What can we do to support people having meaningful work to do in God's world?**

These activities that we have listed are all ways to fight poverty, even though we often do not see them that way. They fight poverty by working to restore and reconcile broken relationships. Certainly we can say that giving money, building hospitals, and treating sickness are all part of fighting poverty as well. But it is crucial for us to focus on activities of reconciliation in our ministries as we work against poverty.

We also need to focus on reconciliation as we measure our success in our work against poverty. What does success look like? It does not mean that our African nations begin to look like foreign countries. For example, the United States might be wealthy in money, but there is material poverty there as well. Over 500,000 Americans are homeless, living on the street.[1] Americans also experience many broken relationships, and some do not believe in God at all. Many Americans suffer from depression, drug abuse, and high rates of divorce and sexual immorality. The goal **should not** be to make Africa look like the United States or any other Western country. That would not be success. Success is seeing people reconciled in all of their broken relationships, whether in the U.S. or Africa or the rest of the world. We want to see people who glorify God by living in right relationship with him, with self, with others, and with the rest of creation. This reconciliation will lead to a reduction in material poverty as well.

Let me give you a short statement or definition to summarise how we fight against material poverty. **Fighting material poverty is working to reconcile the four relationships so that people can fulfil their calling of glorifying God by working and supporting themselves and their families.**

Notice something in this definition. Fighting material poverty involves more than just making sure that people have enough material things and money. It involves the much harder task of empowering people to earn enough to meet their material needs through their own meaningful work in God's world. When people earn what they need instead of receiving handouts, we help them move closer to being the people that God created them to be. We will look at work more deeply in a later lesson.

Now let's look at how to work on reconciling the four relationships in more detail.

Reconciliation with God

A person's relationship with God is the foundation for all the other relationships. So the most important goal is reconciling people to God, and that is where we must begin. This is for two reasons. First, if people do not have forgiveness and eternal life, then it does not help them much to be well fed, healthy, and materially rich only for this short life. Second, once we come to know God, repent of our sins, and experience being born again in Christ, every aspect of our lives changes. We are forgiven, we receive the Holy Spirit, we are able to have a proper view of ourselves, we reconcile with other people, and we do meaningful work in God's world for God's glory. Certainly, non-Christians can still work hard at their jobs and also make peace with other people. This is due to God's grace at work in the world in a general way. But if people are not born again in Christ, they are still ruled by sin, and there is not much hope for lasting change in their broken relationships.

This means that the church has a fundamental role to play in fighting poverty. Secular organisations and governments will not have programs and interventions that reconcile people to God. It is only the church, only Christians, who will preach the good news of the gospel and introduce people to Jesus. Read **1 Peter 3:15-16**.

Discussion Questions

1. **Can you think of any situations in which it would be wise to help people with a material need before preaching the gospel to them?**
2. **If people reject Jesus and remain in their poverty of spiritual intimacy, is there anything we can still do to work with them to overcome their other types of poverty?**

Below are some ideas that you could mention throughout the discussions, but only mention them if the participants do not do so themselves first.

For question #1, you could mention that if people are very sick or very hungry, they will not be able to listen well to your gospel presentation. In those cases, it would be wise to treat the sickness or give them food to eat. In this way you also show the love of Christ through your actions. Furthermore, you could mention that it would be bad to give people the impression that they need to become Christians in order to receive material help from us. We need to show love to everyone regardless of whether they are Christians or not. And we do not want people quickly and unthinkingly becoming Christians just to receive food or medicine from us. Similarly, if we give food or medicine to them before preaching the gospel, we need to be careful not to make it look like we are bribing them with material things in order to get them to accept the gospel. We are to preach the gospel through our actions and our words, and allow people the freedom to accept or reject Christ.

For question #2, you could mention that it will be very difficult for people to overcome their various types of poverty without first coming to Christ. But we can still try to help them. We are supposed to keep loving people even if they have rejected Christ. We can still try to help them reconcile with other people, still try to help them have meaningful work to do, still help them to take care of their environment, and still help them with their material needs.

Reconciliation with Self

Reconciliation with self means a person will think of themselves in the correct way, knowing that they are created in God's image, and blessed with gifts and talents. This knowledge removes fear, builds confidence, and helps people to move forward in hope working to change their situation. People should know that they are loved by God and that he has a plan for their lives.

In the last lesson we looked deeply at low self-esteem and god-complexes. To help people reconcile to a proper view of themselves, we need to teach them and counsel them about their value and dignity as people made in the image of God. We need to encourage, build up, and treat materially poor people as equals. For those with god-complexes, we also need to gently challenge or remind them that all of us are equally made in God's image, and we are not superior to materially poor people. Sometimes the best we can do for those with god-complexes is lead by example. We need to repent of our own god-complexes first, and humble ourselves as we care for the materially poor around us.

Reconciliation with Others

We are called to have a loving relationship with our neighbours following the example of God's love for us. We must see each other as created in the image of God. Former Archbishop of South Africa Desmond Tutu once said, "When we see others as the enemy, we risk becoming what we hate. When we oppress others, we end up oppressing ourselves. All of our humanity is dependent upon recognizing the humanity in others."[2]

Christians need to be mediators, working to bring peace between other people, groups, churches, and tribes. Read **Matthew 5:9** and **Romans 12:17-21**. We must set an example by being people who personally reconcile with others, admit our faults, and offer forgiveness.

Through the church's ministry of reconciliation and through love of neighbours, churches build trust in the community. Poverty reigns where there is no trust in the community.

In what ways does a local church build trust in a community?

Reconciliation with the Rest of Creation

Reconciling the relationship with the creation has two parts. First, it means doing good work in the world for God's glory and for the provision of our families. We will wait and talk about that in later lessons. Second, it means taking care of God's creation by being good stewards. We talked in the last lesson about many of the ways that people are destroying the environment and not taking care of God's creation. Reconciliation would mean to begin to care for God's creation in wise and careful ways. For example, we could pick up the rubbish polluting our streets and fields. Christians should be leading the way in taking good care of this world in obedience to God's commands. The result of taking care of this world will make the world more beautiful, healthy, and productive, not only for us, but for our children.

Though the environmental problems we looked at in the last lesson were depressing and might seem overwhelming, there is hope that things can change! Listen to one story of hope from Niger, a place where the desert had been spreading. Wangari Maathai, Kenyan environmental activist, wrote about this story in 2009: "Over the past two decades, following droughts in the 1970's and '80s, women farmers in Niger have planted trees covering 3 million hectares [7.5 million acres], not only holding back the desert sands but re-greening parts of the Sahel. While keeping the trees alive, they also provide themselves with food, fuel, and income as they sell off branches for firewood."[3]

Anthony's story

We've now looked at the ministry of reconciliation as applied to the four types of broken relationships. Let's look at another example. This time from the other author, Anthony, who was trying to help a beggar in a market in Uganda. As I share the story, pay attention to what Anthony did well and what he could have done differently.

> There is a beggar that I often saw in the market. He looked like he was in great need. I had given food to him a few times. But one day I decided to talk to him. I found a merchant to translate for me. I shook the beggar's hand, introduced myself and we had a brief conversation. I found out that he had the ability to make ropes out of old bags, which is something I have no idea how to do myself. I affirmed that he was made in the image of God and it was God who gave him his gifts and skills. So I bought him some used bags for 3000 shillings. With the bags I gave him, he could make enough ropes to earn about 18000 shillings. I figured that helping him work to earn food was better than just giving him food which would keep him in the situation of begging. I talked to him about God and found out that he was a fellow Christian. I affirmed his gifts and dignity, and encouraged him to go back to working with his hands. I was proud of myself for having spent an hour helping this person instead of just giving a handout. Next time I went to the market I could not find him and a merchant told me he was no longer begging and was out selling ropes. But unfortunately, after a few weeks he returned to begging again. I now realise that although what I did was better than just

giving a handout, it was not enough, and there was more I should have done.

1. **What did Anthony do well in this story?**
2. **Did Anthony try to help reconcile all four of the beggar's relationships? Explain.**
3. **What did Anthony do wrong, or what more could he have done?**

It is okay for the participants to criticise Anthony in this story. None of us help others perfectly, and we are all continually learning together. Here are some points you can note in the discussion if the participants do not bring them up themselves:

For question #1 – He affirmed the dignity of the beggar, talked to him, shook his hand, and affirmed the gifts and skills God had given to him. He did not simply give money but looked for a way for the beggar to earn money himself.

For question #2 – He did not really do much to reconcile the beggar to God. He did not find out whether the man attended church or ask any follow up questions after finding out that the beggar was a Christian. Anthony did try to help the beggar have a better view of himself. He did try to help him with his relationship to the creation by helping him find work to do. He did not do much to help reconcile him to others. He could have introduced him to a local pastor, invited him to church, or continued to meet with him personally and be the beggar's friend.

For question #3 – Anthony did not find out the beggar's real home situation, whether he was staying with his family and was just begging for his daily job, or whether he was living on the street in a desperate situation. Anthony did not do any follow up. He expected to be able to help him in only one hour rather than building a long-term relationship with the man. He did not teach him anything about budgeting or business, or find someone to help him with these things. In the end, the beggar might have felt even worse about himself and more ashamed than before. Perhaps he thought to himself, "*This nice person was willing to help me, and I still failed. I can't do anything right.*"

Focus on the People

Since we have seen that the main work of fighting poverty is actually the work of reconciliation, then this means that fighting poverty is not so much about material things, but it is about people.

Focusing on people means we will have to take the time to build relationships. Let's go back to **Isaiah 58:10** again. We must spend ourselves in order to truly help materially poor people. This means we must spend our time. We must take the time to build real relationships with people, to really get to know them and love them, and in turn let them know us as well.

Helping Without Hurting in Africa

Many times, we focus on programs instead of people. We design programs for materially poor people without their involvement. We might plan a quick church ministry of distributing food during Christmas or Easter. We might have a program to teach materially poor people for one day about agriculture, but then we don't continue in relationship with them.

Instead of making detailed plans about what "we" want to do for a community, we have to spend time with the poor and hear what their needs are and what they want to do. We shouldn't be forcing our programs on a community or an individual person. We need to get to know materially poor people before we can help them. Relationships are necessary for reconciliation to happen. Programs have a difficult time creating reconciliation!

We must walk together with materially poor people. We must work against our god-complexes and remember that we all have poverty, just in different ways. We and materially poor people need to go to God together to ask him to fix all of us. Instead of just offering our programs to materially poor people, we need to be together with them asking God to transform all of us.

Take-Home Activities for Lesson 5

The facilitator should provide detailed guidelines and clear instructions on how to go about the take-home activities. For most lessons, there are two take-home activities for participants to choose from depending on whether they are a church leader or not. But in this lesson, the activities are for all of the participants. Read them aloud and encourage the participants to do all of them, but tell them that each participant should at least choose two of the activities to do.

1. **Personally memorise Isaiah 58:10. If you are a church leader, see if your whole church would be willing to memorise it together. Explain to the congregation that we need to focus on building relationships with materially poor people rather than always making quick programs for them.**

2. **In order to have a better view of yourself, read Psalm 139 and think about how God carefully created you and how much he values you. Write down five things that you appreciate about yourself, about the person God made you to be. Then tell your spouse or a friend five things that you appreciate about them, who God made them to be.**

3. **To improve your relationship with God's creation, plant a tree somewhere in your community or at your church, especially in a place that will benefit others more than yourself. Make sure to give the new tree some protection so it doesn't get destroyed by animals.**

4. **Share the gospel with at least one non-Christian friend or acquaintance.**

Small Group Discussion Questions (20 minutes)

- Inform the participants that they will be going into small groups to discuss together the questions listed at the end of Lesson 5 in their manual.
- Read out loud the questions that they will be answering and make sure they understand them.
- Divide them up into groups of 5 people (anywhere from 3-6 people per group). They can be the same groups as before, or you can put them into new groups. They will not be presenting their answers to anyone.
- If you have organised the whole workshop to take longer than what has been outlined, then feel free to give the participants a longer time for discussion.
- Remember to move around and listen in with the groups as they discuss. Be available to answer their questions. You can give guidance or input if necessary during their discussions, but they have heard you talk a lot, so try to let them do the talking now. Remind them periodically about how much time remains for their discussion.

Small Group Discussion Questions

1. **What do these passages teach us about building relationships with the materially poor?**
   a. Matthew 25:31–46
   b. Luke 14:12–14
2. **In your church or ministry do you build close relationships with the materially poor or do you focus only on quick programs? Explain.**

Further Reflection

Read this section at home for further learning.

- **Forgiveness**

Forgiveness is one of the most important components of reconciliation. Forgiveness is crucially important in dealing with poverty of community and broken relationships.

Reflect on this question: What Does It Really Mean to "Forgive" Someone?

1. Forgiveness is about your heart and what you feel towards the other person and not about how the other person responds. Therefore, you can still forgive someone even if full reconciliation is not possible. We cannot control how a person responds, but we can control our own response.

2. Forgiveness means we try to think well of the person, we leave the judgement of that person to God, and we ask God to bless the person. Reflect on **Romans 12:19-20.**

3. We remember that we are equally sinners before God along with the other person. We forgive because we have been forgiven by God. As God has shown us mercy, we show mercy to others. Read **Ephesians 4:32.**

4. A person can be truly forgiven but still experience painful consequences for their actions. For example, a murderer can go to prison, but the victim's family can forgive the murderer from their hearts while the murderer has to remain in prison.

5. When we forgive, we should try to forget, even though that is not always possible. We should try to not keep thinking about the offence and we should not repeatedly speak about it again. We do not hold on to our bitterness.

6. Forgiveness can be a long process in which we keep asking God to change our heart and feelings towards a person who has hurt us.

7. If we are truly born-again Christians, we will forgive others. God says that if we don't forgive others, we will not be forgiven. Read **Matthew 6:14-15**.

Is there anyone in your life that you need to forgive? Take time to pray right now. Ask God to change your heart towards that person. Ask God to give you the strength to forgive them. Ask God to bless that person and give them grace and peace.

- **Focusing on People and Reconciliation: Hamida's Story**[4]

Here is an inspirational story that reminds us to focus on people and relationships rather than quick programs.

Hamida lives in Malawi. She and her seven siblings moved to stay with her grandmother after her parents passed away. Hamida helped her grandmother in her business of collecting and selling firewood. Although Hamida worked hard, they were not earning enough money for the family. Her siblings had to drop out of school. As men started to approach Hamida for sex, she resisted at first. But as the family became desperate for money, she decided she would try sex work. For over four years, Hamida gave her body to be used by men in order to feed her family.

An organisation called Word Alive wanted to reach out to Hamida and other girls like her in the community. Word Alive formed a girl's group for them to support one another. At first, Hamida was suspicious. But she joined the group and was glad to meet other girls who shared her experiences. The group became a safe place to ask questions and learn new information. They formed very close relationships. The group encouraged Hamida to get HIV tested and supported her decision to stop engaging in transactional sex. She went through some more training and learned how to lead small groups. She started teaching other girls about sexual reproductive health and cultural practices that are harmful to girls. Now Hamida is a peer mentor and leads a group of 17 girls. She has been helping other girls to stop engaging in transactional sex and find other work to do. She receives a small stipend from Word Alive while she uses her time to mentor other girls. She and her peers are getting business training and are planning to start a business together to support themselves and their families.

We can learn from Hamida's story how important relationships are. We must focus on the people. Although Word Alive's ministry involves programs, the core of the ministry is about people. The focus is on the relationships between mentors and peers. It is these relationships that gave Hamida the support she needed to have hope and see change in her life.

Helping Without Hurting in Africa

Facilitator Manual

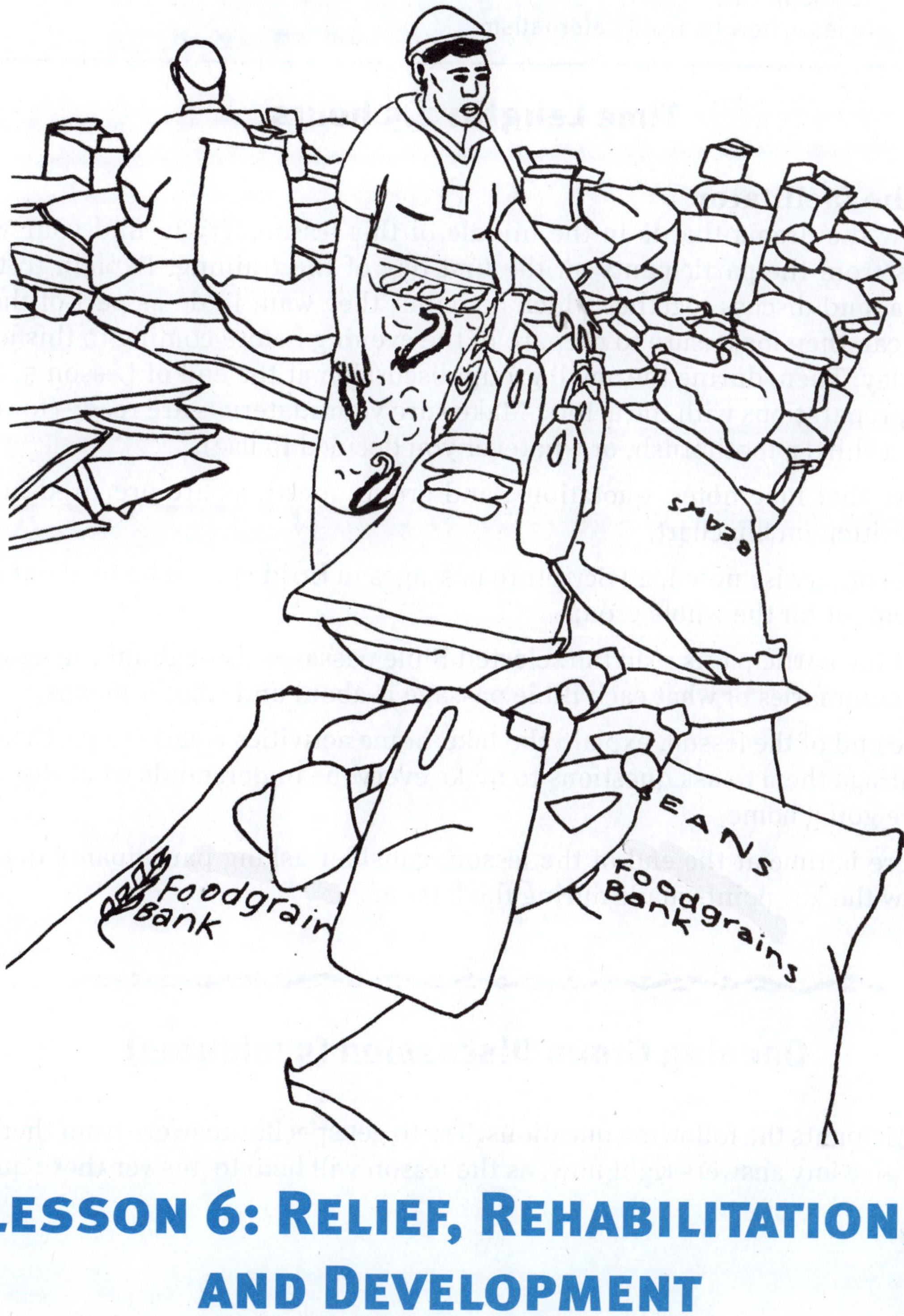

Lesson 6: Relief, Rehabilitation, and Development

Lesson 6: Relief, Rehabilitation, and Development

In this section, you will find:

- Discussion of the best ways to actually begin to help without hurting.
- Stories of success, but also failure.

Lesson Objectives:

- To understand the different approaches of relief, rehabilitation and development.
- To learn how to avoid paternalism.

Time Length: 2.5 hours

Notes to the facilitator

- Review the drama that is in the middle of this lesson. Try to find your volunteer actors from the participants on the first day of the training. Explain to them the drama, and discuss together which activities they want to do as part of the drama. They can then make sure to prepare in the evening before coming to this lesson the next day. Then, during the small group discussion at the end of Lesson 5, make the final preparations with the actors. Make sure your materials are ready (for example, food, a shirt, a toothbrush, or whatever you decided to use).
- Ensure that long notes, quotations, and group questions are prepared in advance and written on flip chart.
- Unless otherwise noted, all Scripture passages in **bold** should be read out loud by a participant for the whole group.
- When the participants read the selected Bible passages throughout the lesson, make brief summaries of what each Bible passage is about and what it means.
- At the end of the lesson, explain the take-home activities clearly to participants and encourage them to ask questions to make everyone understands what they are to do before going home.
- If there is time at the end of the lesson, consider asking participants questions to review the key points made during the lesson.

Opening Group Discussion (5 minutes)

Ask the participants the following questions. Try to get specific answers from them. You do not have to give any answers right now, as the lesson will help to answer these questions.

1. **In what situations should we give money to people in our community who ask for help?**
2. **In what situations should a visitor from a foreign country give money to people in our country?**

Facilitator Lecture: Relief, Rehabilitation and Development (65 minutes)

In this lesson we will look at three types of responses or approaches to helping people who are experiencing poverty. These responses are termed "**Relief**", "**Rehabilitation**", and "**Development**". It is critically important to know in which situations to employ each type of response. Let's think about an example that will help us to define and understand these three different approaches.

- You read in the newspaper that a mudslide destroyed a community in your region killing hundreds and leaving thousands of people without food, clothing, or shelter. Then you read another article in the newspaper about the ongoing problem of homeless people in your country's capital city. These people also regularly struggle to get enough food, clothing, or shelter. Imagine your church wants to do more to help both groups of people. At first glance, it seems like your responses to these situations would be very similar.

- The people in both situations have similar needs. Giving food and other resources to both groups of people seems to be the obvious solution. But actually these people are in different types of situations and need different types of help. What principles about fighting poverty can help us figure out the correct response in each case?

- The first step is to understand the situation and figure out whether it calls for ***relief***, ***rehabilitation***, or ***development***. Skipping this important step is one of the reasons why so many poverty fighting efforts end up doing more harm than good.

Relief

This is the temporary emergency aid given to reduce immediate suffering from a natural or man-made problem. People needing relief are unable to help themselves, just like the people affected by the mudslide. Without help their situation would just keep getting worse and may result in death. Relief tries to "*stop the bleeding*". For the mudslide victims we would urgently give them food, water, clothing, and shelter to make sure that they could survive.

In relief, one person is a provider who gives assistance to the receiver, often in the form of material things. Even though this is not the main point of the passage, the parable of the Good Samaritan, in which the Samaritan bandages the helpless man who lay bleeding and dying in the road, is an example of the relief response to poverty.

Ask for a volunteer among the participants to quickly summarise or retell the parable of the Good Samaritan from memory. Then summarise how the story demonstrates the points you mentioned above about relief.

Rehabilitation

Rehabilitation begins as soon as the "bleeding" stops. This is the attempt to bring people and their communities back to the same normal conditions they had before the disaster or emergency. For the mudslide victims, rehabilitation would be the next step after the emergency relief. During the rehabilitation response, we would work together ***with*** the mudslide victims, not ***for*** them, so that they also participate in their own recovery. For the people affected by the mudslide, we might work together to rebuild their homes and replant their fields.

Development

Development is the process of change that moves people to a better way of life than they have ever experienced before. It is taking them from their normal level and raising them to a higher level. Christian development should not be only concerned with raising people's income, but should primarily focus on moving people closer to being in right relationship with God, self, others, and the rest of creation. As materially poor people develop, they are better able to fulfil their calling of glorifying God by working and supporting themselves and their families.

As in rehabilitation, development is not done ***to*** people, and not done ***for*** people, but done ***with*** people. Development is a process of empowering all the people involved, including the people helping, to become more of what God created them to be. In the situation of the mudslide, development would take place after rehabilitation was finished, after people were restored back to their normal situation. Development for these people could include introducing new farming and tree-planting practices to better avoid future mudslides, starting new churches, introducing savings and loans programs to be better prepared for future emergencies, and many other possible activities.

Let us look at this diagram below for better understanding.

- The person at the beginning is in his normal living situation, and he has regular struggles and challenges, but there is no urgent need of help. He has room for improvement in the four relationships, and he may be materially rich or poor. But he is not in any immediate danger nor completely helpless. His life continues as it always has.

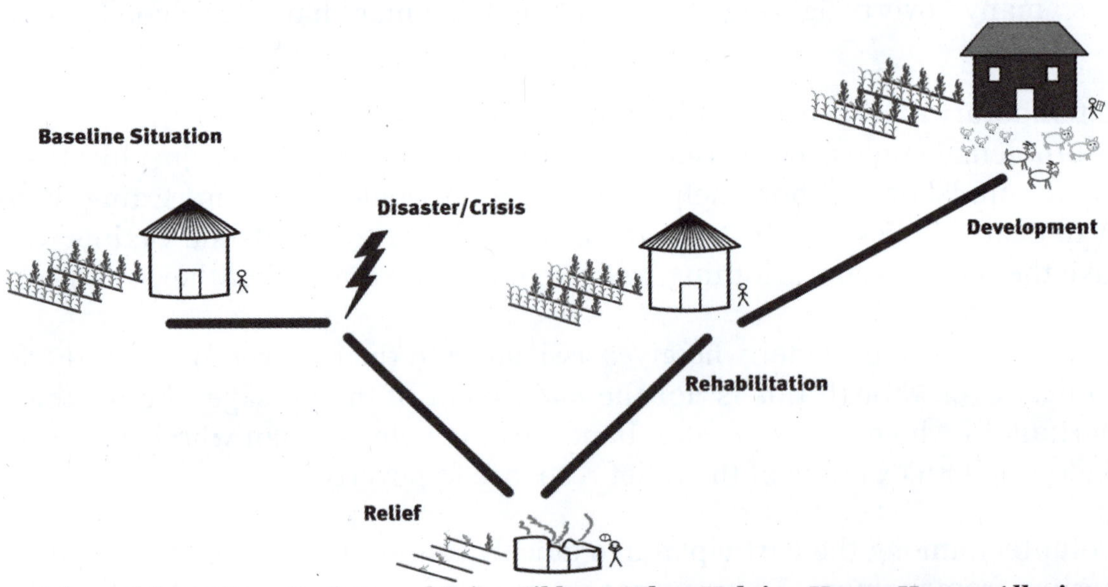

Fig. 5.1 Adapted from Steve Corbett and Brian Fikkert, When Helping Hurts: How to Alleviate Poverty Without Hurting the Poor...And Yourself, 2nd edition (Chicago: Moody Publishers, 2012), 100.

- But then, disaster strikes! This is represented by the lightning bolt. The disaster could be a storm, a war, the collapse of a nation's economy, or a vehicle accident. Whatever the disaster, this person cannot meet his own needs for survival. This person is "bleeding". He will probably die eventually without help. Relief is stopping the bleeding by giving the person whatever is necessary for survival.

- Next in the diagram is rehabilitation. This is helping to bring the person back to where he started. After giving rehabilitation, the person will be back to what his life was like before the disaster. In rehabilitation, we might still give money or resources, but we will be sure to ask the person who is receiving the help to contribute to their own recovery, as they are no longer helpless. Remember, the goal is always to reconcile the four key relationships, and asking people to use their own gifts and abilities as much as possible is part of this process.

- Next in the diagram is development. As we said before, this is when we help an individual or a community to improve their four relationships beyond where they have normally been living. Development could be started with an individual or a community after the rehabilitation phase has finished. But development can also be an approach to helping an individual or community that is just in their normal situation and has not experienced a disaster. In fact, when we want to help people experiencing poverty, development will almost always be the correct approach and in most cases it will not be after a disaster.

- Let us look at some examples of relief, rehabilitation, and development. I'll ask you to tell me what type of response each example is to see if we are all understanding.

1. **When we teach people new methods of sanitation? (development)**
2. **When we take someone to the hospital who has been bitten by a snake? (relief)**
3. **When we help someone rebuild their house after a flood? (rehabilitation)**
4. **When we send a missionary to a community to preach the gospel? (development)**
5. **When a child soldier escapes and returns home, and we give him counseling? (rehabilitation)**
6. **When we find an abandoned child who is starving and we feed this child? (relief)**
7. **When we give farmers a sample of new cassava stems to try out? (development)**

- Out of the three responses, relief is the one where resources and money are simply given to the person without expecting them to contribute anything because they are helpless. Money and resources can also be given or utilised in rehabilitation or development, but this should only be done in a way that complements the people's use of their own assets. Notice in the last example that even though we are giving handouts to farmers, this is development, not relief. There is no emergency. We are simply trying to help them improve their situation. The gift is a one-time gift, and it requires the farmers also to participate and do the work. If money is utilised in rehabilitation and development, it will be done in partnership, with the people being helped also contributing what they are able.

- Now that we understand these three approaches, let us go back to the other newspaper example. We've discussed what we should do for those affected by the mudslide. But what is the correct approach to helping those in the capital city?

Do the homeless people in your capital city need relief, rehabilitation, or development?

Discuss.

Let the participants discuss for a while. Generally, try to help them understand that the people need rehabilitation or development. Because they are not helpless and can contribute to their own improvement, relief is generally the wrong intervention. Responding with relief, that is, treating people as helpless and simply giving handouts, is not going to change the situation of the homeless, and it fails to move them towards stewarding their own gifts and abilities. Rather, they need improvement in the four relationships, work to do, skills training, inexpensive housing, counseling, reconciliation with their families, etc. You can mention how some of them might be suddenly homeless due to a crisis and could need relief. Others might have received relief already from other sources, but need rehabilitation. Be sure to discuss how other organisations and churches have been responding to these people. If they are already receiving the handouts they need to survive from many sources, then what they really need now is development to change their situation. Last, you could note that some of the homeless people really are in genuine need of relief, for example mentally disabled people living on the street, those with debilitating diseases, and those facing starvation.

As I help you through this training, am I giving you relief, rehabilitation, or development?

Hopefully the participants are able to note quickly that the training is development. Explain to them that development is done in partnership, just as the training is being done in partnership. You have offered your time (and possibly your own resources) to facilitate the training. But they have also paid for their own transport, accommodation, food, and manual. They were not in a situation needing relief. They were not helpless, needing you as a facilitator to pay all the expenses for them.

Now, let's take some time to look at deeper principles that will guide us in how to do relief, rehabilitation, and development well.

Doing Relief, Rehabilitation, and Development Well

Relief

1. **Relief is infrequent**. This means it is "not often". There are very few situations in which people actually need relief. So relief will only be done once in a while, in emergency situations.

2. **Relief needs to be immediate**. If people cannot help themselves, then a quick response is important. When a natural disaster happens, the victims cannot wait weeks while your church or organisation figures out what to do to help. People will need food, water, and medicine right away. Or imagine a person has a heart attack. You need to immediately take the person to the hospital, not wait around discussing who is going to pay for everything. It is helpful to plan ahead. Have your church or organisation think about what types of disasters and crises people in your community could face. Decide which ones you want to be ready to respond to and then make a plan so that you will have financial, material, and human resources ready to help in such a situation.

3. **Relief is temporary**. Relief is only provided during the time that people are unable to help themselves. Determining when to stop relief is difficult. We don't want to stop our assistance too early. But if we give for too long we can create unhealthy dependency that is harmful. We are all dependent on other people for certain needs. There is nothing wrong with that. But unhealthy dependency is when people are dependent on others for basic needs that they should be able to obtain on their own. They end up feeling like they cannot live without the one who is providing resources to them. It is wise to have policies in place to guide your church workers about how long relief should be given so that unhealthy dependency does not develop.

For the following question, ask for only one story for the sake of time. At most, let two people share a story if they are both short.

Can anyone share a brief story of a community or an individual that became stuck in dependency because relief was given for too long?

So in conclusion relief needs to be infrequent, immediate, and temporary.

Rehabilitation

1. **Rehabilitation is done *with* people not *for* people**. The work should be done in partnership. Everyone should participate and contribute something. The people being helped should be involved in designing and running the program. For example, if you are trying to help the mudslide victims rebuild their homes, they should contribute whatever materials they are able to contribute, even if you also provide some financial assistance. They should be the primary ones to do the actual work of rebuilding the homes. As much as possible, we need to treat people as the responsible stewards that we want them to be.

2. **Do an assessment at the beginning to get an understanding of the disaster situation**. The emergency is over, but you need to know the real situation on the ground before you rush in to help. Find out the needs and what other churches and organisations are already doing to help. Do not just get a group of volunteers in a bus and rush off to the affected community. Learn about the situation first. This principle actually applies to relief as well, though in a relief situation you have to act more quickly.

3. **Respond when the people in need are not already being helped by local people and local organisations**. This means we only help when there is a need and the local organisations cannot help or they refuse to help. If the organisations of a local community are already able and willing to do rehabilitation in their own community, then we should stay away and let them do it. We can always still partner with them if they ask for more help. The local organisations will have a better understanding of how to get the job done. And the goal of development work is for local people to take charge of their individual lives and communities. Furthermore, when local organisations help, they are able to build up good relationships, unity, and goodwill in a community. If we try to help as outsiders when the local organisations are able to help, we might only get in the way or in some cases actually crush the efforts to help by the local organisations.

Unfortunately, this has been done in many places in Africa by foreigners. Though almost always done unintentionally, some NGO aid and some aid from foreign governments has destroyed the good initiatives of local organisations by dumping in large amounts of money at one time, making the efforts of local organisations look insignificant in comparison. This creates dependency and makes people feel worthless, contributing to low self-esteem. **We have to be very careful that as we strive to be generous, we do not let our generosity destroy the generosity or good stewardship of others**.

We can see from some biblical texts that the first people responsible to help a person are those people who are closest to him or her in terms of family relationship, church, or location. **1 Timothy 5:8** teaches us that family members have the first responsibility to care for their own family members. **Galatians 6:10** teaches that caring for believers, who are part of God's family with us, takes greater priority than caring for those outside the family. This chart, called **Circles of Priority**, gives us some helpful guidelines in looking at the order of priority of who should help first, and second, and third, and so on. The family members should help the victim first, but if they are unable to help, then the next circle can help, and if they are unable to help, then the next circle, and so on. Those closest should help first.

Circles of Priority

Fig. 5.2
Circles of Priority Original diagram by Anthony Sytsma.

The idea of the circles of priority is also important because we all have limited time and resources. We simply cannot manage to help every person and cannot respond to every problem in the world. If we do not have any focus but try to immediately help all the people and problems we hear about, we become overwhelmed and paralysed. We may become filled with guilt because we cannot help everyone. But the circles of priority give us guidance and show us where our greatest responsibilities are. Of course, when we have the ability, the love of Christ still compels us to sacrificially help others who are far away from us.

Listen to this story which shows the importance of the circles of priority and shows the joy that local people can experience when giving.[1] In 2010, nearly half of the population of Niger was food insecure and in need of some relief. An international Christian organisation donated grain and worked with a local Christian group, SEL, to sell that grain to people in need in several communities at a highly discounted price. In the past, during times of food insecurity, the international organisation had provided some grain that would be given freely to individuals in greater need, for example people with disabilities or chronic illnesses. But this time, the international staff challenged SEL to consider raising funds locally from churches to purchase the grain that would be distributed freely. At first, the SEL members were sceptical, not imagining that there was anything they as poor Christians could do on their own to help others. But the Christians gave generously and were able to purchase grain for 98 people who had the most need in the several communities being helped by the international organisation. In the end, SEL thanked the organisation for encouraging them to help their own community members. They said, "It was such a privilege to help, to know that we weren't just distributing somebody else's gift, but it was from our own pockets, and from our own hearts. Everyone in the village knew that it came from us."

How do you think this community might have changed because the 98 people were given grain by neighbours instead of from foreign donors?

Development

Development is the process of moving people to a better way of life where they are better able to support themselves and their families by working, and they are growing in their relationship with God, self, others, and creation. We will look at development principles in the next lesson, and you can read more about development in the "Further Refection" section at the end of this lesson.

Large Group Activity
Examples of Relief, Rehabilitation, and Development

This activity should take between 5 and 10 minutes. Ask the participants to give examples of activities that would fall under relief, then activities that would fall under rehabilitation, and then last activities that would fall under development. Write their answers on your flip chart. Use one sheet for relief, one for rehabilitation, and one for development. Try to get at least 5-10 examples on each page. You can write down the situations that need the type of response (someone's house burned down and they are destitute is an example of a situation needing relief). Or you can write down the activities that qualify as the type of response (giving someone food and shelter after their house burned down and they are destitute is giving relief). It's okay to write down both situations and also activities as examples.

Here are some examples in case the participants are having difficulty. Under relief you could mention these examples: Taking someone to the hospital after a car accident, sheltering a woman whose husband is beating her and threatening her life, and giving shelter to refugees fleeing their country during a war.

If participants have difficulty with rehabilitation, tell them to think about next steps that would come after each relief example. Some examples for rehabilitation could include—making someone crutches after they get out of the hospital from the accident, helping refugees to find work to do in their new location, giving seeds and planting a field together with a farmer who had lost everything in a flood.

If participants have difficulty with development, have them think through each of the five types of poverty. For material poverty—building roads and hospitals, digging wells, savings programs, etc. For relationship with God—planting churches, discipleship, teaching. For relationship with people—community groups, counseling others, tutoring children, peace-building, etc. For relationship with self—counseling, preaching on the image of God, community initiated projects, etc. For relationship with creation—planting trees, picking up rubbish, helping people find jobs, etc.

Explain to them how some of their examples are difficult to determine which category they fall into. That is okay. Fighting poverty is complicated. Most of the suggestions will be easy to categorise, but a few may be difficult. Tell them it is okay for us to have different opinions. Explain to the participants that some activities could be either relief, rehabilitation, or development, depending on "how" they are done. The key thing to remember is that relief is done for people who are unable to help themselves, and with rehabilitation and development, the help will be done with the participation of the people being helped.

Common Mistakes

One of the biggest mistakes we often make in fighting poverty is giving relief in situations that actually require rehabilitation or development. When relief is needed, we must give quickly and generously. But when relief is no longer needed, we can cause harm when we keep on giving it. Giving relief to those who do not need it can cause them to feel helpless and ashamed. In some cases, they will become dependent, stop looking for work to do, and therefore not fulfil God's purpose for their lives. Sometimes we give relief to those who do not need it because we lack wisdom even though we have a feeling of love. Other times we may give relief to those who do not need it just to feed our pride and god-complexes and to look good in front of others. Many of the people coming to your church for help will say that they need emergency financial help to pay for housing bills, school fees, food, or transportation. Is relief the right response to these people coming to you? Maybe, but maybe not. There are several things we need to consider.

1. Is there really an emergency? If you do not give immediate help, will there be serious negative results or a life-threatening situation? If not, then rehabilitation or development may be the correct option. If it's not an emergency, then there is time for the person to take action on his own behalf with your partnership.

2. Is the person helpless, or can they contribute to their own improvement? If the person is not helpless, then relief is not the right response. Simply giving money might prevent him from being a steward of his own resources and abilities. But this does not mean you don't help at all. It just means that you might help by using rehabilitation or development, asking them to contribute something to their own improvement. There are other ways to help besides giving a handout.

3. How responsible was the individual for their situation? If people are helpless, then we should provide relief whether they are partly to blame or not. But if they are not helpless, then the manner in which we do rehabilitation or development might be partly determined by the extent to which they are responsible for their own situation. For example, if a person is struggling because they lost a lot of money gambling, then we might want to be more careful about introducing outside resources than if they were struggling because insects had destroyed their crops. Having a conversation with people whose irresponsible behaviour has led to their pain can make them realise their mistakes and reform. Of course, we need to have compassion and understanding and help even those who make mistakes. The point is not to punish the person for mistakes or sins he has committed, but to be sure that lessons are learned.

Can one person share an example of when you refused to give money to someone so that they could experience the consequences of their unwise action and learn from it?

4. How much relief has this person been receiving from you or others in the past? How likely is he or she to be receiving such help in the future? This person may be going from one church, to an NGO, to another church, so that your one-time gift might actually be the tenth gift this person has received.

Many foreigners who visit Africa give relief at the wrong times, thus contributing to the problems of shame and dependency in Africa. They see people living very differently from how they live in their home countries, and think that people need relief. This can easily destroy the initiatives and projects of the local people. In some cases, widespread handouts from foreigners may even drive some people out of business in the community. For example, if an NGO decides to give everyone a free mosquito net, what happens to the local person who receives his income from making and selling mosquito nets? As Africans, we need to be willing to speak up and gently confront foreigners when we see them giving in an inappropriate and harmful way.

It is helpful for your church to have a set of policies in place about when and how to help the poor who ask for help. This way, when a situation comes up, you have some guidelines to follow. Your policies should come from the mission and vision of your church and be consistent with a biblical view of the nature of poverty. It is sometimes difficult to say "no" to someone even if you know it is the right thing to do. This is a very sensitive issue in Africa because of the culture of extended family and community obligations where you are expected to help without asking many questions. With policies in place, a person asking for help cannot personally blame the pastor or deacons if they say, "no". The pastor can say, "Our church's policy is not to give out money for this type of request." This way the church will not be accused of favouritism for helping some people and not others.

Large Group Discussion

Ask the participants the question below and record their answers on a flip chart.

What types of people need ongoing handouts of financial assistance and resources?

The reality is that only a small percentage of people in the entire world require regular relief. Besides victims of disasters and emergencies who clearly need relief, some groups of people regularly need handouts of food or financial assistance to survive. These would include: some people with physical disabilities or chronic illness, some of the elderly, young children, orphaned children, and some people with mental disabilities. Some people in these categories are unable to do any work that earns money and they need assistance regularly in the form of handouts.

But most people are not completely helpless, so they do not need ongoing relief. And when we treat people like they are helpless, we do them more harm than good. Even many of the people in the categories we just discussed are able to do something to work in this world and help others, even if they cannot do it for money. Someone who is physically disabled might not be able to do work in the garden or drive a vehicle, but maybe they can sit and make baskets or nets. The elderly can teach their knowledge to the next generation. Some people with mental challenges can still do hard physical work in the garden. Children can help their parents with chores around the home. It is okay to provide ongoing assistance to such people to complement their use of their own gifts. This is actually a developmental approach, since we are doing things ***with*** them. They are contributing what they can, and we are coming alongside of them to help them with the things they can't do for themselves.

Sometimes we look at people and assume they are helpless, and assume they can only survive on handouts. But our assumptions can be wrong. For example, often when Christians see beggars they think the only way to help them is to give them money or food. But most beggars do not need relief, they need development. Listen to this story:

> Jim was a Christian development worker in the country of Haiti.[2] Haiti is one of the most materially poor countries in the world. People would often come to Jim's home and ask him for money. One day, a beggar named Eddy came and knocked at the gate

at his home. He wanted a few coins. But Jim knew that simply giving him a few coins would not really help. So he said, "Eddy, my garden needs fertilizer, and I do not have time to get it myself, so it would help me if you could bring me manure. I will pay you for it, and you will have a way to earn money for yourself." Eddy agreed, but Jim did not know if he would really do the work.

But Eddy did go and collect manure from the streets in the city since so many people had their cattle pass through town leaving manure. Each week he would bring Jim some more manure and Jim would pay him. Jim was getting what he needed, his garden was healthy, and Eddy was very happy. He actually had a job. He no longer begged for money. Even Eddy, someone with no education who had been begging for years, was able to do something meaningful to help others and earn income. Jim helped him to overcome his poverty of being. He no longer felt ashamed of himself. For us, collecting manure might not sound like a great job, but for Eddy, it was a huge improvement in his life.

But one day, there was a knock at the gate, and Jim went and looked. It was not Eddy but a different beggar. And he had collected manure and wanted money for it. So Jim paid him. Jim thought it was strange, but was okay with it. The next week, again it was this other beggar and Eddy was not there. So Jim asked the beggar, "My friend Eddy used to bring me this manure, do you know where he is?" The beggar took Jim into the city to find Eddy. In the city, Jim found Eddy sitting like a king. He was directing other beggars to go collect manure to sell to people. He had developed himself and become a manager. He no longer did the collecting himself, but now had created jobs for other beggars. Because of Jim's creative way of helping Eddy, now there was a whole group of former beggars doing real work and finding joy in having work to do.

What if Jim had only given Eddy a few coins for food? Nothing very good would have happened. But since Jim realised Eddy did not need relief, Eddy's life changed dramatically. He not only overcame his material poverty, but he overcame his poverty of being and poverty of stewardship. Let's all try to be creative in helping people like this.

Facilitator Lecture: Avoid Paternalism (20 minutes)

All of these terms and principles we've been discussing can get confusing. So we will now learn one simple rule that will be easy to remember and can help us know what to do in most situations.

The rule is: **We should avoid paternalism.**

Paternal means "*fatherly*". It means acting like you are a parent and treating the people you are helping like dependent children. It means that you think you are mature and they are not. You are wise and they are not. You think you are the one who has to do everything. It means you treat them like children who cannot take care of themselves. We don't want to treat people that way!

Generally, avoiding paternalism means: **Do not routinely do things for people that they can do for themselves**. Of course, in day to day life, the Holy Spirit calls us to serve our family members and neighbours, and do things for them that they could do for themselves. But when it comes to trying to solve issues of poverty, routinely doing things for materially poor people that they can do for themselves creates dependency, lowers people's self-esteem, and only keeps them stuck in poverty. The loving thing to do is actually not to keep doing things for people that they can do themselves.

Drama

The drama will be done by 2-3 volunteer participants, and the facilitator should help them to plan for it the day before. The drama should be brief, around 3-5 minutes. The purpose of the drama is to show how foolish and frustrating paternalism is. The drama will show someone doing a normal every day activity that he (or she) can do for himself. But then the other actors are the friends who will be constantly trying to help the person do that easy activity. The drama should show that it makes people feel silly and ashamed to have someone help them do these activities when they do not need the help. People want to be treated as capable adults, not as infants.

- Choose which activities you want to do based on what materials you have available. Some ideas include: Helping the person to eat their breakfast, including actually using their hands to put the food in the person's mouth and helping them chew the food. Helping the person to put on their shirt. Helping someone to brush their teeth, including keeping their mouth open and using the toothbrush. Helping someone to wash their hands with soap. Helping someone to take a drink of water.

- These activities can be accompanied by the actors telling the person how to brush their teeth, take a drink of water, or whatever activities you chose. This kind of unhelpful guidance really helps to show the paternalism, even more than the actions, since clearly an adult would know how to do these things already and does not need the guidance. Remember the purpose is not to show acts of helpful service. The purpose is to show unhelpful acts of service, doing things for people that they are better off doing on their own.

- At the end, ask the participants:

How do you think the person felt who was being helped?

- The participants should note that the person feels embarrassed and ashamed that the friends thought they needed help to do such simple things. Ask the participants to think back to childhood, to remember how good it feels for a child to learn to do things on their own without needing the help of their parents, such as the first time they could tie their shoe laces on their own, or the first time they cooked their own meal.

Varieties of Paternalism

Paternalism has a few varieties:

1. Resource Paternalism

This is giving resources or money to people when they have access to their own resources. Sometimes, a lot of outside money is given when the real need is for the local people to utilise and develop their own resources. In some regions of Africa, foreign missionaries have given out many free Bibles over the years, with the result that it is difficult for bookshops and Bible societies in Africa to sell Bibles, even at a very discounted price. It is common to find some Christians without Bibles even when they have the money to purchase one, because they prefer getting them free from their community church or foreign missionaries.

Sometimes it is good to give something to people once, even if they could buy it for themselves. For example, if we are working with a materially poor community, we might encourage them to take a deworming medication so that they can be healthy. If it is something new and strange to them, they might not be willing to spend their own money on it. But if we were to give them the deworming medication one time, they could experience the health benefits, and then in the future use their own money to purchase it. Resource paternalism means we **routinely** give people resources that they could get for themselves. Giving is not bad, but we have to be careful about making harmful expectations for future giving. Robert Lupton explained it well in his book *Toxic Charity*: "Give once and you elicit appreciation; give twice and you create anticipation; give three times and you create expectation; give four times and it becomes entitlement; give five times and you establish dependency."[3]

One easy way to avoid paternalism and avoid creating dependency is to charge a small fee for resources that you want materially poor people to receive. For most people, when they receive something for free, it is more difficult to value it or take ownership of it. But when they pay something for it, even if they only pay 5% of the true cost, they tend to value it more and take good pride in the fact that they bought it for themselves. Perhaps it is not a coincidence that the Kiswahili word "bure" for "free" also has another meaning of "worthless". When we try to help materially poor people, perhaps they cannot afford all the resources that they need, but they can probably afford to pay something small for what they need. Another benefit of this approach is that it gives materially poor people dignity and a voice. Rather than simply receiving whatever we want to give them, they will be able to show and tell us what they really want and really value because they are paying something small for it. This approach will show us what is truly helping people and what they really value, whereas if we only gave things for free, we would not know if people were really valuing the things.

2. Spiritual Paternalism

This is when we assume that we are more spiritually mature than poor people and therefore we should be the ones to preach or lead in times of prayer. Being poor often has nothing to do with being weaker in faith; indeed, the poor are often much stronger in faith than the rich. When you are helping a materially poor person, be open to the fact that God might want to use that person to teach you something new or inspire you in your walk with Jesus. Also, in our churches, let us not show favouritism and only give leadership positions to those who are rich. A materially poor person, rich in faith, still has the ability to preach, lead worship, or evangelize.

3. Knowledge Paternalism

This is when we assume that we have all the best ideas about how to do things. But this is not always true. Some people are materially poor but they still have a wealth of knowledge. We should not try to do all the thinking for them. Sometimes they might know better than we do the best way to manage their business or the best way to plant their crops. And the materially poor people know better than we do what it is like to be poor. Sometimes we do have important knowledge we need to share with materially poor people, but as we do so, let us be open to their ideas as well.

Let me share with you a true story about the harm of knowledge paternalism.

> Some villages in West Africa received a loan to earn money by buying cattle at a cheap price, fattening them, and selling them at a higher price. Some cattle experts said that they should buy a special breed of cattle in the north of the country that would get a very good price in their area. So the villages sent a group up north to buy 100 cattle and pay for them to be transported south. They took enough money to buy 100 cattle, but when they arrived up north, the price was much higher than they expected, so they bought only 76 cows. When the cattle arrived, six of them were sick and soon died. The rest did not like to eat the kinds of grass in the south, and they could not be sold at a good profit since the purchase price and transport and buying food for them had cost a lot. The villagers and the agency evaluated the cattle fattening program. They learned that some farmers bought cattle at the nearby market and were getting more profit than the people who had received the 76 cattle from the north. They decided to make another grant proposal, and this time have farmers in the loan group buy bulls one at a time at the market.[4]

How does this story illustrate knowledge paternalism?

4. Labour Paternalism

This is when we do work or labour for people who could do the work for themselves. When we help a family or a community, we should not assume we have to do all the work for them. In fact, even in very difficult situations, there might be work people can do. For example, when refugees flee from their home country to another country, they often rely on government aid in order to survive. But they can still take part in the work of distributing goods, building the temporary shelters, and digging the new pit latrines. There is no reason that they should sit and watch NGO or government workers do these things for them. Doing this work for themselves brings dignity.

5. Managerial Paternalism

This is when we plan, manage, and direct activities to help poor communities when people in those communities could do those things on their own. We have to be careful not to assume we should always be the ones in charge. We may be the one supplying resources, but the people we are helping can take part in managing the project or ministry. We need to encourage active participation and community leadership.

Large Group Discussion

Does anyone have stories of paternalism you would like to share, either in your family, your church, your community, or your country?

Try to take only about two stories for the sake of time. Clarify any aspects of paternalism that seem to be misunderstood or unclear to participants.

Take-Home Activities for Lesson 6

The facilitator should provide detailed guidelines and clear instructions on how to go about the take-home activities.

1. **For church leaders**
   Together with your other church leaders, deacons, and staff members, write down all the organisations and churches you can think of in your community who are trying to help the poor. Are they doing relief, rehabilitation, or development? Do the people in your community need relief, rehabilitation, or development? Is there a mismatch between what the organisations are doing and what the people need? How can your church address this mismatch? Make a plan for what your church will do. Then have your leadership communicate to the entire church what your plan and focus will be. Pray for God's help and direction in that ministry.

2. **Alternative for development or government workers**
   Do the same activity in #1, but with your colleagues from your work. Discuss what other organisations are doing.

3. **Alternative for other individuals**
   Analyse your own extended family relationships. Identify whether you or other family members are practicing paternalism in your relationships with other family members. Make a plan on how to address it so that a change can be made.

Small Group Discussion (30 minutes)

While the small groups discuss the questions below, go around and listen to their answers. As they discuss question #5, try to challenge them to think deeply about why they might not be giving financially to support good organisations. For some people, it may be that they do not give because they think that they have nothing to give, which is not true. For others, they may think that the foreigners supporting the organisations have unlimited resources and do not need the assistance of local African people. Help them to think these ideas through as they discuss, but we will also be looking at some of these ideas in the next lesson.

Small Group Discussion Questions

1. **Have you ever tried to help a materially poor person without really listening to his or her opinion because you thought you had all the knowledge and solutions? Explain.**

2. **Is your church being paternalistic in any of your ministries? Explain.**

3. **Are you aware of any government programs for the poor that are using the inappropriate response (for example—giving relief when development is needed)? What specific actions can you take that might start to bring about some change in these programs?**

4. **Think about the materially poor people in your community. Do these people need relief, rehabilitation, or development? Has your church been helping in the appropriate way?**

5. **Are you personally giving any money to the organisations in your community that are doing good work to help the poor? If you said "*no*", then why are you not giving?**

6. **Pray together. Repent of any paternalism and ask God to guide you and empower you to help in the right ways.**

Further Reflection

Read this section at home for further learning.

- **Principles of Good Development**

  1. **Development is about all five types of poverty**. Don't forget that development is not only about reducing material poverty through creating new roads, new buildings, and increasing people's incomes. The real goal of development should include people growing in their relationships with God, self, others, and the creation. The goal is not to have our country become a rich but immoral, unhappy, and godless nation. The goal is to glorify God and have healthy relationships.

  2. **Participation starts at the beginning**. As with rehabilitation, development is done ***with*** people not ***for*** people. The people should be involved in every part of the process. Don't just go into a community and start a project. First get to know the people. Figure out together with them what the project should look like and what they can contribute to the project (money, time, talents, materials, etc.).

3. **Start small**. Make sure the project can be managed by the community mostly on its own. Don't make the development project so big that it cannot continue on its own without ongoing outside assistance. You do not want to rely too much on outside resources or outside people. You want the project to be sustainable and continue even after the outside funding has stopped.

4. **Help people learn how to learn**. Instead of just instructing people in one new technology or one new practice, teach people how to learn and experiment. It's easy to tell a farmer to use a new variety of maize, and he might use it and have some success. But what happens if a disease destroys that maize? Then the farmer might just wait for you to come back and tell him what to do. Instead, we want to teach people how to experiment, be innovative, how to learn and manage different situations. That way if a disease destroys one crop, the farmer might try out new crops on his own without waiting for you to come again.

5. **Encourage the community to mobilise its own resources**. A community can't rely 100% on outside donors from other countries. If all the money and resources are coming from other places, local people won't feel involved in the project, won't have a sense of ownership and won't manage it well.

- **Finding Your Role**

It is extremely difficult for any one person or church to do all three types of responses to poverty in their community—relief, rehabilitation, and development. All three are very different things and require different skills and different programs, and they all take time. It is best to focus on one group or one community that you are trying to help. And then you should focus on either meeting the relief needs, or the rehabilitation needs, or the development needs, but not all three. If your church is known as the place that gives out free food to those who desperately need it (relief), then your church probably would not be the place that was also working on helping people find meaningful jobs (development). It's best to focus on one and to do it well. Other churches and organisations may be meeting other needs that you aren't. Together we can make a big difference.

How can you decide what your church should do? The first step is to figure out what kind of services are already being provided by organisations or other churches in your community. Second, study your community to figure out what the needs are of the materially poor in your community. Are they in danger of losing their lives so that relief is needed, or can they contribute to their own improvement? Most of the time the people in our communities are not in need of relief, but rather development. We suggest that you consider focusing on development after taking this course because most churches and organisations have not thought thoroughly about these issues and give mostly relief.

- **Stories**

1. Analyse this story and consider how it illustrates the importance of the circles of priority you learned about in this lesson.

> In Uganda, there were two tribes with a history of conflict. The North Eastern tribe had continually stolen cattle and killed people during raids into the tribe west of this North Eastern tribe. After many years of government intervention and church initiatives, peace was finally made, and reconciliation between the two tribes was achieved. The violence stopped. But soon after, there was a desperate famine experienced by the North Eastern tribe. Some of the churches of the tribe west of this North Eastern tribe pooled their efforts together in order to bring food and other resources to the North Eastern tribe. They knew this action would show their forgiveness and love and help to heal the old hurts. However, after they gathered the resources, the United States government beat them in the race to help. The USA sent many tons of relief food, so much so that the local Ugandan church's efforts became redundant and unneccessary. The foreigners ruined this opportunity for the Ugandan church to exercise their responsibility and good stewardship, and destroyed this opportunity to show love and forgiveness and create more reconciliation between the two tribes.[5]

2. This is an inspiring story about reconciliation and good rehabilitation ministry.

> After attending a Vision Conference in Rwanda in 1998, a pastor challenged the members of his church to assist returning refugees who had fled Rwanda as a result of the 1994 genocide. The church members welcomed these returnees, helped to rebuild their homes, brought them food and water, and helped their children return to school. The former refugees were astounded by the sacrificial love and generosity of the church members. Many in the church had friends or family who were murdered in the genocide, and the likelihood was high that the returning refugees included perpetrators of genocide. Still, these devoted Christians reminded the returnees that reconciliation comes by hearing the Word of God and demonstrating his love by loving those who have even killed our relatives.[6]

Helping Without Hurting in Africa

Facilitator Manual

Lesson 7: Asset-Based Community Development

Lesson 7: Asset-Based Community Development

In this section, you will find:

- A discussion of the difference between needs-based and asset-based approaches to poverty.
- A study of Bible passages encouraging us to be faithful with God's good gifts.

Lesson Objectives:

- To understand Asset-Based Community Development.
- To become good stewards of the gifts that God has given to each of us.

Time Length: 1.5 hours

Notes to the facilitator

- Make sure you carefully review the "Parable of the Talents" Bible study in this lesson so that you can carefully guide the group on verses that are difficult to understand during the discussion.
- Ensure that long notes, quotations, and group questions are prepared in advance and written on flip chart.
- Unless otherwise noted, all Scripture passages in **bold** should be read out loud by a participant for the whole group.
- When the participants read the selected Bible passages throughout the lesson, make brief summaries of what each Bible passage is about and what it means.
- At the end of the lesson, explain the take-home activities clearly to participants.
- If there is time at the end of the lesson, consider asking participants questions to review the key points made during the lesson.

Opening Discussion (5-10 minutes)

Ask the participants the question below and listen attentively as the participants describe their communities. Record both their positive and negative answers. You can take general answers from all participants, or you can choose 1 or 2 participants to answer specifically about each of their communities.

Imagine someone from another region or country visits and wants to help your community. If he asks you to tell him about your community, what would you say?

In many groups, the answers will tend to be about the problems and challenges of their communities. It is common for most of us to immediately go to the negative characteristics of our communities, rather than saying what is positive. After the initial discussion, ask the group these questions:

1. **Were most of your answers positive or negative? Why?**
2. **How do you feel when someone describes your community and only talks about all the problems, sins, and challenges in your community?**

Explain that when we focus only on the negative characteristics, it adds to our shameful feelings about ourselves and makes our poverty of being worse. Explain that it is important to first identify the gifts, resources, and good things that are happening in communities. This is important even in a situation in which someone is looking to help a community. Rather than only identifying the problems and looking for solutions from outside the community, the foreigner could also hear about the good things God is doing in the community already, and then see how to work together with the people and their resources to accomplish even more together. Go over these points just briefly, telling the participants that these concepts are what this lesson is all about.

Asset-Based Community Development (10 minutes)

In this lesson, we are going to carefully study an approach to development called, "Asset-Based Community Development", or "ABCD" for short. It is an approach used by both Christians and non-Christians. However, this approach to development fits with biblical teaching and we will examine some important Bible passages together. But first we will look at each letter in ABCD to make sure we understand all the terms.

- **A and B = Asset-Based**. An asset is something that we own and possess. Assets are the things that God has blessed every individual and every community with, including: possessions, money, land, social structures, knowledge, animals, intelligence, schools, creativity, production equipment, other people, and more. Asset-based means that as we do development we start by focusing on people's assets instead of starting by focusing on their problems and needs.

- **C = Community**. A community is any group of people in a specific location. But we can also think of a community as a group of people in one place who share a set of common values. In this lesson we are looking at community development, but the principles also apply to **individual development**.

- **D = Development**. We learned in the last lesson that development is the process of change that moves people to a better way of life. Christian development is concerned with raising people's income, but is even more focused on moving people closer to being in right relationship with God, self, others, and the rest of creation. As materially poor people develop, they are better able to fulfil their calling of glorifying God by working and supporting themselves and their families.

- **ABCD = Asset-Based Community Development**. We can now give a full definition of ABCD, by putting the terms together. ABCD is a long-term process in a specific community, ideally initiated by local people, and always directed by local people. In this process, the local people first identify their assets, and then they try to better utilise their assets for their own development. This results in measurable change in the community, including a reduction in material poverty, and improved relationships with God, self, others, and the creation.

Often, churches, development organisations, and governments use a different approach to development that we can call **Needs-Based Development**. They might begin working with a community by first determining or asking about the needs and problems. They may carry out a "**needs-assessment**" through research or through interviews.

But there is a problem with the needs-based approach. If we go into a community and begin the relationship by talking about their problems, it is as if we are telling the people, "Hello, what is wrong with you? How can I fix you?" And if we think about what we've learned through these lessons, we can imagine how damaging those statements would be to materially poor people. It would make them feel even more depressed and inferior.

Asset-based community development is very different. In ABCD, we begin by focusing on the gifts God has given to the people in the community. We begin by asking, "What good things are you doing in your community? What gifts has God given you that you can use to improve your life and the lives of your neighbours?" This reminds the people that they bear God's image and are on this earth for a purpose. They can contribute. It is a way to appreciate the good they are already doing, and give them more hope for the future.

If you begin by looking only at the needs, you might think the only solution is to have donors from other regions give a lot of money to a community even though this does very little to help people develop and take ownership of the changes in their community. But if you help people to use their assets, people will feel good about using the abilities and resources God has given them to develop their own communities. They will not feel helpless or dependent.

This does not mean that it is bad to identify a community's needs. We already learned in this training that you cannot properly treat a problem unless you first understand the real diagnosis. You need to know what is causing poverty in a community. A needs-assessment can be a helpful tool, but it is important to focus on people's assets first, even if later we identify needs and problems. After the community has identified its assets, the next step is to ask the people these questions: "What problems do you see that must be solved? How can you use your assets to address those needs and to solve those problems?" Once the problem is identified, the community can use its assets to come up with a plan and start working on making things better.

We can also think of Asset-Based Community Development as being consistent with God's story of Creation-Fall-Redemption-Consummation (as discussed in Lesson 3). We start by looking at the *good* of God's **Creation**, and then we look at the *bad* as a result of the **Fall**. After this, we seek to apply Christ's **Redemption** to reverse the effects of the Fall on the goodness of creation as we long together for his return and the **Consummation** of all things. By contrast, if we start with a needs-based approach, it is almost like cutting Genesis 1-2 out of the Bible and starting God's story with the Fall in Genesis 3. This doesn't make sense! Start the way God starts. Start with the good of creation and then move forward.

- If we as leaders and pastors in Africa are trying to help our own communities, we need to begin by looking for the good things God is already doing in our communities. We must look to identify the gifts and resources and opportunities in the community, and then encourage people to utilise them and work together.

- If we as leaders are trying to help another community as outsiders, we must be careful with our financial assistance. If it becomes obvious that the community will need a little financial or material help, then it is okay for the outsiders to contribute generously and help in partnership or to seek for government or foreign donors. But it is important to first utilise the community's own resources and skills and support the good things that they are already doing.

Bible Study - The Parable of the Talents (20 minutes)

Let's look at an important parable of Jesus, the Parable of the Talents. In this parable, Jesus teaches us about his kingdom and about stewardship. But this parable also teaches us some principles that relate to ABCD.

Divide the participants into groups of five and ask them to read and discuss **Matthew 25:14-30**. They should discuss the question below and write down their answers. They will be reporting their answers to the large group afterwards. Give them 10 minutes to discuss in their small groups before you have them report to the larger group.

What lessons do we learn from Matthew 25:14-30?

What does this passage teach that might relate to community development in some way?

After the 10 minutes of discussion, write down the answers from all the groups. To do this, write down one principle or lesson at a time on your whiteboard or large sheets of paper. Take only one answer from a group who is reporting until you've received at least one answer from each group. Many of the groups will have the same answers, so you do not need to rewrite answers that another group has already reported.

These are some principles that you can bring up if they are not able to think of them on their own:

- We all have gifts and abilities. God has given all of us something. No one can say, "I have nothing."
- We all have been given different things. The distribution is not totally equal.

- We are only caretakers of God's possessions. It all belongs to him.
- God wants us to be good stewards of what he has given. We have to use our gifts appropriately.
- God enables us to produce even more with the gifts and skills we've been given. We honour him when we obey him in trying to multiply what we have for the glory of God, the Master.
- Though hiding our gifts for ourselves may seem prudent to some, it is actually disobedience to God to treat the things he has given us as though they belong to us and not him. Some people, by being lazy, afraid to use their gifts, or afraid to take risks, dishonour God. He commands us to overcome that fear by trusting in him.
- God will hold us accountable for how we use our gifts because they belong to him and not to us. There is possibility of reward or of punishment.
- Good stewardship can result in greater blessings and responsibility. Poor stewardship sometimes results in losing even the little we had. If we are good stewards with little now, when Jesus returns again we will be given more to steward in the Kingdom of God. God can also give us more resources to steward right now if we are using his gifts wisely. But while God often does this, it is not a guarantee. We know from many other Bible passages that sometimes godly people suffer a lack of resources during disasters or persecution. For example the apostle Paul was often hungry—**1 Corinthians 11:27**. Later we will talk about this more in our lesson about the prosperity gospel.

Conclude the Bible study with these summary statements:

- In the Parable of Talents, the first two servants understood the instructions and the character of their Lord. They both trusted their Master and used their resources to make more profit for the benefit of their Master. But the third servant had mistrust and fear, and so he failed to obey the Master's instructions. He buried the money in the earth and returned the original amount. The two servants who utilised what they had been given were praised by the Lord, given even more responsibilities, and invited to enter into the joy of their Lord. The fearful disobedient servant was scolded, rejected, and punished. This teaches us that those who believe God, trust him, and faithfully utilise what God has given them will be rewarded in his kingdom. Those who do not trust God but only fear, and do not use what God has given to them, they will be rejected and judged. When we forget that Christ is coming back, treating his gifts as though they are our possessions or as though they only matter in this life, we are disobeying him.

- Jesus said, "For everyone who has will be given more, and he will have an abundance. Whoever does not have, even what he has will be taken from him." This might sound like Jesus wants to take away even the little that poor people have and make rich people richer. But this is not what Jesus meant. If we have received salvation as a gift and are obedient followers of Jesus in his kingdom, being good stewards of God's resources, we will receive blessing after blessing. Those blessings might not be increased health and wealth in this life. However, we will be rewarded with eternal life when Jesus comes again and maybe more responsibilities in this life. But if we have rejected the kingdom, if we are not good stewards of God's gifts, then even the little that we have in this life right now, we will ultimately lose and then experience eternal punishment.

- Among other things, this parable teaches us about the responsibility entrusted to us as those who have received God's good gifts and the serious consequences of failing to obey God's instructions. We are all stewards entrusted with gifts to use for God's glory, for our own benefit, and the benefit of others. Those that do a good job will ultimately be rewarded and those that don't will ultimately receive judgement. If we are truly born again in Christ, and we have true faith, our faith *will* produce fruit. We will be people who are obedient in being good stewards of the resources God has given to us.

- God is the owner of everything, so all we have belongs to God. We are responsible for using all of the resources we've been given to bless others and to give God glory. We do this with our time, our money, and our skills. Additionally, as Christians we have been given the Word of God and the good news of the Kingdom of God, the most valuable resources of all, and we must share them with others.

- You can see how all of our answers about what this passage teaches connect to ABCD. As leaders, we want to help people identify the gifts that God has given to them, and then help them to use those gifts wisely in order that they are multiplied. We need to help people use their resources wisely and productively to benefit themselves, their families, their communities, and their churches for God's glory. We need to teach people that God will hold them accountable for how they use what they have. For those who are afraid to use their gifts, we need to encourage them to trust in God and help them to find peace and freedom in Jesus Christ. And for those that say, "I have nothing", we need to help them see that this is a lie, and that they have also been given talents by God, even if they have been given different or less talents than others. To focus only on what we lack is to forget God's provision, power, and authority.

Story of Pastor Gideon

One of the authors, Anthony, taught these principles to a group of pastors in Uganda, and a couple weeks later one of the pastors put what he learned into practise.

> A young man visited Pastor Gideon and complained about his poverty. He wanted the pastor to give him money. But Gideon first asked, "What do you have?" The young man said, "I have nothing." Gideon said, "No, you must have something even if it is little. What do you have?" The young man said that he had only 1000 shillings (about 30 cents USD). The pastor told the young man that God could help him use that little 1000 shillings to bring development in his life, and so the pastor did not give him any money. Gideon said that the young man had ability to buy and sell, had good health to be able to travel, so he should be able to purchase some honey in his village area and then travel 15 kilometres by bicycle to the major town nearby to sell the honey for profit. So the young man did this. He bought honey for 1000 shillings, then was able to sell it for 3500 in the town. He found out that this could be a way to keep earning money, so

he continued and after only a couple trips he had made already 35,000 shillings profit! And he felt great about earning that money for himself using what God had given him!

Large Group Activity—Inventory of Assets (10 minutes)

Sometimes we do not feel like we have many gifts or assets. Many of the people in our churches also think they have very little. Some people don't give anything to church or to other people, and if you ask them why, they will respond, "I have nothing to give." Or if we want someone to identify their assets so that we can help them, they might say, "I have nothing and there is nothing I can do to change my situation. You just need to give me money." Therefore, one of the most important things we can do is to help someone create what is called an "inventory of assets", or some people call this process "asset mapping". We can do this with an individual or with a whole church or community.

We will practise doing this together right now. Then you will know how to do it with the people you want to help. We are going to take a few minutes and list all of the assets that we can think of that are in our community (or communities).

Go through one category of assets at a time. Explain to them what types of things are in each category. Then together list what assets are in their community (or communities), according to each category. Write down their answers on the board or large papers. Try to have them exhaust their answers before you provide answers that they did not think of. If they get stuck, give them one or two examples and then again wait for them to give more answers. They should be able to just shout out answers without raising their hands while you quickly write them down.

Make a list of the assets in our communities:

1. **Financial resources:**
2. **Physical possessions:**
3. **Human resources:**
4. **Natural resources:**
5. **Knowledge and skills:**
6. **Local Institutions and infrastructure:**
7. **Cultural and social resources:**
8. **Spiritual resources:**

Here are some answers for you to draw on as a facilitator if the participants get stuck. The answers will vary from region to region throughout Africa, but these examples will help you to generate more good ideas. If a participant mentions an asset that is hard to classify into a category, just record it in more than one category. The important thing is to list assets, not to worry so much about how to sort the assets into categories.

Financial resources: cash, bank accounts, loans, wages, pensions.

Physical possessions: homes, property, shops, buildings, furniture, clothes, food, bicycles, motorcycles, vehicles, Bibles, books, utensils, dishes, soap, hoes, tractors, baskets, cattle, pigs, chickens, ducks, goats. For this category the list is almost endless.

Human resources: life, people, children, large population, unemployed people eager to work, healthy bodies, good ideas, human creativity, courage to try new things, willingness to work hard, thinking and reasoning, human reproduction.

Natural resources: time, seasons, sunshine, rain, cultivated land, open land, seeds, rocks, trees, forests, wildlife, rivers, lakes, fish, birds, termite mounds, clay, soil, minerals, oil, gems.

Knowledge and skills: ability to buy and sell, business skills, carpentry, pottery making, agricultural knowledge, livestock knowledge, hairdressing, mechanics, using computers, computer maintenance, tailoring, medicine, making crafts.

Local Institutions and infrastructure: local churches, church leaders, government officials, government programs, non-governmental organisations, community leaders, chiefs, development organisations, police officers, judges, sports teams, clubs, libraries, schools, hospitals and health clinics, electricity, running water, boreholes, dams, roads, bridges, markets, cell phone towers.

Cultural and social resources: good relationships, family members and relatives, generous neighbours, caring friends, teachers, employers, good reputation in the community, cultural traditions, social networks, foreign missionaries.

Spiritual resources: faith, hope, love, prayer, worship, fellowship, Bible study, the Holy Spirit living in us, spiritual gifts, God's power, God's protection, God's provision, God's love, God's grace, God's plan to use us.

1. **Describe how you feel after listing all of these assets?**

2. **What changes might result in your community if you did this exercise together with all the members of your community?**

Reflecting on Asset-Based Community Development (20-25 minutes)

It is not true when people say they have nothing. God has given all of us many gifts, resources, and skills. Each of us has been blessed with different things. So even if you have things that someone else does not have, or they know how to do something that you do not know how to do, nobody needs to feel inferior. We are all created in the image of God and God has a unique purpose for each of our lives.

It is not our job to compare ourselves to each other, but rather to be faithful with what God has given to each of us, and to our communities. If we spend our time comparing ourselves to others, we will feel envy. We will get frustrated. We will feel shame and low-self-esteem. We will not change and will stay in poverty. Instead of comparing ourselves to others, we should focus on what God has given to us, and use what he has given for his glory.

If we focus on what we have instead of focusing on what we lack, we will be able to make changes and grow. If we focus on what God has given, our prayer lives will be full of gratitude and thanksgiving and full of joy. If we focus on what we do not have, then we will only spend our time complaining to God. Think about children. You enjoy it most when they thank you for what you've given to them, but you don't appreciate if they spend all of their time complaining about what they do not have. Similarly, God appreciates our gratitude. Read **1 Thessalonians 5:16-18**.

You can see that when we focus on the things we have, this takes away low self-esteem. We don't feel so desperate and helpless. We don't feel dependent or inferior. Focusing on what we have makes us feel better about ourselves. It helps to take away our poverty of being. So when you go and help people in your community to recognise what God has given to them, it will help to reduce their poverty of being and give them hope for change.

After people identify their assets, the next, more difficult step is to figure out how to use those resources and skills to develop and change. Sometimes we as leaders will have good ideas to suggest to people about how to use those resources. Other times the people who we are helping will have better, more creative ideas themselves. Other times, experts and consultants can come and teach people how to utilise what they have. In some situations, the community members will have to get organised and work together in order to make use of the resources in their community. This curriculum cannot give you all the answers for how communities should utilise their resources. God has given each of us wisdom and creativity to figure that out within our own places and cultures. But at the end of all the lessons, I will give you some recommendations of further trainings and projects you can do in your community which will give you more technical assistance and ideas.

Listen to this story from a slum in Nairobi, Kenya:

John Mwangi grew up in a slum but was fortunate to be sponsored to study organic farming after high school. He returned to Nairobi and wanted to help the young men living in the slums. With very limited money, it was difficult to see how to help. But he realised that one resource they had in abundance was garbage. Most people don't view garbage as a resource but John was creative. He gathered a group of young men and they began to sort out the natural waste (like vegetable cuttings and fruit peels) from the rest of the garbage. Then they took that waste through a 21-day process, finally having it turn into usable compost suitable for horticultural farming. Now John has 15 groups producing compost in 7 different slums. His workers are making good money selling the compost to farms! Their motto is, "Garbage is income, give it to me."[1]

I'm not sharing this story with you just so you try to do exactly what they did, but I want to encourage all of us to use our creativity to look at the things around us in new ways, and to help other communities to do the same. Most communities have far more resources than garbage to use. **We need a changed perspective**.

What do you see?

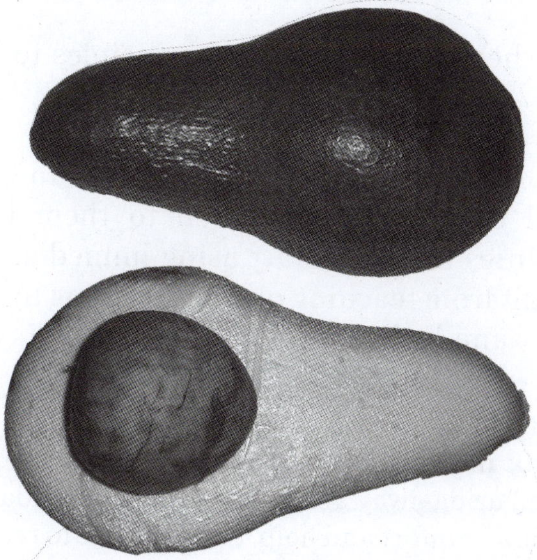

Fig. 6.1
Public Domain Image

- Some people look at the picture and see a single avocado and its seed. But someone else with more creativity and vision sees a whole forest of avocado trees by looking at what that one seed could eventually become. This shows us something amazing about God's creation. Wealth and resources are not always as limited as people think. If someone else becomes rich, it does not mean that I must become poor. It is not a competition. If we have two avocadoes, we do not have to fight over them, but we can each take an avocado and get a whole tree of avocadoes with it. Through God's good design, our creativity, hard work, and cooperation can develop and produce more new things. There is potential for amazing reproduction of wealth because of the way God's creation works.

What does this mean?

"You can count the number of seeds in a mango, but you cannot count the number of mangoes in a seed." – Traditional Kenyan Proverb.

- The avocado seed is like one talent, in the Parable of the Talents. Can you trust God to utilise that one talent and make it reproduce many more? We need a changed perspective. We need to help people take notice of common things that they have come to ignore, and help them to see these things as resources that they can utilise.

We need to teach people a new perspective. Realise what you have, utilise the assets that God has given to you, build upon those resources and skills, and trust in God to multiply your efforts for the good of your family and his kingdom.

Principles of Asset-Based Community Development

To summarise what we've learned in this lesson, here are four general principles to help us implement ABCD well:

1. Identify and utilise the skills and resources of the individual or community. Look at materially poor people as people full of possibilities, given to them by God. Sometimes people have resources and abilities they can start using immediately with encouragement. But often people may benefit from teaching or skills training to develop their God-given potential and ability. For example, listen to this story from Egypt:

   Farida was born into a poor family in Egypt, and got married when she was 20 years old. Unfortunately, her husband died only six months into the marriage, and she had become pregnant. The husband's family drove Farida away and took her baby. Farida was heartbroken and turned to God and the church for comfort and help. She was able to recover her baby. Additionally, through the church's ministry and partnership with an organisation called Tearfund, Farida was able to join a widows's group in which the widows were given skills-training. She received training to be a hairdresser. Now, Farida is thriving. "I am the only women's hairdresser in my community", she says, "It generates a very good income for me." But she is not focusing only on her own development. God has been using her to help others. She has been giving loans to help other poor families in the community, and also teaching women in her village how to read and write.[2]

2. Look for resources and solutions to come from within the individual or community as much as is possible, rather than from outsiders. Ask good questions, and listen well to the people and their ideas. And trust that the people care deeply about their communities and want to make change.

3. Try to build up the relationships among local individuals, organisations, churches, businesses, schools, and government. God intended for the individuals and institutions in communities to be working together.

4. We should only bring in resources from outside the community when local resources are not enough to solve pressing needs. And we need to be careful about bringing in outside resources too early in the process, and be careful not to bring in too much. While outside assistance is often helpful, we must be careful not to weaken the community's effort to utilise its own resources and abilities. Listen to this encouraging story from West Africa:

   An American organisation was working with a local development organisation in a very materially poor region in West Africa. The local organisation wanted the American organisation to provide them with a new motorcycle in order to continue to do their development work effectively. The American NGO workers firmly believed that the work needed to be done in partnership and up to this point the Americans had provided all of the funding for the development projects. So although the Americans had raised money to cover part of the purchase of the motorcycle, they suggested that it was possible for the community members of the various villages to raise the remaining money needed for this motorcycle. It seemed impossible. The local organisation's workers said that people didn't have any money to contribute, but reluctantly they said they would ask. One of the workers went to the first village, and with some shame, asked the people if they were willing to contribute towards the motorcycle. The response was shocking. "Why of course we'll contribute towards your new motorcycle" the villager said excitedly, "your visits are very important to us. In fact, I'm going to go to surrounding villages and tell them that you need a new motorcycle and that they can contribute towards it." Before the workers could even visit and ask all the villages, the money started streaming in from all over. Within six weeks their goal for the motorcycle had been met and even surpassed by 30%. The people had been struggling with food shortages, and receiving food assistance from the American NGO through the local organisation, but even in their time of need, they were able to do something themselves, and that brought them amazing joy.[3]

To conclude this lesson listen to this quote from a philosopher of ancient China. He was not a Christian, but what he taught fits well with ABCD and with what God wants us to do.

Lao Tzu a 6th Century Chinese Philosopher said, "Go to the people. Live with them. Learn from them. Love them. Start with what they know. Build with what they have. But with the best leaders, when the work is done, the task accomplished, the people will say 'We have done this ourselves.'"[4] **But as Christians, we need to add: "With the help of God!"**

Take-Home Activities for Lesson 7

The facilitator should provide detailed guidelines and clear instructions on how to go about the take-home activities. Read aloud the two activities and explain that pastors should probably choose #1, and others attending the training should probably choose #2. If the participants are meeting only periodically, then they could do this activity before they come back for the next lesson.

1. **For church leaders:** Preach a sermon on the parable of the talents in your church. Then, during the Sunday service or at a different church event, instruct all your church members to identify and write down the assets and abilities of the whole church. Talk about both physical resources and spiritual gifts. Discuss together how to best use everyone's gifts for the good of the church and the community.

2. **For individuals:** Do a Bible study on the parable of the talents with your family or with your community group. Identify and write down the assets and abilities of your family, or the assets and abilities of your community group. Discuss how you can use them together to overcome material poverty. Make a plan on how to address it so that a change can be made.

Small Group Drawing Exercise (20 minutes)

- Divide the participants into small groups of four or five people. Make sure each group has one large sheet of paper and several markers or pens of different colours. Instruct the groups to do the activity below, and emphasize that they will only get 10 minutes so they will have to work very quickly and have each person in the group contributing to the drawing at the same time. After the 10 minutes are finished, take away the markers so that each group has equal time. Part of the fun of this activity is that the drawings will not be perfect or fully finished. Have each group take turns presenting. Each group should select one person who will show the drawing to the large group and explain how the drawing shows a community developing in one minute or less.

In your groups, draw a picture of a community that is developing. You cannot use any words, only pictures. Be creative. Remember that development should include not only a reduction in material poverty, but an improvement of the four relationships.

- This is intended to be a fun exercise. Keep the mood relaxed and humorous. For example, you might point out which communities lack water, trees, or a church. Or if the drawing lacks any animals you could say, "Did the people in this community kill off all the animals?"

- However, it can be very instructional. As the facilitator, analyse each drawing. Point out what good things you see, point out what things are missing. Or ask the large group, "In this drawing, do we see an improvement regarding material poverty?" "In this drawing, do we see an improvement in people's relationship with God?" etc.

  - For material poverty (people having their needs met).
  - For poverty of being (people doing things for themselves, using their own resources, and feeling good).
  - For poverty of spiritual intimacy (people beginning to worship God, churches planted).
  - For poverty of stewardship (people finding work to do and caring for creation, the land, animals, and plants).
  - For poverty of community (people beginning to work together and being at peace).

- It also can be helpful to point out if a community in a drawing is using their own resources or if the community is being assisted by an NGO, or both.

Conclude on a more serious note by talking about how what they have drawn are things that are achievable for their communities. They are really possible by using the local resources that people already have. Take time to pray for the group and for their communities that God would help them to realise these visions before you continue to the next lesson.

Further Reflection

Read this section at home for further learning.

- **Africa is Blessed**

Part of having a changed perspective is looking at our continent differently. Because of the history of the slave trade, and because of all of the aid from foreign governments and donors that has been given to our continent, many of us have internalised the idea that we are poor, helpless, and inferior to the rest of the world. Some of us have even wondered if Africa is cursed. Some foreigners in the past claimed that the people of Africa are cursed using **Genesis 9:24-27**, but this is a lie. They called it the "Curse of Ham". But in fact, the curse in this passage was on Ham's son Canaan, not Ham. Canaan was the ancestor of the Canaanites, so this passage is not about Africans. It's true that Ham had other sons who were ancestors of the Ethiopians, the Egyptians, and the Libyans, but they were not cursed.[5] And the curse was not really about ethnicity, but it was about how the Israelites would eventually conquer the wicked Canaanites in the Promised Land.[6] We are not under the curse of Canaan, but even if we were, we experience blessing that overpowers that curse and any other curse once we come to know Christ. Jesus is more powerful than all curses. Jesus's death and resurrection even conquers the original curse of death.

The reality is that God has richly blessed Africa. Some of the assets God has given to Africa include: many unique cultural heritages, a large population, natural resources like oil and minerals (for example—diamonds, gold, and also coltan, a very rare ore containing minerals used in making mobile phones), beautiful animals and national parks, some of the world's greatest rivers, productive agriculture, and a huge land area.

Africa is rich in gifts from God. Unfortunately, sometimes these resources have been forcefully misused by foreigners, or mismanaged by corrupt leaders in Africa. But we must realise how much God has blessed our continent and utilise well what he has given us by working together. Doing this is our best hope at overcoming our continent's dependency on the aid from foreign nations. Aid can be helpful and we can still partner with foreign countries as we try to help our people, but we must not remain dependent on that aid. It is not a long-term, sustainable solution, nor is aid something that builds up the dignity of our people. If we want to be obedient to God by being good stewards, we must learn to focus on and utilise the gifts God has given us. We must take responsibility for the development of our own communities and nations.

- **Inspiring Stories of Asset-Based Community Development**

1. In Ethiopia, Kale Heywet Church in the Arba Minch region found a way to use the little resources they had to make a nice profit for the church. Originally the church land was given to them by the government. The government said it was full of rocks and no one would be able to do anything with it. So the government leaders thought

they might as well just give the land away. The land is 20 hectares in size and large rocks cover the surface all over. But one of the church leaders realised that these rocks should be looked at as assets, not as a curse. He thought maybe the rocks could be sold for construction projects. He and the other leaders calculated and researched how this could be done. Today construction vehicles can be seen on the church property breaking up the rocks to be sold. Now the church enjoys a regular profit from these rocks! With a new perspective, things that some people see as worthless can be seen as assets given by God.[7]

2. Hellen and her husband live in Turkana County in Kenya, a place that is hot and arid and where there is no electrical grid. She and her husband are both partially blind but they feed fifteen people in their household every day. How do they manage this? Hellen joined a VSLA (Village Savings and Loan Association) in 2015. A VSLA can be like a community funded and managed bank. Members encourage each other, save together, and offer each other low interest loans. A VSLA allows people to use the little resources that they have, and multiply them by working together. Hellen used her first loan to buy a shaving machine and started a barber business earning about $4 USD per day. After she paid off that loan she continued saving. She then took out two more loans to purchase a solar panel, a television, a video machine, speaker, amplifier, and a battery, which she quickly used to open a video-showing business and a phone-charging business, which have added another $4-10 per day to her household income. After paying those loans off, she took another loan to buy water pipes to bring water to her house so her family has regular access to water. Now she sells water to her neighbors as well and earns $1-2 a day.

   Hellen's husband was motivated by these successes. With the VSLA's loan-lending at capacity, he secured a loan from a bank and, together with Hellen's savings, they have invested in another business venture with the purchase of a maize-milling machine. Their milling brings in about $4-8 USD, per day. Hellen's five businesses have added up to $24 USD per day to her family's income. Her life has changed. She can afford to feed, educate, and clothe her extended family, and gives cheerfully to the church. Hellen is encouraged by her success and isn't ready to stop; she has plans to invest next in a water tank. This story shows us one method of helping people to multiply the little resources that they have so that they can support themselves. We will examine VSLAs in a future lesson.[8]

3. Dinnah, also known as "Termite", lives near the city of Soroti in Uganda. Before she came to know Christ, she used to be a serious alcoholic. She brewed alcohol and she would drink and smoke up to 12 hours a day. Today she looks back and feels like it was such a wasted life full of bitterness and quarrels with other people. But in 2010, she came to know Jesus personally. Her life completely changed! She became full of joy and peace, and she made peace with her family members as well. But she remained materially poor, especially since she gave up brewing alcohol. After she attended a Bible study about the importance of working with her hands, she knew she needed to find productive work. She tried to think hard about what resources and skills God had given to her that she could use to make an income. She saw termite mounds around her community, and as a child she was taught how to catch the termites from the mounds. She decided to catch and fry termites to sell to people. Some people in her community

think of this kind of work as shameful. But her life and success prove those people wrong. Dinnah started to make a lot of money especially since she has her own unique recipe: fried termites with onions and spices. She has been able to take care of all her family's needs through selling these termites, and now it is her normal business. She has built a house with the income as well as paying school fees for her children. Now people in her church and community call her "blessed" and admire her for the change in her life. People affectionately call her "termite" in the local language. The author, Anthony, is one of her customers and he can testify that she can really cook!

Helping Without Hurting in Africa

Facilitator Manual

Lesson 8:
Opening Exercise Evaluation

Lesson 8:
Opening Exercise Evaluation

In this section, you will find:

- A review of the plans participants made in Lesson 1.
- Instructions to participants on how to proceed with the other lessons of the training and how to schedule future training sessions.

Lesson Objective:

- To improve the plans made in the Lesson 1 Exercise so that they can be implemented effectively in the participants's communities.

Time Length: 1 hour

Notes to the facilitator

- This lesson is for evaluating the plans the participants made in Lesson 1. You will be asking participants to look over their plans in their original groups of five people. You will then be asking participants questions about their plans.
- During the evaluation, periodically remind participants that the purpose of the evaluation is not to insult groups and their plans, but rather for all of us together to learn from our mistakes. You can even tell them about your own experience of this activity when you were first trained and how you learned from your mistakes.
- Periodically remind the participants that although they are seeing mistakes that they had made in their plans, they will now be able to put revised plans into action in their real communities, and help people in a wiser way.

Evaluation

We are now coming to the end of our first training session of this curriculum. We will now evaluate the plans we made to help materially poor people at the very beginning, during Lesson 1. In this way we will be able to learn from our mistakes, while at the same time reviewing the important principles we have learned from each lesson so far.

Some people do not like evaluations or critiques, but if we have the right attitude, this can be a helpful exercise. Our goal is not to insult one another or feel bad about the mistakes we made in our plans. The goal is to reflect on what we have learned and think about what we would do differently now in our plans. Just like materially poor people, we and our ministries are broken. We don't need to try to cover this up. Rather, we can relax in the good news that God knows we are broken and that he can transform all of us—the materially poor, ourselves, and our ministries—into something new! We will discuss it later, but the take-home activity for this lesson is to go home and make changes to your plan and then try to really carry it out in your community.

Why should we be willing to listen to other people who criticise and evaluate our ministries and plans?

Let's read and reflect on **Proverbs 12:15** and **Proverbs 19:20**.

What kind of attitude should we have when evaluating other people's ministries and plans?

Let's read and reflect on **Ephesians 4:29** and **1 Corinthians 13:1-2**.

- It is common for Christians to criticise one another, especially Christians of different churches and denominations. Unfortunately this has often not been done in love. Sadly, at times we do not see other churches as part of the same team, but as competition, even though we will be living in the New Creation together. But despite these failures, God does call us to hold one another accountable. We should be correcting each other in love and helping each other to follow Christ more fully.

- It is common for Christians to disagree and discuss theological differences and worship practices, but it is rarer for Christians to hold each other accountable concerning how to care for poor people. Perhaps most Christians think that if someone is actually trying to do anything at all for poor people they should be thanked rather than criticised, especially since so many people neglect poor people completely. But think about all you have learned so far. Poverty is complicated. It is so easy to make mistakes that actually harm poor people rather than help them. All of us must be more willing to offer constructive suggestions to one another in love. We will do that now as we go through our plans. But mostly we will each evaluate the plan our own group made. It's good to learn how to evaluate ourselves before we evaluate other people.

- But later, when we all go home we must be willing to speak up and tell the truth. We must guide other Christians, churches, and ministries so that they also will help poor people wisely, in a way that glorifies God and brings real change. This is extremely difficult, and having an attitude of humility is crucial. We must be quick to listen, and slow to speak. Even after this training, we do not have all the answers. But we need to ask good questions of other Christians, and be willing to speak the truth. We should speak with gentleness and respect, and we should be sure to thank Christians for their care for the poor. Many Christians are trying to help poor people with sacrificial love, but they need more guidance on how to do so wisely. As we guide other Christians, and even challenge them on some of their practices, we must maintain an attitude of love and try to stay together in unity. Let's read **Ephesians 4:2-3**.

Tell the participants to gather into the small groups that they were in for Lesson 1 on the first day. Make sure that each group is close enough to listen to you and see you as the facilitator.

Once the groups are assembled and everyone is quiet, read aloud again the scenario that you had chosen for them in the first lesson.

- **Scenario 1**—You must plan how to help the **beggars** in your city. One of the pastors in your city recently preached about giving to the poor, and many people in the church were convicted and wanted to do more to help the poor. Particularly, members of your church have felt a burden to help the beggars who they always see in the market. Up to this point, the church members have mostly ignored the beggars and avoided them, but a few church members sometimes give them some coins. The beggars beg for food while sitting on the ground. Some have physical disabilities while others seem healthy. Many of them are old. Your church really wants to give generously and help them.

- **Scenario 2**—You must plan how to help the **widows** in your village community. A church member recently announced her opinion that your church should be doing more to assist the widows in the church. The other church members agreed, and added that the church should also at least do something small for the widows in the wider community who don't belong to the church. Many of the widows in the community are struggling, even though the cultural expectation is that their children and relatives are supposed to be taking care of them. Some very elderly widows are struggling, and some widows with small children lost their husbands at a young age.

- **Scenario 3**—You must plan how to help **street children** in your city. Street children have been spending their time near your church. On Sunday, as people are coming to church, they beg for money and food from church members as they walk and drive to church. This annoys the church members very much. At times, the street children have even written graffiti on the church building. All the church members have agreed that the street children have become a problem, so something must be done. The church leaders have suggested that the church tries to love and care for them rather than calling for the police to intervene. The church members agreed to try.

Hand back the papers that each group wrote their original plans on, if you have kept them for the participants. Have each group read through their answers and discuss the evaluation questions. While doing this, they should not be changing what they had written, but they could write down a few brief notes in answer to each question. Give the groups about 30 minutes to go through the questions together. This is about 2 minutes per question.

Once the participants have gone through all the questions, break up the groups, and have everyone return to their seats in the large group. Now in the large group, go through the questions with everyone in about 20 minutes. You'll only have one or two minutes for each question. Do not have every group answer each question as this would take many hours. Instead, just have any one or two participants answer each question. Since we tend to learn best by learning from our mistakes, try to rephrase many of the questions just for the large group discussion. For example, for #2.b., you could say: "Was there any group who realised they did not address poverty of spiritual intimacy in their plan?" Suggestions will be given to you as the facilitator below, listed as "**Alternative Questions**".

- As you go through each question, give them some ideas of things they could have done in order to help people in a wise and effective way. A few general suggestions will be given to you in the facilitator notes in the following page. You can make these suggestions more specific by applying them to the scenario that was chosen for your training group.

- Try to appreciate the good answers of the participants, but even when someone acknowledges a mistake in their plan, thank them for their honesty.

- This evaluation exercise is a great time to review concepts from all the lessons covered so far. Take time to stop periodically and ask participants to define terms or principles that relate to the questions being covered, for example "poverty of stewardship" or "assets".

- As participants respond with answers and comments, write down on the flip chart important insights, observations, and things people have learned.

Evaluation Questions

1. Mention some good things you see in your plans. In what ways did you plan well?

2. a. Did you address material poverty in your plans? Explain.

This concerns helping people to meet their physical needs such as food, clean water, shelter, income, medicine, or other necessities.

2. b. Did you address poverty of spiritual intimacy in your plan? Explain.

Alternative Question—Was there any group who realised they did not address poverty of spiritual intimacy in their plan?

This involves improving people's relationship with God and could include good activities like evangelism, counselling, sharing God's love, proclaiming the gospel, and inviting people to church.

2. c. Did you address poverty of community in your plan? Explain.

Alternative Question—Was there any group who realised they did not address poverty of community in their plan?

This could include activities like inviting people to church, mentoring, connecting people to community groups, reuniting people with their families, reconciliation, adoption, and making new friends.

2. d. Did you address poverty of being in your plan? Explain.

Alternative Question—How did you help people feel less inferior and ashamed? Or would your ministry plan have made people feel even worse about themselves?

Addressing poverty of being could involve counselling, making friendships with materially poor people, showing respect to materially poor people, listening to the people who you are helping, giving them meaningful work to do in the community or in church, and affirming that they are made in the image of God and have value, gifts, and abilities.

2. e. Did you address poverty of stewardship in your plan? Explain.

Alternative Question—Did you help people find meaningful work to do in God's world to support themselves and their families?

Good activities for addressing poverty of stewardship include helping people to take care of their land and environment. Also, we could help people find jobs, or find meaningful work or service to do. We could go to job interviews with people and give job skills training. We could help children go to school, be responsible, and do productive things with their time.

3. Do you see any evidence of a god-complex in your plan (thinking that you are better or more intelligent than the people you were trying to help)?

Alternative Question—Who can be brave and share honestly about a god-complex in your group's plan? We will not judge you, but we can learn together from your sharing.

A god-complex could be shown by telling the beggars, widows or street children exactly what to do without listening to them. Or it could be trying to do things for them without their participation. Or it could be helping them while feeling superior to them.

4. In your plan, did you focus on people, reconciliation, and building relationships over a long period of time? Or did you focus only on short programs to help the poor as quickly as possible?

It is good to build friendships with people who are poor instead of just doing something quick to help them. This may involve having a conversation with them, worshipping together, and visiting their homes. It means that we do not look for a quick-fix to a problem by quickly giving out things, but we plan to stay in these relationships and walk with these people for a long time.

5. a. In your plan, were you responding to the people with relief, rehabilitation, or development?

Remind the participants that they might give financial assistance in any of the three approaches, but relief is characterised as helping people in an emergency situation in which the people are not capable of participating in their own development. In rehabilitation and development we work together with people, and they also contribute their own resources. For example, if you see a ministry plan that was just planning to give handouts and do things for beggars, without actually working together with them, then that ministry plan would have been trying to give relief (even when relief was not appropriate).

5. b. After what you have learned, what do you think the people really need - relief, rehabilitation, or development?

It is helpful to get a show of hands from the participants, to find out how many participants say that they need relief, how many say rehabilitation, and how many say development.

Explain that it is not always easy to determine which response is the right one. It's okay for groups to have some disagreement about this question as long as they are properly understanding the three approaches. If the beggars were in danger of death and incapable of helping themselves, they may need relief at the beginning, especially if they are weak from hunger, but the relief should transition to rehabilitation and development. Other beggars are able to do something to participate and so what they need would actually be rehabilitation or development, even if that development includes financial assistance. Some elderly widows and street children may need relief because they are not able to take care of themselves. But other widows may be able to work and participate in their own development. Some street children may have families that they should be with, and they need reunion with their families, not handouts.

6. In your plan, do you see any paternalism (doing things for people that they could do for themselves)?

Look for evidence in plans of treating people as helpless or ignorant. Were the beggars, widows, or children treated with respect? Was their advice taken in how best to improve their situation?

7. a. Did you encourage people to recognise their gifts and assets?

Alternative Question—Was there any group who did not try to utilise the gifts and skills of the people they were helping before giving handouts?

Good activities for this could involve job skills training, identifying people's assets, abilities, and skills, helping guide children about schooling and how God can use them, and identifying social structures and people who can care for and help the people.

7. b. If you gave out resources, did the resources come from the local community or from outside donors?

For most of the groups – widows, beggars, and street children – there may be families and relatives that could help these people. We should look first to the local community and family to help before getting the help of outside donors.

8. What have you learned about yourself or your church from this exercise?

After going through the questions above, ask each group to give themselves a mark/grade on a scale of 100. This can be just for fun, but also it helps you to measure how much the participants have learned since the beginning of this training.

Take-Home Activities for Lesson 8

Take-home with you your written ministry plan that you evaluated during this lesson, as well as your notes and answers to the evaluation questions. Have a meeting with your fellow church leaders or colleagues. Over the next several months, revise your ministry plan and correct any mistakes you made using what you've learned in Lessons 1-7. Improve the plan and then actually go and try to implement it in your church and community.

Please do not do this alone, but ensure that you work with your community or church. Commit your plan to God and continue to ask for his guidance. Go forward in faith and in confidence that our powerful God will be with you and use you in mighty ways to bring transformation in the lives of people in your community!

Optional: Testimonies, Evaluation, and Prayer (30 Minutes)

This is an optional section especially for groups who planned to only pass through Lessons 1-8 and do not plan to complete all the lessons in *Helping Without Hurting in Africa*. This time of testimonies and evaluation will function as the ending of the training for those groups. In addition, some groups that are planning to complete the whole curriculum may still decide to use this section. If your group is finishing their first training session at this point and is planning to schedule new days for completing the remaining lessons, then this section can be a fitting conclusion until the next time your group meets. It is optional. There will be another opportunity for evaluation and testimonies at the end of the whole curriculum. Make a decision based on how much time you have available and how you have scheduled the training sessions for your group.

Encourage the group members to take a few minutes to discuss with you about whether they would like to plan another training session with you in order to complete the remaining sessions. Depending on how you have structured the training, you may need two or more additional training sessions. Remind the participants that only those who complete all the lessons in *Helping Without Hurting in Africa* receive the certificate. Only those with the certificate are qualified to facilitate and teach other groups.

Let me remind you of all the lessons still remaining in this curriculum:

- **Lesson 9**: Working for God's Glory
- **Lesson 10**: Worldview Transformation
- **Lesson 11**: Broken Systems
- **Lesson 12**: The Prosperity Gospel
- **Lesson 13**: African Culture and Money
- **Lesson 14**: What Causes Change in Someone's Life?
- **Lesson 15**: Participation of the Community
- **Lesson 16**: Church Benevolence Ministry
- **Lesson 17**: Urban Ministry: Opportunities and Challenges
- **Lesson 18**: Mission Trips within Africa
- **Lesson 19**: Foreigners, Missionaries and Sponsors
- **Lesson 20**: Seed Projects and Further Resources

I hope and I pray that all of you will go home and put into practise the take-home activities in your churches and communities so that we can see real change! The take-home activities are the most important out of everything else in this training. Remember also to review the lessons at home, and take time to read the "Further Reflection" sections that we did not cover. You might want to consider meeting with a friend and discussing the material together.

Testimonies

We will now have a time of testimonies. Anyone is welcome to share with me and the group what you have learned so far in this training and how it will benefit you going back home. You can also share if you plan to teach some of these principles to people in your family or church. If you would like to write a written testimony and give it to me, that is also very helpful. I, the authors, and the Chalmers Center who published this curriculum would all appreciate it. Just write your testimony on the testimony page and give it to me later. You are also free to email me. Or you can wait and write a written testimony after you have finished all the lessons.

Encourage participants to be brief and concise in their testimonies so that more people have time to speak. Point out to participants the authors's email addresses in the Participant Manuals on page 87 and tell them that should they have any questions or testimonies for the authors, they are invited to email them.

Evaluation

Now we will spend just a few minutes hearing feedback from you so that this curriculum can continue to be improved. You can share what you really thought was good in the training, and you can share what you think needs to be improved. You can also share about how I myself can improve as a facilitator. Remember what we said about criticism earlier. Please speak in love, but know that I, as a facilitator, and those who wrote this curriculum very much value your advice as we seek to always serve Christ more faithfully and make this a very effective curriculum.

There is an optional evaluation page in your manual that you can write your evaluation on. You can complete it after we close today, tear out that page, and give it to me. Or you can use any other piece of paper. If you plan to complete other lessons in *Helping Without Hurting in Africa*, you could wait and complete one evaluation form at the end of the whole curriculum.

Evaluation Questions

1. **Is there anything we have discussed that you are confused about? Do you have anything you want help to understand before we leave?**
2. **What lessons or activities did you appreciate most in the lessons so far?**
3. **Do you plan to complete the remaining lessons in *Helping Without Hurting in Africa*? Why or why not?**
4. **What can be improved in this training or in my facilitation?**
5. **Would you recommend this training to a friend? Why or why not?**

Consider giving the participants your contact information so they can call you later with follow-up questions and ideas. If you have time, stay around after the training finishes so that you can answer individual questions people have for you.

Prayer

Be sure to close this training session with prayer, but pray in the way that you and your group sees fitting. Pray that God would give everyone time to meet together again to continue with the remaining lessons. Pray for the revised ministry plans and also for the take-home activities that the participants will go home and do. You want the participants to go home equipped with God's power and with courage and confidence to put into practise what they have learned. You want them to go home with a deep love and compassion for people struggling with poverty. Commit them and their plans to our mighty and loving God who is willing to use even people like us for his work in this world!

Helping Without Hurting in Africa

Facilitator Manual

Lesson 9: Working For God's Glory

Lesson 9: Working For God's Glory

In this section, you will find:

- A biblical framework for understanding work and business.
- A discussion of ethics, tithing, and how we can all engage in our work for the glory of God.

Lesson Objectives:

- To understand the biblical importance of work.
- To become people with integrity in our work.
- To understand business as an appropriate Christian calling.
- To become people who give generously from what God has provided.

Time Length: 2 hours

Notes to the facilitator

- Ensure that long notes, quotations, and group questions are prepared in advance and written on flip chart.
- Unless otherwise noted, all Scripture passages in **bold** should be read out loud by a participant for the whole group.
- When the participants read the selected Bible passages throughout the lesson, make brief summaries of what each Bible passage is about and what it means.
- At the end of the lesson, explain the take-home activities clearly to participants.
- If there is time at the end of the lesson, consider asking participants questions to review the key points made during the lesson.

Opening Discussion (10 minutes)

In the previous lessons we said that fighting material poverty primarily involves reconciling the four relationships so that people can fulfil their calling of glorifying God by working and supporting themselves and their families. In this lesson, we now need to look more deeply at our relationship with creation, specifically the nature of "work" and how to do our work for God's glory.

Ask participants the following questions and take brief notes of their responses on a flip chart.

1. What is "work?"

2. Is work a gift or a punishment?

For question #1, encourage the participants to give a clear definition of work. Also, prompt them to discuss whether work includes only activities that earn money, or whether it can include other types of activities that do not earn money (for example, a wife who takes care of the children and does chores at home while the husband earns money through a job). You could also have them discuss whether it is possible for an activity to be considered work for one person but not for a different person. For example, counselling people is part of the daily work of a pastor, but for other Christians it could be something they do in their free time. Planting crops is the work of farmers, but planting in a garden could be considered a restful activity for someone who works in an office all day.

For question #2, just summarise their answers, but don't give them your answer yet, as you will explain further in the lecture. The correct answer is that work is a gift from God. However, though work is not in and of itself a punishment or a curse, it has become difficult because of the Curse that fell on creation after Adam and Eve sinned.

Facilitator Lecture (1 hour)

Work in Genesis

What is "work"? Work is an activity involving mental or physical effort done to achieve a purpose or result. It is a means of earning income.[1] We usually think of work as what people do from day to day in order to earn money, but not all types of work involve earning money. Sometimes we work to take care of ourselves, or to help others, or to make this world a better place. However, in this lesson we will primarily look at work as any activity done in order to support a person's basic needs and the needs of their family.

Let's look at what the Bible says about work in Genesis. Read **Genesis 2:1-3**. In this passage we learn that God was the first one to work. He worked in order to create this world and then he rested. He was happy about his work and pleased with the result. Read **Genesis 1:31**. If God worked, we should follow his example and also work. This tells us that work is not a bad thing, not a punishment, and not a curse. In fact, it is a godly activity.

Read **Genesis 1:28** and **Genesis 2:15**. We can see clearly that God wanted Adam and Eve to work. Work was a gift from God so that Adam and Eve could have meaningful lives. In fact, out of all God's creatures, only humans were given a job to do. They were created with a purpose. They were to manage the Garden of Eden, rule over the animals, and fill the earth. As God is the creator, people who are made in his image also continue to create new things. People develop God's world. People create culture, write songs, build houses and roads, cultivate fields, and create social institutions. We utilise God's creation for our benefit and for God's glory.

Of course, there is a problem with our work today and that problem goes all the way back to Adam and Eve in the Garden. When Adam and Eve disobeyed God, sin came into the world and stained everything. The whole world became broken and corrupt. And God gave them a punishment for their sin. We call this punishment, "the Curse". Let's read just part of the Curse, **Genesis 3:17-19**. Even today all people experience the consequences of humanity's fall into sin.

In verses 17-19, we see that the work of farming was made difficult. But it is not only farm work that has become difficult. All work has the potential to be stressful, or boring, or dangerous, or frustrating.

We must understand that work is still a gift even though it has become difficult. The same concept is at work in childbearing. Childbearing is difficult and painful, but giving birth to children is still a beautiful gift from God. Work was cursed and made difficult, but work is not a curse in itself. Work is a godly activity, and it is one of the things God created us to do. In fact, recent research studies have shown that people who have work to do are far happier than those without work to do.[2] We need work. Even when Jesus returns and his kingdom is complete, we will still be given work to do.

When their work became difficult, did Adam and Eve become hopeless in their work? No. God continued to bless them and be with them. Adam and Eve were able to work and provide for themselves, even outside the Garden of Eden. They were able to bear children and reproduce. God did not abandon humanity. Even though work is difficult, God still provides for us through our work and continues to give us his blessings. **Read Psalm 104:10-14** about how God cares for us.

Many people and cultures in Africa have viewed work as a curse or a punishment. Even some Christians have misunderstood the Bible and believe that work is a punishment for Adam and Eve's sin. The result of these beliefs is that some people view work as a burden and try to only do enough work to be able to survive. This is one of the beliefs that causes a lot of materially poor people to remain in their poverty.

Do you know any people or communities who have this belief?

In order to help materially poor people, we need to try to reconcile their relationship to God's creation. This means that we try to help materially poor people find meaningful work to do in God's world, work that can financially support them and their families. We want them to be able to view work as a gift not a burden. We should not help them to find work just because we are tired of being generous in our financial assistance. Instead, we want them to have work to do so that they can be the people God created them to be—people made in God's image who work just like God works. Helping people to find work can include encouraging people to use their assets and skills, and sometimes it means educating and training people in new skills so that they have more work opportunities.

Working for God's Glory

Ask the participants these questions and take brief notes of their responses on a flip chart.

1. **What does it mean to work for God's glory?**
2. **Practically, how should we as Christians work differently from others, in a way that honours God?**

For question #1, you can discuss with participants what the word "glory" means. Glory refers to honour, praise, thanksgiving, and exaltation. The word suggests fame and beauty. Discuss the connection between our work as humans and God's glory. Try to help them see that we should be working as a way to praise and thank God, working for God's fame and beauty, not our own.

For question #2, you can simply summarise their answers because you will discuss this more throughout the lesson. They probably will give answers like: we need to work hard, work honestly, do quality work, work humbly, etc.

We must realise that one of the ways we worship God is by honouring God in our daily work. We often think of worship as only singing to God, but we are to worship God in every aspect of our lives. Read **1 Corinthians 10:31**. We spend only a few minutes or hours each week singing to God, but spend most of our time working. We need to be honouring God throughout the week, not only on Sundays. God created us to work and so we honour God when we are faithful to his call to work. We'll now look at a number of ways to do our work so that it gives glory to God.

Ways to Work for God's Glory

1. Do work to please God not people. Read **Colossians 3:23-24**. We serve Christ not only people. Our work is a way to worship God by using the skills and opportunities he has given us. We should do our work with a positive attitude knowing that it pleases God when we work well. He has also promised to reward our faithful work. We should do our work knowing that God is watching us and is with us. Listen to this quotation from the German reformer Martin Luther talking about the work of a parent.

   > "God, with all his angels and creatures, is smiling—not because that father is washing diapers, but because he is doing so in Christian faith."[3]

What does Martin Luther mean by this statement?

2. Look to Jesus as our example in work. Before Jesus began his public ministry, he worked as a carpenter. Then he worked in his ministry all the way to his death on the cross. Read **John 5:17**. Because of his work, we are saved. In gratitude for our salvation, we should follow his example and work.
3. Commit work to God. Read **Proverbs 16:3**. We should commit our work and plans to God, knowing that we need his help and his blessing to get through the difficulties and challenges in our work.
4. Do work to provide for our own needs and the needs of our families. Read **Acts 20:34** and **1 Timothy 5:8**. The Apostle Paul made it clear that it is not good for us to be dependent on others, but that it is right for us to work. Read **1 Thessalonians 4:11-12**.
5. Do work so that we won't be tempted to sin. Read **Ephesians 4:28.**

What are some of the reasons that make people steal in your community?

6. Work hard. We should be on time. We should do a full day's work. It is more common for people to rob their employers by being lazy than by stealing cash. Even if we do not have

a boss and we run our own farm or business, we must still work hard, looking for new initiatives and ways to improve. Read **Proverbs 10:4.**

7. Work with the gifts and skills God has given us. God has given each of us unique callings, skills, talents, gifts, and opportunities. We need to see our daily work as a calling, even when it is hard. We need to be good stewards and utilise the gifts God has given in our work, whether that work is at home, at the office, or at the church. Read **1 Peter 4:10.**
8. Do good quality work. When we do good work, whether it is cleaning well, or making good chairs as a carpenter, or administrating well in an office, we honour God. God is the Creator who called the creation "good". We honour him when we also do good quality work. We should give our very best in everything we do.

Imagine you are the owner of a shop. Which gives more glory to God: running a profitable business well, naming the shop, "Praise Jesus Supermarket", or both?

DIscuss.

9. Don't look down on certain types of work. In the Greek culture of the New Testament, the people who did manual labour were considered inferior. But this is not a biblical idea and the Apostle Paul set a good example by working with his hands and making tents. In some of our regions in Africa, there is a similar idea that manual labour is inferior to office work, or working as a doctor or teacher. In some places, certain jobs are considered as suitable for only certain tribes. Generally, in our world today, jobs that earn higher incomes are considered superior to those with lower incomes. Even in the church, people often view pastors as doing more important work than everyone else. We have to resist these types of comparisons that cultures make. Jesus was a carpenter and his disciples were fishermen. Every vocation is important to God and to the development of a community. Don't look down on people who have different work from you or people who earn less money.

What type of work is viewed as inferior in your community? Is this mind-set contributing to material poverty?

10. Do work with thanksgiving and try to enjoy it. We should thank God when we have work to do, even if it is difficult, because God provides for us through our work. We should be thankful and humble. Read **Ecclesiastes 2:24-25**.
11. Love other people in the work place. We must show love to our co-workers, employees, bosses, and customers, loving all regardless of status.
12. Take good care of God's creation as we work. As we discussed in previous lessons, we must avoid deforestation, pollution, and other environmental problems as we go about our work. We are to do our work in God's world in a way that will make God's world more beautiful, healthy, and productive.
13. Do work according to the rules. We need to do the right thing and obey the rules of our supervisors and the laws of our respective countries. We must obey even if we do not have any danger of being caught, even if the laws are not being enforced, and even if everyone else is breaking the rules. As Christians we must try to obey all the laws as long as they do

not go against God's Word. Read **Romans 13:1-2**. Imagine you are a bus or taxi driver. It is more important to drive safely according to the laws than to play Christian music on the radio and write "Jesus saves" on the vehicle. If we do not do our work with integrity, we are denying Christ through our actions. Read **Titus 1:16**. We actually become hypocrites by shouting to people that we are Christians, but then not living like Christians.

What rules and laws are not being obeyed in your workplace and in the nation? Are Christians obeying them?

14. Bless others with the fruit of our work. God designed the world so that our work benefits people and benefits the community as a whole. When we grow food, or make chairs, or sell mobile phones, other people are benefittting from the work we do. Our products and services should actually help people and make their lives better, and not be wasteful or draw people away from God.[4] Furthermore, God calls us to be good stewards of his material blessings by giving financial support to others. Working and giving generously to others is satisfying and brings us a blessing. Read **Acts 20:35**. We also work hard to support the ministry of the church, which we will talk about later.
15. Use the work place as a mission field. Our work place is our most important mission field. We spend most of our time at work with colleagues or neighbours. Look for opportunities to encourage others, share the gospel, or disciple other Christians you work with.
16. Rest from work. Read **Exodus 20:8-11**. Sabbath was a gift from God for the Israelite people, showing that they no longer had to work like slaves in Egypt. Sabbath was about freedom. Today, we worship on Sunday, the Lord's Day, instead of Saturday, because Sunday is the day Jesus rose from the dead. But the principle of resting on the Sabbath should be applied to Sunday. Resting is good for us, allowing us to recharge our energy and do better quality work.

    It is becoming a problem among the middle and upper class in Africa for people to overwork and be too busy. Some of us don't rest because we are chasing riches. Other times overworking is a sign of sinful pride. We say "yes" to every request. We do too many different jobs, take part in too many organisations, and serve in too many volunteer positions. We don't know how to say "no". We love the feeling of being important and needed. The result is a group of people doing way too much work, and another group of people without enough work opportunities. We must resist this attitude and realise God is in charge of the world; we cannot do everything ourselves. When we don't rest, we are sinning by breaking God's commands. Overwork can also cause us to neglect our families. Additionally, resting shows that we trust God to provide for us. If we don't rest, it may mean that we lack faith in God's promises.

Is overworking a problem for you? How can we change?

17. Do work honestly and with integrity. We must have integrity in everything we do. Integrity is not perfection; we all still struggle with sin, but our faithful honesty at work, home, and church shows the real relationship we have with Christ. We must resist corruption. If we are dishonest in the little things, we will also be dishonest in the big things. If you are dishonest in anything, you are not a trustworthy person. Read **Luke 16:10-12**. Our integrity and honesty can lead others to know Christ. Read **1 Peter 2:12**. Keeping our

integrity can be difficult. In some positions we may lose our job if we fail to participate in the corruption of others. Read **1 Peter 4:12-16**. If we are true followers of Christ, we will be willing to suffer for his name. In a later lesson, we'll discuss how to overcome corruption in society in order to help the materially poor and allow for development. But in this lesson, we are focusing on doing the right things in our places of work.

Daniel's Story

Let me share with you a story about integrity. I hope we can all follow the example of Daniel.[5]

Daniel grew up in a materially poor family in Ethiopia. Daniel came to know Christ personally at the age of twenty. By working hard in school as a youth, he was able to go to a university where he obtained a degree in Accounting. Upon graduation, Daniel applied for a number of jobs, but during the interviews he told the employers that if they asked him to change a number "3" to a number "8", he would say no. It took him a long time before he finally received a job.

He finally got a job at a seed company which imported and exported seeds. Daniel watched with discomfort as his boss bribed officials in order to falsely state that certain seeds were of a good quality. When Daniel's boss went back to school, Daniel knew he was going to have to take his place and be the one paying the bribes. But Daniel could not imagine doing this as a follower of Christ. So instead of taking the boss's place and earning a lot more money, he quit the job completely. The owner was shocked and asked Daniel to stay. Daniel said that he could not do anything unethical so he could not take that position. The boss valued Daniel's integrity so much that after Daniel quit the job, he hired Daniel as a tutor for his children.

Later, Daniel went back to school to get training in something besides accounting because he feared that any job with accounting would involve corruption. He got a degree in medical laboratory work. In school, Daniel refused to cheat on exams and assignments, and through his integrity he led several classmates to Christ! Daniel finished first in his class and got a great new job as a manager of a laboratory at a newly opened government hospital. Unfortunately, he again faced issues of corruption. Supervisors, even Christian ones, suggested he make some extra money by buying inexpensive and less effective equipment, while writing up invoices with a greater amount so he could pocket the difference. Daniel refused and faced a lot of hardship, but he set up an excellent lab. Then, doctors would request unnecessary tests for patients who had very little money and no insurance to increase the profits. Daniel challenged the doctors but there was no change. Daniel felt so bad about how the customers were being cheated that he finally left this job as well.

Later Daniel went to work as an assistant for an owner of a business. Today Daniel works as the manager of that business and earns $100 a month. With that income he supports his ten children. About his life he said recently, "I don't give. God is the only giver. I simply share what God has given. I know that someone somewhere is looking for me to show him or her Christ. So I am waiting for God to show me the next move."

Discussion Questions

What hardships did Daniel experience because of his integrity?

What blessings did Daniel or other people experience because of his integrity?

What will you do differently in your workplace after hearing this story?

After the discussion, conclude with:

We can see that God continued to provide for Daniel and his family even in those hardships. Because of Daniel's integrity he was not able to become financially rich, but he is a man who knows the riches he has in Christ. He is a man at peace with himself and with God. He knows he has done the right things and he continues to trust in God to provide for him.

Business for God's Glory

How does the church view the business world?

After they discuss, you might suggest that Christians often view people in business as people who love money, who are corrupt, or who are concerned with worldly things, etc.

How does the business world view the church?

After they discuss, you might suggest that many business people think the church is made up of beggars who don't understand how to work hard and create wealth.

Is it possible for a Christian to be highly successful in business?

One of the most common ways that people work to earn money is by being involved in business. At times, the church has looked down on business as something secular and unchristian. But the mere fact that many people have done their business in ways that dishonour God, does not mean that business is a bad thing. Business can be a very good thing when it is done in a way that honours God. In fact, business is an important part of development.

Basically, business is about creating wealth. Some people tend to think of wealth as a limited cake, that there is only a certain number of slices to divide up among everyone. But wealth is not limited like this. God uses us, his people, to develop the creation and create wealth. It's true that we are not supposed to chase after wealth to have a meaningful life. We are not supposed to seek wealth by oppressing other people. And we are not supposed to try to get rich in order to depend completely on ourselves. We are supposed to depend on God. However, money and possessions are not evil. God wants us to make use of his creation to provide for our needs and others around us. It is God who gives us the ability to produce wealth and money. Read **Deuteronomy 8:18**.

Listen to several principles from the Wealth Creation Manifesto created by the Lausanne Global Mission Movement and BAM Global[6]:

1. Wealth creation is rooted in God the Creator, who created a world that flourishes with abundance and diversity.
2. We are created in God's image, to co-create with him and for him, to create products and services for the common good.
3. Wealth creation is a holy calling, and a God-given gift, which is commended in the Bible.
4. Wealth creators should be affirmed by the church, and equipped and deployed to serve in the marketplace among all peoples and nations.
5. Wealth creation through business has proven power to lift people and nations out of poverty.

Do any of these points surprise you? And if so, why?

Creating wealth and focusing on business is a lot more productive than focusing on aid from other people or foreign nations. Aid is good and can be very helpful. But aid is not sustainable in the same way that business is. We need to focus on creating jobs. Unemployment is above 25% in some African countries.[7] Aid will not take away unemployment. But starting new businesses can create wealth and provide jobs for people in need.

Listen to this quotation from George Ayittey, a Ghanaian Economist, "The Cheetah Generation is the new and angry generation of Africans who can see that their leadership has failed them"..."They're not going to sit there and wait for governments to come and do things for them. As a matter of fact, they're not going to sit there and beg for foreign aid, because they can see that every social need in Africa is a business opportunity. The Cheetah Generation is entrepreneurial."[8]

Can you think of examples of social needs that creative Africans turned into business opportunities?

If the participants cannot think of any good examples, you could mention Mpesa in Kenya as one example (Mpesa is mobile banking through mobile phones). There was a need for people to save money safely and easily, without having to travel far to banks or pay high bank fees. In addition, Mpesa has allowed people to pay for services and products quickly and easily.

We need to complain less about the problems in our society and try to see the new jobs and businesses that will be created by responding to those problems. We can create a better life for all through creativity and using what God has provided. Anglican Bishop John Rucyahana in Rwanda said, "Instead of training job seekers, we train job makers", he says. "We need to be able to move from aid to production."[9]

We need to encourage Christians in our churches that business is not evil. Of course, some people use business to exploit people, destroy God's creation, or for greedy purposes. But business can be done in a God-glorifying way, and business as a form of work is necessary to help people out of material poverty. Businesses provide jobs that help materially poor people climb out of poverty, become generous stewards, and bless others with the fruits of their work.[10]

Sometimes Christians have viewed business negatively because of the competition involved in it. It is true that people can make an idol out of defeating their competitors or out of making the highest profits possible. But also consider how competition in sports encourages teamwork and pushes our bodies to new physical accomplishments. Similarly, competition in business can produce innovation, creativity, and good quality products and services. When done well for God's glory, business can also contribute to trust, fairness, and discipline in a society.[11] And when done with integrity, the products of business not only benefit the seller, but they also provide something to the customer. Listen to Herman Chinery, a businessman in Ghana, nicknamed the Bill Gates of Ghana – "In every business you do, it has to be win-win. The person who is buying your service must win, and you must win. Otherwise, it's not sustainable."[12]

What would be a "win-win" for both buyer and seller?

Business is work that honours God because it is using wisely the things in God's creation in a way that helps people. Pope Francis wrote: "Business is a noble vocation, directed to producing wealth and improving the world. It can be a fruitful source of prosperity for the area in which it operates, especially if it sees the creation of jobs as an essential part of its service to the common good."[13]

Christians are also able to honour God in business by earning more money to support Christian ministry and to help take care of the poor. John Wesley, an English preacher, famously said, "Earn all you can! Give all you can! Save all you can!"[14]

Tithing and Giving the Fruits of Our Work

Let the participants discuss the two questions below and then continue with the lecture which will try to answer these questions.

1. **What does tithing mean?**
2. **Are Christians commanded by God to tithe?**

A tithe refers to the voluntary giving of 10% of your financial income, or 10% of what you produce, such as 10% of the food that you grow. In the Old Testament, God commanded the Israelites to give a tithe, as well as other offerings. The tithes were given to support the priests, Levites, and the work of the temple, and also to provide for widows, orphans, and foreigners living in Israel. In the New Testament there is no clear command given to Christians to tithe, yet it seems likely that Jesus and the apostles expected Christians to continue the practice of tithing. When Jesus criticised the Pharisees, he accused them of faithfully giving the tithe while neglecting justice and the love of God (Luke 11:42). Jesus told them to continue to tithe, but also to practise love and justice.

The Apostle Paul also made clear that pastors and evangelists should be supported out of the giving of Christians, just as the priests were supported through the tithe (see 1 Corinthians 9 for more information). In addition, in many places of the New Testament, Christians are called to be generous with their money. Since we have so great a salvation and have been blessed far more than the Israelites, our grateful response should be to give away far more than 10% of our money. It is good for us to look at the example of Zacchaeus who was transformed by grace and gave away half of his possessions. Some Christians in history have turned things around and made a choice to live on only 10% of their income and give away 90% to the church and to help others!

As Christians we don't give out of guilt or as a burdensome obedience to a law, but out of thanksgiving. We should not be giving in order to earn salvation or God's acceptance. Instead, we give out of thanksgiving after receiving forgiveness and love as a free gift. We give cheerfully out of gratitude. Read **2 Corinthians 9:7**. In our joy, we should give as much as we possibly can, thinking of 10% as a beginner's guideline. As Tim Keller, a pastor in the USA, says, "If Jesus had only tithed his blood for us, we would still be lost. But Jesus gave all his blood for our salvation, far beyond the tithe."[15] In response, do we want to only give 10%?

Paul also taught that people should give according to what they have been given. Read **2 Corinthians 8:11-12**. This fits with the principle of tithing, giving a percentage of what we have received.

Some Christians teach that we should give tithes and offerings to the church so that God will bless us with more money. We will discuss this topic at greater length in the lesson on the Prosperity Gospel.

As we honour God in our work, we are also to honour God in our tithing and giving. Tithing is one way to worship God. Singing is easy, but sacrificing our money or possessions is much more difficult and is therefore a very meaningful act of worship. God wants us to use all the resources we have in a way that honours him, whether that is through supporting the needs of our family, or giving back to the ministries of the church, or showing compassion to materially poor people.

Today, around the world, tithes and gifts of Christians are used to support church ministries and pastors, to send out missionaries, translate and publish the Scriptures, take care of the sick and those in prison, lift up materially poor people, provide for community development, and so much more.

Does your church use most of the tithe and offering money for the church building? What percentage of offering money is used each month to take care of materially poor people in the community?

Tithing gives us a regular reminder that we are dependent on God. By tithing we show that we trust God to be our provider. Everything we have is not really ours, but it all belongs to God. When things are going well in our lives, tithing shows our thankfulness to God for his abundant provision. When we are struggling financially, tithing becomes a test of our faith, reminding us to trust God to take care of us.

1. **When Christians do not tithe, what does that say about their faith?**
2. **Should materially poor Christians tithe?**

While Christians may not all agree on whether materially poor Christians should tithe, hopefully the whole group will be able to agree that everyone is able to contribute something to the church and to help others, whether that is money, produce from harvests, skills, or time. Everyone is able to be generous to others and there is great joy and blessing in giving, even if it is a little. At the same time, we should not force materially poor Christians in our churches to give when they are struggling just to feed their families. And, as they do give generously from the little they have to the church offerings, the church members likewise should have compassion and give them financial assistance when possible.

When we experience the joy of receiving salvation and God's grace, it changes us and makes us want to give generously, even to the point of giving in a situation of extreme poverty. Most of us have seen elderly and materially poor people come to church every Sunday full of happiness with their humble tithe or offering. Maybe they give a basket of mangoes or some maize or eggs. They are faithful in their giving and church attendance. Some even have great difficulty walking to church but they ensure that they start the journey to church early so that they are not late for service. May we all learn from their examples!

Take-Home Activities for Lesson 9

The take-home activities will include assignments or activities that the participants should carry out in their communities, churches, or place of work, applying the lessons they have learned. The facilitator should provide detailed guidelines and clear instructions on how to go about the take-home activities. For most lessons, there will be two take-home activities for participants to choose from, mainly determined by whether or not the participant is a church leader or not. Read aloud the two activities and explain that pastors should probably choose #1 and others attending the training should probably choose #2.

1. **For church leaders**: Preach a sermon about the importance of work and how to do our work for God's glory.

2. **For others**: Consider having your church start a training program to train people in the community on job skills and income generation, with the goal that they will be able to find work and take care of their families. Some ideas:

    a. Training program on basic job skills, work ethic, budgeting, and saving.

    b. Training program on one of the following: mechanics, carpentry, baking, hairdressing, business, brick-making, IT (computers), tailoring, photography, etc.

Closing Activity: Ethical Quiz[16] (20 minutes)

Let's close this lesson by discussing in small groups about difficult ethical situations we face in our daily work and also in church ministry. We are supposed to follow the rules, work honestly, and work for God's glory. Discuss whether each person's behaviour is ethical (morally right) or unethical (morally wrong). Take 15 minutes to discuss in your small groups and then we will come back together to as a large group and I will tell you my answers.

Ethical Dilemmas in the Market

1. A lady selling sugar charges you for 1 kilo of sugar and sets her scales to give you less (unethical; see Leviticus 19:36).
2. You borrowed money from a friend to start a new business. You promised to repay that money the next month, but never repaid nor mentioned the loan again (unethical; see Matthew 5:33–37).
3. You think your employer does not pay you a fair wage. You are tempted to take some work supplies home to compensate for the difference. Instead, you ask your employer to meet with you and talk about increasing your wages. (ethical)
4. You hire four men to harvest maize in your field and you promise to pay them for their work at the end of the day. At the end of the day, the amount of maize harvested is far less than you expected. When you find one worker sleeping in the field around midday, you wake him up and send him home with half of the full day's payment (ethical). You pay the other three workers the full payment despite the smaller harvest (ethical).
5. Your manager gave you 1,000 shillings to purchase some items for work in town. You spend 950 shillings and use the other 50 shillings left over to buy a cup of tea for yourself (unethical).
6. Your neighbour borrowed your hoe to work in her garden. When she finished, she returned it to you broken with apologies and a promise to replace the hoe next month (ethical). When the next month came, she came to you and explained her financial problems. She then asked to give you a basket of maize as payment. You agree (ethical).
7. You asked the electric company to install wires all the way to your business for 6,000 shillings. After they agreed and installed the wires, you gave them 4,000 shillings and explained that was all the money you had (unethical).

Ethical Dilemmas in the Church

1. A visitor from another region gives the church a gift agreeing that it would be used for church construction, but the pastor spends that offering on a sound system after the visitor leaves (unethical).
2. A member borrows money from the church funds to pay hospital fees and fails to repay on time (unethical). The pastor then approaches the member and arranges a repayment schedule (ethical).
3. A member finds the pastor walking along the road and gives him some cash, saying that it is a gift is for the church. Using that money, the pastor buys tea and a newspaper on his way home, considering it "the church's support of his ministry" (unethical).

4. The pastor tells church members the cost to pour a cement floor in the church. The funds are raised, the floor is poured, but the cost is different than what the pastor expected and there is money left over from the money raised. The pastor announces to the members about the extra money and together the members decide how to use the money (ethical).

Further Reflection

Read this section at home for further learning.

Inspiring Stories about Work:

1. Grace, a young woman in Tanzania, is an example of a person who was helped out of material poverty by finding meaningful work to do in God's world. Grace lives with her elderly parents who are materially poor. Grace completed secondary education but unfortunately was not able to go to university because her parents did not have money for her school fees. After returning home, Grace could not think of any way to earn money to meet her needs. Finally, she became desperate and took up sex work in order to meet her food and clothing needs. Later on, she heard about an organisation named ACHAMA which helps young girls who are sex workers. The staff of the organisation agreed to let Grace into their program and they taught her vocational skills. Grace learned how to make soap, fabrics, baskets, chalk, wallets, and more. Today she uses her new skills to make four baskets a day and she sells them in the market. Grace has said – "I am very happy with my newly gained skills because they enable me to meet my needs. I am also happy because I was able to leave sex work with its high risk of HIV transmission." Grace advises other girls who are still depending on sex work to leave it behind; there is other work that they can do![17]

2. A Christian sister who is a senior civil servant in the government of Benin attended a Vision Conference of Samaritan Strategy Africa. During the conference, she learned that God wanted her to glorify and honour him in all areas of life – not just her spiritual life. This began to have a dramatic effect on her work ethic. She became more diligent and punctual. These changes were challenging. She was met with opposition from her colleagues and subordinates who were convicted about their own lax work habits. However, her diligence was observed by her superiors, and within three months, she was promoted to the position of Deputy Minister of Industry and Commerce. She went on to hold a cabinet position in the national government, the first woman to hold such a position. She is so thankful for God's work in her life and for the Vision Conference.[18]

On Business and Job Creation:

Reflect on this quotation. The first female Nigerian Finance Minister, Ngozi Okonjo-Iweala said, "The best way to help Africans today is to help them to stand on their own feet. And the best way to do that is by helping create jobs."[19]

Read this recommendation of the Lausanne Mission Movement: "We call upon the church world wide to identify, affirm, pray for, commission and release business people and entrepreneurs to exercise their gifts and calling as business people in the world – among all peoples and to the ends of the earth. We call upon business people globally to receive this affirmation and to consider how their gifts and experience might be used to help meet the world's most pressing spiritual and physical needs through business as mission."[20]

Helping Without Hurting in Africa

Lesson 10: Worldview Transformation

Lesson 10: Worldview Transformation

In this section, you will find:

- A review of how worldviews shape our thinking and contribute to our 4 relationships.
- Comparisons between three key worldviews.

Lesson Objectives:

- To understand the definition of "worldview" and how a person's worldview can contribute to their poverty or their development.
- To understand how teaching the Christian worldview is an important step in helping materially poor people.

Time Length: 2 hours

Notes to the facilitator

- Look through the list of false beliefs that keep people in poverty. Take some good time to think on your own first about Bible passages that correct each false belief before you ask the participants during the lesson.
- Ensure that long notes, quotations, and group questions are prepared in advance and written on flip chart.
- Unless otherwise noted, all Scripture passages in **bold** should be read out loud by a participant for the whole group.
- When the participants read the selected Bible passages throughout the lesson, make brief summaries of what each Bible passage is about and what it means.
- At the end of the lesson, explain the take-home activities clearly to participants and encourage them to ask questions to make sure everyone understands what they are to do before going home.
- If there is time at the end of the lesson, consider asking participants questions to review the key points made during the lesson.

Opening Discussion (10 minutes)

The facilitator should ask the participants the questions below and write the answers on a flip chart.

When you look at a cow, what do you see?

Give the participants some examples of answers that will help them to understand the question better. You could say: *"For example, you might look at a cow and see food, or maybe you see it as a source of income."*

Let a couple people answer the question. And then ask them:

"How might people of other cultures see the same cow?"

After a few participants respond, you can suggest other ideas such as the following. Some people look at cows as a symbol of high status. Some people see owning cows as part of their identity, others see a cow as a source of dowry, some people see cows as security, and some people may see the cow as just a dirty animal. Some see the cow as a creature made by our God for his enjoyment. Some people, such as Hindus in India, see the cow as a sacred animal that should not be eaten. Some Buddhists believe that the cow could be a person who has been reincarnated.[1] A Jewish person might look at a cow and remember how they were used in sacrifices to God in the temple.

We can see that people look at cows in extremely different ways. And this is not simply because of a lack of knowledge about cows. All of these different views about cows are held by people who understand cows and most likely know how to take care of them well. People look at cows differently because they have different "worldviews". People around the world with different cultures have different ways of seeing the world and the things in this world.

What is a worldview? **A worldview is all the beliefs that someone has that affect how they live and act**. Our worldviews are the glasses through which we see the world. Imagine how things look different for a person with clear glasses and a person wearing shaded glasses. Our worldviews shape the way we relate to God, ourselves, others, and the creation. Our worldview includes our beliefs on the big questions of life – Who is God? Why were humans created? How should people live and behave? Is there life after death? A person's worldview also shapes a person's every day decisions and behaviour. While every individual person has a slightly unique worldview, people generally share worldviews together with other people of the same culture.

Why is it important for us to consider a person's worldview when we are trying to help him or her out of poverty?

Give the participants time to think of some reasons and then write down the answers on the flip chart. And then continue with the lecture.

The basic answer to this question, which we shall explore in this lesson, is that often people's beliefs contribute to keeping them in poverty or to taking them out of poverty. People can remain trapped in unhelpful practices because of their worldview. People's beliefs will always influence their decisions and actions and how they relate with God, themselves, others and the rest of creation.

We would say the correct way to view the world is through the **lens** of our Christian Faith. We as Christians have a Christian worldview, or we can call it a biblical worldview, based on the truths of God's Word. Other people have some true beliefs and also some false beliefs. But we need to remember that it is also possible that we as Christians have some false beliefs, so we need to keep reading God's Word to correct ourselves. We should continually seek to be renewed in our minds by the Holy Spirit through reading God's Word. Read **Romans 12:2**.

Because false beliefs and false worldviews can contribute to people's poverty, part of our work in fighting poverty is to teach people the Christian worldview. We must teach people the truth about this world and our place in it. This teaching should not only be about giving people the knowledge they don't have, but it should be a source of learning, encouragement, and enlightenment to non-Christians, so that they come to see that the Christian worldview is the correct one. This calls for gentleness and patience as we try to lead people to know Christ personally.

Once people trust in Jesus and have been taught the Christian worldview, they will be better able to have good relationships with God, self, others, and creation. If people have a false worldview about any of these four relationships, it can cause them to remain stuck in any or all of the five types of poverty.

Facilitator Lecture: Worldviews (80 minutes)

To understand why having a false worldview can contribute to poverty, we need to think about some examples.

Let's first look at a false belief concerning humanity's relationship to God's creation. In the cultural beliefs of the Basotho in Lesotho, the traditional belief is that if farmers weed their fields during the day between 10:00am and 3:00pm, then there will be hailstorms. So the farmers do not weed during that time and much of their time to work hard and plant their fields is wasted. Another belief they have is that if women wash their clothes during the day or breast feed their babies during the day, there will be hailstorms. So they only do these activities at night. You can see how these beliefs would cause the people to be unproductive. This can change when people are taught the biblical worldview. We must teach people that God created them to rule over the creation, not that the creation should rule over people. Also, we can teach that God is in control of his creation and the weather, and he is the one who told people to work for six days every week. Christians in Lesotho who have been taught a Christian worldview based on the Bible are no longer afraid to carry on with their work during the day and are able to get more work done.[2]

People can also have false beliefs about God which keep them trapped in either one or all of the five types of poverty. If a person believes that witchcraft is more powerful than God, she might waste a lot of her money on sacrifices and rituals with the witchdoctor. The rituals and witchcraft will not result in healing or blessings, but only in wasted resources, evil bondage, and material poverty. When people come to know Jesus, they are taught to trust in God to take care of them, to work for his glory, denounce evil and not to participate in witchcraft.

A person's worldview will always influence their opinion on what is good or bad and what is right or wrong. A person's worldview will also shape the way they look at poverty and development. Sometimes, it may be a whole community or nation that shares a similar worldview and similar beliefs, beliefs that contribute to keeping them in poverty or beliefs that contribute to their good development. Therefore, understanding a person's worldview or a community's worldview is very important in helping people without hurting them.

In your community, what false beliefs do people have that are keeping them in poverty?

List their answers on the flip chart. If a participant simply states a belief, ask him or her to explain how that false belief keeps people in poverty.

As these examples show, false beliefs can contribute to people experiencing all five types of poverty. And these false beliefs greatly reduce the possibility of development in someone's life. This means that worldview transformation is important in fighting poverty! In fact, in some cases it might be very difficult to bring any progress at all until people have changed their worldview. This reveals to us, once again, what a unique role the church has in fighting poverty. It is Christians who will share the good news of the gospel that totally changes our worldview! It is Christians who will teach people God's Word and how to think about God, God's creation, the purpose of life, the image of God, the nature of work, how to have harmony in relationships, and so many other topics.

We will now look at some more examples of false beliefs. But let's first discuss how each belief can contribute to any of the five types of poverty in people's lives. Second, let's discuss what the truth is on each point, and if you can, try to mention what the Bible teaches.

Large Group Discussion

In some cases, you may choose only one person to comment on a belief before moving on to the next one, and for other beliefs listed, a longer discussion might be appropriate. Spend more time discussing the false beliefs that are common in your community. If any of these beliefs are repetitions from the beliefs the participants identified earlier in their community, then you do not need to discuss them again.

False beliefs that keep people in poverty:[3]

1. **"If you are poor, you will always be poor. If you are poor, it is because God wants you to be poor. It is your destiny."**
2. **"Our family is cursed." Or, "Our community is cursed." Or, "Our tribe is cursed." Or, "Africa is cursed."**
3. **"God only cares about spiritual things."**
4. **"We are so poor that we are unable to give to others. Other people should give to us."**
5. **"There are different classes of people. Our people are inferior and we deserve the standard of life that we have."**
6. **"Work is a punishment. We should do as little work as possible."**

7. **"Products from other countries are better than local products."**

8. **"There is no poverty in America, Europe, and China. There are unlimited resources there. It is their job to take care of us."**

9. **"I am powerless to change my situation."**

10. **"Women are inferior to men."**

11. **"Death, accidents, and poverty are always caused by other people, curses, spirits, or witchcraft."**

12. **"Working hard and making money is dangerous. Other people will attack me or bewitch me and I will be worse off in the end."**

These are some of the false beliefs in our communities keeping people in poverty. You can see that many of these false beliefs relate to poverty of being. For most of these false beliefs, it is helpful and important to teach about how God made all people equally in his image. Also, teach that God has created each person with a purpose. He has given talents to each person; everyone has different skills and gifts to use in this world to glorify God and help other people. We should be giving people hope that God is in control, and that he has the power to change their situation.

But it is not only the poor who have the challenge of false beliefs. Sometimes it is we, who are trying to help the poor, who have false beliefs. These false beliefs are not only a problem in our lives, but they can also cause us to hurt the people we are trying to help. Let's look at some examples of these false beliefs. Discuss how each belief might cause us to hurt people. In other words, how would these beliefs hinder our efforts to fight poverty?

Divide the participants into four small groups. They can just turn their chairs to face each other instead of going to other locations because the discussion will be brief. Assign one group to look at beliefs 1-3, another group to look at beliefs 4-6, another group to look at beliefs 7-9, and the last group to look at beliefs 10-11. If you have a large number of participants, you can make more than four small groups. Just assign more than one group the same numbers. For example, if you have enough people for eight groups, you can assign two groups beliefs 1-3, two groups beliefs 4-6, etc. Then tell the participants the instructions below.

Discuss the beliefs assigned to you for 5-10 minutes with your group. Choose only one false belief to present to the large group. A representative from your group will take only one minute to summarise for us how this false belief causes problems or hurts as we try to help materially poor people. The presenter should also explain if we see this false belief in ourselves.

False beliefs that cause hurting while helping:[4]

1. **"The poor have nothing. They are so desperate. It is so sad and terrible. We must give them a lot of resources and money."**
2. **"The poor are uneducated and do not have many skills. There is nothing they can do to help themselves."**
3. **"What leaders say is always right."**
4. **"Real development requires a lot of money in order to have a big impact."**
5. **"God does not work in the lives of poor people until we come to them as the solution to their problems."**
6. **"Many poor people know Jesus, but we who are trying to help are more spiritually mature than them."**
7. **"All of those people are corrupt. It's nearly impossible to help them or work with them."**
8. **"If the poor would just listen to all of our good ideas, then their situation would finally change. We have all the answers for them."**
9. **"Our time is more important than the time of the poor people in the community we are visiting and trying to help."**
10. **"The local church is unable to make a real difference regarding the community's physical needs. They can care for one or two families, but real change takes place only through large NGOs or government programs."**
11. **"We have more resources because we are blessed more than them." Or "because we are better." Or "because we have worked harder and earned it."**

Make sure that each group presents in one minute or less. Remember that the participants will be able to further study this list of beliefs on their own at home. After the presentations continue with the lecture below.

When we want to help the poor, it is extremely important that we not only focus on teaching other people the Christian worldview, but we also need to make sure that our own worldview is correct as well. Some of these false beliefs require us to go through a mind-set change. We need to be renewed in our minds by God's Word. Remember Romans 12:2. If we are honest, some of these false beliefs are the result of our god-complexes, the result of sin and pride in our hearts. We need to take time to confess this sin and repent.

Have people stand up to pray. Either you yourself, or a participant, can pray a brief prayer of confession and repentance.

Comparing Worldviews

There are many different worldviews and in fact each tribe and people group have their own general worldview. Beyond that, each individual has their own unique beliefs and assumptions about the world. However, in this lesson we'll look at three general worldviews: Secularism, which is held by people in Western countries, African traditional religions, and the biblical worldview. Looking at how both the Western and African worldviews differ from the biblical worldview will help us think through poverty and development in a deeper way.

The Western secular worldview is held by many but not all non-Christians in North America and Europe. The African traditional religions (ATR for short) worldview is held by many but not all non-Christians throughout Africa. Some have also called this type of worldview "animism" but animism is a broader term that covers many cultures and religions around the world. African traditional religions is a more fitting term for Africa. Both secularism and ATR as worldviews contain some truth that fits with what the Bible teaches. For example, one of the beliefs of ATR is that there is a Creator God. The Bible also teaches this. But for the most part, secularism and ATR are competing worldviews with the biblical worldview. To believe the biblical worldview means we must reject many of the beliefs and perspectives of secularism and ATR. So we want to pay attention to how these worldviews are different from the biblical worldview.

Although Christians hold to the biblical worldview, many Christians in Western countries are still affected in their thinking by secularism, and many Christians in Africa are still affected in their thinking by ATR. However, secularism is becoming strong in parts of Africa. Many people on the African continent today might be more influenced by secularism than by ATR. Some Westerners are also moving away from secularism and embracing new forms of spirituality that look similar to ATR in some ways.

We need to understand these worldviews and how they relate to poverty and development. We shall begin by looking at the different beliefs they each have about God, about humanity, and the problems in this world.[5]

In each of these sections below, the large group discussion question is, "In contrast, what does the biblical worldview teach?" You are given facilitator notes in answer to this question for each topic – God, humanity, the earth, etc. However, in most cases you will not need to read these answers because the answers will hopefully come from the group members themselves. Instead, you can just fill in whatever points they miss, or summarise the answers that they give.

View of God

Secularism: Secularists do not believe that gods or spirits exist. Or, if they believe there is a god, they view God as unknowable and very distant from the world.

ATR: In ATR, people believe in many gods and many spirits. They also believe there is a supreme god who is the creator and provider. But he is often seen as too holy, powerful, or distant to communicate with. This makes it necessary to use other spiritual beings or ancestors as mediators between people and God. The spiritual beings are often viewed as having control over the earth and the activities of people. In order to escape from bondage to these spirits, people try to manipulate the spiritual forces, and try to use them for their benefit instead. People may also try to bribe God through offerings and sacrifices to get what they want from God.

In contrast, what does the biblical worldview teach?

The Bible teaches that there is one God, who is a Triune God of three persons, Father, Son, and Holy Spirit. God is eternal, almighty, perfectly holy, and perfectly good. God is the personal Creator God who loves his creation. He is separate from his creation as the Creator, but he is intimately involved in the workings of the creation. He provides food for the birds and is the one in control of the sunshine and the rain. God is perfectly holy and just and he cannot be bribed. God is to be worshipped for who he is and not to get material things from him, because he deserves our worship, and because having a relationship with God is the ultimate good thing in this world.

View of Humanity

Secularism: Secularists view humanity as a species that randomly evolved in this world. There is nothing more special about humans compared to animals, except that we have evolved to be superior to them. Most people with a secular worldview think that people are just physical and there is no such thing as a soul.

ATR: In ATR, people believe humans were created by God, but they view humans as subject to the powers of the spiritual forces. People often live in fear of the gods or spiritual forces. They may be fatalistic thinking that the place of humanity is one of slavery and there is not much humans can do to change their situation. They believe people are victims to gods, spirits, natural forces, curses, and witchcraft, and so they do not take much responsibility for their own situation.

In contrast, what does the biblical worldview teach?

The Bible teaches that humans were created by God, body and soul, and that they are "good". All humans are equally made in the image of God, and are different from the animals. They are the crown of God's creation. But humans have fallen into sin, and fell from the holy life that God intended them to live. We need to be redeemed through the life, death, and resurrection of Jesus Christ. As people made in the image of God and redeemed in Christ, we are to rule the creation and we live in freedom, not in bondage to the earth or to spirits.

View of the Earth

Secularism: Secularists think we need to make use of the earth's resources for our benefit. But many secularists argue that we should also take care of the earth because if we destroy it, we will also destroy ourselves.

ATR: In ATR, the earth is thought to be intimately connected to the spiritual realm. There is much overlap. Events in the spiritual realm are able to be discerned through physical things, such as animal entrails. Much of the earth is viewed to be the realm of spirits who have control of certain resources, mountains, forests, and rivers. Sometimes people are afraid of these spirits and so they do not make use of these parts of the earth. Many things and events in the earth are believed to be beyond people's control, which leads people to a fatalistic attitude, thinking that there is nothing they can change about their situation on this earth.

In contrast, what does the biblical worldview teach?

The Bible teaches that God created the earth for his enjoyment and glory, but also for our benefit. God wants us to continue to develop the earth, fill it, and be good stewards of it. We should not live in fear of the earth, but realize that God has given us dominion over it. And God is almighty and in control of the creation. God is also the one who created the spirits and they are under his control. This means that God can work through us to make real change in our life situations.

View of Work

Secularism: Some people with a secular worldview worship work and find their primary identity, status, and meaning in life through their work. Others view work as a necessary evil in order to obtain the money and possessions they want. They look to possessions to give them a happy and satisfied life.

ATR: In ATR, people view work as a punishment by God or by the spirits. Work is done as a necessary evil, but work is avoided when possible. This is, however, gradually changing as we now see some influence of secularism in Africa, where some people have begun worshipping their work and looking at work as a form of identity and status.

In contrast, what does the biblical worldview teach?

The participants should be able to answer this one easily after the previous lesson!

View of Morality and Sin

Secularism: Secularists do not believe there is such a thing as sin, because they also do not believe in God. People with a secular worldview tend to be relativistic. They think there is no objective moral standard, but each person or each culture decides on their own what is right and wrong. Others look to human reason to teach us what is right and what is wrong, but because of cultural change, their view of morality shifts over time and place.

ATR: In ATR, right and wrong is determined by the traditions, or influenced by the tribe's and clan's beliefs and norms, and what will please the ancestors. Actions are good if they bring honour, and bad if they bring shame. It is seen as a deep betrayal to act against the expectations of the community. Morality is also determined by the results of actions. People do what "works". *Actions are good if they bring me rewards and bad if they cause me problems. I should live in a way that will avoid suffering, curses, and punishments from parents or ancestors or spirits.*

In contrast, what does the biblical worldview teach?

The Bible teaches that we sin when we do anything that displeases God, or when we fail to do what we are supposed to do. The Bible teaches us that we are all sinners, in need of God's grace and forgiveness. There is a universal morality, for all people, which is determined by God, not by tradition or the community. There are right actions and wrong actions, which we learn from God through his commands in the Bible. The Bible teaches us to obey God, even when it is hard, and even if it causes us to suffer.

View of Other People

Secularism: Most secularists try to care for other people because they believe it is the right thing to do and the best way for all of us to live together in harmony. But others mistreat people in order to get ahead, since they believe life is all about survival of the fittest. Some cultures are viewed as superior to other cultures which might be seen as "primitive" or "undeveloped".

ATR: In ATR, people believe they are intimately connected to other people, even the dead who have become revered ancestors. They respect the tribe and clan, and the fear of upsetting other people, the community, or the clan makes it hard to do anything new even if it will be beneficial to the people. This can make change slow and difficult. Humans are not all equal to each other. One's tribe is viewed as superior to other tribes and peoples. In most cases, witchdoctors, chiefs, and elders are seen as special or superior. Ancestors are to be honoured and obeyed. Men are generally seen as superior to women. The community is viewed as more important than the individual. But people outside of the privileged or superior positions are expected to remain the same together. There is what some people call PHD syndrome – "Pull him Down".[6] People should not try to get ahead of others, or develop ahead of others, and if they try, the community will try to pull them back down.

In contrast, what does the biblical worldview teach?

The Bible teaches that God made all people in his image, both male and female. While the Bible teaches that each person is different and we have different roles and positions in society, we are all equal in dignity and value before God. God wants us to live together with other people in love and harmony, loving our neighbors as much as we love ourselves. The Bible teaches that God values community and wants humans to live in community with each other, but that God also values individuals and has made each person with a unique purpose and with different gifts and talents. God values people from every tribe and language, but every culture needs some worldview transformation.

View of the Problems in the World

Secularism: People with a secular worldview think that problems of the world are due to ignorance, lack of resources, and lack of technology. They seek the help of medicine and technology in order to find healing from sickness, or to solve the problem of poverty. They do not look for help from a god or from prayer. They think that, with enough time, human reason and technology will be able to solve most of the world's problems.

ATR: In ATR, the problems in the world are caused by gods, spirits, ancestors, curses, and witchcraft. The solution to these problems is to try to manipulate these powers in the world for our own benefit rather than to our hurt.

In contrast, what does the biblical worldview teach?

The participants should know the answer to this question because they learned about it in the first few lessons of this curriculum. Remind them to think about how the Fall into sin of Adam and Eve caused broken relationships in the world. While demons or a lack of technology can cause problems in the world, the main problem is broken relationships. And the solution to these problems is Jesus, who reconciles us to God, and works through us to bring reconciliation in the other relationships as well.

Christians can make use of technology and natural things to make people's lives better, but they see that these are gifts that ultimately come from the hand of God. Christians also see that technology can cause as much evil as good, because all people are sinful, and it is people who use technology. Christians know that demons do cause problems in the world, but that in Christ we have power over them. (If participants want to discuss demons, curses, and witchcraft, you can let them if you have enough time, but tell them that there is a section about demons and spirits in the "Further Reflection" section to read at home).

1. **What beliefs or perspectives of ATR do you see in your country and are they contributing to any of the five types of poverty?**
2. **What beliefs or perspectives of Secularism do you see in your country and are they contributing to any of the five types of poverty?**
3. **Concerning your answers in #1-2, how will teaching people a biblical worldview bring change and development?**

If participants struggle to see how these worldviews can contribute to poverty, remind them that it is not only about material poverty, but also about how these worldviews affect people's relationship with God, with others, with self, and with the creation.

Culture

Some of us might be finding this lesson uncomfortable and feel like our culture is being challenged. **This is because our worldview is directly linked to our culture and traditions.** Every culture has elements in it that are pleasing to God and elements that are not pleasing to God. Every worldview has some beliefs which are true and fit with what God teaches us in his Word, and every worldview has other beliefs which are not true according to what God teaches us in his Word. Therefore, no matter who we are, God's Word challenges our culture in some way. In the Bible, the Jews became Jewish Christians, and the Gentiles became Gentile Christians. You see, to be a disciple of Jesus, we do not have to abandon our culture completely, but we have to change any cultural practices and beliefs that do not conform with the Word of God.

In some places, it is very difficult to go against the expectations and beliefs of the culture. It is hard to change as individuals, and it is also hard to face ridicule and anger from others in our family or tribe. Our African culture values community and family relationships so much. Some people will not like it when we embrace the biblical worldview and Christian way of living. Some Christians fear going against their parents's or clan's wishes, and worry about punishment, witchcraft, or curses as consequences. As we teach people the truth, we will face challenges. In Africa, it is easy to preach to people and see people become born again. "But in addition to 'born again' hearts, Christians need 'born again' minds."[7] It is not easy for people to be born again in their mind, but we can find comfort in the knowledge that it is not up to us to change people's hearts or minds. That is the work of the **Holy Spirit**, and we have the privilege of being used by God in a small way in that work.

Would one person like to share a brief testimony about when you chose to obey Christ over the expectations of your culture? Did you suffer for it and how did God help you through that suffering?

Following Christ can cause us to suffer. We may lose friends, jobs, or even our very lives like the apostles in the Early Church. But we remember that Jesus told us to take up our crosses to follow him. Following Jesus will include suffering and sacrifice, but we know that God uses our suffering for good (see **Romans 8:28**). Through suffering, God draws us closer to him, grows us in our patience and character, and uses us as witnesses to others. We also know that God will give us strength to endure the suffering and he will be with us as we go through the valley. Our suffering is temporary, and Jesus has promised to return soon. In the meantime, we must accept suffering as part of the Christian life. We must put Christ first and our culture second even when it is hard. During the small group time, we will reflect on some more Bible passages about this.

Worldview Transformation

Because every culture has a worldview that does not perfectly line up with the truth of God's Word, we all need worldview transformation. We must have our minds renewed by Christ. This is true for all people, whatever country they are from. For some of us, maybe we need to repent of certain beliefs and behaviours that we inherited from ATR that do not conform to the truth of God's Word. For others, we may have to repent of some of the perspectives we have unconsciously inherited from secularism. Let's take a moment to pray together that God will continue to renew our minds according to his truth.

You or one volunteer can pray a quick prayer on behalf of the whole group.

Teaching Technical Knowledge

Besides teaching a biblical worldview, it is also important to teach general knowledge and technical knowledge to people as part of our holistic approach to fighting poverty. For example, even if people have been taught a biblical worldview, it is still of great importance for them to learn new methods of agriculture, proper sanitation techniques, and the ability to read and write.

Listen to this quote from former Secretary-General of the United Nations, Kofi Annan, "Knowledge is power. Information is liberating. Education is the premise of progress, in every society, in every family."[8]

We need to teach people knowledge and new skills. Sometimes we need to teach how diseases are spread, how to treat HIV-AIDS, how to make a budget, how to advertise for a business, and how to harness solar power. But as we teach these things, it is important to teach about them from a biblical worldview. For example, think about what happens if you teach people about pills that treat malaria without integrating a biblical worldview in your teaching. People might look to the medicine as an alternative solution, an alternative God, to replace both witchcraft and Christ. In fact, it is secularism that teaches people to look to science and technology to solve the world's problems, rather than looking to God. Instead, teach people that God made the plants of this world for our benefit, and it is from these plants we get these medicines. God wants us to use these medicines to treat our sicknesses. When we are healed from sickness through medicine, God is still the one doing the healing, but he is healing using things he has created, rather than healing miraculously. We can appreciate God healing us in any way that he chooses to do so. Whether you teach about healthcare, business, agriculture, or savings programs, make sure to teach about these topics with an **integrated biblical worldview approach**.

If participants would like access to good curricula about agriculture, business, or other topics that integrate a biblical worldview, email the Chalmers Center to get suggestions for resources. There are also suggested further resources in the last lesson of this curriculum.

Have you been teaching anyone technical knowledge without integrating a biblical worldview? Explain.

Take-Home Activities for Lesson 10

The take-home activities will include assignments or activities that the participants should carry out in their communities, churches, or place of work, applying the lessons they have learned. The facilitator should provide detailed guidelines and clear instructions on how to go about the take-home activities.

1. **For church leaders** – Preach a sermon about the biblical worldview using one of the Bible passages mentioned in the lesson or in the small group discussion questions. Speak about the need to be born again in our minds as well as our hearts. Be sure to talk about how we need to put Christ first, above all other gods, including putting him ahead of the expectations of our culture. It is important to talk about the reality that this might cause suffering, but also that God will be with us in this suffering.

2. **For others** – Plan to teach people in your church, or your community, or in your family about a topic or skill you are knowledgeable about. It may be related to health, business, agriculture, carpentry, sanitation, budgeting, cooking, etc. But before you start teaching, make sure your prepared lesson has integrated the biblical worldview. This is not always easy to do. You might have to spend time in deep reflection about your topic as well as meditating on Bible passages which relate to your topic. If you are having trouble connecting your topic to the biblical worldview, talk to a pastor, a friend, or an expert in your topic, to see what ideas they have.

Small Group Discussion (30 minutes)

Read out loud the questions that they will be answering and make sure they understand them.

Divide them up into groups of 5 people (anywhere from 3-6 people per group). They can be the same groups as before, or you can put them into new groups. They will not be presenting their answers to anyone.

If you have organised the whole workshop to take longer than what has been outlined, then feel free to give the participants a longer time for discussion.

Remember to move around and listen in with the groups as they discuss. Be available to answer their questions. You can give guidance or input if necessary during their discussions, but they have heard you talk a lot, so try to let them do the talking now.

Remind them periodically about how much time remains for their discussion.

1. **What do the passages below teach us about the importance of having a Christian worldview?**

   a. **Ephesians 4:17-24**

   b. **Colossians 2:6-10**

2. **Read and discuss 1 Peter 3:14-16 and 1 Peter 4:12-16 about the role of suffering in the life of a Christian. Are you willing to put Christ first, and live differently than other people in your culture, even if this means you will suffer? Explain.**

3. **We have talked already about the beliefs of secularism and ATR in our country. But in what ways do you see secularism or ATR having an influence within your church today?**

4. **What technical knowledge would benefit the people in your community? Who in your church or in this training group with you might be able to teach them?**

Further Reading

Read this section at home for further learning.

More information about the differences between secularism, ATR, and the biblical worldview:

1. ***They have different views on "the meaning of life"***.

Secularism: Some people with a secular worldview think there is no meaning to life, but that humanity just evolved randomly from nothing. Some think we should just try to enjoy material things and our possessions for as long as we can, because we are all going to die. Others try to create their own meaning in life by trying to see how humans can progress and advance through science. They want to be the best humans they can be. Secularists do not believe in an afterlife so they live completely for this life.

ATR: In ATR, most people focus on power as the most important element in life. It is about the "*—power of the ancestor to control those of his lineage, power of an evil eye to kill a newborn or ruin a harvest, power of planets to affect earthly destiny, power of the demonic to possess a spiritist, power of magic to control human events, power of impersonal forces to heal a child or make a person wealthy.*"[9] *The goal is to use the power of the spiritual beings for the benefit of you and your family* in this life. There is belief in an afterlife. But, generally in ATR, people are much more concerned with getting daily needs met, finding food, healing, etc. than thinking about the afterlife.

In contrast, what does the biblical worldview teach?

Both secularism and ATR focus on power. Secularism looks to the power of humans and

ATR looks to use the power of the spirits. "Animists seek to manipulate spiritual powers by means of magic; secularists manipulate their environments by means of technology."[10] But the Bible teaches that the meaning of life is not to look for power, but to spend our time worshipping God and enjoying his love. Both this life and the afterlife are about God and his glory; we live to serve him and we receive his love. It's also a problem to focus on power because power can be counterfeited.[11] Just think of the power that Pharaoh's magicians showed to Moses. Power cannot always be trusted. But truth cannot be counterfeited. It is better for us to focus on the truth of God's Word, than to trust in power.

2. ***They have different views on "spirits".***

Secularism: Secularists do not believe in any spiritual world, so they do not live in fear of spirits nor do they try to make use of their power.

ATR: In ATR, there is belief in many spirits, some good and some bad and some indifferent. Humans must try to discover these spirits and then appease them in order to gain benefits from them. These spirits can help a person obtain a good job or give a miraculous healing from a sickness. Many people live in fear of these spirits and in fear of what other people can do to them using these spirits.

In contrast, what does the biblical worldview teach?

The Bible teaches that God is sovereign and almighty. He is the one who created all spirits and he is in control over all of them. Some spirits are angels who worship God and are obedient to him. Some spirits are demons who have rebelled against God. God has allowed them to continue to exist and cause harm in this world, but he has only allowed them to do this for a short time. The day is coming when Jesus will return, when all demons will be thrown into the lake of fire (Matthew 25:41). As we wait, we still have to struggle against demons, even as Christians, (Ephesians 6:12-13). But even right now, those in Christ do not need to live in fear of demons. Christ has overpowered Satan through his death and resurrection. Through Christ living in us, we have power over demons (Colossians 2:15, Luke 10:18-19, 1 John 3:8, and 1 John 4:4). We no longer need to be afraid. (1 John 4:18, Romans 8:38-39).

It is true that some poverty can be caused by demons. Demons cause problems in the world for individual people, and they even work through groups and institutions to make systems more inefficient, corrupt, and unjust. We must recognise the authority and power we have with Christ living within us, and overcome these demons. This means that part of fighting poverty is liberating people from demonic influence through the power of Christ. We must put on the armour of God, truth, righteousness, the gospel, faith, salvation, the Bible, and prayer (Ephesians 6:10-20).

Some people avoid trying to develop because they fear other people will bring them down through witchcraft or curses. But we do not need to live in fear of witchcraft or spirits or curses. Jesus has overpowered them. Jesus is in control of our lives. Jesus is the victor. Jesus is the King!

More Information Regarding Worldview Transformation:

Worldview transformation is extremely important, and that is why we have a whole lesson on it, but we should also not fall into the error of thinking that as long as we teach people a biblical worldview, then everything will be okay, and people will immediately come out of poverty. Even if a person has correct beliefs, they can still struggle with poverty. Here are some reasons why:

1. The Bible teaches that Christians will still experience suffering, including poverty, even if they love God, have faith, and have the right beliefs.

2. Having the right worldview about how relationships are supposed to work does not automatically make those relationships work well in the way that they should. I might know how I am *supposed* to have good relationships with my neighbours, but that does not mean there won't be conflict.

3. The entire creation is cursed because of the Fall. That means that earthquakes and hurricanes and famines and floods still happen and affect us even when we have correct worldviews.

4. Sometimes other people actively work against the efforts of a poor person to change his situation, even if the poor person has a Christian worldview.

5. Broken systems can cause poverty as well, even for people with a Christian worldview. Corruption and broken systems are discussed in Lesson 11.

Helping Without Hurting in Africa

Facilitator Manual

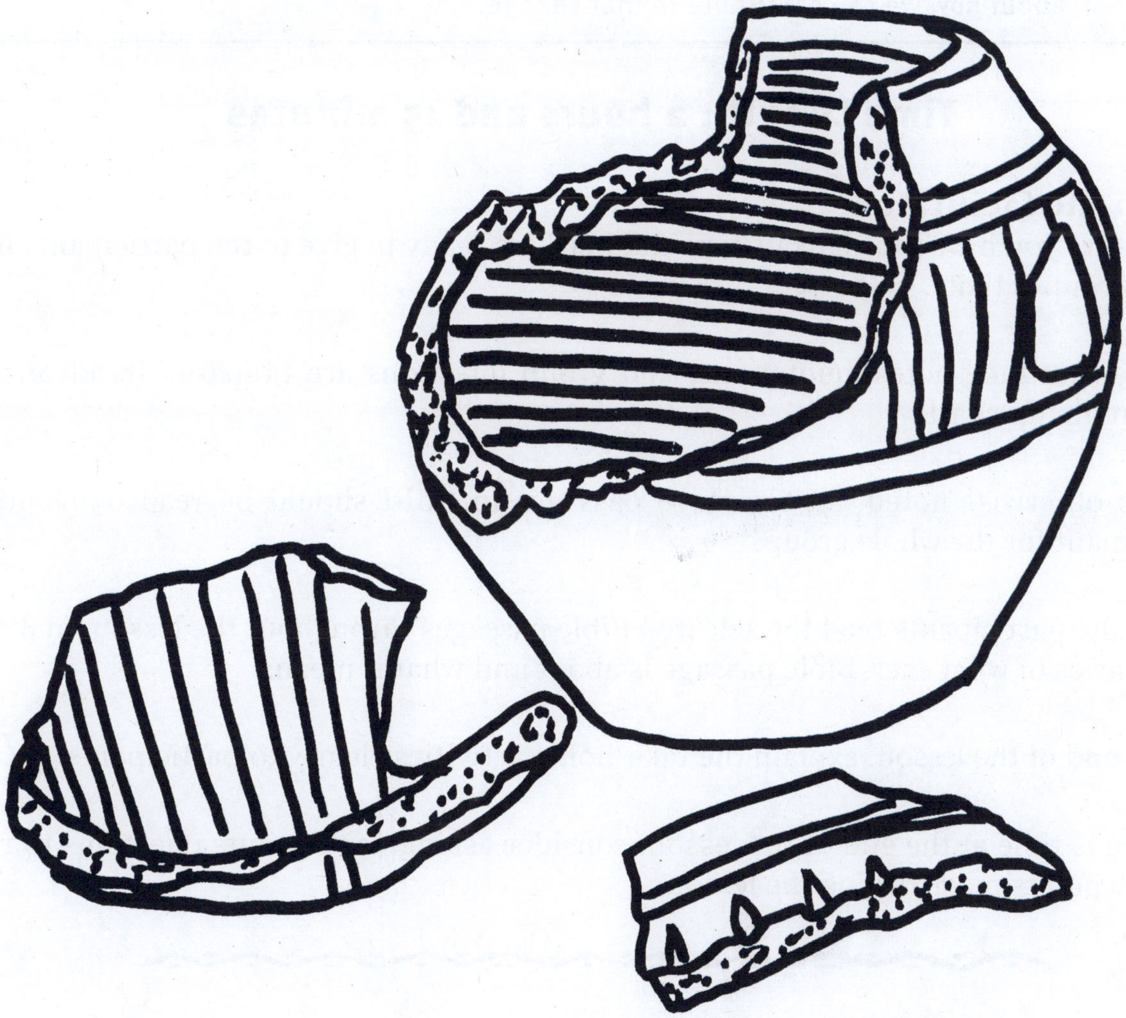

Lesson 11: Broken Systems

Lesson 11: Broken Systems

In this section, you will find:

- A review of the various broken systems we live in and how they keep the poor trapped in poverty and communities from developing.
- Suggestions for overcoming corruption and broken systems.

Lesson Objectives:

- To understand the different broken systems in Africa and how they contribute to poverty.
- To build hope that broken systems can be changed, and to learn some ideas about how we can contribute to that change.

Time Length: 2 hours and 15 minutes

Notes to the facilitator

- Make sure you have flip chart papers and markers ready to give to the participants for the small group activity.
- Ensure that long notes, quotations, and group questions are prepared in advance and written on flip chart.
- Unless otherwise noted, all Scripture passages in **bold** should be read out loud by a participant for the whole group.
- When the participants read the selected Bible passages throughout the lesson, make brief summaries of what each Bible passage is about and what it means.
- At the end of the lesson, explain the take-home activities clearly to participants.
- If there is time at the end of the lesson, consider asking participants questions to review the key points made during the lesson.

Opening Discussion: Broken Systems (10 minutes)

Ask participants the question below and encourage them to include examples in their answers. You can take brief notes of their responses on a flip chart.

When you hear the term "broken systems", what comes to your mind?

Broken systems refer to structures, policies, and programs that are not effectively promoting human flourishing: **they are not helping people to live in proper relationship with God, self, others, and creation**. Systems can be broken because they are no longer fulfilling the good purpose for which they were created. And systems can be broken because they were designed to give preferential treatment to some groups of people while disadvantaging other groups. For this lesson, we will categorise broken systems into three types: political systems, economic systems, and social systems.

Political systems refer to the institutions, laws, and policies governing a nation. Also in this category we include the voting system, the police force, public education, and public healthcare. Economic systems refer to local or international systems of trade, markets, banking, wages, and management of resources in a country. Social systems include the family, the clan, the church, and other cultural systems and expectations.

All of these systems are very significant and have a big impact on whether people remain trapped in poverty. The systems of a country can either contribute to development or hinder development. Systems are good when they provide basic services that people, communities, and nations need. But when broken, these systems can keep people trapped in poverty through no fault of their own.

Earlier in this training we had a lesson about relief, rehabilitation, and development. In that lesson, we learned to be very careful about blaming people for their poverty because sometimes people are poor due to natural disasters, accidents, and robberies. And now, again in this lesson, we learn to exercise caution in blaming people for their poverty because some people are poor due to broken systems. A man may be a follower of Jesus, honest, and hardworking, but still suffer from poverty because of a corrupt manager at his workplace.

The statistics presented in Lesson 1 indicated that many people are still in dire material poverty despite the vast resources in Africa and the generous foreign support. This can partly be attributed to the breakdown of political, economic, and social systems in Africa, and also the unfair systems and policies of other countries outside of Africa.

As Christians we must care about broken systems because God cares about them too. Remember that Jesus is King over everything in this world, from our gardens to our governments. He cares about everything, including our systems. Throughout the Bible we see that God cares about nations and how they treat people through their policies and systems, especially how they treat the poor. In the book of Amos, we read that God is angry at the nation of Israel for how they were exploiting the poor among them. Read **Amos 2:6-7**. Israel had broken systems that were denying people justice. Read part of God's response in **Amos 5:24**. A large part of working for the justice that God wants is trying to correct and repair broken systems. That is what this lesson is about.

Small Group Activity (15 minutes)

Divide the participants into groups of 5 or 6 to do the activity explained on the next page. Give to each group flip chart paper and markers so that they can write down their answers. The discussion and writing should take 10 minutes. Then take another 5 minutes to have each group briefly present to the large group. Instead of reading their entire list, each group can simply mention the top three broken systems from their list.

Make a simple list of the broken political, economic, and social systems that you see in your country or community that are contributing to keeping some people in poverty. Arrange them in order, starting from those that contribute to keeping people in poverty the most, to those that contribute to keeping people in poverty the least (#1 should be the most harmful broken system in your country or community).

From our discussions, we can see that some of the broken systems we listed are common to countries throughout Africa, and even the rest of the world. But we also see some broken systems in our lists that are perhaps more unique to our communities. In this lesson, we will look more deeply at a few broken systems and how they keep people in poverty. And then we will try to figure out how, by God's grace, we can bring at least some small change to these broken systems.

Facilitator Lecture: Broken Political, Economic and Social Systems (45 minutes)

Political Systems

In many countries in Africa, broken political systems are probably the most damaging broken systems. Just think about the incredible damage done by prolonged insecurity, a political coup, or by one war. The damage done in one week can undo the development of twenty years. In many of our countries, we also experience poor governance, dictatorship, and the extreme centralisation of power in the hands of a few people or tribes. In some of our countries, the state fails to advance and protect human rights such as freedom of the press and freedom of speech. Many government programs meant to help the poor don't work as they should and benefit only a few people while excluding others. Some countries don't have free and fair elections. In some places, there is a great amount of corruption involved as governments make policies and elect leaders. Many of our countries also have a lot of corruption in our police forces. We'll look at corruption in more detail at the end of this lesson. But right now, let's look at five political systems that are broken in many countries of the world: public education, public healthcare, infrastructure, rule of law, and bureaucracy.

Public Healthcare

Public healthcare exists in most African countries but it is often a system that is not functioning very effectively or fairly. Problems sometimes include:

- Limited access to health facilities especially in rural areas, and poor-quality health services due to weak and under-resourced health centres.
- Lack of drugs in hospitals. Because the drugs aren't available, patients must pay for drugs at private clinics and pharmacies.
- Lack of accountability and monitoring of health facilities and personnel. This encourages absenteeism of health workers and also theft of drugs from public hospitals. Additionally, this allows for corruption during the procurement of medical products resulting in low quality drugs.
- Low investment in health services and health research by governments.

- Health workers are paid poorly, so sometimes they charge extra for services that are supposed to be free. They are also overworked because of a lack of medical personnel. And many end up leaving for jobs in other countries where they will be paid better and not overworked.

Is the public healthcare system broken in our country in any of these ways? Which ones?

How do these problems especially hurt materially poor people compared to the rich?

Public Education

Public education exists in most countries in Africa, usually as a free public service,[1] but it is often a system that is not working well. Problems sometimes include[2]:

- Lack of school infrastructure and lack of adequate facilities, especially in rural areas.
- Lack of trained teachers. In 2012, the average pupil/teacher ratio in primary school was 42:1 in Africa. That statistic has not changed since 1999.[3]
- Failure to enforce education policy and standards. Many schools that don't meet the required standards and lack qualified teachers continue to be formed.
- Teachers are paid poorly, resulting in frequent strikes at all levels from primary schools to universities. Teachers sometimes migrate to other countries where they are better paid.
- Lack of monitoring and supervision by government which leads to corruption, as well as leaked examination papers, and forgery of academic transcripts.
- No government system of loans to help people pay for higher education.
- Schools which are supposed to be free sometimes still charge large fees for food or textbooks, resulting in many materially poor families still being unable to send their children to school.
- Families with financial means send their children to better private schools, resulting in less community investment in the public schools. Since the public schools are filled with the children of materially poor families, it is left to materially poor families with little power to advocate for the development of these schools.

Is the public education system broken in our country in any of these ways? Which ones?

How do these problems especially hurt materially poor people and their children compared to the rich?

Infrastructure

In many countries on our continent, there is a problem of infrastructure because governments have not invested enough in the development of their nations. The result is that many countries lack a good power network, good telecommunication networks across the whole country, clean water and sanitation, and an extensive road network with regular maintenance and repair. Sometimes it is only the wealthy areas of the country that get to experience the benefits of good infrastructure, while rural areas and city slums are neglected. In the past, money from foreign countries was given in the form of aid or loans to many countries in Africa for the purpose of infrastructure development, but unfortunately that money was often unethically spent by government leaders on other things.

What tribes or regions in your country are the most disadvantaged concerning lack of infrastructure?

Rule of Law

By the "rule of law" we mean that there is authority and laws in a country that are enforced. People cannot do whatever they want, but rather people who break the law are punished. Every citizen should be subjected to the law, whether rich or poor, even government officials at the highest levels. Laws should be clearly written and made known to all citizens. Property rights should be upheld. Voting rights should be upheld and elections should be conducted freely and fairly. Term limits should be respected. The rulings of judges should not be influenced by bribes or threats. People should be treated fairly by courts and government officials, regardless of tribe.

In places where laws are not enforced, how are materially poor people more disadvantaged compared to those who are rich?

Bureaucracy

A bureaucracy is an organisation made up of many departments and divisions that are administered by a lot of people.[4] Government bureaucratic systems were established in Africa to promote good monitoring and efficiency of service to the people of our countries. But bureaucracy can become unhelpful when the administration becomes needlessly complicated with too many forms, procedures, and inefficient processes. Unfortunately, some administrative systems in Africa have been abused by people in power for their own benefit. Instead of trying to make systems as efficient as possible, some systems are intentionally made inefficient in order to create opportunities for corruption or to justify redundant positions. The end result is that materially poor people cannot navigate the endless processes and procedures, while the rich can pay a simple bribe and bypass all of this extra work.

We have now analysed several broken political systems and seen how they particularly disadvantage the poor. But another way to look at this issue is to analyse how these broken political systems also have an impact on potential investment in our country. Think about the problem of bureaucracy and people who want to come and work in your country. A country might say that it takes 14 days to get a work permit, but in reality, the process might take over a year. Think about this example: "In Cameroon, it takes an investor who seeks a business licence on average 426 days to perform 15 procedures." In the USA, it would take only 40 days to perform 19 procedures.[5]

Explain how infrastructure, rule of law, and bureaucracy would influence foreign governments and foreign companies looking to invest in Africa. How will they choose which countries to work in and invest in?

Significant change is possible if we can convince our leaders to address these issues. Listen to this hopeful example. "The Commission for Africa noted that Uganda's economy grew by around 7 per cent between 1993 and 2002 when the country improved its regulatory climate. It also reduced the number of people living on less than a dollar a day from 56 per cent in 1998 to 32 percent in 2002 after the government introduced measures to attract investors." [6]

Economic Systems

An economic system refers to the processes and innerworkings of production, resource allocation and distribution of goods and services within a society or a given geographic area.[7] In other words, we are looking at systems of trade, money, and managing resources. Remember that we learned in the lesson on asset-based development that Africa is one of the wealthiest continents in the world in terms of having vast natural resources such as diamonds, gold, minerals, and wildlife. Unfortunately, many African countries are struggling with material poverty, and this is partly due to broken economic systems which do not allow making effective use of these resources.

Broken economic systems can include:

- Low wages for workers.
- Lack of access to banking, especially in rural areas.
- Inadequate revenue for the government due to a small tax base.
- The lack of infrastructure, particularly roads and other types of transport, means some people do not have the ability to transport their harvests and products to markets within country or for export out of country.
- Population growth is far exceeding the pace of job creation in many countries; thus, unemployment is very high.

But some of the broken economic systems are the result of the policies of foreign countries or international agreements. Some of these policies benefit the rich more than the poor. For example:

- Foreign governments and foreign companies take advantage of the willingness of people in Africa to work for very low wages and to sell natural resources for minimal prices. The result is that many African countries do not see a good profit from their export of natural resources. To make matters worse, sometimes corrupt government leaders in Africa are the only ones to benefit from the sale of natural resources while the local people watch their resources being taken away. For example, Nigeria has pumped more than 400 billion dollars's worth of oil since it was discovered there in the 1950s – enough to cancel all of Sub-Saharan Africa's debt. However, more than 80 per cent of oil revenue has accrued to just 1 per cent of the population, while the majority of the population have got poorer, leading to a violent rebellion in the oil-rich Niger Delta.[8]
- There is limited participation of leaders in Africa in determining the terms and conditions of international trade. This allows for the possibility of other countries making policies and tariffs that are in the best interests of their people, but not for

the people of Africa. For example, "in Senegal, almost half of all chicken farms have gone out of business as a result of a 1,000 per cent increase in imports of poultry from the European Union." "These chicken imports are heavily subsidized by the European Union and have dramatically displaced domestic production."[9] In other words, it's hard for farmers in Africa to compete with farmers in foreign countries in the global market.

Loans and Debt

One international economic system that affects countries in Africa is the system of loans and debt. African countries have received aid and also a large amount of money in loans from foreign governments and banks. Sometimes this money has been used to develop infrastructure in African countries, but other times it has been misused. Because of high interest rates and little money received in taxes, many African countries are finding it impossible to pay back their loans. In some cases, the loan payments exceed the amount of money the countries can collect from taxpayers.[10] With the problem of unpayable debt, it's hard to know who to blame. Sometimes it was corrupt African dictators who took the loans and misused them for their benefit or to buy weapons. Other times foreign countries gave the loans unwisely and expect too much interest in the repayments. Either way, it is now the common citizens of these countries who have to try to pay back these loans even if they had no voice in choosing whether to take the loans.

There is a lot of discussion in the world today about what to do with these loans that are proving impossible to pay. Some leaders in foreign countries and in Africa argue that the best plan is to simply cancel the loans to take this burden off the backs of poor citizens. Others argue that forgiving the loans just adds to the problem of dependency. Further, they say that forgiving the loans sets a bad example for other people, showing that there are no consequences if you don't pay your loans. It's also possible that foreign countries will want to stop loaning to African countries in the future if they don't receive their money back. But to some extent this may be difficult to stop because some western countries also benefit from the loans they advance to African countries. Other leaders suggest reducing interest and giving more time to repay the loans, but not cancelling them completely.

Broken Social Systems

What do you think is the best solution to these unpayable loans?

Should your country continue to take loans from foreign countries?

Many times when we talk about broken systems, we tend to look beyond ourselves and blame others such as the government, other tribes, or donors. We easily forget that we are responsible as well. We will now look at broken social systems like the family, the church, and our traditional cultures.

Family

Every one of us was born in a family and should belong to a family. Family is the foundation of every society and if things go wrong in the family, this will also affect the rest of the nation. The breakdown of family systems can be seen in separations and divorces in marriages, single parenthood, child-headed families, child neglect, child abuse and labour, and in street children and violent youth. **The church must try to bring to broken families the peace and reconciliation only found in Christ.** Christians also need to model healthy family life to the rest of the nation.

The Church

The church is the Body of Christ, and yet as Christians and as churches we continue to struggle with sin and make mistakes. Sometimes we run our churches with traditions, policies, and systems that are not pleasing to God. Some of our practices particularly disadvantage materially poor people. Depending on the location and type of church, some examples might include:

- Most leadership positions and opportunities are given to materially rich people, denying materially poor people the opportunity to serve.
- Churches mostly welcome rich or well-known people during Sunday services. These people are given nice chairs to sit in and chances to speak. Poor people are not always given the same treatment.
- People who give a large amount of money in offerings or church fundraisers are highly recognised and thanked, while poor people who give small amounts but with great generosity are hardly recognised.
- Church leaders and church members show more support and attendance at burials and parties of rich people from the church rather than materially poor people.
- Weddings in church are expected to be big celebrations that everyone can enjoy. Therefore, poor Christians may have to wait many years before marrying in the church while trying to save up money to meet everyone's excessive expectations.
- The church often finds it easy to discipline the materially poor people, but for the rich who give money to church, church discipline is not done. Their sins are tolerated.
- Some pastors prefer visiting, guiding and caring for the rich over the poor in their churches. They know they might receive financial gifts or food from the rich person's home, but the materially poor from their church might offer nothing.

Explain how each of these practices contributes to the five types of poverty for poor people in our churches?

The take-home activity at the end of the lesson is about overcoming these unjust systems in the local church. I pray you will all engage in the take-home activity very earnestly.

Traditional Culture

For the questions and cultural systems below, there are no answers provided in the manual. The systems will differ greatly from one country and culture to another. It is best for the participants and facilitator together to discuss these difficult issues and see what answers they can come up with themselves. We suggest that you as a facilitator encourage participants to reflect on the cultural systems in light of biblical principles and specific Bible passages. All that we do should be evaluated through Christ and our Christian faith.

There is a wealth of value in our traditional cultures. We would do well to learn wisdom from our ancestors and keep many of our cultural traditions alive. But at the same time, some of our cultural systems are broken and are keeping people trapped in poverty. Some of the cultural systems may need to be discouraged and rejected. While other cultural systems can be kept as valuable traditions, they may need to be adjusted so that they truly work well, benefittting all people. Let's think about these examples and answer these questions for each one:

As Christians, is this a system in our culture that we should reject or should we continue to take part in it? If the system is good and should be continued, do we need to adjust anything about it so that it does not get abused or disadvantage some people?

a. Polygamy

b. Clan punishments for crimes or disobedience

c. Dowry/bride-price

d. Widows not inheriting land when a husband dies

e. Royal leaders who represent, guide, and lead each tribe

Can you think of any cultural broken systems we have not discussed yet?

Partner Discussion: Corruption (5 minutes)

Tell the participants to discuss this question with the person seated beside them.

Have you ever been a victim of corruption? How did it make you feel about the other person, about yourself, and about your country?

Facilitator Lecture: Corruption in Africa (35 minutes)

Corruption is still a big problem in many African countries and it has greatly hindered economic development. It has created and increased poverty and exclusion of people. While corrupt individuals might enjoy a materially luxurious standard of living, millions of other Africans are deprived of their basic needs like food, shelter, education, and healthcare. Of the ten countries considered most corrupt in the world, six are in sub-Saharan Africa, according to Transparency International. A 2002 African Union study estimated that corruption costs the continent roughly $150 billion a year. Compare that to the amount of aid given to Africa each year. For example, $22.5 billion was given in aid to sub-Saharan Africa in 2008.[11]

Let's dream together. What could you do for your continent with $150 billion to address poverty and encourage development?

Some Africans say that we have a disease, and it's called "grabiosis". We have a culture of wanting to grab everything we can for ourselves. This goes from top to bottom. Whether we are powerful rich politicians, or simple farmers in rural areas, many of us try to grab as much as we can. We embezzle money, try to steal our neighbour's land through the courts, or even lie to a seller in the market just to save a few shillings.

In the eyes of our God corruption is an evil sin of greed and deceit. But there are at least three other reasons why corruption must be challenged and reduced:[12]

1. Corruption breeds inefficiency. Where services are only rendered after the payment of bribes or business can only be transacted with "under the table" payments, time is wasted, bureaucracies multiply, costs increase, and quality is compromised.
2. Corruption leads to loss of revenue by governments since money gained by corrupt means is not taxed and is often diverted into foreign bank accounts.
3. Corruption frustrates potential investors leading to missed business and employment opportunities.

It is easy for us to criticise corrupt politicians and policemen, but let's look at ourselves first. Have we ever stolen anything? Have we ever lied?

Which is the bigger sin, for a politician to steal a million shillings from a public fund, or for someone to steal a chicken from their neighbour?

We should not get stuck looking at the amounts. Both actions should be considered stealing and both are sinful. Whether we steal a little or a lot, we are guilty of stealing. Whether we lie a little or a lot, we are guilty of lying.

Sometimes, we start off sure that we will never fall into corruption at our place of work. But then slowly but surely, we change until one day we are surprised at how corrupt we have become. It is like a frog in a pot who doesn't realise the temperature is slowly changing until it dies.

> Organizational ethics works in much the same way. In many companies plagued by scandal, employees consistently expressed surprise about how they got to the place where they were breaking the law. They took it one small step at a time, and the steps were so small that they did not notice where they were ultimately headed or how close they were to getting there. In organizations where corruption is endemic, this is a part of an intentional strategy to bring people into unethical and in some cases illegal behaviour.[13]

And sometimes we rationalise our behaviour by saying to ourselves, "Everyone else is doing it, so what is the big deal if I do it too?"

Let's discuss these difficult questions and search our hearts as we answer:

Do we expect preferential treatment when we have a relative in a senior position, but then at the same time criticise others when they get preferential treatment? Explain.

Do we criticise others for only voting for members of their same tribe, but then do the same thing ourselves? Explain.

Do we criticise politicians for making false promises and lying to our country's citizens, but at the same time we lie to our own spouses and friends? Explain.

Not only is corruption a sin that God hates, but it is harming our witness in the world. It may be that corruption is the greatest obstacle today to evangelizing the world. "If our lives do not express integrity, wholeness, freedom from corruption, if there are inconsistencies and cracks, people will not believe or welcome our message. They will reject the good news as too good to be true, or as obviously not relevant. If people do not feel they can trust what we will do or say, if they are not assured that we are working for the common good, or for their personal good, they will not take seriously what we say about anything else, including the good news of Jesus Christ."[14]

Feel free to adapt and change the time of prayer according to your context and according to the time that you have. Consider asking one person to close in prayer after people have had a time of silent confession.

We need to take time to confess and repent to God for our own sins as individuals, before we look at trying to change other people. Let's take a moment of silence to pray and confess to God in our hearts.

Facilitator Lecture: Bribery and Extortion

As we talk about the evil of corruption, it is important to discuss the difference between bribery and extortion. A **bribe** is a gift or an offer in exchange for a favour or service from someone working in the government, or a non-governmental organisation, or in a business. With a bribe you are giving something in order to receive some benefit you do not deserve, such as asking for your forms to be processed before all the others who gave their forms ahead of you. A bribe can also be giving something in order to get out of a penalty that you deserve, such as when you give money to the police so that they don't write you a speeding ticket. In both cases you are trying to cheat the system for your own benefit. Bribery is always wrong and detestable to God.

It is important to see how extortion is different. **Extortion** is the act of obtaining money, property or something from another person wrongfully through either use of force, threats, violence, or fear and intimidation. This is normally done by people in power or positions of authority that wrongfully take advantage of their positions to intimidate and extort money or property from others. Extortion is when you have done nothing wrong, but money is still being demanded of you. You were not trying to cheat the system, but you are being forced to give money. This can happen when a government official demands extra money or else he will revoke your business license. Another example is when a police officer waves you down on the road and threatens to give you a ticket or arrest you even though you have not committed any crime or traffic violation.

We all agree that to give a bribe is wrong. But is it sinful to give money in a situation of extortion?

We should not view giving in to extortion as sinful in the same way as giving a bribe. This is because sometimes we are left with no other option, and it is better to give the money than to risk our lives or the lives of our family members. You are being forced and so you do not need to feel the same kind of guilt you would feel when bribing. But it is important to keep in mind that if everyone gives in to extortion, then extortion is actually encouraged. If we always give money to those who extort us, they will continue to do so, and even extort others as well. It is better that we resist extortion, publicly announce those who are extorting others, and sometimes face the penalties for doing so. If the worst that can happen when we resist a situation of extortion is getting a ticket or spending one day in jail, we might want to consider enduring this suffering because of our walk with Christ, in order to make a small change in the system over time. People who extort others may eventually give up trying when instead of getting money, they have to waste their time taking people to jail. Hopefully, this will then raise questions about their behaviour.

Giving bribes and extorting others are both criminal offences. Unfortunately, many times these types of corruption are tolerated and accepted as normal. Both bribery and extortion arouse the wrath of God and they greatly hinder development. We must do all in our power to stop them.

Overcoming Corruption and Broken Systems

Explain specifically which practical steps we can take to personally resist corruption and also what we can do to overcome corruption in our country?

We have discussed in detail the broken systems in Africa and how they hinder economic progress and increase poverty. Right now, you might feel despair that the problem of corruption is too big for us. You might feel hopeless looking at all the many broken systems and wonder if any of us can really make change. If it was up to us alone, there would not be much we could do. But we worship an Almighty God who works in this world and is willing to work through us, his people.

If we all come together with boldness and determination to change, first by working at changing ourselves, and then working together to change broken systems, there can be real change. God will help us. Change has happened before and it can happen again.

Let's think about what happened in South Africa where for much of its history the rulers were the white minority.[15] In 1948, the government set up a system called "apartheid", not only a broken system but an evil system. Apartheid refers to a set of laws that made sure there was strict racial segregation. White South Africans and black South Africans were kept divided. At times, black South Africans were forced from their homes which were then demolished so they could be relocated to new areas. Throughout the years South Africans as well as the international community protested against apartheid. But it seemed like it was just the "way things were" in South Africa and that there would never be change. Black South Africans continued to riot, boycott, and protest, and they had to be willing to suffer to do so. Many were killed or put in prison. One such leader put in prison for almost thirty years was Nelson Mandela, who went on to become the first black president of South Africa when apartheid finally ended in 1994. Apartheid was able to end because of significant pressure from other countries and because Africans were willing to protest, sacrifice, suffer, and even risk their lives for things to finally change. Apartheid was a racist and evil broken system that looked like it was going to be there forever. But change came! After apartheid ended, Mandela and former Archbishop Desmond Tutu went on to help the country heal from all the past hurts and atrocities through the Truth and Reconciliation Commission.[16] "Here's how it worked: Victims told their stories of atrocities. Then, the perpetrators got a chance to own up to their crimes, and by doing so, became eligible for amnesty. All they had to do was tell the truth."[17] At home, you can read more inspiring stories about broken systems being challenged and changed in the "Further Reading" section at the end of the lesson.

How should we go about trying to overcome corruption and bring change to broken systems?

1. We need to first focus on **reconciling our own broken relationships** with God, self, others, and the rest of creation. This will change us as well as setting a good example. And we must then allow God to use us in bringing reconciliation to other people in their relationships.

2. We need to **strengthen our institutions** and ensure that competent people with integrity and the right skills are hired for their jobs. We also need to make sure that institutions are properly funded and that government workers in the police force, and hospitals, and schools are paid adequately and on time so that they won't be as tempted towards corruption.

3. We need **good laws and policies** that attract investments and growth, and that create a good working environment, avoiding too much unnecessary bureaucracy.

4. We need to **encourage our leaders** to enforce the laws at all times, and we need to **speak up** whenever we see laws not being enforced.

5. We should reward those in leadership who **have integrity and avoid corruption**. Congratulate them publicly and support them in their work.

6. We need to publicly **report corruption** wherever we find it, whether in the church or the government or in business. We need to stand against any corruption we see, whether that of Africans or foreigners or donor organisations.

7. As Africans, we need to **speak up for our rights in international forums**, regarding international policies, organisations, structures, and trade agreements.

8. We need to **ask for God's grace and strength** so that we have the courage to experience suffering as we resist and report bribery, extortion, and corruption of all kinds.

Take-Home Activities for Lesson 11

The take-home activities will include assignments or activities that the participants should carry out in their communities, churches, or place of work, applying the lessons they have learned. The facilitator should provide detailed guidelines and clear instructions on how to go about the take-home activities.

1. **For church leaders** - Together with church leaders and members, identify the broken systems in your church and discuss the practical steps that you can take to overcome them. Make an action plan that includes the problems, the solutions, the people responsible and the time frame. Present the action plan to the church members.

2. **For others** - Identify one broken system in your community or country that you would like to see changed. Discuss together with your colleagues and write a plan of action together to try to bring change.

Small Group Discussion (25 minutes)

Read out loud the questions that they will be answering and make sure they understand them.

Divide them up into groups of 5 people (anywhere from 3-6 people per group). They can be the same groups as before, or you can put them into new groups. They will not be presenting their answers to anyone.

If you have organised the whole workshop to take longer than what has been outlined, then feel free to give the participants a longer time for discussion.

Remember to move around and listen in with the groups as they discuss. Be available to answer their questions. You can give guidance or input if necessary during their discussions, but they have heard you talk a lot, so try to let them do the talking now.

Remind them periodically about how much time remains for their discussion.

1. What do the passages below teach us about resisting and overcoming corruption?

a. Exodus 23:8

b. Deuteronomy 1:17

c. Proverbs 11:1

d. 1 Peter 2:12

2. What do these passages teach us about trying to change broken systems and bringing justice and fairness to all?

a. James 2:1-7

b. Isaiah 1:17

c. Isaiah 58:3-7

Further Reflection

Read this section at home for further learning.

Trade Versus Aid

Concerning the topic of international economic systems, there is a vigorous debate among world leaders about what would help people on the African continent the most: better trade policies or more foreign aid or both?[18]

What do you think? Would it be more helpful to fix some of your country's broken economic systems and change the trade policies to be more favourable to your people? Or would it be more helpful to receive large gifts of financial aid to your country?

There is no simple answer to this question. Trade and aid are both very important in helping a country to develop. Aid is usually a short-term intervention to address an urgent need while trade is a long-term relationship that promotes economic growth of a country. Trade is what will help countries to develop in a sustainable way, so that they are earning what they need themselves. Look at the pros and cons of aid and trade.

Pros of Aid

- Aid is essential in helping countries deal with their urgent issues such as famine, natural disasters, epidemics of disease, and budget deficits. Many countries in Africa face such situations that require foreign financial aid since they may not have the capacity and resources to handle them.
- Aid can give a country the start-up capital it needs to build up infrastructure for later development.

- Aid can help the very poor and vulnerable, people who would not benefit from new trade policies.

Cons of Aid

- Aid can easily become a tool by foreign donors to make leaders in Africa do what they want. Sometimes conditions are attached to the aid to try to manipulate Africans to change their culture and values.
- Countries can become dependent on aid and this dependency can hinder motivation to change and develop.
- Aid can actually foster insecurity and corruption. When those in power receive aid, it can stir others in the country to rebellion. There is competition over who will control the aid and how it is used.[19]
- Unfortunately, many leaders in African nations have used aid in the past to hoard wealth for themselves rather than using that aid to help their countries.

Pros of Trade

- Trade is necessary for economic growth and sustainable development.
- Trade helps countries to become self-reliant, and therefore helps them to feel less shame and inferiority.
- Trade promotes partnerships and interdependency between countries.
- Trade increases access to economic resources that a developing country needs, through the exchange of goods and ideas.
- Trade creates employment for the population as it attracts investments and foreign companies.

Cons of Trade

- Trade does not necessarily benefit the people who are very materially poor, but mostly the middle and upper classes, those with good work and access to markets.
- Free trade is risky to fragile developing economies.
- Trade may require an initial investment through aid in order to be profitable.
- Some countries in Africa are not peaceful and stable enough to benefit from new trade policies.

Different countries may have different answers about whether trade or aid is needed. But generally, the correct answer is probably that we need both trade and aid, but we need them done wisely and fairly. However, because so many countries in Africa have focused for so long on aid, we recommend that we focus more on trade today so that Africa can develop.

Consider these words from Senegal's President Wade in 2002 – "I've never seen a country develop itself through aid or credit. Countries that have developed – in Europe, America, Japan, Asian countries like Taiwan, Korea, and Singapore – have all believed in free markets. There is no mystery there. Africa took the wrong road after Independence."[20] And this statement from Kofi Annan, former secretary general of the United Nations - "Open markets offer the only realistic hope of pulling billions of people in developing countries out of abject poverty, while sustaining prosperity in the industrialized world."[21]

Inspiring stories about how broken systems and corruption can be overcome:

1. This story is a quotation from the book, *The Bottom Billion*, written by Paul Collier. Collier wrote:

> The heroes are Emmanuel Tumusiime-Mutebile, now governor of the central bank of Uganda, but in the mid-1990s permanent secretary of the Ministry of Finance and Planning, and Ritva Reinikka, a former student of mine. The story begins with Reinikka devising a survey to track public expenditure (the same survey that was done in Chad). She initially devised it for Uganda, where it came up with rather depressing results: only around 20 percent of the money that the Ministry of Finance released for primary schools, other than for teachers's salaries, actually reached the schools. In some societies the government would have tried to suppress information like this, but in Uganda, far from suppressing it, Tumusiime-Mutebile used it as a springboard for action. Obviously, one way would have been to tighten the top-down system of audit and scrutiny, but they had already been trying that and it evidently wasn't working too well. So Tumusiime-Mutebile decided to try a completely different approach: scrutiny from the bottom up. Each time the Ministry of Finance released money it informed the local media, and it also sent a poster to each school setting out what it should be getting. Tumusiime-Mutebile is a practical man who wanted to know if things were working, so three years later he repeated the tracking survey. Now, instead of only 20 percent getting through to the schools, 90 percent was getting through. In state-of-the-art statistical research that analyzed this experiment in detail, Reinikka and her colleague Jakob Svensson were able to demonstrate that the media had been decisive – in this case reports in newspapers. So scrutiny turned 20 percent into 90 percent – more effective than doubling aid and doubling it again.[22]

2. This story is a quotation from the book, *The Challenge for Africa*, written by Wangari Maathai. She wrote:

> In Kenya in 2002, a coalition of political parties finally laid to rest the presidency of Daniel arap Moi, and the first new administration in twenty-four years came into power. A newfound spirit of enthusiasm pervaded the country; in fact, there was so much goodwill when the new government was formed that something extraordinary happened: across Kenya, the "social machine" began to move again. Here is just one example. For years, policemen had cadged bribes from the drivers of matatus, the cheap, private minivans that, given the generally poor state of public transit, are the main means of transportation for millions of Kenyans. To the drivers, the bribes were an accepted cost of doing business – allowing them and not another driver to ply a certain route, or ensuring that police officers would ignore any infractions in the vehicle's condition or running. Matatus had become extremely unsafe; high-speed accidents were common, and thousands of lives were being lost every year. And yet, people had few other alternatives but to continue riding in them. After the 2002 election, matatu passengers began to challenge any policeman who demanded a bribe from the driver.

Inspired by the new government, which had vowed to make fighting the corruption that riddles society from top to bottom a priority, ordinary citizens stood up and demanded that neither the police nor the drivers conduct business as usual. This reached a point where policemen stopped asking for the bribes, either because they feared the reaction of the matatu passengers, or possibly, because even they embraced the new spirit and did their part to facilitate the service without demanding a kickback. Matatu drivers also began obeying speed restrictions and agreed to abide by the new government's directive to install seatbelts, a practical safety measure that also limits the number of passengers. (Previously, drivers would pick up as many people as they could, even when riders were literally hanging out of the doors.) This was evidence of the "new Kenya" that citizens wanted to work for and believed was possible, after decades of a government devaluing their aspirations for a more honest and just society. But as soon as it was clear that individuals in the new government were not honest and refused to honour the promises they made to each other during the campaign, this spirit was suddenly lost; and unfortunately, before too long many people went back to the bad old habits.[23]

3. This story is told by an American missionary, Renita Reed, about a businessman in Ethiopia. (His name has been changed for confidentiality). Moses worked as a manager in a furniture company for fourteen years. He was known as a manager who would not compromise his ethics. Eventually he felt God calling him to leave this business and start his own. Moses began importing high quality office furniture from China, working primarily through contracts (also called "tenders") from various government offices, businesses, or institutions. Businesses who work through contracts or tenders tend to be plagued with potential corruption, as the contract will often go to the one willing to bribe the people in charge of decision making. Moses and his wife decided when opening this business that they would not pay bribes or receive bribes. Moses said, "Each bribe has two parties - a giver and a receiver. If we all would stop being givers, what could the receivers do?" This was not an easy decision for them. Moses lost so many contracts because he was unwilling to pay bribes. But over time, and because he insisted on selling high quality furniture, he began to be known as a business man with integrity whose products would outlast his competitors. This has opened doors for him to have many conversations, especially with government officials (even those who are Christian) about doing work with integrity. But one of the main things that has allowed him to keep his integrity is the fact that he and his family have decided to live below their means, so that they will always have the option of saying no to contracts that demand bribes. Moses said, "My joy is not from money in my business but rather in the satisfaction of doing a job well." Moses is an example of someone having the courage to be light in a dark place.[24]

4. The city of Gulu in Northern Uganda has some of the highest alcohol consumption rates in Africa, and there are endless stories of people who have had their lives destroyed by alcohol addiction. It used to be popular to sell alcohol in tiny colourful plastic sachets of 100ml. Children were able to buy them and hide them in their pockets. In early 2015, a local group, Wakonye Kenwa decided it was time for a change. For many years, religious leaders, different NGOs and community groups had cried out about the alcohol problem. A united, strategic effort was needed. Together Christians collected data and personal stories from the community about the impact of alcohol. They submitted a report to the District Government, demonstrating the need for new laws. A petition was signed by Gulu's top religious leaders

calling for a ban on the sachet alcohol. Over 10,000 signatures were collected. Pastors and other community leaders marched through the city to present the petition to the officials. The district leaders announced to the crowds, "We will not fail you." Finally, the law was passed in October 2016. But it is easier to pass a new law than to enforce it. After a few alcohol seizures, powerful national politicians and police leaders became angry. Efforts were made to thwart the law through bribes and political pressure. But Wakonye Kenwa and other community leaders did not give up on trying to make change. Finally, they were able to convince district leaders to form an elite team to make sure the laws were enforced. Today, sales of sachets of alcohol have greatly been reduced and can only be bought in secret. There is now much less drunkenness seen in the city's streets. It took years to make the change, but with perseverance, working together, and the power of God, change is possible![25]

5. Listen to this true story by Mary Crickmore in her curriculum called "Shalom: A Manual for Christian Workers." The names have been changed. Crickmore wrote:

> Mary was a young woman whose husband became very sick. She worked hard to support the family since her husband could not work. After some time, he died. The husband's brother came and told her to leave the house because he needed it. He and his other relations came and took all the furniture away. Because this was an ethnic group that had a tradition that all property belongs permanently to the husband's relations, no one stopped them from doing this. This had been done to many other widows in that town. And because many people in that place had AIDS there were many widows. Mary's church denomination decided that they wanted to help widows. They set up a micro-loan program, but they found that they also needed to address the root cause of why so many widows were poor. They made a rule for all of their churches that no one should take a house or furniture away from a sister or daughter-in-law who was widowed. And they began AIDS prevention teaching in the churches.[26]

6. Go to this website to see how Kampala Pentecostal Church in Uganda decided to reach out in love to the police force through a Police Appreciation Day - https://www.youtube.com/watch?v=SolSAzqWp_8

Helping Without Hurting in Africa

Facilitator Manual

Lesson 12: The Prosperity Gospel

Lesson 12: The Prosperity Gospel

In this section, you will find:

- A summary of the claims of the prosperity gospel.
- Arguments against the prosperity gospel and summaries of how various aspects of the prosperity gospel are false.

Lesson Objectives:

- To understand the prosperity gospel and how it contributes to poverty.
- To understand the role of suffering in the life of a Christian.

Time Length: 2 hours

Notes to the facilitator

- Review the role play that is near the end of this lesson. If possible, during a break between previous lessons, find one or two people who are willing to be actors in the role play. You can tell them what to expect. Otherwise you can still ask for volunteers later, as the preparation should not be very difficult.

- Ensure that long notes, quotations, and group questions are prepared in advance and written on flip chart.

- Unless otherwise noted, all Scripture passages in **bold** should be read out loud by a participant for the whole group.

- When the participants read the selected Bible passages throughout the lesson, make brief summaries of what each Bible passage is about and what it means.

- At the end of the lesson, explain the take-home activities clearly to participants.

- If there is time at the end of the lesson, consider asking participants questions to review the key points made during the lesson.

Opening Discussion (5 minutes)

Ask participants the question below and take brief notes of their responses on a flip chart.

Briefly explain how you would define "the prosperity gospel", also known as "the health and wealth gospel".

Facilitator Lecture: The Prosperity Gospel (65 minutes)

What is the *prosperity gospel* or *health and wealth gospel*? It is a "gospel" (or good news) claiming freedom from sickness, poverty, and all suffering in this life. Yes, Christ's death and resurrection are comprehensive in scope, overcoming the effects of the Fall on our bodies, souls, and even on the entire cosmos. Indeed, one day believers will live in a new creation where there will be no sickness, pain, or poverty. And sometimes God provides financial and physical prosperity in this life as well. But the prosperity gospel is a false gospel because it promises that *all* God's people will have material prosperity here and now in this life. The prosperity gospel further teaches that Christians have a right to the blessings of health and wealth, and these blessings are obtained through positive confessions of faith and the sowing of seeds through financial or material giving.[1]

The increase of prosperity gospel preaching and teaching around the world and especially on the African continent should be of major concern to all Christians because it is greatly impacting the way our churches and communities interpret the Bible and relate to God. In addition, it changes the way people look at poverty. As we have seen in these lessons, material poverty is still one of the greatest challenges facing Africa. Some leaders and teachers of the prosperity gospel contribute to this poverty out of greed, in order to take money from the poor. But other leaders, with good intentions, also make Africa's material poverty worse because they have mistakenly thought that the prosperity gospel is the major solution to the problem of poverty.

Since many people feel desperate in their situations of poverty, they are eager to reach out for solutions to their problems, and the prosperity gospel gives them a potential quick-fix to their problems. Yet as we will see in this lesson, the **prosperity gospel only ends up hurting the poor**. As Christian leaders in Africa, we must make a unified effort to stop the spread of the prosperity gospel. We need to preach the true gospel, educate people on the errors of the prosperity gospel, and teach people *real* biblical solutions to the problems of poverty. We know from these lessons that **poverty does not have a quick and easy fix, but there is still hope** for change when we apply what we've learned from God's word and focus on Christ.

In this lesson, we will look more deeply at the prosperity gospel and why it does not fit with what the Bible teaches. We will then look at the role of suffering in the Christian life. And last, we will examine how the prosperity gospel actually keeps people in poverty rather than being a solution to poverty.

Large Group Discussion

Ask participants to answer the questions below and take note of their responses on a flip chart. Guide participants to use wisdom in mentioning specific names of people or churches. On one hand, we have to speak the truth and it can be helpful to identify a specific church or popular leader who is preaching the prosperity gospel. On the other hand, we have to be careful not to spend our time judging other people rather than looking at our own problems. It's most helpful to focus on what specific beliefs are right or wrong.

1. What prosperity gospel teachings are being taught in your country?

2. What prosperity gospel teachings have you seen in your own church or among your Christian friends?

3. Have these teachings impacted people you know positively or negatively?

Why the Prosperity Gospel is False

We will now examine twelve reasons why we must reject the prosperity gospel.

1. Prosperity teaching misinterprets Scripture passages by ignoring their context.[2] Oftentimes, prosperity preachers quote specific verses of the Bible which seem to reinforce their message and then they treat those verses as absolute promises of God. But often the individual verses are taken out of context and misunderstood. This results in a man-made message which twists the Word of God, whether done intentionally to mislead people, or unintentionally out of ignorance.[3] **John 8:31-32** says "if you abide in my word, you are truly my disciples and you will know the truth and the truth will set you free." We must therefore genuinely seek the truth in God's Word and he will set us free from the lies of prosperity gospel.

There are many verses in the Bible which prosperity preachers quote, but we only have time to discuss two passages.

a. **Jeremiah 29:11**. Prosperity preachers love this verse, and indeed many of us do too. Perhaps you even have it memorised. Prosperity preachers will tell someone who lost their job, "Don't worry, God has good plans for you. Pray with faith and tomorrow God will provide you with a new job." They think this verse is a promise that our lives will be easy, that we will be prosperous, rich, and healthy. But what if we look at the context? This was Jeremiah's letter written to the exiled Jews living in Babylon. Let's read **Jeremiah 29:10-14**. It took 70 years for verse 11 to be fulfilled for the Jews. It was 70 years before the Jews returned to Israel their home. It was a promise to the Israelites that God, according to his plan and time, would restore his people. They did not "prosper" right away. This wonderful verse is similar to **Romans 8:28**, and can be a comfort to us today that God is in control of history and working for our good. But it does not mean that we will get what we want right away, and it does not mean that God will remove all suffering from our lives. Yes, when Christ returns, there will be no more suffering for believers, but until that time there will still be suffering, even for believers. So we wait in hopeful expectation that Christ could choose to heal us now but also knowing that he might ask us to wait for such healing until he returns and ushers in a new heaven and earth in which there will be no more suffering.[4]

b. **2 Corinthians 9:6-15**. Prosperity preachers love to talk about sowing and reaping. They focus on verse 11 where Paul says that when we give, God will give us all that we need and we will be made rich (verse 11). So they tell people to give a lot of money so that God will provide you with all the possessions that you want and you can live a comfortable rich life.

What do prosperity preachers misunderstand about this passage?

Let the participants answer first, but then you can give this answer. The prosperity preachers make at least two mistakes. First, they think of sowing and reaping too simply. The Bible teaches us to sow for eternal life, not for treasures during this life now (**Matthew 6:19-21**). Paul is not only talking about reaping material possessions here but reaping glory and honour to God (see verse 11 and 12).[5] Second, the context of this passage makes clear that God will give to the Corinthians not so that they can enjoy a comfortable rich life, but God is going to provide for them all that they need so that they can continue to sacrifice in being generous to others (see verse 8, 11-12). Paul earlier told the Corinthian Christians about the Macedonians who were materially very poor but still gave generously (**2 Corinthians 8:1-2**). God gave grace to the Macedonians which allowed them to give even in their poverty. Paul is encouraging the Corinthians that God will also give them grace so that they can give generously even if they are materially poor.

2. Prosperity teaching promotes a manipulative relationship with God. Instead of seeing God as our Loving Creator and Heavenly Father, worthy of our worship, the prosperity gospel makes God into an object we need to manipulate to meet our needs. In this teaching, God's promises are seen as binding him, in that when the Christians follow the right procedures, God is expected or bound to produce desired results. But this is not how we should relate to God. The gift of the gospel is the forgiveness of sins and the joy of reconciliation with a Holy God, not a means to financial gain. The true gospel promises a close fellowship with God in which we submit to our King out of love, respect, and allegiance. In contrast, the prosperity gospel teaches that our relationship with God is just a means to an end in which we try to use God for our own selfish purposes. God is viewed almost like an ATM. I do my part, inserting the card into the machine, and the money comes out. Some prosperity teaching seems to teach that people should bribe God. If you do this for God, he will do that for you. But we know that God cannot be bribed.

Some Christians have seen similarities between African traditional religions and the prosperity gospel. Is it true that both seek to use rituals and sacrifices to manipulate spiritual powers to meet our needs? Explain your answer.

Surely God answers prayers and nothing is impossible for God (**Luke 1:37**), but we must leave room for the freedom and sovereignty of God. God is not a tool. The Triune God is a living God and a personal God.

3. Prosperity teaching fails to identify correctly humanity's greatest need.[6]
The prosperity gospel emphasizes our physical and financial challenges as the main problems that we need God to fix. Christ is only preached as a means to solving those problems. The prosperity preachers say, "Come to Jesus and he will heal you, he will provide you a husband, he will give you children, he will give you a promotion at your job. Just have faith in him!" This contradicts what the Bible says about man's greatest need. Humanity's greatest problem is our sin, God's judgement of our sin, and our broken relationship with our Creator. We need to be forgiven for our sin, have our punishment taken away, be reconciled to God, and given eternal life. This is very important for us to understand because many people go to church not to seek a personal relationship with Jesus, but to seek a quick solution to their financial challenges. The goal of our salvation is God himself, and not money or gold. We should focus on God for who he is and not just for the things we want from him. We exist to serve God and to give him glory, not the other way around.

4. Prosperity teaching claims that poverty is directly related to the sins of people. While it's true that the root cause of all poverty is sin entering this world and Creation becoming cursed at the time of Adam and Eve (see Lesson 3), this is very different from saying that a person's poverty is always a direct result of their own sins or their unspiritual life. Some prosperity preachers claim that only sinful Christians are poor or that it is sinful to be poor. But we see that most of God's people in the Bible were poor, and even Jesus was materially poor. We know from our lessons up to this point that there are many causes of poverty in addition to a sinful life, including such things as natural disasters, demonic forces, and broken government systems to name a few. Of course we all struggle with sin and sometimes that causes us to experience material poverty, but much of the time, material poverty or suffering in our lives is not the direct result of our personal sins. This is actually one of the main teachings of the book of Job. Job's friends assumed that Job was suffering in poverty because of some great sin in his life. But by the end of the book, we learn that Job was a righteous man and God was not punishing him. God had a greater mysterious plan for why he allowed suffering in Job's life. The prosperity preachers make the same mistakes as Job's friends by accusing all poor people of committing sins that led to their poverty.

5. Prosperity teaching falsely claims that spiritual maturity can be measured by material wealth and that material wealth is always a sign of God's blessing.[7] Prosperity teachers look at wealth as a sign of holiness and say that someone who is wealthy has been blessed by God. In contrast, the Bible makes it clear that sometimes the righteous suffer, and sometimes evil people prosper. Good health and riches should not necessarily be taken as signs of God's blessings. Read **Proverbs 28:6** and **Deuteronomy 32:15**. The Bible shows examples of godly people who were materially poor and rich people who were corrupt and evil. In our world today, we see the same thing. We can see faithful Christians who work hard worshipping God in the slums. And we can see corrupt leaders in our countries who have become rich through exploitation and oppression of their communities.

The prosperity gospel attributes one's wealth, position, and health to his or her level of faith. It is true that generally speaking, a person who comes to know Christ and stops certain sinful behaviours such as laziness or sexual immorality, will likely experience an improvement in their health and financial situation. But since there are other causes of poverty besides personal sin, we cannot judge a person's holiness or spiritual maturity by looking at how much money they have.

When you see a church leader or community leader driving around in a vehicle, what is your first impression about his or her spiritual maturity? When you see a beggar sitting on the ground, what is your first impression about his or her spiritual maturity? What specific things can we do to work on changing our assumptions?

6. Prosperity teaching urges people to give primarily to receive material gain. Prosperity preachers proclaim that the more you give the more you receive. If you sow, you will reap. It is true that there are biblical passages that talk about how God will provide for us, especially when we give with generosity. But remember 2 Corinthians 9 was not about how God is going to reward us and make us rich. Rather God provides for us so that we can continue to be generous to others. We should give cheerfully (**2 Corinthians 9:7**) because we love God, we love the poor, and as a way to worship and glorify God. We give because all that we have belongs to God already, and we give to show our thanksgiving for all that God has already done for us. Our motive should not primarily be to receive personal gain. Prosperity preachers are focused on only material gain as the blessing they will receive from God. But there are many types of blessings that we receive from God, and the spiritual and eternal blessings are far more important than treasures in this world that will not last.

When the pastors preach about giving at your church, what motive do they tell people to give with?

7. Prosperity teaching makes an idol out of money and encourages greed. Prosperity preachers promote greed and covetousness by encouraging people to focus on accumulating wealth for themselves. They promote a materialistic mind-set in which the focus in life is on accumulating possessions. Unfortunately, we see church conferences and outreaches organised with the main purpose of collecting money instead of winning people to Christ. Christians are urged to come to church so that they will be blessed with more money, rather than coming to church to worship the Almighty God. Prosperity preachers encourage Christians to focus their minds on becoming rich, even though the Bible repeatedly warns against this idolatrous desire. Read **Matthew 6:24** and **Luke 12:15**. Surely it is important to earn money and develop ourselves and our communities. That is what this curriculum is about. But we must be careful not to make something good into an idol. Money is not a bad thing, but prosperity teaching places the desire for money central rather than making God central.

In what ways can the prosperity gospel contribute to corruption in Africa or to the widening gap between the rich and the poor?

If they get stuck on this discussion question, you can help them by suggesting that they look at the connection between greed and feeling entitled to riches, and committing theft or corrupt actions. Concerning the gap between the rich and poor, you could help them to see how the prosperity gospel does not encourage the rich to help the poor, and how the prosperity gospel sometimes makes poor people lose even the little that they have to prosperity preachers.

8. Prosperity teaching does not include the message of self-denial. Prosperity preachers do not preach very much about personal sacrifice and living a simple life in order to be able to give away more of our money to help materially poor people in our communities. In churches that preach the prosperity gospel, there are often many rich people. While some might see this as evidence that the prosperity gospel is effective at making people rich, it could actually be the case that rich people choose to attend prosperity preaching churches. Rich people may attend prosperity preaching churches so that they can feel comfortable with their extravagant lifestyles. If you surround yourself with others who have the same expensive clothing and vehicles as you, then you do not have to feel guilty about having so much wealth. The prosperity preacher will tell you that all your possessions have been given to you by God because you deserved them on account of your holy life, strong faith, and the offerings you gave to the church. If you are simply enjoying the possessions that you earned from God, then you can enjoy them by yourself without feeling guilty that you are not giving anything to others. But the Bible emphasizes the need for a very different kind of Christian character. Our lives should be characterised by self-denial, taking up our crosses, and loving others sacrificially. The prosperity gospel calls us to deny Jesus to follow our materialistic lust and yet, Jesus calls us to deny ourselves and follow him.[8]

9. Prosperity teaching misunderstands what it means to have strong faith.[9] Prosperity teaching views faith as a self-generated spiritual force that leads to or creates prosperity.[10] There is a particular prosperity teaching called "word of faith" theology. In this theology, our faith has the power to create reality. We can speak our desires into existence if we have faith. We become masters of our own destinies as long as we have enough confidence. Faith then is not about God, but it is a sign of human achievement. This is wrong. The Bible emphasizes that we need to have strong faith, but our faith should be trust in God's love and God's power, not trust in the power of ourselves or our words. See **Matthew 9:28-29; Ephesians 2:8-9**.

10. Prosperity teaching values humanity's will over God's will. Prosperity teaching emphasizes that God is ready to do for us anything we want, as long as we have enough faith. Prosperity preachers look to Jesus's words in **John 14:13-14**. Yet we see in the Bible that sometimes we don't receive what we ask for in prayer. Read **2 Corinthians 12:7-10**. And we know that all Christians in the Bible suffered at times, and all of us have suffered at times. How then do we understand Jesus's words that we will receive whatever we ask for? It is important to interpret confusing Bible passages by comparing them to other passages. We need to look at a similar passage, **1 John 5:14-15**. Notice that it is not that we simply get anything we ask for, but what we ask for also has to fit into God's will and plan for our lives. If we ask for something that we want but God does not want it for us, we will not receive it. If we look again at **John 14:13-14** we see that we need to pray in Jesus's name. Praying in Jesus's name does not involve magical incantations but rather expresses alignment of one's desires and purposes with God.[11]

Prosperity teachers emphasize that we pray for our own will to be done. Yet Jesus himself said, "Yet not my will, but yours be done" (**Luke 22:42**). And when Jesus taught us how to pray, he told us to pray for God's will to be done, not our own (**Matthew 5:10**). The prosperity gospel is a false gospel that is pleasing to people's ears because it makes people believe that their will is God's will. Instead, we need to seek and submit to God's will for our lives. And even when we do not get what we ask for, we can trust that his plan for us will be good. Read **Romans 8:28**. As human parents know how to give good gifts to their children, but still have to say no to some requests, so also God as our heavenly Father knows how to give us good gifts, but will sometimes say no to our requests. If children ask their parents to only let them eat sugarcane and sweets and nothing else, loving parents will say no because they want them to be healthy. They have a better plan for their children. Similarly, when God does not give us what we want, we must trust in him that he has a good plan for us, even when we do not understand it. See **Matthew 7:9-11**.

Have you ever asked God for something that you did not receive? What did God teach you through that experience?

11. Prosperity teaching falsely promises healing from all sickness in this life for faithful Christians. Believers of the prosperity gospel say that there is a connection between good health and one's spiritual righteousness. Prosperity preachers look to **Isaiah 53:5** to promise that Jesus's death on the cross provides full healing for all of us in this life. And they are partially correct. We know from the rest of Scripture that Christ's death and resurrection ensure that both our bodies and souls will be fully whole when Christ comes again. So healing is promised to us through Christ. But the prosperity gospel is wrong in promising that we will be healed from all sickness right now in this life. If we read this verse in context, we can see that this passage is all about Christ dying so that we can be forgiven for our sins. In this passage, "healing" is probably a way of talking about being cleansed from our sins, which is also how Peter looked at it in **1 Peter 2:24**. Prosperity preachers say we will be healed every time we ask if we have enough faith. This, unfortunately, causes Christians to accuse sick people of sin or weak faith instead of caring for them. Surely God has the power to heal and all of us can testify to God's healing in our lives. Yet we know that we are not always healed every time we want it. We are healed according to God's plan and God's will for our lives. Even Paul was not healed every time he asked. Remember what we read in 2 Corinthians 12:7-10. And instead of telling Timothy to name and claim his healing, he gave him some medical advice. Read **1 Timothy 5:23**. Sometimes we are healed instantly, sometimes we have to wait a long time for healing, and sometimes we are not healed at all in this life. We will all die eventually, but we will all be healed eventually too. We wait for our full and perfect healing at the resurrection of the dead.

12. Prosperity teaching does not account for the Bible's teachings about suffering in the Christian life.

1. **According to the Bible, what types of suffering should we as Christians expect to experience sometimes in our lives?**
2. **Think of people in the Bible who were materially poor. List as many of their names as you can think of.**

Prosperity preachers largely neglect the very important biblical theme of suffering. They make it sound like real Christians live comfortable rich lives without sickness or suffering. What does the Bible teach? Let's look at a few important biblical principles about suffering.

a. The ultimate cause of suffering and poverty in this world is sin. We suffer because of the curse that came when Adam and Eve sinned. Remember what we learned in Lesson 3 about the four broken relationships. We suffer because we sin against God and we hurt one another. Because Jesus is at work in this world, we can hope to see some transformation and development in this life, but we will all continue to experience some suffering in this world until Jesus returns.

b. God is sovereign and in control of this world. He knows the future. Nothing takes him by surprise. He is almighty and supreme. Therefore, whatever happens, even when evil things happen, they all fit somehow into his overall plan for this world. Read **Proverbs 16:33** and **Matthew 10:29-30**. We know that God is powerful enough to use evil and suffering for good. Read **Genesis 50:19-20** and **Romans 8:28**. We do not always understand God's plan, but we know that his plan is good because God is good, loving, and perfect. Thankfully, we already know the end of his plan. Our suffering is temporary. In the end, we will experience resurrection and eternal life in his New Creation and we will have no more pain or poverty.

c. When we suffer, we learn from the Psalms, for example **Psalm 13**, that it is acceptable for us to cry out to God honestly about our pain. But as we cry out to God, we should still trust in him. And whether he takes away our suffering or not, we must continue to praise him and obey him, trusting in his good plan for our lives.

d. We should expect to suffer because our Lord Jesus also suffered and we are united to him. Many passages talk about this but let's read **Romans 8:17**. We should even try to rejoice in suffering because God uses it for our good. Read **James 1:2-4** and **Romans 5:3-5**. How can God use our suffering for good? He can use our suffering:

- To help others.
- To discipline us so that we grow in holiness.
- To teach us patience.
- To test our faith like Job.
- To make us less tempted to sin.
- To help us learn to depend on God and trust in him.
- To draw others to Christ through our testimony of praising God even in our suffering.
- To help us know how to be better counsellors to others who are suffering.

The best way to understand God's power to use suffering for good is by focusing our eyes on the cross. Jesus dying on the cross was the most terrible, unimaginable instance of suffering in all of world history. Jesus, who is God, was fully without sin and deserved all praise and glory, but he experienced betrayal, torture and death. He experienced the intense wrath of God against humanity's sins. God planned to take the worst suffering that ever happened and make it into the best blessing the world has ever known, our salvation! Surely he can also make good out of suffering in our lives. God is powerful enough to even use evil things for good!

Don't Be Discouraged

Some of us might find this lesson discouraging. In all the lessons so far, we've been emphasizing how Jesus is working to reconcile the four relationships, and we received new hope that it is possible for people to develop and experience less poverty. Are we now saying we can only expect suffering? No. We trust that Jesus is working in our lives and in this world to bring healing and reconciliation. As people come to know Christ and experience some reconciliation in the four broken relationships, we can hope that they will have less material poverty in their lives. In this we can agree with the prosperity teachers. But the problem is that the prosperity teachers promise a life without suffering, poverty, and sickness if a person has enough faith and lives an obedient life. While having faith in Christ and living an obedient life will often lessen one's poverty, it is not always true in every situation. Christians can be materially poor for other reasons besides their sins. We sometimes experience poverty due to broken systems, natural disasters, persecution, or other reasons that fit into God's plan for our lives.

Like the prosperity preachers, we want to see Christians developing and seeing a reduction in all five types of poverty. But the way to go about this is through focusing on God and partaking in the ministry of reconciliation. We should not give people false promises or encourage people to make an idol out of money by thirsting to become rich. Instead, we want people to work for development and wealth creation as a way to serve Christ and a way to increase their ability to be generous to others.

Role play

For this role play you will need help from the participants. You can either do the role play yourself with one participant, or you can get two participants to do it together. The role play will require people who can think quickly and who are ready to try to apply some of the teachings learned so far in this lesson. Participants can have fun with the role play and use their creativity to shape it the way that they want. One person will act as a church member who is coming to see the pastor for comfort and counsel. The other person will act as the pastor. The church member has not been able to find a good steady job due to a recurring sickness or disability that he or she has had for a couple years. This person has been doing various types of temporary jobs and so has been struggling financially. The role play will be divided into two stages:

1. The pastor will give counsel to the church member. For this first stage, the pastor should be a prosperity preacher. Role play what types of things the pastor would say to the person if the pastor believed in prosperity teachings rather than biblical teachings.

2. In the second stage, the person role playing as a pastor should counsel the church member using the true gospel, and using true biblical teachings about faith, poverty and suffering.

When the role play is finished, ask for comments or questions from the rest of the training group.

The Prosperity Gospel Hurts the Poor

Large Group Discussion

1. In what ways does the prosperity gospel specifically hurt materially poor people?

2. If Christians in a local church have taken in some prosperity theology, how might they unintentionally mistreat poor people or sick people in their church?

The prosperity gospel increases poverty of being. It promotes a sense of guilt and shame among materially poor people and sick people. They may blame themselves for their failures in business, or think that they must have weak faith because they are still sick. This may lead to self-condemnation and shame, to the point that the person may quit even trying to make change, and lose all hope that God can change their situation. The prosperity gospel also increases the poverty of being of the rich by inflating their god-complexes. They look to their own strong faith and holiness as the reason that they are rich. This swells their pride and makes them look down on others who do not have as much money.

The prosperity gospel emphasizes individual wealth and success, without the need for community accountability. This has damaged a good feature of traditional African culture, the commitment to care for others within the extended family and the wider social community.[12]

The prosperity gospel causes people to show favouritism to the rich, since financial status is seen as an indicator of a person's spiritual maturity. This causes churches to neglect the poor and give advantages and leadership positions only to the rich. In some cases, it may even promote a church culture where church discipline is only given to materially poor people in the church, but not rich members. Read **James 2:1-7**.

In what ways is your church obeying or disobeying the principles in James 2:1-7?

The prosperity gospel fails to encourage Christians to work hard and be innovative in order to overcome material poverty. Instead, prosperity teaching urges Christians to pray, sit back, and wait for God to simply send them a miracle. This is why many Christians today spend most of their time at church in prayer, requesting pastors to pray for a breakthrough and asking God for wealth, while at the same time ignoring the gifts and abilities God blessed them with. It is common to see many youths in towns spending a lot of time at church, yet they have idle land in their home villages that they could use to farm. It is also common to see youths spending their time doing sports betting, hoping for a quick miracle from God, rather than finding work to do. God has called each of us to use our gifts and work hard in his world, to provide for our families and give God glory through our work.

The prosperity gospel will cause some people to reject God and the church. When people are promised quick and amazing miracles and wealth, huge numbers of people may join a local church. But when they fail to experience what was promised, they will quickly leave the church, never trusting churches or pastors again. Even worse, it may drive some people to question God and reject him completely.

Overcoming the Prosperity Gospel

To overcome the prosperity gospel in Africa we must:

- Repent of how we have treated materially poor people, and repent if we have ever taught prosperity theology.
- Commit ourselves to preaching the true gospel even if it is unpopular.
- Read, study, and be taught God's Word. This will help us to detect and avoid the prosperity gospel and be able to teach others to do the same.

- Give generously to materially poor people in our churches and communities instead of exploiting them as prosperity preachers do. We should give, not in order to get rich, but as an expression of love for God and his people.
- Provide discipleship and teaching especially for pastors and church leaders. Our leaders must learn how to interpret the Bible correctly.
- Make sure that churches have well established accountability structures, so that church leaders and missionaries can be held accountable for what they preach and how they behave. The government may also work with church denominations to set good policies that will prevent prosperity preachers from manipulating and exploiting the poor. Many of the churches and church leaders in Africa today are accountable only to themselves. Some leaders function as their church's treasurer and accountant while also being the pastor. Some local churches have no contact with other churches for accountability. Independent and clear accountability structures for churches and church leaders are very important in enhancing trust, transparency and integrity.

What specific accountability structures are in place for your church leaders and for your local church? Are they functioning well?

Take-Home Activities for Lesson 12

The facilitator should provide detailed guidelines and clear instructions on how to go about the take-home activities. Read aloud the two activities and explain that pastors should probably choose #1, and others attending the training should probably choose #2.

1. **For church leaders, choose one of the following**:
   a. Preach a sermon and clearly proclaim the good news about salvation in Christ.
   b. If you have an adult Sunday school class, teach your church members about the errors of the prosperity gospel as covered in this lesson.
   c. Preach a sermon on one of the passages about suffering from the small group discussion questions.
2. **For others:**

   Ask your pastor if you can start a Bible study at church in which you will guide the group to examine and discuss what the Bible teaches in contrast to prosperity teaching. You can study together the Bible passages identified in this lesson. If you cannot lead a Bible study at the church, then try to form a group of friends, family, and neighbours to study and discuss together on these points and passages. We covered a lot in this lesson in a short period of time, but in your Bible study you can plan to discuss only a few Bible passages or prosperity teachings each time you meet.

Small Group Discussion (20 minutes)

Read out loud the questions that they will be answering and make sure they understand them.

Divide them up into groups of 5 people (anywhere from 3-6 people per group). They can be the same groups as before, or you can put them into new groups. They will not be presenting their answers to anyone.

If you have organised the whole workshop to take longer than what has been outlined, then feel free to give the participants a longer time for discussion.

Remember to move around and listen in with the groups as they discuss. Be available to answer their questions. You can give guidance or input if necessary during their discussions, but they have heard you talk a lot, so try to let them do the talking now.

Remind them periodically about how much time remains for their discussion.

Read the following Scripture passages. Discuss together what each passage teaches in contrast to the false teachings of the prosperity gospel. You will not have time to discuss every passage. Study at home all the passages that you do not discuss in the group.

- **1 Timothy 6:3-10**
- **John 9:1-3**
- **Matthew 5:44-45**
- **2 Corinthians 6:3-10**
- **Matthew 16:24-26**
- **Habakkuk 3:17-18**
- **Luke 13:1-9**
- **Proverbs 23:4-5**
- **1 Peter 3:14-17**
- **1 Peter 4:12-19**
- **Matthew 8:20**
- **Luke 6:20-24**
- **2 Corinthians 11:23-30**
- **1 Peter 1:6-7**

Further Reading

Read this section at home for further learning.

Revisiting: *"Prosperity teaching misinterprets Scripture passages by ignoring their context."*

More examples:

Read **2 Corinthians 8:9**. Prosperity preachers look at this verse as clear evidence that Jesus died on the cross so that we, as his disciples, could become materially rich. But if we compare this verse with what we know from the rest of the Bible, we know that Jesus did not die on the cross to make us rich in this life. Rather, he died on the cross to take the punishment for our sin and to overcome all the effects of the Fall. So what does this verse mean? Christ gave up his heavenly glory, became a human being, and died for us, so that we could be reconciled to God and dwell with him for all eternity. When Christ comes again, we will be fully restored to all that it means to be human: our bodies and souls will live in right relationship with God, self, others, and creation. That gift of full human flourishing is the treasure that makes us truly rich.[13] Let's read another verse in which Paul talks about these true spiritual riches, **2 Corinthians 6:10**. If we look at the context, we can see that Paul is using Christ as an example that we should follow. Paul has just finished talking about the Macedonian Christians who were poor and yet still gave generously to help others (verses 1-2). They followed the example of Christ who sacrificed to help others. And Paul wants the Corinthians to do the same. Far from teaching that Christ will make us materially rich, this passage is emphasizing our need to sacrifice like Christ did, by giving away our money to generously help others!

James 4:2 says "You do not have because you do not ask God." In many churches in Africa, it is very common to hear church leaders preaching about the prosperity gospel and telling their congregation to "name it, touch it and claim it and it is yours!" They use this one verse to justify this message. The idea is that people do not have what they want because they didn't pray with enough faith. But now read the context. Read **James 4:1-6**. In verse 3 we read: "When you ask, you do not receive, because you ask with wrong motives, that you may spend what you get on your pleasures." We see that it is not that the Christians aren't praying enough, but that they want things only for themselves and their pleasure. So in reality James is writing against what prosperity preachers usually tell people to do. Additionally, if we read the rest of the letter, we know we will not get everything we want. For example, at the beginning of the letter in **James 1:2-4**, we learn that we should rejoice in our trials and suffering. If all we had to do was name it and claim it, then we would never suffer. And then James tells the people to expect suffering again in **James 5:10-11**. Clearly James did not expect us to pray for whatever we want and to always get it. Instead, we should pray with faith that God will answer our prayers but also accept that sometimes we will go through trials.

Helping Without Hurting in Africa

Facilitator Manual

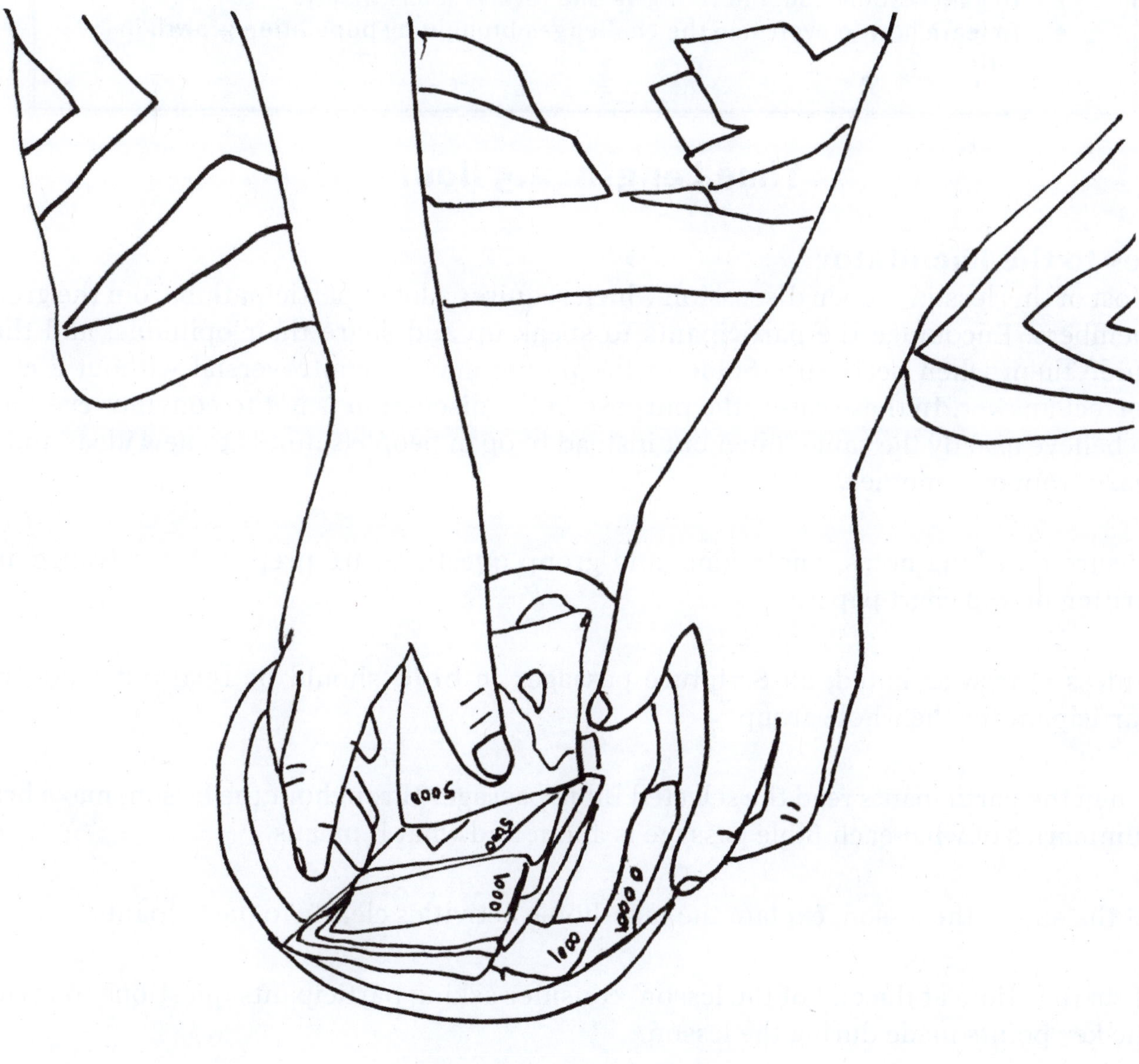

Lesson 13: African Culture and Money

Lesson 13: African Culture and Money

In this section, you will find:

- Listed advantages and disadvantages of various aspects of African cultures.
- Current trends in the African population analysed from a biblical perspective.

Lesson Objectives:

- To understand the similarities and differences between what has been taught in this curriculum and the practices and expectations of African cultures.
- To gain wisdom about how to give and receive loans wisely.
- To learn how to overcome the challenges brought by population growth in Africa.

Time Length: 2.5 Hours

Notes to the Facilitator

- Most of this lesson is open discussion which requires a lot of participation from the group members. Encourage the participants to speak up and share their opinions, and then guide them when necessary. Some of the points may be controversial without a clear correct answer. In these cases, the purpose of the discussion is not to convince everyone to believe exactly the same thing, but instead to open people's minds to new ideas and to learn from one another.

- Ensure that long notes, quotations, and group questions are prepared in advance and written on flip chart paper.

- Unless otherwise noted, all Scripture passages in **bold** should be read out loud by a participant for the whole group.

- When the participants read the selected Bible passages throughout the lesson, make brief summaries of what each Bible passage is about and what it means.

- At the end of the lesson, explain the take-home activities clearly to participants.

- If there is time at the end of the lesson, consider asking participants questions to review the key points made during the lesson.

Opening Discussion (15 minutes)

Ask the participants the following questions and take notes of their responses on a flip chart.

1. Does Africa have a general "African culture"? Explain your answer.

2. Briefly explain how your culture views hospitality and money in relation to maintaining relationships in the family and community.

3. Regarding hospitality and use of money, give specific examples of things that people are expected to do, and things that people are expected not to do.

After the discussion, you can explain the points below in case they have not been mentioned already by the participants.

The African continent comprises of many countries with different ethnic groups, languages and historical backgrounds. The continent is very diverse so strictly speaking there is no such thing as a general African culture. But despite the differences between cultures throughout Africa, we can still see many similar traits that are present in most regions of Africa. These similarities are especially striking when compared to cultures of other countries around the rest of the world. In this limited sense, we can view the cultural similarities throughout Africa as comprising a general African culture. But we should keep in our minds that some cultural traits we discuss will not fit every group throughout the African continent.

Let's analyse some of the cultural similarities we see in many places throughout Africa regarding hospitality and use of money. African cultures are deeply relational. Relationships are valued at all levels and this greatly influences the way that money and other resources are used. Success in any endeavor requires building and maintaining good personal relationships with friends, family members, and other community members.[1]

This relational culture encourages people to support their friends by giving them money or resources, and failure to adhere to this cultural value may harm relationships. For example, in many African cultures, a wealthy person in the community is expected to help those less fortunate. This wealthy person will be considered an important member of the community in good standing if he or she contributes financially to weddings and burials, gives to church fundraisers, and offers loans without interest to those in need. Those who are materially poor in the community can expect to receive handouts of money or food occasionally from wealthy benefactors during times of need.

In African cultures, true friendship includes caring for one another and helping with physical and financial needs. If you help your friend one day in her need, you know that a year later she may be the one helping you in your need. Therefore, giving is a way to help your friend and ensure future help for yourself.

In extended families, we also see cultural obligations. Families and relatives are expected to be the first ones to help other family members who are in need. If family members and relatives are unable to help, then others in the community will be asked to help. Families work together to address their needs. And people in the community work together to address their needs. If family members ask for money or loans, you are expected to give to them. It is your duty to help without asking too many questions or making many demands.

Besides caring for only friends and family, African hospitality also emphasizes care for visitors, even strangers who visit. Preparing meals for others and sacrificing your time and money for those who visit is a strong value. Sometimes people give beyond their means, even borrowing money or resources, in order to host visitors and make them feel very comfortable.

Small Group Discussion (35 minutes)

Divide the participants into groups of five and ask them to discuss and answer the following questions. Give them ten minutes to discuss. Each group will then be given two minutes to present their answers.

We have analysed cultural practices in Africa and expectations concerning hospitality and money and how they are used to maintain relationships. Now think about what you have learned from all the previous lessons in this curriculum.

1. **Make a list of the advantages of these cultural practices and expectations - the ways they promote true development.**
2. **Make a list of the disadvantages of these cultural practices and expectations - the ways they might discourage or block true development.**

Allow the participants to come up with their own advantages and disadvantages. After they have presented their answers, you can explain any of the advantages or disadvantages written below that have not already been mentioned. List them in note form on the flip chart as they are not in the Participant Manual. Be sure to give the participants a chance to comment on any additional advantages and disadvantages that you mention. Some participants might want to disagree with you on a specific point. This kind of debate is encouraged as it helps everyone to analyse and learn.

Advantages

- These practices can build good relationships and promote harmony within the family and community.
- The cultural expectations encourage people to be unselfish with their resources and to think about others who are in need.
- The cultural expectation that family members have the most immediate responsibility to help fits with what the Bible teaches. Remember what we learned about the circles of priority in Lesson 6.
- The emphasis on sacrificial hospitality fosters trust and unity in a community, and is a great example of what it means to obey God's command to "love your neighbour as yourself".
- These cultural practices promote the idea of collective responsibility, encouraging the community to bring resources together to address specific needs.

- When the cultural expectations are being followed, there will be very few people living in extreme material poverty in the community. People might not become rich, but they will not starve since others in the community will feel the pressure to help them.

Disadvantages

- Since family members feel pressured to give money to relatives, they may give without diagnosing the family member's true cause of poverty. For example, if a relative asks for a loan, many might feel obligated to give a loan, even though they are not sure whether the money will be poorly spent on something like alcohol.
- The cultural expectations may promote laziness. Some people might not want to work because they think it's their right to be helped by their relatives or other community members. When they refuse to work and still receive handouts, they are indirectly encouraged to continue in their laziness. For example, many might feel a cultural or family obligation to pay for school fees for a brother's children, even if that brother is not working.
- Dependency can be created when money is given repeatedly by a wealthy family member or community member. The receiver might have initially reacted with joyful thanksgiving upon receiving the first gift, but repeated giving, year after year, could turn into expectation and feelings of entitlement. Failure to continue giving in the pattern that has developed may result in the breakdown of the relationship. Continued giving distorts the good family relationship, turning it into a relationship between a frustrated donor and a demanding, helpless dependent. The cultural expectations can foster paternalism rather than healthy relationships.
- The cultural expectations can promote giving out of fear rather than out of love. People might give only out of fear of being blacklisted by the community. But we should give with a cheerful heart out of love for God and thanksgiving for all he has given. We should give because we have genuine love for people living in poverty.
- The cultural practices may promote god-complexes in those who give. A person might give in order to become a 'big man' and have a lot of power and respect in the community.
- The cultural practices and expectations may create a feeling of low self-esteem among those who are receiving gifts and loans from others. People may start feeling ashamed of themselves as they feel more and more helpless and dependent on others.
- Our cultural values emphasize giving as a way of helping those in need, but some people have abused or misinterpreted these values. Sometimes the receiver thinks that it is his or her right to receive. Sometimes the giver puts conditions on the gifts in order to receive some kind of favour in exchange. The Bible teaches us to give even when we won't receive any benefit in exchange. We are to love even our enemies and even those outside of our own family and tribe.
- These cultural practices focus mostly on material poverty and poverty of community. It is important to focus on these two types of poverty. But we cannot truly help people, and we might actually make their situations worse, if we ignore poverty of spiritual intimacy, poverty of stewardship, and poverty of being.

- The cultural expectations do not always encourage people to utilise their assets to create more wealth so that everyone can see development and growth together. Instead, people with more money and resources are always pressured to give handouts to those with less. People may have the false belief that resources are limited and must constantly be redistributed and shared. This sometimes makes it difficult for one person or family to develop ahead of the others in the community. In a sense, those that try to develop are pulled back down as the family members and community members ask for more handouts. Sometimes the burden and demands of extended family or community may require people to use their extra money to give to others, so they are not able to invest to increase their resources, and are not able to initiate new creative projects that would end up benefittting everyone. Thus, the community may remain mostly stagnant without much material development.
- Some of our cultural values can put intense pressure on people to give and this may drive them to do anything to get enough money to take care of their relatives. This can foster corruption as people struggle to take care and please members of their extended family and community. People are pressured to use their positions and opportunities to cater for their family members, community, and tribe. Showing favouritism in the workplace or engaging in corruption can be demanded by community members who want to see some benefit after having helped the individual or the individual's family in the past.

Facilitator Lecture: Inheritance and Hierarchy (25 minutes)

Let's look at a couple more features of African cultures that relate to the use of money. There are cultural expectations for wealth distribution and inheritance. The head of the family, the father or sometimes the clan leader, has a right to decide who to pass on his wealth or inheritance to when he dies. Inheritance and wealth is mostly passed on to the sons or the elder son and very little goes to the girls. The wife or spouse may be given no voice in choosing who is to benefit from her husband's property in case of death. Unfortunately, sometimes the man may decide to pass his wealth on to those he had a good relationship with and deny other rightful beneficiaries just because they tried to challenge their father. Sometimes widows lose their home and land when their husbands die because the clan inherits the land and chases them away.

1. **As Christians, how should we handle these inheritance issues differently?**
2. **Read Numbers 27:1-11. Does this story guide us about the issue of inheritance today in our culture? Why or why not?**

Hierarchy is another cultural value in Africa that defines how money is used in order to maintain relationships in the family and community.[2] Most people in Africa believe in God as the highest authority, and second to God is man, third is woman, fourth is child, and lastly animals and nature. It is believed that communities and families run smoothly and peacefully when each person knows their roles and authority is respected. Wives should submit to their husbands, children should submit to their parents, and the whole family should submit to God.

This hierarchy may explain why men control all the resources in families and hold the highest positions in the community and government. Any challenge to the man's authority may be seen as disrespect and likewise any demand for equal rights from women or wives may harm the relationship. For example, a wife may fear to hold the husband accountable for the misuse of money because of fear to harm the relationship or fear of being called a disrespectful and uncultured wife. Listen to this Bambara proverb from Mali: "An important man may be wrong but he is always right."[3]

Are you familiar with similar proverbs in your own culture?

Cultural teachings like these may explain why the majority of men control all the resources in their families and also determine their allocation irrespective of whether they worked for it or the wife did. Men may do more work or less work than their wives, but they are still the ones to control how the money is used. And sometimes they use most of it on themselves for things like drinking, betting, or other selfish things, while only giving their wives money for spending on household items from time to time.

1. From a biblical perspective, what is right and good about this cultural value of hierarchy in the family?

For question #1 you can affirm that the Bible talks about respecting authority (for example see **Romans 13:1-7, Colossians 3:18-21**, and **1 Corinthians 11:3**). The Bible teaches that God is our King and he is to be obeyed. The Bible teaches that children should obey their parents. And the Bible teaches that the husband is the head of the wife, although there is considerable debate among Bible scholars as to what 'headship' actually means. You can tell the participants to read aloud some of these key Bible passages during the discussion.

2. From a biblical perspective, what features of this cultural value of hierarchy in the family are not good?

For question #2, you can talk about how both men and women are made in the image of God and are to be co-laborers in stewarding God's creation (see **Genesis 1:27-30**). In contrast to what sometimes happens in our cultures, husbands and wives are supposed to be partners, not acting independently of one another (See **1 Corinthians 7:1-4** and **1 Corinthians 11:11**). You can tell the participants to read aloud some of these key Bible passages during the discussion.

3. Which of these four options describes the common practice of families in your community? Which option do you think is most appropriate for a Christian family?

a. The husband should decide how all the money is used as the head of the family.

b. The husband should decide how all the money is used but should be willing to ask his wife for her suggestions.

c. The husband and wife should discuss and make decisions together for how money should be spent. They each get an equal opinion.

d. The husband should decide what to do with the money he earns while the wife decides what to do with money she earns herself. Both of them should use some of their money for the family's needs, and both of them can use money for other projects as well. But they manage their money separately from one another and don't make decisions together.

Allow the participants to discuss this issue together as a large group. Do not force them to submit to your own opinion as a facilitator. Allow people to agree to disagree. Encourage the participants to think about the results of each choice from a practical perspective. And encourage the participants to defend their answers by referring to what they know about God and what they read in the Bible.

Let's look at some Bible passages and see if they help us with the question we were just discussing. We'll answer some questions very briefly about each passage. Read **Matthew 19:4-6**. The husband and wife should become one flesh.

What does it look like for a husband and wife to live as if they are one flesh?

Let's read **Proverbs 31:10-31.**

What does this teach us about women using money?

Let's read **Ephesians 5:21-33.** We read that husbands are the head of their wives in marriage and that wives should submit to their husbands.

Concerning use of money, how should wives submit to their husbands?

Let's read **Genesis 2:18** and **Hebrews 13:6**. Eve was created to be a helper for Adam. Yet throughout Scripture the same language is used in reference to God as our helper as well.

What does it mean to be a "helper"? What other words in English or your local language mean the same thing as "helper"?

Let's read **1 Peter 3:7**. Peter says that wives are weaker in their bodies, but equal heirs in

Christ along with their husbands. Because they are heirs and partners, Peter says to treat them with respect.

What does it mean for a husband to treat his wife with respect concerning the family's use of money?

Let's read **Romans 16:1-4**. Throughout Romans chapter 16, the apostle Paul is greeting many of his co-workers in the city of Rome. We notice that many of his co-workers are women.

What does it mean to be a "co-worker"? What is another word for "co-worker" in English or your local language?

These Bible passages help us think more deeply about authority and how to work together as married couples. But it still may be hard for us to agree on how decisions about money should be made within a family. Continue to study these passages and pray for God's guidance.

Has anyone changed their opinion after reading these Bible passages?

Allow participants to disagree on this hard issue, but feel free to offer your own opinion. Remind the participants that these are hard issues to figure out and encourage them to keep studying God's Word together. If they feel convicted that they need to make a change within their own families, encourage them to do so even if they grew up seeing something different in how their parents managed money.

Putting Christ First

It can be very hard for us to put into practise what God has been teaching us in his Word and what we have learned in the lessons of this curriculum. Although some of us can imagine going against the culture's expectations, it might look impossible to go against what specific family members and community members tell us to do. We might be afraid of breaking relationships or having people look down on us because we do not do what is expected. Yet we are called to put Christ first. Christ is the King, not our individual cultures. We cannot make our culture into an idol. We can appreciate the good in our culture, but we must be ready to obey Christ instead of our culture when they are in conflict.

What counsel could you give to another Christian who is having difficulty obeying Christ over his or her culture? What Bible passages would help this person?

Is anyone willing to share a story about how you went against the expectations of your culture in order to obey Christ?

If no one is able to tell a personal story, then you can share the story about Stephen Kwakeye below.

Listen to this story about someone who went against the expectations of his culture. Stephen Kwakye is a Ghanaian who went to live in the United States.[4] He felt the cultural pressure to send gifts home to his family and community in Ghana. For 19 years, he sent over $20,000 worth of products in shipping containers back to Ghana. But later he realised these shipments of things produced no lasting change in his home community. Instead, these handouts only created dependency. He learned that he needed to go against the expectations of his community and culture. He decided to do something different. The money that he would have previously spent on shipping containers he has invested into the purchase of land in Ghana. He plans to start a farm to provide work and sustainable income for rural people. He is committed to supporting his home community in Ghana, but he is willing to go against the expectations of his culture and community in order to help people in a better way.

Debts and Loans (20 minutes)

Raise your hand if you are owed money by friends or family members. Now raise your hand if you owe money to friends or family members or institutions. Clearly for most of us, loans are a big part of our lives. They benefit us personally and also those we help.

One of the most common ways that we care for our relatives and friends is through giving loans. In most cases, this is done without charging interest. This can be a powerful way to help others at times of crisis. Giving a friend a personal loan means that they can avoid bank loans and loan companies that charge crippling interest. Some of the interest rates make it nearly impossible to pay the loans back.

Why are loans an effective way to help people who are in need? What are some of the possible good results of giving people loans?

Let the participants answer first. But you can point out anything that they do not mention.

1. Loans help people when they need money urgently. Even wealthy people might need loans at times to pay for unexpected hospital bills or vehicle repairs before their next paycheck.
2. When loans are repaid it can strengthen a relationship as both the person giving the loan and the person paying back the loan are building trust in one another.
3. Loaning can teach people good stewardship of money as they learn to budget, plan, and carefully pay back their debts.
4. Loans can be a good way to reduce low self-esteem. If someone receives only handouts, they might feel shame. But a loan gives a person dignity, since they will feel like they are doing something themselves for their own development with only a little bit of help.
5. Dependency is less likely to develop when giving loans instead of repeated gifts.
6. Loans are a way to keep using the same money to help people over and over, as you can re-loan the money again each time you are paid back by someone.

What are the disadvantages of loans? In what ways do they harm relationships?

Let the participants answer first. But you can point out anything that they do not mention.

1. Loans are far more complicated than gifts. It can be difficult to structure and give loans wisely.

2. We feel stuck and full of guilt and shame when we cannot pay back our own loans. We might feel so much shame that we avoid ever seeing the person to whom we owe money.

3. When friends or family cannot pay us back for loans we've given to them, it makes us frustrated. Sometimes we lose relationships with people who have abused our trust or failed us too many times.

4. When we forgive loans to save the relationship, we still remain frustrated at the loss of money.

Let's share our wisdom with each other and try to answer these difficult questions.

1. **What should we do when a friend is unable to repay a debt to us?**
2. **What should we do when a friend is unwilling to repay a debt to us?**
3. **What could be the result if we forgive debts very often?**
4. **What kind of repayment agreements do you suggest when loaning to friends or family members?**
5. **When someone feels pressured to say "yes" to giving a person a loan, but he really thinks he should say "no", what could he say? How should it be handled?**
6. **For what needs do loans work well? For what kinds of needs should we avoid giving a loan and give a gift instead?**

Population Growth and Development (35 minutes)

Let's look at the reality of population growth that our world is facing today. Here are some facts:

1. In 1500AD the population of the world was only 425 million. In the year 2000, it was 6 billion. Today it is 7.6 billion. By 2050 there will be about 9.2 billion people in our world. The population is increasing at an ever-faster rate.[5]

2. The population is increasing rapidly because people are living longer than before. This is due to better healthcare, improved food production, and other helpful technologies.[6]

3. We have consumed more of the earth's natural resources in the last 50 years than all people combined who have lived in the world before us.[7]

4. If everyone in the world lived like a middle class American, then our planet could only support around two billion people.[8] Our large population combined with the way that we live is putting great pressure on the environment. We are quickly using up oil, trees, groundwater, and the fish in our oceans. As the population rises, we can expect even tougher competition over scarce resources, especially water resources and land for settlement.

5. While the population is exploding in some countries, in wealthy nations the birthrate is dropping. As people become less materially poor, they would be able to support more children, yet research shows that wealthy people generally have less children.[9] As a country develops economically the birthrate drops. This is thought to be due to several reasons:

   a. As a country develops economically, women become more independent and want fewer children in order to also have careers.

   b. An economically developed nation will have a higher rate of people going into higher education which causes many to postpone starting their families until they are older.

   c. More people are migrating to urban areas for work instead of farming at home. In addition, modern farming methods have reduced the amount of human labour needed in agriculture. The result is that large families are not needed as often to work on family farms.

   d. In a wealthy nation there are less children dying at a young age, so people feel less pressure to have many children.

We are going to discuss some difficult and controversial issues - population growth and family planning. Most likely we come here today with many different perspectives and opinions. Even after we finish our discussion we should not expect that all of us will believe the same thing on these hard issues. Today the most important thing is for us to learn how to bring these issues into the light and discuss them openly. We cannot hide from them just because they are controversial. This is just the beginning of a conversation. We need to be slow to speak and quick to listen to one another. There is much that we can all learn from each other even when we have some disagreements.

We will have an initial large group discussion about the general issues. Then we will go to small groups to examine some Bible passages that relate to these issues.

Large Group Discussion

Ask the participants the following questions and allow them to discuss and give examples to support their answers. Give them plenty of time to discuss each question. Facilitator notes are provided for you below for each question. Use these notes to help you facilitate and guide the group discussion, but you shouldn't lecture from these notes. Your goal is to help participants learn how to discuss these issues peacefully, and to open their minds to new perspectives and ideas. Record some of the important participant responses in note form on the flip chart.

1. What are your cultural values concerning family life and bearing children?

2. What are the advantages and disadvantages of a family bearing many children?

3. Is population growth in a country good or bad for development? Explain.

4. Is family planning appropriate for Christians? What kind of planning is acceptable and what is not acceptable?

For question #1, make sure that participants discuss the expectations that relatives and communities have on families and how many children they should have.

- Are children viewed as a gift or a burden?
- Do most people desire to have few children or many children?
- Is there any status or power attached to having a family with many children?
- How are people treated if they have few children or no children?
- There are couples suffering from infertility due to medical issues. How are they treated by relatives and the community?
- Are children desired for labour to work on family farms?
- How is the desire for many children connected to polygamy?
- How is the desire and pressure to have a boy (an heir) connected to people having large families?

For question #2, here are a few ideas:

Advantages

- Children are a blessing, so having more children is also a blessing.
- Many children can provide more labour for the family business or farm.
- Bearing many children ensures that the parents will have some children reach adulthood, since some children may die young due to sicknesses. There is still a high infant mortality rate in many areas of Africa today.

Disadvantages

- Many children might strain the family's financial resources as more people means more money is needed for food and healthcare.
- Many children might cause the parents to have to spend a lot more money paying school fees, or they might be forced to make hard choices in sending only some of their children to school due to lack of resources.

- Many children results in the family's land being divided into smaller and smaller portions with each successive generation of children. So a farmer today might have only 5 acres for his family, while his great grandfather had 50 acres for his family.
- Many children sometimes results in increased conflicts as family members compete for the scarce resources. For example, children and parents might fight for control of the land or children might fight amongst themselves over small pieces of land.

For question #3, make sure that the participants look at both the positive and negative ways that population growth can be viewed.

Possible Advantages

- People are a resource. New people mean new ideas. People can create wealth. Wealth is not a limited cake that must be divided between all people. God can multiply our assets. The earth supports more people now than it ever did. We are able to support a lot of people through our advances in technology.
- Many children means there will be a large available labour force in the future. Labour prices will remain low.
- The larger the population in a country, the more taxes a country will receive to implement government programs and public infrastructure.
- A large population can attract investors and companies from foreign countries, since they will be drawn to the inexpensive labour force. This provides economic development as well as new jobs.
- Population growth can sometimes lead to economic growth as there are more people spending money on products, healthcare, education, and transport.

Possible Disadvantages

- Population growth can lead to unemployment if the government and private companies are not able to provide enough jobs to the growing population. This is a common problem in many countries in Africa. It can lead to a large population of idle youth who feel hopeless and restless.
- Population growth in a country can lead to the devastation of land and natural resources and even cause the extinction of animal and plant species. In some countries, there has been severe damage to the environment because of deforestation, over-utilised land, waste, and pollution.
- Population growth may indirectly cause wars over intense competition between land and resources.
- Population growth in a country can lead to rising land prices, housing prices, and food prices.
- Population growth can lead to increased pressure on the services provided by the government. If economic development cannot keep pace with population growth, many people will be deprived of access to basic services like good healthcare, education, shelter, transportation, and clean water.

- Population growth can lead to a situation in which there are very few adults who are working compared to the large number of children in a country. This puts great strain on the whole society of adults to care for all the children who cannot take care of themselves. For example, in Niger 56.8% of the population is 18 years old or younger.[10] A young population can also put pressure on society and on families to make children work, even if there are child labour laws in place.

- In some countries, rapid population growth has resulted in widespread unemployment of the youthful labour force. This can lead these youths to crime or drug abuse as they try to deal with their hopelessness.

A Response to the Disadvantages: It could be argued that population growth is not the real problem, but instead the problem is that some people live extravagant, wealthy lifestyles and use too many resources. If people lived more simply, a large population could live comfortably together on this earth.

For question #4, make sure everyone understands what is meant by "family planning". It can refer to simply planning well to take care of your family, or it can be another word for "birth control". Here are some ideas to talk about:

- The Bible makes clear that children are a blessing, not a curse.
- The Bible makes clear that marriage and bearing children is God's plan for most people. However, celibacy is also acceptable to God and even advantageous (see 1 Corinthians 7, if necessary). And if Paul gave up marriage for the sake of his ministry calling, might it be possible that some couples give up having a large number of children because of their callings?
- Planning for the future is a good thing. God has a plan for this world. If God makes plans, we should too. We should make good plans for our families and take care of them well.
- Abortion is not an acceptable form of family planning or birth control. It is the murder of an actual child; therefore, it is sinful.
- Children are a gift from God, and no one should be coerced or forced to not have children. People should be free to bear children. Therefore, Christians reject government programs of forced sterilization or forced birth control.
- Some Christians believe that since children are a blessing, we should only bear as many children as we are able to properly love and take care of. We should not have so many that we cannot know them personally. We should be able to provide food and education and healthcare for all of our children.
- There are birth control methods that do not involve abortion that allow Christian couples to plan how many children to have, or to plan spacing in between children. Some of these are very natural and simple, such as the rhythm method, which is just planning to refrain from sex at the time of each month when the wife is most susceptible to becoming pregnant. Other methods involve making use of man-made technologies such as condoms, other barrier methods, birth control pills or injections, and sterilization techniques such as vasectomies for men.

- Christians take advantage of technology and medicine to treat their sicknesses. These medicines are developed from God's creation and are viewed as gifts from God. Should we think of birth control technologies in the same way, or are they different?
- The Bible never says anything about the correct number of children that every couple should have. Some Christians argue that we should leave it all up to God to give us the number of children he wants to give us. And then our job is to be content with the number of children that we receive. Other Christians argue that it is a matter of wisdom and it is a personal decision for each couple that they make together in prayer. Some Christians also note that 10-15% of all couples in the world are unable to conceive a child according to some studies.[11] This seems to suggest that there isn't a required number of children for every Christian family.

Let's read **Genesis 1:28** together. Christians take this command in different ways. Some Christians use this passage to argue that using birth control is being disobedient to God. But it is possible to read this verse with other interpretations. We may not all agree, but let's ask ourselves these questions:

1. **Is this a command to each individual person to fill the earth, or is all of humanity supposed to fill the earth together?**
2. **Is the earth filled yet? How do we know when we have fully obeyed this command?**
3. **How should we view and respond to couples who are infertile?**
4. **Are couples disobeying this command if they choose to only have a few children?**

Conclusion

These are difficult issues that we have discussed – cultural expectations, inheritance, marriage, debts, and family planning. We may not all agree, but at least we have all heard new ideas today that have opened our minds. We must be ready to challenge the expectations of our culture whenever it doesn't line up with what we learn in God's Word. In most cases, cultural principles influence and shape our thinking, behaviour, and personality, but we must let God's word be primary. In our small groups, we will examine Bible passages together and see if they help us think more deeply about family planning and population growth.

Take-Home Activities for Lesson 13

The take-home activities will include assignments or activities that the participants should carry out in their communities, churches, or place of work, applying the lessons they have learned. The facilitator should provide detailed guidelines and clear instructions on how to go about the take-home activities.

Try to do at least two of the following activities of your choice:

1. Analyse your relationships with your family members and relatives. Because of

(Continued on the next page)

cultural expectations, are you too dependent on one of your relatives? Or are some of your relatives unhealthily dependent on you? Have an honest conversation with the people involved and try to make a change. Remember to focus on the four important relationships – with God, self, others, and the creation.

2. Take more time to analyse how money is handled in your family. Talk to your wife or husband about the discussion you had during this training about the different ways that couples handle finances. If you have been convicted that a change is needed, gently talk with your spouse and try to implement that change.

3. Think about your relationships that have become broken due to unpaid debts. It might be because you failed to repay a debt or because someone failed to repay a debt to you. Call the other person on the phone and arrange a time to meet together and reconcile. Either arrange for forgiveness of the loan or make a plan to resolve the situation. But most importantly, pray together and ask for God's help to restore the broken relationship.

4. Talk with your spouse about what you learned about family planning. Ask your spouse their opinion and then listen well. Study the relevant Bible passages together. Pray together about it. Discuss and make a plan together for your family.

Small Group Discussion (20 minutes)

Read out loud the questions that they will be answering and make sure they understand them.

Divide them up into groups of 5 people (anywhere from 3-6 people per group). They can be the same groups as before, or you can put them into new groups. They will not be presenting their answers to anyone.

If you have organised the whole workshop to take longer than what has been outlined, then feel free to give the participants a longer time for discussion.

Remember to move around and listen in with the groups as they discuss. Be available to answer their questions. You can give guidance or input if necessary during their discussions, but they have heard you talk a lot, so try to let them do the talking now.

Remind them periodically about how much time remains for their discussion.

Read and discuss these Bible passages together. Do any of these passages help us to better understand what we should believe about population growth or family planning? Continue to discuss together your different perspectives about family planning as you study these passages.

a. Psalm 127:3-5

b. Proverbs 14:28

c. 1 Timothy 5:8

d. 1 Timothy 3:1-5

e. Proverbs 17:6

f. Proverbs 11:29

Helping Without Hurting in Africa

Facilitator Manual

Lesson 14:
What Causes Change in Someone's Life?

Lesson 14: What Causes Change in Someone's Life?

In this section, you will find:

- An overview of the change cycle and triggers that cause a person to change.
- Best practices for encouraging change within different personality types.

Lesson Objectives:

- To learn strategies that will bring about change in a person's life.
- To learn whether it is biblically acceptable to help someone change by not giving to them.

Time Length: 1.5 Hours

Notes to the Facilitator

- Make sure you have flip chart paper and markers ready to give to the participants for the small group activity.
- Ensure that long notes, quotations, and group questions are prepared in advance and written on flip chart.
- Unless otherwise noted, all Scripture passages in **bold** should be read out loud by a participant for the whole group.
- When the participants read the selected Bible passages throughout the lesson, make brief summaries of what each Bible passage is about and what it means.
- At the end of the lesson, explain the take-home activities clearly to participants.
- If there is time at the end of the lesson, consider asking participants questions to review the key points made during the lesson.

Opening Exercise: (10 minutes)

Tell the participants to write their names down on a piece of paper. Wait a moment, and then tell everyone to write down their name again but using their other (non-dominant) hand. After they have written their name again, ask them: "Does everyone feel comfortable writing with that other hand, or was that a bit more difficult?" Explain to them that even though it was basically the same action, we are all used to writing with a particular hand. When we try to change and do an activity in a new way, it can be difficult and uncomfortable.

This was only a simple activity, but in life there are some changes that people need to make that may be very challenging and even painful.[1]

1. Why is it so hard for people to change their behaviour?

2. What kinds of experiences cause people to change their behaviour? You can use your own life example to explain.

As we work with materially poor people, sometimes we can see that certain behaviours are causing them to be materially poor, or causing them to live in dependency and shame. We encourage them to change how they behave, but we become easily frustrated when people refuse to change. When we see people suffering year after year from the same mistakes, we might feel like giving up on them. Indeed, many people in the world have given up on trying to help materially poor people, and they simply leave them in their suffering. As Christians, we must have a deep love for the poor and we must not give up trying to help them.

In our previous lessons, we learned that development is a process of change in which people move closer to being in right relationship with God, self, others, and the rest of creation. The most important change in someone's life is meeting Christ and being empowered by the Holy Spirit! So if we want to see people change, we must preach the gospel and enfold people into the church. If people are not reconciled to God, they will make very little change in their relationships with other people, self, and the rest of creation. But when people meet Jesus and are born again, the Holy Spirit will help change every area of their lives.

Briefly, give one specific example of how your relationships or your behaviour changed after you came to know Jesus.

Let a few participants answer briefly. If your group is small you could have every participant answer the question in one sentence each. For example, one participant might say, "When I became a Christian, Jesus helped me to overcome my alcohol addiction."

When we first trusted in Jesus, he transformed our lives. But in the Christian life, there are always more ways we need to change. We are not yet perfect. The Holy Spirit continues to work in our lives to help us become more holy and obedient to Christ. As leaders in our churches and communities, we want to see our people continue to change so that they can live in the way that God wants them to live and be the people who God wants them to be. How can we best encourage them to change? What should we do or stop doing to bring about change in people's lives? The first task is to pray. We need to pray for God to work in people's lives so that they will have the motivation and power to change. All our efforts to help materially poor people should begin and end with prayer. But what can we do in addition to praying? In this lesson, we will examine what kinds of forces and experiences cause individuals and communities to change. And then we will look at ways that we can help bring about these experiences and changes.

Facilitator Lecture – The Change Cycle (20 minutes)

Take a moment to look at the diagram in your manual called "Change Cycle for Individuals and Communities." It is a simple diagram, but it will help us to think about the process of change in people's lives.

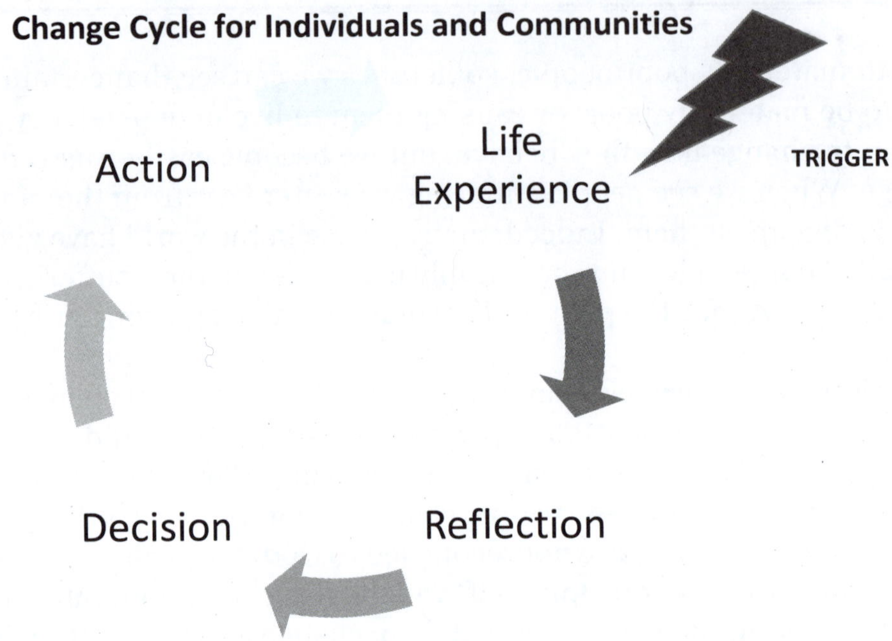

In the diagram we see that change starts with a trigger. A trigger is something that sets off a reaction. A trigger can be a person, thing, or event. A trigger could be new knowledge a person has obtained, or a crisis that a person has gone through. The trigger will cause someone to stop and reflect on his or her current situation and about the possibility of a better situation in the future. This reflection may result in the person making a decision to live in a different way. The decision will then result in new actions. Hopefully, they will begin to live in a more productive way and in a way that is obedient to Christ.

After this, the cycle begins again. New triggers will come. These new life experiences will begin the process of reflection, decision making, and action again. The reality is that all of us are in this cycle all of the time. We are constantly analysing the things that happen to us, and constantly making new decisions and planning new actions. But if we can understand this change cycle well, we will not only understand ourselves better, but we will know how to effectively encourage other people to change.

This change cycle applies to all kinds of behaviour change in our lives. But in this lesson, we want to focus on helping materially poor people to change. We want them to be able to grow in their relationships with God, self, others, and creation, and be able to support themselves and their families through productive work.

Types of Triggers that Cause Change

We will now examine five types of triggers that can cause people to reflect and make changes in their lives. For each of the five types, we will be given an example of a materially poor person experiencing that type of trigger. Then we will discuss how we can best interact with that trigger to encourage the person to change his or her behaviour.

Facilitator notes will be given to you under each example, but you do not need to read them unless participants need more help in answering the question.

1. A recent crisis. This could include sickness, losing a job, the death of a family member, an accident, a theft, or a natural disaster. This type of trigger affects both individuals and communities. Consider how a community which has experienced a devastating mudslide will reflect together on how to prevent such disasters in the future. The Bible teaches that suffering is one of the tools that God uses to help us change in our character and grow in maturity. Suffering through a crisis is an excellent opportunity to learn how to change. But because crises are painful, some people ignore the opportunity for growth and instead they might become more depressed and create more brokenness in their four relationships. Therefore, it is very important that we walk together with people who have suffered from a crisis and give them our love and compassion. If we have listened to them well and mourned with them, they might be willing to listen to our guidance and counsel about how they can experience positive change through the painful experience.

> **Example** – A materially poor neighbour in your community has been arrested as a thief for trying to steal someone else's goats. He is now in jail. You are going to visit him.

What could you say to this neighbour to help him reflect on his choices so that he becomes willing to change?

Being in jail would be a crisis in his life because he is experiencing the consequences of his actions. You could ask the neighbour why he tried to steal the goats. You could help him consider what is more productive: looking for a new job, working hard on his farm or at his job, or trying to steal. Which one will yield the better result? This would also be an opportunity to share the gospel with the neighbour and point him to Jesus to receive forgiveness for his sins and the power of the Holy Spirit to make positive changes.

2. Experiencing small problems over a long period of time. Sometimes it is not a sudden crisis that causes a person to change, but rather an extended period of experiencing the same small problems and frustrations over and over. Eventually, the person will get to a breaking point where they feel too frustrated to continue. Then they will figure out what they can do to try to change the current situation. A person may be tired of regularly feeling hungry so they finally become willing to try a new type of work. A person may be tired of having their crops die from droughts year after year, so they finally become willing to pay more for drought resistant seeds.

> **Example** – Ali is your nephew who has been regularly asking for financial help from you. He uses this money to help pay for his mobile phone and transportation. He has a degree in accounting but has not found an accounting job yet. You have been trying to convince him to do casual work while still looking for accounting jobs, but he has refused.

How could you facilitate a trigger in Ali's life so that he will change and begin to work?

One option is to simply stop giving Ali any money. This would create a trigger for change. Ali would begin to feel frustration over a long period of time of regularly not having money to pay for his mobile phone, transportation, and other needs. At some point, he would hopefully become frustrated enough that he would begin working at another job, while waiting for a good accounting job. If you continue to give him money, he may continue to be idle and refuse to work.

3. Learning something new. This could be something as simple as seeing a new type of product or invention while walking through town. Or the trigger could be that a person gained a new perspective from a seminar. Or a person could learn a new skill from a friend. Or a person could learn some kind of technical knowledge through a book. Exposure to new skills and ideas is an extremely important trigger for change not only for materially poor people, but for all of us.

> **Example** – As a pastor you see that your church members are complaining that a certain kind of worm is destroying their crops. You have prayed for them and visited their homes and farms. You want to help them further but you aren't sure how to advise them.

How could you help the congregation learn something new so that they know how to change their farming practices in response to the worm problem?

The pastor could ask an agricultural extension officer to come and speak to the church about how to kill the worms. Or the agricultural officer may advise them to plant a different kind of crop that the worms do not eat. In this case, you create a trigger for behaviour change by having your church members exposed to new knowledge from this expert.

4. Reward or punishment. People often are willing to change their behaviour in order to earn a reward or to avoid a punishment or consequence. The reward or punishment is the trigger that can cause someone to reflect and change. We have to be careful with rewards and punishments when working with materially poor people since we want to avoid paternalism and do not want to treat them like they are children under our authority. But rewards and punishments can work well when trying to help our actual children to change their behaviour, or when working with people we employ at our business.

> **Example** – You are the manager of a shop which employs 10 workers. You are frustrated with the work ethic of the employees. Many are lazy. They are not friendly enough to customers and are not quick to help customers find what they need. Customers have complained and you know you are losing out on sales.

What kind of reward trigger could you implement to encourage your employees to work harder?

You could give promotions to the employees that have shown good work ethic, and give them new titles, new responsibilities, and higher payment. You could also try to find ways to help the employees feel ownership of the business and work together. For example, you could say that every month that the profit of the business reaches a certain level, every employee will receive an equal bonus in pay.

5. Relationship. Relationships have probably been the most important factor into making you who you are today and making you behave the way you do. We change through interacting with people. Think about all that you have learned from your parents and how your relationship with them has shaped your character. Think about how much someone changes when they get married. And remember that we discussed how all of our lives changed dramatically when we began a relationship with Jesus. As we have emphasized throughout this entire curriculum, we must focus on building relationships with materially poor people. As we walk with them over a long period of time, our relationship will prompt behaviour change in their lives, as well as change in our own lives.

> **Example** – Samia is a single mother with two young children. She earns a little money each day washing clothes for people while her children are at school. But her life is very difficult and it's hard to earn enough money to take care of her family. She feels alone and ignored and without hope.

If you and your family began a relationship with Samia's family, how might this new relationship change Samia and benefit her?

Having a friend will completely change Samia's life. She will no longer feel alone and she will feel like someone cares about her. Your family could also encourage her that she is taking good care of her children and give her affirmation and hope. You could share with her about Jesus and the good news of the gospel. Your family could invite her to church with you where she will meet more friends, and possibly even receive new job opportunities or financial help in times of need through these new friends. You or your older children could help Samia once in a while by watching her children so that she has time to rest and time to do more work. You may also find opportunities to serve Samia by helping her make a budget, doing home repairs for her, teaching her new skills, and giving her advice.

Principles for Encouraging Change (10 minutes)

Principle 1 - Promote trigger events that will cause someone to reflect and change.

As we've been discussing, we need to create triggers in people's lives that will cause them to change, or counsel and encourage people when they have already experienced a trigger.

Principle 2 - Live by example.

We must practise what we preach. We must be continually willing to make changes in our own lives as we try to grow in our relationships with God, self, others, and creation. We must be obedient to Christ and grow in holiness. As people see us change, they will also be encouraged to make change themselves and emulate our behaviours and attitudes.

Principle 3 - Mobilise supportive people.

When people try to change, sometimes the people around them will discourage them because they feel threatened or jealous. Because of this, people need a lot of encouragement and support when they try to change how they live. We need to pray for them, listen to them, and give them help when they need it. We have to be willing to walk the long journey of change with people. As pastors, development workers, or even as neighbours, when we are trying to help materially poor people to make changes in their lives, we need to mobilise people who can give support and encouragement to them.

Sometimes this can be done through forming peer groups of people who are all trying to make the same change together. For example, you could form a group of alcoholics who all want to support each other in giving up drinking together, along with others who have already found freedom from the addiction. Or you could form a village savings and loans group for people to learn how to budget and save their money together with mutual support and encouragement.

Principle 4 - Start small.

Start by helping people to make small changes in their lives. If you try to help an individual or a community make many changes to their lifestyle all at once, they may get overwhelmed and give up on making any change at all. But if you can begin by helping people make one small change, they will see the benefit of change when they see the positive results. This change can be celebrated and people will be ready to try making another change. It is also wise to start with changes that are easy to make with results that will be seen quickly. After people have made several small changes and seen the positive results of each one, you could consider helping someone to make a bigger change that will show positive results only after a longer period of time.

Principle 5 - Start with the people who are most willing to change.

Development can only happen with people who are willing to change. If people do not believe they need to take any action to make positive change in their lives, then it will be very difficult to see any development in their four relationships. Even if someone is in a difficult situation through no fault of their own, if they are not willing to take any new action themselves to make positive change, then it will be very challenging to see any development in his or her life.

It is also important to start with the people who are most willing to change because these people will be an example to others who are much more resistant to change. Listen to this story.

A Christian organisation was working in West Africa, training people in poultry farming. It was already common for farmers to raise chickens for selling eggs and meat. But their chickens were susceptible to disease and often died. During the training, participants learned how to take care of chickens, how to vaccinate them, and learned about some typical diseases. As part of the training each participant was to bring a chicken from home so that they could learn how to vaccinate it. One lady, Lydia, came with a very tiny chicken. Her husband was sure that the vaccination would kill the chicken, so he told her to bring the smallest chicken they owned. Lydia learned how to vaccinate her chicken, and then went home to her village. Because of her husband's mistrust, this was the only chicken she vaccinated. Several months later an epidemic spread through the village, and all the chickens in the entire village died. The only one that survived was the scrawny chicken that Lydia had brought to the training! Everyone from her village wanted to know, "What did you do to that chicken when you brought it to town a few months ago?" She explained about the training and the vaccination. Amazingly, all of these people asked Lydia to vaccinate their chickens! As people in her village began buying new chickens to replace those that had died, Lydia vaccinated every last one.[2]

How did this amazing change happen in the lives of so many people? It began by the organisation working with just a few people who were willing to change and try something new even when others were afraid.

If people are not willing to make any changes in their life, then we might want to consider not helping them at all and instead wait patiently until they are willing. There are two reasons we should consider this. First, we are limited in our time and resources. Remember we learned how long it takes to walk with one person, truly getting to know them, and finding out why they are materially poor. We simply cannot help everyone. Unlike God, we have limits. We have to say "no" to some people. So it makes sense to prioritise helping those people who are willing to change and who will set a good example to others. Second, if we stop giving hand-outs like food and clothing to people who are unwilling to do anything to try to change their lives, we may help them experience a trigger for change. This might seem harsh, but sometimes not giving money to people is actually the loving thing to do. Not giving might be the only thing that will make them tired enough of their situation that they are willing to change. And then when they are ready to change, we should be ready to walk with them and help them make those changes.

But doesn't the Bible say we need to always give? Are we really allowed to say "no" to someone who asks us to give them money or help? That is the topic of our next discussion.

The Bible's Teaching about Giving (20 minutes)

Large Group Discussion

Ask participants the discussion question and take note of their answers. Encourage them to share examples from their real life experiences. Encourage them also to cite specific Bible passages to defend their answers.

When people ask for money or resources from us, is it biblically acceptable for us to say "no" in specific situations? Please explain your answer with examples from your life and from Scripture.

You don't need to discuss this question until the group reaches consensus. After they have discussed for a little while, continue with the lecture which will help participants to be able to answer this question.

Some people may want to answer this hard question by quoting **Matthew 5:42.** Let's read it together. For some people this verse by itself is enough to clearly answer the question and end the discussion. It seems to be clear that we should always give. But it is not that simple. When we come across a difficult passage like Matthew 5:42 we can only fully understand it in the context of the rest of Scripture. We need to read other passages on similar topics and also think about the broad themes of Scripture.

In this Sermon on the Mount, Jesus makes many strong statements besides this strong command about giving. For example, in **verses 27-30** he says that we should remove our hands and eyes to avoid sin. Surely Jesus didn't mean for us to literally cut off our hands! It is sinful to destroy our good bodies that God has made. Jesus is making a strong point about sin and temptation, but his point must be understood in the light of the rest of Scripture. Similarly, Matthew 5:42 should not be taken as a literal command for every situation in our lives. Jesus's main point is that we should be incredibly generous people, and care for all kinds of people, even our enemies. But sometimes it is the right thing to do to not give a hand-out. There are at least four reasons why Matthew 5:42 (as well as other similar Bible verses) should not be understood as a command to give in each and every situation.

1. Remember we learned in earlier lessons about the story of the whole Bible and the themes we see throughout the Bible. Our goal is not just that people would have money, but our goal is **to help people fulfil their callings of glorifying God by working and supporting themselves and their families.** Our goal is that people would be reconciled to God, themselves, others, and the rest of creation. If we really love people and want them to be who God wants them to be, we cannot be simplistic and think that giving money is always the answer. If we give people money, but cause them to feel shame and turn to sinful behaviours, then we have not truly helped them. We must give generously, but we need to be holistic in our approach and keep the right goal in focus.

2. There are other Bible passages that clearly teach us "not to give" in certain situations. We must obey the whole Bible and not focus only on one or two verses. In **1 Timothy 5:3-16,** Paul told the church that they should not give to widows who had children or grandchildren, or to any widows under 60 years of age. Was God being unloving towards these widows? No. If those widows received such financial support they would become "idlers, but also gossips and busybodies" (verse 13) rather than working to support themselves. Similarly, **2 Thessalonians 3:6-15** gives us a very serious command to never give to people in the church who are not willing to work. If someone does not work, they should not eat. The Bible cannot contradict itself. Passages like these and others teach us that we need to use wisdom in our giving, and sometimes the most loving response is to say "no" to giving someone hand-outs. So even as we obey Matthew 5:42, we should give with wisdom and not say "yes" to any request.

3. No one is able to give to everyone who asks, simply because we all have limited resources. For example, Peter could not give money to the crippled man who was begging in **Acts 3:2-6**. But Peter still responded to him with love.

4. Even in a situation where we do not give someone a hand-out, it does not mean that

we turn away from them. Our message should be - "*We love you enough to give you far more than what you are asking from us right now. We want to be part of your life and to walk with you and help you overcome the situation you are in. It would be easy to give you money, but we are going to do the harder thing of sharing our lives and energy with you to truly help you, because you are worth it in God's eyes.*" Sometimes, we may want to give a hand-out so that we do not have to deal any longer with the person in need, but that is not how Christ taught us to love. We need to be committed and have patience and love for those in need. If people decide to walk away and refuse this help, they are the ones turning away from us, not us from them. If this happens, we should not be discouraged, but instead keep praying for them until they return to us again.

Take a minute to find out if everyone is now at peace on this difficult issue. Does everyone agree together now? Does anyone have more questions?

Personality and Change (10 minutes)

People differ in their reaction to change because of their personalities and backgrounds. We can categorise people into five groups.[3]

1. **Risk-takers**. These people generally view change positively and with excitement. They will always be the first to try out new methods, actions, or beliefs. They are comfortable standing out from other people, and sometimes enjoy the fact that they are unique and behave differently than others. Other people are used to risk-takers behaving strangely.

2. **Respected people.** Some people are open to change, if they are convinced that it will be good. These people are considered to be wise and are respected by the community. People follow them and they sometimes have more influence than official leaders. If these respected people accept a change, it is likely to be accepted by others.

3. **Careful people**. Careful people wait and watch what happens when the respected people change. If the respected people experience a good result, the careful people will go along with the change. When the careful people decide to change this is called the "tipping point", because now most people in the community will accept the change together.

4. **Sceptical people**. Some people doubt anything new. They prefer to keep doing the same things they know well. They wait until the majority of the people in the community have made a change, and they continue to observe. After they have seen the change and gotten used to it, they will also change because they do not want to be left out.

5. **Resistant people**. A few people dislike all change. They will hold on to the old ways even when they are going against the majority of the community. Like the risk-takers, they don't care what other people say. But after a very long time, they may get used to the change and embrace it grudgingly.

Large Group Activity

Ask the participants to reflect on the five categories of people and identify which category fits each one of them the best. Have them all stand up. Tell them to stand together in a group with the other people who fit their same category. So there should be five groups. Count the number of people in each group. Then ask everyone this question for a large group discussion:

You want to see a rural community implement a change in their sanitation practices. You are going to facilitate a training, but you only have money for training one group. Which of these five groups would you choose to train if you could only choose one? What are the advantages and disadvantages of the category of people you chose?

It would be good to note that certain categories would allow you to train more people at once. But other categories may be more strategic if you want to see change in the whole community. The respected people group is probably the best choice for a training group even if they are few in number. The risk-takers are quick to adapt and change but other people may not necessarily follow their examples because they always act differently from others anyway.

Take-Home Activities for Lesson 14

The take-home activities will include assignments or activities that the participants should carry out in their communities, churches, or place of work, applying the lessons they have learned. The facilitator should provide detailed guidelines and clear instructions on how to go about the take-home activities.

For Everyone – Try to do all three.

1. Identify two people in your workplace, church, or community who you have seen make a difficult but positive change in their lives. Write them a card or note to encourage them and appreciate them for setting a good example for others.

2. Determine one change that God wants you to make in your own life. It could be something simple like getting more exercise or reading your Bible every day. Try to encourage several friends to join you in making this change in their lives as well. Then meet together once a month to encourage each other and hold each other accountable to this change.

3. One of the triggers for change is when people learn about something new. Who could you invite to a special church event to teach something new to your church members? (For example: teaching about agriculture, healthcare, business, or computers.) Make a plan to invite this person in the next few months.

Small Group Discussion (20 minutes)

Read out loud the questions that they will be answering and make sure they understand them.

Divide them up into groups of 5 people (anywhere from 3-6 people per group). They can be the same groups as before, or you can put them into new groups. They will not be presenting their answers to anyone.

If you have organised the whole workshop to take longer than what has been outlined, then feel free to give the participants a longer time for discussion.

Remember to move around and listen in with the groups as they discuss. Be available to answer their questions. You can give guidance or input if necessary during their discussions, but they have heard you talk a lot, so try to let them do the talking now.

Remind them periodically about how much time remains for their discussion.

1. **Does your church mobilise supportive people to walk with and encourage people who are courageously trying something new to change their lives? Explain. If not, how specifically could your church be doing this better?**
2. **Take turns sharing with the group about a person in your life whom you have been trying to help but who is very resistant to change. Let the group members give you advice about what you can do to encourage this person to change, and what triggers would help this person to reflect and decide to do something different. Pray together that the Holy Spirit would give these people courage to change.**

Helping Without Hurting in Africa

FACILITATOR MANUAL

LESSON 15: PARTICIPATION OF THE COMMUNITY

Lesson 15: Participation of the Community

In this section, you will find:

- Best practices for true participation from *all* in community planning.
- A guide to resource mapping.

Lesson Objectives:

- To understand why community participation is essential for success in community development.
- To encourage Christians to listen to the opinions of all types of people in their communities and to give a voice to the voiceless.
- To learn how to create a simple resource map in a community.

Time Length: 1.5 Hours

Notes to the Facilitator

- Find and prepare a location outside of your training building for the large group activity of making a resource map. A small open dirt area or grassy area is sufficient.

- Make sure you have flip chart papers and markers ready to give to the participants for the small group activities.

- Ensure that long notes, quotations, and group questions are prepared in advance and written on flip chart.

- Unless otherwise noted, all Scripture passages in **bold** should be read out loud by a participant for the whole group.

- When the participants read the selected Bible passages throughout the lesson, make brief summaries of what each Bible passage is about and what it means.

- At the end of the lesson, explain the take-home activities clearly to participants.

- If there is time at the end of the lesson, consider asking participants questions to review the key points made during the lesson.

Opening Discussion (5 minutes)

Ask the participants this question and take brief notes of their responses on a flip chart.

Important visitors are coming to your home, what would you need to do to feel like you fully participated in hosting them?

Participants might answer with statements like: "I would need to help determine what to buy, I would want to make sure that each family member helped in the food preparation, and I would want to make sure the chairs were clean and set up well. Then during the visit, I would welcome them, eat with them, talk to them, and I would pray for them before they left. Then, I and my family would clean the dishes and home together."

Encourage them to keep their answers simple and brief. Tell them to think about how they would participate in the planning, the preparation, the actual visit, the clean-up and the family discussion about the visit afterward. After they have given their brief responses, ask them this question:

"How would you feel if your family did not include you in the planning, or the preparation, or the visit, or the discussion afterward?"

Let the participants respond and then conclude with the summary below.

To successfully host a visitor, the whole family must come together with the shared goal of showing hospitality to the visitor. And naturally, each of us would want to personally be involved in every aspect of hosting a visitor, and that is the only way we will feel like we have fully participated. In the same way, the community or materially poor person we are trying to help should be involved in every aspect of the process. They should be involved in the planning, preparation, implementation, and evaluation of any activity or project. The people we are trying to help are image bearers who are called to live in right relationship with God, self, others, and creation. So they should be empowered to make decisions for themselves, and they should take charge of mobilising, identifying, and managing their resources to contribute to their own development.

In this lesson, we will learn why participation is important and also learn about strategies and a tool for encouraging better participation. But first, let's look at a story together from Eastern Uganda.

Story from Eastern Uganda (10 minutes)

An international organisation wanted to help a tribe in Eastern Uganda and noted that the people there did not have pit latrines. Most people defecated in the bush out in the open. The organisation planned to give the people ventilated pit latrines in order to improve the sanitation of their environment. The pit latrines were constructed and handed over to the people. Later, a development worker from a different organisation visited the area and used one of the latrines. Surprisingly the latrine was perfectly clean inside. Unfortunately, the development worker discovered that this was not due to regular cleaning by the community. It was due to the fact that no one in the community was using the latrines. They did not want them. They all preferred to defecate in the bush. In fact, for this tribe, using latrines was considered a taboo. There was even a cultural belief that women would not bare children if they used the latrines.

Although we have not been given all of the information about this project, this short story can help us to learn important principles about how to wisely help materially poor communities. Let's discuss these questions together:

1. What are some of the reasons this project did not work out well?

The biggest problem is that it appears the organisation did not even ask the people if they wanted latrines and if they would use them. Participants should also note that the community did not have much participation in this project. The organisation did not take the time to learn about the local culture and its needs. We don't know for sure, but it appears that they did not try to teach the community members or leaders the benefits of using pit latrines, nor did they try to teach them a Christian biblical worldview which would help them to overcome their false cultural beliefs that were keeping them from using the latrines. The organisation did not involve the community in mobilising their own resources and labour to help build the latrines. This is very important. If you offer a free gift to a community, they may say "sure, you can give us those things" even if they do not really want them. Who turns down a free gift? But they would not have said "yes" to a gift that required their labour and resources unless it was a gift that they saw as valuable and helpful.

2. Do you think the local people were involved in the planning, preparation, implementation, and evaluation of this project? Explain how you determined your answer from the story.

The clear answer is "no". It appears as if the local people were not involved in any part of the process. If they were involved in the planning, they would not have said "yes" to the latrines without being first convinced of their value. Or they might have asked for help with something that they saw as a more urgent need. Or they and the organisation may have decided to use a different type of latrine that perhaps would not have offended the people. For more ideas, see the notes for question #1.

3. In your region, have you seen similar situations in which organisations or churches did not involve the local people they were trying to help in the planning and implementation of projects? Briefly share your examples.

Facilitator Lecture – Community Participation (10 minutes)

Through these stories we have learned the critical importance of community participation in the process of development and in all of our attempts to help materially poor people. Let's summarise the positive results of community participation.

Positive Results of Community Participation:

1. **Ownership**. Materially poor people and communities are just like other people in that they are more likely to appreciate and take responsibility for a project if and when they participate from the beginning of the project to the end. If we work together ***with*** the community for their own development, they will feel ownership. But if we do work ***to*** them or ***for*** them, they might only be passive recipients.

2. **Sustainability**. If people feel ownership of their own development, then there should also be sustainability. Even if the individual or organisation who is helping moves away, the people will continue to make changes by themselves, now that they have learned the responsibility and joy of taking charge of their own development.

3. **Self-esteem and confidence**. If an individual or community has fully participated, then they will feel good looking at the changes that have taken place in their lives. They will see that God has given them the power to continue to make changes in their lives, and this will give them confidence for the future. Participation in a project, even if the project is not fully successful, will reduce a community's poverty of being and give them more self-esteem.

4. **Knowledge sharing**. Materially poor people and communities are often not well understood by the people intending to help them. For example, a beggar understands the challenges of being a beggar far better than a local church does! He knows much more about why certain people become beggars, how often beggars are able to find real work, about the types of people who give to beggars, where the best places are to beg in the city, etc. It would be unwise for a church to plan how to help beggars in their neighbourhood without first talking to the beggars. We must listen carefully to materially poor people, learn about their context and culture, and share knowledge. Knowledge sharing will help us to plan successful initiatives together.

5. **Equitable distribution**. Sometimes when churches or organisations try to help materially poor communities, only certain groups within the community benefit, and the people who need the most help might be overlooked. Participation of the whole community will help ensure that resources are distributed to those who need them most. With full community participation, opportunities for corruption and favouritism will be reduced.

6. **Resource mobilisation**. When the people who are being helped participate, they are able to offer their labour, materials, and money for the project. This greatly reduces the cost for the church or organisation that is trying to help and produces community ownership.

7. **Teamwork and Accountability.** When everyone in a community is participating together to see change happen, there can be a great spirit of teamwork and harmony between the community members, government officials, churches, and organisations. Because everyone is aware of what is happening, each member can be accountable to the others. The organisation that is helping and the community itself can hold each other accountable to doing good work that glorifies God.[1]

Have you ever heard of a community calling government officials or organisations to account concerning the way they tried to help that community? Share your story briefly.

Community participation is essential in order to help people without hurting them. One of the most common mistakes that churches, missionaries, governments, and development organisations make is that they try to help people without the full participation of the people they are trying to help. What are the consequences of this mistake?

Consequences of not having community participation:

1. **God-complex.** If we try to help people without letting them plan and participate with us, this shows that we do not respect them. We will be communicating to them that we are superior and have all of the right ideas. This means we have a god-complex. At the end of the work, our god-complexes will only be made stronger and the people may feel even more inferior and have more shame.

2. **Dependency.** If we help people without their participation, they will not feel any ownership. They will view new assets like a church building, school, or a well as the property of those who built it for them. They will feel little responsibility to manage and repair such assets. They might say: "But you built this. It is yours. We are waiting for you to fix it." Since they did not participate in their own development, they will continue to wait for outsiders to bring them more gifts.

3. **Failed Project**. When outside church leaders and organisations try to help other communities, they often make the mistake of thinking that what worked in one community they helped will automatically work in other communities. But this is not always true. Every community has different personalities, needs, assets, land, and cultures. When we come into a community with a know-it-all attitude or I-have-done-this-before attitude, our attempts to help will likely end in failure. We need to appreciate the process of discussing and planning together with the people, instead of rushing in with our predetermined plans. Too often we are in a hurry because we are excited to help or because we are trying to meet the expectations of donors. If you have the participation of the community in the entire process, things will take longer and require more patience, but it's better to go slow and truly help the people.

Case Studies (15 minutes)

1. Project Signs.

In some communities, it is common to see signs that read – "This project was donated by organisation ABC" or "This classroom was built by organisation ABC."

Can you think of such examples in your region? What do signs like this tell us about community participation? Are these projects still functional?

Imagine a different type of sign that reads, "We, ABC church, constructed this building with the assistance of organisation DEF."

What does this type of sign tell us about community participation?

2. A true story: A literacy centre built by Muslims and Christians together.

In an area of West Africa where the people are a mixture of Catholic, Protestant, and Muslim, a church agency received many requests to teach literacy in the villages. The agency director knew a Christian development organisation from Canada and asked for help. The Canadian organisation gave them funds to pay teachers in just five of the villages for a test project. The villages had to build their own literacy centres and pay some fees for their books. When the literacy classes in those five villages were almost completed, the Canadian organisation sent two experts who had experience working with literacy programs in neighbouring countries. They visited the five villages, and suggested many ways to make the teaching and the classes better. They also wrote a report. Using that report, the Canadian organisation helped the church agency write a grant proposal to a donor. The donor accepted the proposal and made a written agreement to fund enough teachers and supervisors to work in 30 villages over three years. About a thousand people, Catholic and Protestant and Muslim, learned to read together, and they were very happy with their new skills.[2]

What is your reaction to the story?

What does it teach us about community participation?

3. A true story: A broken generator.

A development organisation in West Africa wanted to help women by making their labour easier. They decided to give generators to rural villages that could be used to grind grain as well as pump water into water towers. They went to many villages and offered to give them generators, and said it would be the responsibility of the villages to do the maintenance. There was a village where this organisation donated a generator and built a water tower. The people contributed labour as the organisation required them to do. But after a short time operating, the generator needed maintenance. Each time it broke they had to collect money and send someone to the city to buy parts. After they had repaired the generator four times, when it broke the fifth time they decided that it was not worth it to fix and they left it sitting broken. The expensive water tower is standing in the village empty.[3]

What is your reaction to the story?

What does it teach us about community participation?

Try to help the group bring out the idea that although the community participated with their labour in the construction, they were not part of the planning process. If they were, they might have explained to the organisation that they would not have the necessary money needed for the regular repairs of this complicated generator. This project seemed like a good idea to the organisation, but it was too big of a project for the community to sustain. It would have been better to start by listening to the community about what they really wanted, and then work with them to start a small sustainable project to meet that need.

4. VSLA programs - village savings and loan situations.[4]

> **1. Can someone please explain to us very briefly what a Village Savings and Loans association is?**
>
> **2. Why are Village Savings and Loans associations spreading rapidly in poor communities throughout Africa? What makes them so successful?**

Let the participants answer first and then explain other ideas that they did not mention. VSLAs work well because the central feature is community participation. It is about people coming together to save together and help each other. They encourage collective responsibility and help communities take charge of their own development. They also focus on people's assets, making use of available resources, rather than waiting for outside help.

Listening to the Voiceless (30 minutes)

Small group activity

Divide everyone into smaller groups, but this time people should be divided based on either sex or age. If you have a wide range of ages, divide everyone into four groups, with each group representing a different age group. One group will have the youngest people, another group the oldest people, and others in the middle groups. Alternatively, you could make two groups of men and two groups of women. It doesn't matter if some groups have a few more people in them compared to other groups. If you have a training group that cannot be divided easily by sex or age, then choose a different distinguishing trait that will result in groups having various perspectives.

Give the groups 10 minutes to discuss. All the groups should answer the question below and write down their answers. Each group will then be given 2 minutes to present their answers.

> **If a donor gave $1,000 USD to our training group today, how should that money be spent to benefit our group and improve our training location?**

Allow each group to present their answers and then lead a discussion about the differences in their answers. Point out to the participants that men and women have different perspectives and ideas. Different age groups have different perspectives and ideas. (Although no money is actually being given to the training group, you as the facilitator should discuss the suggestions that were given with other leaders and organisers of your training group at another time, perhaps in the evening after the session is finished for the day. Discuss whether you are able to act on any of the recommendations to improve the training experience for the participants.)

This activity shows us why it is important to listen to and involve all types of people in a community, whether it is our own community or a community in another region we are trying to assist. The answers our small groups gave were very different from one another, and we are generally like-minded people. Imagine all the different perspectives we would get if we interviewed a whole community, asking people how to spend money to develop their community!

If we want to help a community, or even just one neighbourhood around our local church, we need to talk to and listen to the different types or categories of people. We will hear many different ideas, but it is not that one group of people is right and another group is wrong. All of the opinions are valuable. In the end, we won't be able to do everything that every person suggests and hard decisions will have to be made. But we shouldn't make those decisions without first putting in the work of really listening to different people, and their various needs and priorities.

When trying to help a community, it is very important to have people participate irrespective of their gender, education, race, age, religion, or disabilities. To disregard any group in the community will result in us missing vital information and possibly cause us to hurt some people while trying to help the community.

We need to take special care to not only talk to the people in power, but also to those who are disadvantaged and voiceless. By voiceless, we don't mean people who are unable to speak. We are referring to people who are not listened to by other people, particularly people with power and money. Voiceless people do not have much power and influence due to social isolation, feeling inferior, or unfair treatment by the community.

What types of people are often voiceless in our communities?

If the participants have trouble answering this question, remind them of this statement you already made: "When trying to help a community, it is very important to have people participate irrespective of their gender, education, race, age, religion, or disabilities." It should bring to their minds certain groups of voiceless people.

We need to take special care to appreciate the contributions of the voiceless and also agree on the way forward together with them. This will help them feel loved and valued, and their knowledge and skills will allow for better planning to help the community. We must listen to them ourselves, but also try to give them opportunities to speak so that others will listen to them as well. This is "giving a voice to the voiceless".

Let's consider a few verses from the book of Proverbs. Read **Proverbs 31:8-9** and **Proverbs 21:13**.

1. What do these verses teach us about how to help the voiceless?

2. Discuss how you personally or your church, organisation, or government can give a voice to the voiceless? Be specific.

Resource Mapping (20 minutes)

There are various techniques that can be used to promote community participation and the choice of technique will be influenced by the different situations, communities, and institutions that want to help. One effective tool for promoting community participation is called a resource map. We will learn how to make one together now.

A resource map or asset map is a tool that enables us to identify and learn about the community and its resources. At the same time, it is a useful way for the community itself to think about its resources and to explain what is important to them. The resource map will show their assets and their locations. A resource map is generally more suited to rural areas, but it can be adjusted to work for urban areas as well.

The resource map can be drawn on paper, but in many contexts it is more useful for community members to draw the map on the ground using locally available materials. The map they make can be transferred to paper later for record keeping.

A resource map is a good way to help the community to identify their resources so that they can better use the gifts and skills God has given them for their own development (remember Lesson 7). After making a resource map with our own community or with another community we are trying to help, we can together plan with the community members how to address pressing needs starting with available resources. It is a good first step in planning and partnering together to bring change in their lives and their community.

Resource mapping is only one tool with a limited but important objective. It will help the community to reflect on their assets and what resources, opportunities, and needs are prioritised by various types of people in the community. But it is only a tool for gathering information, and it will not guide a community through the process of deciding how to use that information. In the last lesson of this curriculum, there are recommended further resources that may help organisations and communities in the decision-making process.

How do you develop a resource map?

1. Make sure that you have representation of various interest groups and different types of people from the community present in the meeting, especially those who are often voiceless.

2. Divide the community members into smaller groups. For example, you could place the older men alone, the older women alone, the younger men alone, and the younger women alone. In some places you may want to divide people into smaller groups based on other factors. It is very important to have all community members participate irrespective of their gender, education, race, age, or disabilities. Everyone's perspective is important. Disregarding any of these categories of people may result in us hurting certain people in the community as we try to help the whole community.

3. It is helpful to have each of the small groups draw a separate resource map. They will all draw a map of the same area but each group will highlight different assets and different challenges in their maps.

4. Tell the groups to draw their community, highlighting the assets, natural resources, water sources, trees, roads, institutions, and facilities of the community and their locations. There are many different types of assets that you can remind them about (remember Lesson 7). The map should be drawn on the ground using readily available materials such as stones, sticks, leaves, fruit, water bottles, etc. They should also mark

areas of challenges and needs and areas that offer potential solutions. For example, they might mark a water source that has become polluted. If you are an outsider discussing this with the community, listen patiently and allow time for the members to discuss. Ask probing questions to stimulate their thinking about various types of assets, and ask questions about the objects they've put in their map.

5. After drawing the resource map, the smaller groups should discuss what the top five pressing needs are for their community. They should rank them according to priority. If possible, they should identify assets they drew which might be used in some way to bring a solution to the need. For example, a resource map might reveal that there are very few trees to use for firewood. But the same map might reveal plentiful water sources, and large open spaces in which to plant trees.

6. Each smaller group should present their map to the other community members. They can explain what each object is in the map, emphasizing their most important assets, as well as explaining the pressing challenges or needs.

7. The resource map should give the community encouragement and confidence that they have resources they can use to bring change. The information can now be used by the community and other outside helpers as they plan together for future projects and initiatives. Various communities will use the information gained from the resource mapping in different ways, and every community and culture has different methods in how they plan what they will do and how they will do it. But every community should be encouraged not to neglect what they have learned from the typically voiceless groups in the community during the resource mapping. If we pretend to give a voice to the powerless by including them in the resource mapping activity, but then they find out that their views did not influence any of the actual planning that was done later by community leaders, they will feel like their voices were not really heard at all. They may feel even more hurt and marginalised than they did before, and they might not bother to show up at future community meetings.

Large Group Activity- Creating a Resource Map

Find out if you have a number of training participants that are coming from the same community. These participants will be the ones to create a resource map of their community while the whole training group observes. The other training participants should participate by asking good questions and reminding the community members about the various types of assets. They can also assist in collecting objects to use in the map (for example, a water bottle could represent a water source, and a Bible could represent a church). Instruct the community members to make the resource map following the steps that were outlined.

When they have finished making the map, discuss it briefly with the participants. You are now finished with the lesson, but don't forget to explain the take-home activity.

Take-Home Activities for Lesson 15

The take- home activities will include assignments or activities that the participants should carry out in their communities, churches, or place of work, applying the lessons they have learned. The facilitator should provide detailed guidelines and clear instructions on how to go about the take-home activities.

1. **For Everyone** - Go home and practise using the resource mapping tool. Begin by gathering your family members and then reflect together on the assets of your family. Think about your family's land, buildings, household possessions, and other physical assets. But you can also consider specific opportunities and skills that are unique to each family member. Also, take time to hear from each person about pressing needs and challenges. Then make a plan together as a family to address the most important challenges using the assets and opportunities that you identified. Be sure to consider every family member's interests as you make the plan together.

2. **For Church Leaders** - Try to gather church leaders and church members from several other churches and organisations close to you in your neighborhood or area. Lead them in utilising the resource mapping tool to reflect on the assets, opportunities, and needs in your neighborhood or area. Discuss if there is a way you can work together to use your assets to try to address one of the pressing needs. Try to make a specific action plan, being sure to determine the responsible people for each task, and the time frame in which the tasks will be done. Present the conclusions of the group to your church, pray for your plan, and carry out the plan you have made.

Helping Without Hurting in Africa

Facilitator Manual

Lesson 16:
Church Benevolence Ministry

Lesson 16: Church Benevolence Ministry

In this section, you will find:

- Principles for guiding and implementing a church benevolence ministry.
- Sample intake forms for a church benevolence ministry.

Lesson Objectives:

- To learn why benevolence ministry is important in the life of a local church.
- To learn how to create clear policies and procedures for benevolence ministry in a local church setting.

Time Length: 2 Hours

Notes to the Facilitator

- Make sure you have flip chart paper and markers ready to give to the participants for the small group activities.
- Ensure that long notes, quotations, and group questions are prepared in advance and written on flip chart.
- Unless otherwise noted, all Scripture passages in **bold** should be read out loud by a participant for the whole group.
- When the participants read the selected Bible passages throughout the lesson, make brief summaries of what each Bible passage is about and what it means.
- At the end of the lesson, explain the take-home activities clearly to participants.
- If there is time at the end of the lesson, consider asking participants questions to review the key points made during the lesson.

Opening Discussion: Benevolence Ministry[1] (10 minutes)

Does anyone want to try to give a definition of benevolence ministry?

Allow a few people to answer the question and then proceed. Write brief notes about the definition on your flip chart.

Benevolence ministry is one of the many ministries a local church can engage in. It is a program that provides financial or material assistance to those in need, especially members within the local church but also to other people in the community. One of the ways we honour God is through sharing Christ's love by helping people in a tangible way. Let's look at two Bible passages that very clearly demonstrate the importance of benevolence ministry. **James 1:27** and **1 John 3:16-18**. If we truly love God and have experienced his love for us, we will also be people who love our brothers and sisters in the church as well as our neighbours in the community.

Today, churches in Africa and all over the world are faced with the challenge of many people coming to the church to ask for financial help. This is a good thing because it gives us an opportunity to preach the gospel and show the love of Christ through our care for people. Unfortunately, many of our churches today in Africa do not have a benevolence ministry, and those that have a benevolence ministry of some kind often do not have clear structures, procedures and policies. The result is that the decisions of a church about who to help are inconsistent. Without clear policies and an organised benevolence ministry, people may be helped at random, or worse, only influential people in the church will be helped.

It is important to remember that the church is made up of people and people will often be in need of assistance, and many times the expectation is that the church will be the first to help. Our churches need to be ready to help with money, resources, and time. We need to care for people not only by preaching to them, but also supporting them in times of need. Our local churches need an organised benevolence ministry with clear policies so they know to whom they should and should not give money. And remember, even when we say "no" to giving someone money, we should still seek to walk with them and partner with them in other ways.

Ask participants the question below and take brief notes of their responses on a flip chart.

1. **Does your church have a benevolence ministry?**
2. **If yes, how does your church decide whom to give money to and whom not to give money to?**
3. **If no, does your church help people with material needs in other ways?**

Facilitator Lecture: The Purpose of Benevolence Ministry (30 minutes)

What is the purpose of having a benevolence ministry? The purpose of benevolence ministry is to love people as a response to God's love for us. Jesus served his disciples by washing their feet and ultimately by dying for them for their salvation. Jesus told us to serve one another also. The intended result of our service will be that someone will have been helped with a material or physical need, and also at the same time that they would have grown in their relationship with God. In fact, benevolence ministry that is done well should help people grow in all four of their fundamental relationships – with God, self, others, and the creation.

Who should benefit from our benevolence ministries? The Bible is clear that our responsibility is first to those who are with us in the local church. Remember the circles of priority from Lesson 6. We have a responsibility to first help those closest to us including our families and fellow Christians in our church. Read **Galatians 6:2** and **6:10**. We are supposed to bear one another's burdens. We are supposed to take special care to do good to those who are with us in the family of believers. This means that church benevolence ministry is right to first focus on helping church members with their needs and challenges. These challenges could include not having enough food, needing an expensive medical operation, needing help with school fees, needing help with burial or wedding costs, or needing assistance to find a job.

While benevolence ministry can prioritise the needs of the church members, we must be careful that we do not become too focused on ourselves. We must not only look inward, but also outward. Even Galatians 6:10 says to do good to all people. We must not forsake the Great Commission. The church is not a social club where we only care about our own members. We are also supposed to reach out with love to our neighbours like the Good Samaritan did. We are supposed to seek out the lost sheep. We are supposed to befriend the outcasts of society like Jesus did. So even as we care for church members, we must make sure that we intentionally set aside a portion of our resources to help those in the community who are not members of the church.

We should care for non-church members as an act of obedience and out of love for them. But a good benevolence ministry can also be a central feature of a church's mission. What better way to point people to Christ than to show them how the church is salt and light in a community as it cares for the hurting and desperate? When people see the way your church cares for the poor, it draws people to want to be a part of the church and find out what is causing you to be so full of love. A good benevolence ministry draws people to Christ and can cause a church to grow.

However, a good benevolence ministry can also bring challenges. As your church attracts new members through the benevolence ministry, you should be prepared that many of the new people at your church might be materially poor. They might be the very people your church has been helping in the community. The result might be that your church has many people who are rich in faith, and yet materially poor. Be prepared for this and do not let it discourage you. It is the way the church has often been throughout history. Read **James 2:5** and **1 Corinthians 1:26-29**.

1. **What do these Bible passages teach us?**
2. **Some church leaders do not want their churches to be known for having many materially poor members. Why do you think they feel this way?**

Large group discussion

Ask participants the following questions and encourage them to give examples which support their answers.

1. In benevolence ministry, why should we usually avoid giving cash to the person in need of help?

2. What are the benefits of a local church giving loans to church members who are in need? What are the potential problems and complications from doing this?

As the facilitator, you can summarise the key points below if they have not already been spoken by the participants. But it is better for learning if the answers come from the participants themselves. Let them speak first, then add the ideas from the notes below that they did not mention.

In our benevolence ministries, we should generally avoid giving cash to people who come to us with material needs. Giving food, medical care, shelter, or the actual item needed is a better option. In situations where cash is required, it is better that payment is made directly to the source instead of giving it to the person requesting for help. For example, if the need is for school fees or for a hospital bill, the payment should be made directly from the church benevolence ministry to the school or hospital, but not given as cash to the student or the hospital patient. This will limit the possibility of the money being misused for other things. And doing this will limit the number of people who will try to take advantage of your benevolence ministry, people who are just looking for ways to get easy money. If the community finds out that you hand out cash, then you will never know who to trust when many people come to the church asking for handouts of money.

When you as an individual are helping a friend in need who you know well, it can be good to give cash directly as this builds trust in the relationship, showing that you respect them and trust them to use the money in the right way. The person receiving the money then practises being a good steward, making wise decisions to use that money for the purpose it was intended. But we must not think it works the same way with church benevolence ministries. Often the people who will request help are not in a personal relationship with the volunteers in the benevolence ministry. And remember that the relationship is really between the person in need and the entire church through the benevolence ministry. Every church has limited resources to give to members and to the community, so a church must not regularly hand out cash to people in need.

Loans are a very effective way to help people if you have a structured microfinance organisation, savings group, or if you are personally giving a loan to a friend you have a relationship with. Loans provide people with money at just the time they need it, so that they have enough capital to succeed in their businesses or educational opportunities. But churches with a benevolence ministry should avoid giving loans to members of the congregation and to people in the community. Loans do not work very well when being given by a church. Why is this?

First, most churches are not well equipped and trained to handle the complications of being money lenders. There are many difficult issues that will be raised such as record keeping, accountability, determining who receives loans, determining the sizes of the loans, figuring out a method of money collection, figuring out what to do when people don't repay their loans, and legal issues resulting from disputes between the church and people who have received loans.

Second, in some cases around the world where churches have given loans, it has hurt the witness of the church in the community. This happens because church members have to chase down people who have not repaid the loans. If they are strict and force people to pay with tough penalties then they receive a bad image in the community, rather than being known as a church that focuses on preaching the gospel. If they are not strict in forcing people to repay loans, then those with debts do not feel the need to repay and the church ends up losing a lot of money. It is difficult for churches to enforce loan repayments.

Third, many times church members will find themselves unable to repay the loans that they borrowed from the church. To deal with their shame and embarrassment, they will simply leave the church. They are then deprived of their community and place to hear God's Word because it was the church that gave the loans. It makes a lot more sense to leave this task of giving loans to organisations and banks so people do not get cut off from the church community simply because of failure to pay back loans.[2]

Benevolence Ministry Procedures and Policies (50 minutes)

As we mentioned at the beginning, it is important that we write policies. Benevolence ministry policies[3] are brief statements that capture the overall guidelines and procedures that will be applied when helping or offering assistance to people in need. Policies could also be thought of as rules governing the ministry.

Give some examples of policies that could be used for a church's benevolence ministry. Each policy statement should be one sentence long.

Allow the participants to answer, but you might need to give them a couple examples to get them started. You can give your own examples, or use some of these below. This is not the time to create a whole set of policies. It's only important that the participants hear several examples of policies in order to make sure that everyone understands what is meant by benevolence ministry policies. Examples include:

- We do not ever give cash directly to someone in need.
- We do not give cash directly except for when helping church families with burial expenses.
- 50% of our benevolence ministry funds should be used to help widows.
- 30% of each church offering is to be given to the benevolence fund.
- We do not help people with school fees.
- When helping someone with a medical bill, we will pay the hospital directly.

- We will give a report to the church once every month about how funds in the benevolence ministry have been used.

- Before giving to anyone, someone from the benevolence team will do fact-checking about the person's story.

It is important to have clear and well thought out policies for our benevolence ministries for several reasons:

1. Policies prevent us from giving and helping in inconsistent or random ways.

2. Policies prevent us from giving with favouritism. In some churches, only well-known families in the church receive any help at times of need. In other churches, it is only the rich or influential people who decide who to help and how to help.

3. Policies will help us to be good stewards of the limited resources that we have. We can give in the ways that will be the most effective.

4. Policies can ensure that we take into account all four fundamental relationships as we try to help. The policies will help us to avoid the mistakes we have learned about in *Helping without Hurting in Africa*.

5. Policies will allow the ministry to function smoothly and quickly, without needing an extra church meeting with all the church leaders every time a new need arises.

6. Policies will guard against benevolence ministry workers being attacked or criticised when they say "no" to giving money to someone who asks. A benevolence team representative can say: "According to our policy, we are unable to give you money at this time for your specific request. This is not just my own policy, but one that the whole church agreed upon together."

Have you noticed any of these problems in your church's ministry because you didn't have policies in place? Explain.

In summary, we need benevolence policies in order to guide our churches about when assistance should be given, who it should be given to, and how it should be given. The primary goal of benevolence policies is to give a concrete basis for decision making to those who are on the frontlines of your benevolence ministry.[4] Let's now look at some of the specific types of policies each church benevolence ministry should have.

Specific Policies

One of the most important procedures or policies for church benevolence ministry is the use of intake forms. An intake form is a sheet of paper that will be filled out when someone requests for help. Usually the intake form will be filled out by a member of the benevolence ministry team while they interview the person who is asking for assistance. An intake form allows the interviewer to gather more information about the people asking for help and what their specific needs are. Sometimes simply the process of discussing what is in the intake form will help the person in need to come up with solutions to their problem. Other times, going through the intake form will quickly reveal if the person is lying. Regardless of the situation, going through the intake form interview is an opportunity to begin building a relationship with the person in need.

The form ensures that the interview is not rushed and the benevolence ministry team will not forget to gather all the types of information necessary for making a good decision. After the intake form is filled out, the members of the benevolence ministry can meet together and decide what to do. In your manual, you can see an intake form that you can use in your church, but you can feel free to modify it. For many churches, you might choose to have a simpler and shorter form.

Review some of the key questions in the intake form, but you don't need to discuss everything in it with the participants. They will be able to read it at home.

BENEVOLENCE MINISTRY INTAKE FORM[5]

Date of First Interview ________________ Date Intake Form Completed _________

Date Benevolence Team Notified _________ Date of Response to Request __________

Information fact-checked by ________________________ Date ___________________

SECTION 1: Identifying Information

Name: ____

Age _____ Male _____ Female _____ Couple _____

Address: ___________________________________

____

Work phone: __________________ Cellphone: ____________________

Email: ____

Spouse's name: ____

Children's names and ages:

____

____

Other family members living with person:

____

Church member? ____ yes ____ no. If yes, how long? _____

If no, regular attender? ____ yes ____ no If yes, how long? _____

If not a regular attender, is this person connected to the church in any way?

____

Has this individual been previously assisted by the church? _____ yes _____ no

If yes, when?____

What was the help for? ____

What help was given and to what degree?

____

____

Did the individual receive financial assistance? _____ yes _____ no

Has this individual received assistance from other churches/agencies in the past year?

_____ yes _____ no

If yes, what was the help for and what form did the help take?___________________

____

List names and phone numbers of personal or pastoral references who could be contacted for further information regarding this individual (ask for verbal permission to contact these references):

____

____

SECTION 2: Current Situation and Reason for Request

What is the presenting problem as stated by the individual?

____

____

____

____

____

How long has this problem been going on?

____

Has the individual recently been victimized by abusive or corrupt people in ways that have created or contributed to the problem?

____

____

Has the individual done or not done anything that has created or contributed to the problem?

____

____

____

Other important details of the situation:

____

____

What steps has this person taken to remedy the situation?

____

____

____

What is the individual's specific request of the church?

____

____

What does this person think needs to be changed in the situation and/or in themselves?

____

____

Is this person willing to work with the church to create an action plan aimed at solving their current problems as well as working to help prevent this problem from occurring again?

____

____

This form was started by: ____________________________
on (date) ______________

Person assigned to follow up: ______________________________

SECTION 3: Detailed Context and History

(You may want to wait until future meetings to obtain some or all of the following information)

Education/Work History

Current job held: ____________________ How long at present job? __________

Work history:

____

____

Highest level of education and degrees held:

____

Other training certificates or programs completed:

____

Financial Position

Assets

Current Savings in the bank ____________________________

Cash on hand and Mobile Money ____________________________

Food reserves at home ____________________________

Vehicle assets ____________________________

Animal assets ____________________________

Land assets ____________________________

Other assets ____________________________

TOTAL VALUE OF ASSETS = ____________________________

Income

Monthly Income ____________________________

Monthly gifts from relatives, friends ____________________________

NGO support ____________________________

Government assistance programs ______________________

TOTAL MONTHLY INCOME = ______________________

Monthly Expenses

Food ______________________

Water ______________________

Housing ______________________

Electricity ______________________

Cooking Gas / Charcoal / Firewood ______________________

Telephone airtime ______________________

Transportation costs ______________________

Ongoing medicine and treatments ______________________

Supermarket expenses like soap, toothpaste, sugar, paper, etc. ______________________

Animal Feeds and treatments ______________________

School Fees ______________________

Clothing / Shoes ______________________

ATM fees / Bank Fees / Other organisations or clubs fees ______________________

Personal giving to church and other charities ______________________

Insurance ______________________

TOTAL EXPENSES = ______________________

Housing Situation

Does this person rent or own? ______________

Who do they live with? ______________________

Does this person have any dependents living with them? If so, who?

____

Is this person homeless? ______ yes ______ no

Spiritual, Social, and Emotional/Mental Health

Describe person's Christian experience/spiritual journey, if applicable:

____

____

What sort of social supports does this person have?

____

Does this individual have any family living nearby? ______ yes ______ no

If yes, who? ______________________

Does this individual have a church small group? ______ yes ______ no

If yes, name and phone number of leader ____________________________________

Do one or two close friends know of the person's situation? ______ yes ______ no

Is this person seeing a counselor? ______ yes _______ no

If yes, who? ____

Has this person ever been diagnosed and/or treated for a mental illness?

______ yes ______ no If yes, explain: ______________________________________

____

Is this person currently taking any prescribed medications? ______ yes ______ no

Has this person experienced trauma at some point in their life? If yes, describe:

____

____

SECTION 4: Church Assessment and Response to This Request

- Remember that poverty has multiple causes: the individual's behaviour, abusive or exploitive people, oppressive systems, and demonic forces. In many cases, more than one of these causes are at work.

- However, to the extent that the person's own behaviour is a contributor, you should try to gauge their receptivity to taking actions to make positive changes in their life. In such cases, check the one that most applies:

This person/family believes:

1. ______ There is no deep-seated problem that I/we need to address.

2. ______ There may be a problem, but I'm/we aren't the one(s) who need to change.

3. ______ Yes there is a problem, but I'm/we doubtful it can be changed.

4. ______ Yes there is a problem, and I/we can be a part of making changes.

5. ______ Yes there is a problem, and I/we are very ready to take steps to make changes.

Category 1 or 2: This person/family is not ready to do the hard work of: (1) identifying areas that they need to change, and (2) making those changes with your church's help. They are not ready to create an action plan. Their lack of readiness to change might disqualify them from receiving assistance from the church at this time. But that doesn't mean ignoring them. Through continued contact and conversation, they might develop more openness to change.

Category 3–5: This person is ready to create an action plan.

You may find that people in category 3 or 4 complete the action plan but then do not follow through on their goals. Do not give up! They will probably need extra encouragement and support, and their goals and time frames may need to be adjusted. If they do not make sufficient progress on their goals even with repeated encouragement or help, then you and your church may need to stop providing the material and possible human resources that you committed to in the action plan. But you would continue to encourage them and build the relationship.

Initial church assessment of issues that need to be dealt with that contributed to the current problem:

____

____

____

____

1. Will a failure to provide immediate assistance likely result in serious harm to this person? ____

____

2. Is the person largely responsible for their situation? ________________________

____

3. Will providing immediate financial assistance help or hinder such empowerment (in the 4 relationships)? _________________________

In addition to receiving assistance, is the person willing to discuss an action plan and way forward to make changes to their situation with the help of the church?

____

____

Initial decision made by the benevolence ministry:

____

____

____

Report on the response made by the benevolence ministry and the impact:

____

____

____

____

Report from future follow-up visit and conversations:

____

____

____

Intake form filed in records by __________________________

Date________________________

You can see that the intake form mentions an "action plan". An action plan is a written plan made by the person being helped together with the benevolence team. The action plan consists of goals which are changes the person wants to see in his or her life, together with activities which the person will do to see the goals achieved. There is a sample action plan form in the "Further Reflection" section at the end of the lesson. Do not read it now, but read it when you go home, and your benevolence ministry can feel free to use it together with the intake form.

Find out if they have any questions about the intake form and then proceed.

After completing the first interview and intake form, it is important to do at least a little fact checking to find out if the person's story is true. Sometimes this can be as easy as calling the school or hospital to find out that the person truly has a bill that needs to be paid. Other times it may necessitate a visit to the person's home and family. Visits should be done as a team when possible.

As a member of the benevolence team, why is it important to visit someone's home with at least one other member of the team?

Some answers could include: for security, for more than one set of eyes, so that the person/family cannot pressure one person to do what they want, so that the one person cannot be accused of favouritism or making a bad judgement on behalf of the benevolence team, and so that you don't have one person visiting another person of the opposite sex alone.

You will need many other good policies that will set clear standards and guidelines for the benevolence ministry. When you go home, you should ask the members of your church benevolence ministry team these questions in order to come up with your policy statements. These are some examples, but you might think of more questions to consider as well.[6]

1. What is our purpose statement for our church benevolence ministry?
2. What is our definition of poverty?
3. Who will lead and participate in the benevolence ministry? Will they be church leaders or volunteers or both?
4. How will the money used in the benevolence ministry be raised? What percentage of the church budget or offerings will go to the benevolence ministry?
5. What percentage of the benevolence ministry budget will be spent on church members and what percentage spent on others in the community?
6. What will our intake process look like as people come with requests?
7. Will we always require the person we are assisting to make an action plan for change? Or are there some cases where an action plan is not necessary?
8. Who are the target groups that our church feels called to help?
9. Will we give assistance to those who are not Christians, like Muslims, Hindus, and those practicing African traditional religions?
10. In what situations will we respond with financial or material assistance?

11. How many times will we help the same person or family with financial or material assistance?
12. Will we focus on relief, rehabilitation, or development, or a little of each?
13. How will our ministry help people grow in their relationship with God? With others? With self? With the creation?
14. When people ask for our help but they do not have a job, what steps will we take to help them find meaningful work?
15. How will we respond to people who are capable of working but are unwilling to work?
16. How will we publicise our policies to our church and discuss together in order to ensure their agreement?
17. Will we advertise our ministry to the community? Will we inform the community publicly about our policies?
18. What form will our assistance take? (Cash, food, paying bills directly, etc.)
19. Will we help church members with expenses for weddings or burials?
20. Will we place a higher priority on helping church leaders in need compared to other church members?
21. How will we give regular updates and reports to the church?
22. When we say "no" to giving financial assistance, what kinds of activities can we still do with people in order to try to help them?
23. What steps will we take to confirm people's stories before responding? Who is responsible for doing this fact-checking?
24. When and how will we utilise other ministries, churches, government program, and organisations? Which needs will we try to meet, and for which needs will we send people to other organisations?

Are there any other important questions that you think should be considered when making church benevolence ministry policies?

Even after looking at those questions, it can be difficult to picture what benevolence ministry policies look like in real life. Listen to this example from a church in Nairobi, Kenya called Christ Compassion Ministry. Here are a few of their policies from their benevolence ministry. They call it their "Church Welfare Policy".

- One policy states that money is raised for the fund by having each church member pay 100 Kenyan shillings ($1 USD) to the fund per month. They give to church members in times of crises such as during the death of a loved one and hospitalisation due to sickness.
- One policy states that the amount of financial support given to a family who has lost a spouse, children, or parents will be 20,000 Kenyan shillings.
- Another policy states that the amount given to a family who has lost a brother or sister will be 14,000 Kenyan shillings.
- For times of sickness and hospitalisation, the policies state that in addition to financial

support, church members will visit the sick person in the hospital and pray for healing.

- Another policy states that church members will all be encouraged to enrol in health insurance on a regular basis. The total written set of policies for this church is 6 pages long.

Remember, each of our churches will have different policies depending on their context and how God leads them by his Word and his Spirit. The important thing is that you go home and discuss together with your church members and prayerfully set policies for your benevolence ministry. Making effective and efficient policies cannot be a one-person show but needs the participation of all stakeholders. This will promote ownership. Once the policies are in place, leaders should make sure that the policies are adhered to in order for the ministry to be effective at helping materially poor people.

Concluding Advice

- Remember to try to help people **identify** the gifts and resources God has given to them.
- Give to people in a way that will **avoid creating dependency**.
- Remember to help **holistically**. Even in situations where you don't give money, you can still teach people job skills, watch their children while they work, invite them to a small group at church, pray for them, help them reconcile with people they have hurt, help them plant their gardens, invite them to your home for a meal, etc.
- **Celebrate change**, and encourage people who have followed through on their action plans.
- Sometimes, even after all we have learned in *Helping Without Hurting in Africa*, it is still really hard to know what to do in a given situation. Should we give or should we not give? In such difficult situations, it is better to make a mistake of giving than to make a mistake of not giving. As Christians, God calls us to love people and give generously even to people who don't deserve it, just like God loves us and gives generously to us even though we don't deserve it. **It is better to make a mistake on the side of generosity**.
- Remember the most important thing is to **point people to Jesus Christ**. Do not neglect this when caring for people's physical needs. Take time to pray with people and speak to them the gospel.

Take-Home Activities for Lesson 16

The take-home activities will include assignments or activities that the participants should carry out in their communities, churches, or place of work, applying the lessons they have learned. The facilitator should provide detailed guidelines and clear instructions on how to go about the take-home activities.

1. **If your church has a benevolence ministry:**
   Find out whether there are any policies written down. If you are able, join the benevolence ministry team and help them to write detailed policies using this lesson as a guide, or to improve on the policies already there. Set a good example by contributing financially to the benevolence fund yourself.

2. **If your church does not yet have a benevolence ministry:**
   Consult with the leaders of your church and with church members, and suggest the idea of beginning a church benevolence ministry. If the church agrees to start a benevolence ministry, offer to take the lead by joining the team and helping the team to write detailed policies using this lesson as a guide. Set a good example by contributing financially to the benevolence fund yourself.

Small Group Discussion (30 minutes)

Read out loud the questions that they will be answering and make sure they understand them.

Divide them up into groups of 5 people (anywhere from 3-6 people per group). They can be the same groups as before, or you can put them into new groups. They will not be presenting their answers to anyone.

If you have organised the whole workshop to take longer than what has been outlined, then feel free to give the participants a longer time for discussion.

Remember to move around and listen in with the groups as they discuss. Be available to answer their questions. You can give guidance or input if necessary during their discussions, but they have heard you talk a lot, so try to let them do the talking now.

Remind them periodically about how much time remains for their discussion.

Discuss the following scenarios. What would be the best way to respond and help as a church benevolence team? What benevolence policies would it help to have in place to be ready for such scenarios?

A. Michael is a 20-year-old member of your church. He lost both of his parents to HIV when he was five years old and was raised by his grandparents. They have always struggled to be able to provide for his needs. Michael has been admitted into university to study engineering. He asks the benevolence team if the church might be willing to pay for his school fees. Though he has been working as a casual laborer doing construction work in town, the little money he gets he uses to take care of buying food for himself and his grandparents.

B. Amit and Geeta are a married couple in your church. They are involved in a land dispute with a neighbour who they say is trying to change the boundaries of their land. They do not have money for a lawyer, so they ask the church to give them financial assistance for the lawyer fees. Their neighbour in the land dispute is a member of another church in the area.

C. Grace is 35 years old and not a member of your church. One day she shows up at your church, crying and scared, to talk to the pastor. She is asking the church to take care of her. She has no money with her. Her husband has been abusing her, and you are able to see the injuries to her body. She is worried that if she goes home, he will kill her. Grace admits she has a drinking problem and her husband is angry at her for using money for alcohol.

D. Francis and Rose are a married couple, and faithful members of your church who serve in various ministries. They are well respected. Rose's brother and sister-in-law have a daughter who was born deaf. The daughter has an opportunity through an NGO program to get a cochlear implant that will allow her partial hearing. The heavily subsidized price is $5,000 USD. Francis and Rose ask your church if the church can contribute financial assistance through the benevolence fund or a special freewill offering for the family.

E. Roland and Divine are an unmarried couple who just began attending your church six months ago. Roland talks to your pastor and asks if the church can help him and his family over the next few months. He says he recently lost his job at a phone company when he reported a colleague involved in corruption, but the matter was covered up. He says he is looking for another job, but in the meantime, he doesn't know how to feed his family or pay for his children's school fees.

Further Reflection

Read this section at home for further learning.

On the next page is a sample "Action Plan Form". This is what you could use with a person who will be helped by the benevolence ministry, but who has agreed to make an action plan to work on changing his or her situation. You are allowed to modify the form as needed.

BENEVOLENCE MINISTRY ACTION PLAN[7]

SECTION 1: Reflection

A. Your Future

How would you like your life situation to be different or improved four to six months from now?

Goal 1: ____

Goal 2: ____

B. Abilities and Resources:

What are some abilities and resources you have that could help you get to where you want to be four to six months from now?

____

____

____

____

C. Obstacles:

It is good to be aware of things that might get in the way of you getting to where you want to be four to six months from now. It can be helpful to specifically list possible key obstacles. Doing so can help all of us be aware of them and create plans to overcome them or at least lessen their impact.

Internal obstacles (things about your personality or habits that could block or slow progress)

____

____

____

External obstacles (people or situations that could block or slow progress)

____

____

____

SECTION 2: Planning for the Future Together

A. Things You Want to Do:

Steps that will move you to where you want to be in four to six months:

Goal 1 ______________________________

What specific things can you do? When will you do them?

(a) ______________________________

(b) ______________________________

(c) ______________________________

What specific things can the church do? When?

(a) ______________________________

(b) ______________________________

(c) ______________________________

Goal 2 ______________________________

What specific things can you do? When will you do them?

(a) ______________________________

(b) ______________________________

(c) ______________________________

What specific things can the church do? When?

(a) ______________________________

(b) ______________ ______________

(c) ______________ ______________

SECTION 3: Encouragement and Accountability

A. Supportive People

It is hard for most of us to make changes alone. Therefore, as part of helping you towards your goals, we have an individual/team who would like to support you through prayers and encouragement. They have promised to:

☐ Pray for you every day.

☐ Talk with you at least once a week. This will be to see how you are doing and give you input as you desire.

☐ Keep information confidential as is appropriate.

Would you be willing to have an individual/team support you in your goals? __________

Name of supportive individual/team leader_____________ Phone number _________

B. Follow-up:

Plans fail if they get lost in the busy nature of life, so staying in communication with each other is very important. Normally communication will be more frequent in the beginning of implementing the action plan to ensure that momentum is gained.

When and where can we next get together to check how things are going?

____

Other conditions of agreement:

____

Signature of individual:

____

Date ________________________

Signature of church representative:

____

Date ________________________

Helping Without Hurting in Africa

Facilitator Manual

Lesson 17: Urban Ministry: Opportunities and Challenges

Lesson 17: Urban Ministry: Opportunities and Challenges

In this section, you will find:

- Summaries of the advantages and disadvantages of urban ministry.
- Overview of the issues around caring for orphans and vulnerable children.

Lesson Objectives:

- To understand the church's role in the growth and development of Africa's cities.
- To understand the opportunities and challenges for urban church ministry.
- To understand the risks faced by orphans and vulnerable children in the city and how we can care for them.

Time Length: 2.5 hours

Notes to the Facilitator

- Ensure that long notes, quotations, and group questions are prepared in advance and written on flip chart paper.
- Unless otherwise noted, all Scripture passages in **bold** should be read out loud by a participant for the whole group.
- When the participants read the selected Bible passages throughout the lesson, make brief summaries of what each Bible passage is about and what it means.
- At the end of the lesson, explain the take-home activities clearly to participants.
- If there is time at the end of the lesson, consider asking participants questions to review the key points made during the lesson.

Opening Discussion (15 minutes)

For the first question below, allow every participant to answer. But each of them should answer in only one word. If anyone tries to give an explanation, gently stop them and allow each participant to answer. You can record their answers on a flip chart. Answers might include words like: excited, stressed, or afraid. You can try to give a summary statement afterwards which captures the most common answers.

How does it make you feel to live in a large city or travel to a large city? Tell us your answer using only one word.

After everyone has answered, instruct the participants to pair up with another participant. In their groups of two they should discuss the following questions in 2-3 minutes. The participants will not report their answers to the large group.

Discuss with a Partner

1. What city do you live in or what city is nearest to where you live?

2. What makes you happy about your city?

3. What makes you sad about your city?

Urban Growth in Africa

When we talk about urban ministry, we are talking about ministry in cities. What is a city? Simply put, a "city" or an "urban area" is a place in which a large number of people live fairly close together.[1] When we talk about urban ministry, we are talking about doing ministry in the big cities of our countries. Specifically, in this lesson we will look at how to spread the good news of Jesus Christ through our words and our actions in cities, and we will pay special attention to how to reach out in love to materially poor people in cities. Remember the goal is that people would come to know Jesus Christ, and that they would improve in their four fundamental relationships, with God, self, others, and the creation, and that they would be able to use their gifts and work in order to take care of their needs.

Before we discuss urban ministry, let's examine the recent urban growth in Africa. Cities are growing rapidly because of the continuous mass movement of people from rural areas to urban centres. People are migrating to cities in huge numbers in search of jobs, and looking for better basic services like health care, education, shelter and sanitation. This migration, combined with high birth-rates in many countries in Africa, has led to a dramatic increase in the population of African cities.

Here are some statistics:

- In 1980, only 20% of Africa's population lived in urban areas.[2] As of 2014, that number had increased to 40%.[3] By 2050 it is projected that 55% of people in Africa will live in urban areas.[4]
- In Sub-Saharan countries, on average 60% of the urban populations live in slums.[5]
- Only 16% of urban households in Africa have permanent roofs.[6]
- The percentage of residents in African cities who have access to piped clean water has actually been going down as urbanisation continues. Only 34% had access as of 2010.[7]
- Urban transport in cities in Africa is 42% more expensive than in cities in the rest of the world, largely due to inefficient public modes of transportation such as motorcycles and minibuses or taxis which carry small numbers of people.[8]

- In sub-Saharan Africa, it is estimated that 60% of the urban labour force is employed in informal work such as small-scale selling, minor services, or work in unregistered factories, at extremely low incomes.[9]

These statistics present us with challenges, and they may seem overwhelming, but good things are happening in African cities as well. We will hear some stories of change and transformation in this lesson, and we will look at what our churches can do to make an impact in our cities.

Should Christians Care about Cities? (40 minutes)

Before we go forward, we should stop and ask: "Should Christians care about cities?" Some Christians view cities as evil places, where there is rampant corruption, crime, and sexual immorality. They look at cities as places of sin which Christians should avoid so we are not corrupted by them. These are important concerns. We shouldn't assume that the Bible teaches us to engage in urban ministry.

What does the Bible teach? Let's look at some key passages about cities throughout the Bible. First let's read **Genesis 11:1-9** and **Genesis 13:11-13**. And then we will look at a few other passages about cities as we go through the whole Bible story.

From these two passages in Genesis, what do we learn about some of the first cities?

The correct answer is that these cities in Genesis were pictured largely negatively, as places where people did evil, places where people made names for themselves rather than glorifying God's name. God brought destruction to these cities. In contrast, God's people at this time, like Abraham and his family, were in rural areas and spent a lot of time wandering as nomads.

After God rescued the Israelites from Egypt, he gave them commands about how they should live in the Promised Land. Let's read **Joshua 20:1-3**.

How are cities in this passage pictured differently from the cities in Genesis?

The correct answer is that these specific cities were to be cities of refuge and safety. They are places for people to be kept safe from mob justice and receive true justice and mercy. Cities with walls and a bigger population could protect an accused person and conduct a trial in a way that rural areas could not.[10] Through this passage, we start to see that not all cities were to be viewed as places of evil, especially in Israel.

As we move forward in the biblical story, remember that the Israelite people became a kingdom and a nation. And one city in particular was very important in the nation of Israel. Read **1 Kings 14:21**. Jerusalem was the city where the king ruled, but more importantly Jerusalem became the dwelling place for God's Name. In Babel, people made a city in order to glorify themselves, but Jerusalem was a city God chose for his glory.[11] It became a holy city, the place where the temple was built. It was the place the Israelites had to travel to for religious feasts and festivals for worship. This is an extremely positive view of at least one city. We learn that not all cities are fortresses of evil, but some are places where people glorify God.

Next, let's think about one of the prophets, Jonah. God called Jonah to preach judgement to the Ninevites so that they would repent and be saved from God's punishment. Nineveh was full of very evil people. Here again we have a negative view of a city. But there is more we need to understand from this story. Read **Jonah 3:10** and **4:10-11**.

How would you describe God's feelings towards the evil city of Nineveh?

The correct answer is that although God was angry at the sins of the Ninevites, he still cared about them and loved them. That is why he did not simply destroy them, but sent Jonah to preach to them so that they would repent. God cares about all the people he has made. Because there was a great amount of people living in the large city of Nineveh, God had great concern for Nineveh. Cities are more full of the image of God than any other place on earth.[12] Jonah finally went to the city of Nineveh, but he did not want to. He wanted the Ninevites to be destroyed because they were Israel's enemies. He did not love the city of Nineveh like God loved the city. This story teaches us that if we care about people, we must also care about cities. We should love even the cities that are filled with very sinful people.

Let's keep moving forward in the biblical story. Remember that soon after the Israelite Kingdom was formed, both the kings and the people often failed to worship God rightly. The Israelites continued to worship idols, mistreat the poor, and engage in sexual immorality and corruption. God forgave them again and again with great patience. But finally, God's judgement came upon Israel for their sins. God first allowed the Assyrian nation, and then later the Babylonian nation, to come and conquer all of Israel and Judah. Many of the people were taken away to Babylon in exile. The Babylonian Empire was the major enemy of Israel, and the capital city of Babylon was a city full of idolatry and sin. Many Bible scholars think that Babel and Babylon refer to the same evil city. When the Israelites were taken as slaves to this great city of their enemy, what did God tell them to do? Let's read **Jeremiah 29:4-14**.

What specific commands does God give to the Israelite exiles in this passage?

Allow the participants to answer first, and then teach what follows.

In contrast to what the false prophets were promising the exiles, God spoke through Jeremiah to tell the Israelites that they would be in Babylon for a long time, for 70 years. They were not supposed to sit around and wait for God to save them. Instead, God told them to plan to be there a long time. They were to work hard, plant gardens, get married, and have children. They were supposed to pray for Babylon. And surprisingly, God told them to seek the peace and prosperity of the city of Babylon. If the city prospers, they too will prosper. God did not want them to copy the sinful lifestyles of the Babylonians, but he wanted them to be a witness to the Babylonians. The Israelites were to engage in the life of the city and try to develop it and see it prosper. At the same time, they were to keep their distinct identity by increasing in number, and continue to worship God alone.

Listen to how the author Timothy Keller explains this passage:

> God is still primarily concerned with his plan of salvation. He must establish his people; the gospel must be proclaimed; human beings must be reconciled to him. Yet he assures his people that serving the good of this pagan city is part of this very plan: 'If it prospers, you too will prosper' (Jer 29:7). Loving and serving the city not only shows love and compassion; doing so also strengthens the hands of the people of God, who bear the message of the gospel to the world. Because the Jews in exile obeyed this command, they accrued the influence and leverage needed to eventually return to and restore their homeland. God ties, as it were, the fortunes of the people of God to the effectiveness of their urban ministry.[13]

We must consider that today we are in a similar situation to the Jews in Babylon. Our citizenship is in Heaven, yet we remain in this broken world which rebels against God. But instead of running away from the world by running away from cities, we should love the cities of our nations. We must engage in the life of those cities and seek to see them prosper. As we do so, it is part of the way we witness to the people in those cities. Christians must work in cities for the peace, justice, and prosperity of their neighbours, loving them in word and deed.[14]

Let's move ahead now to the New Testament. We see in the book of Acts that the gospel was primarily taken to new places through cities. Paul and the other missionaries travelled from city to city to plant churches. Paul viewed the cities as the key areas that needed to be reached in order for the gospel to also travel to the rural areas. In fact, after reaching the key cities, Paul was willing to say he had no more work to do in those regions. Let's read what he says in **Romans 15:18-24.**

Last, let's think about the end of the Bible, Revelation chapters 21 and 22. We won't read those chapters right now, but they give us a beautiful picture of eternal life. We see a new Heaven and new Earth, and God and his people joined together. The central image in these chapters is God's Holy City, the New Jerusalem. We read about the city's size, the city's beauty, the tree of life in the city, and the Lamb living in the city. We saw at the beginning of the Bible that God's people were wandering nomads. Abraham travelled around without a permanent home, and later the Israelites wandered in the wilderness. But then God directed his people to build cities, and to build a nation.[15] Later, God even wanted his people to love the cities of their enemies, Nineveh and Babylon. After Jesus died and rose again, he sent his apostles out in mission and they targeted the great cities of the Roman world. Finally, at the end of the biblical story in the book of Revelation, we find that the perfect home for God's people is a city, a city where God dwells.

In your region, what are the key cities that need more churches so that we can reach the entire region with the gospel?

In the biblical story, God's people begin in a garden, but they end up in a city. The movement is not from a garden to a garden. And it is not from a garden to a city and then back to a garden. The overall movement in God's redemptive plan is from a garden to a city, so urban ministry plays a very special role in God's story.

Summary

From the biblical story, we have seen that some cities are set up in rebellion against God and they can be places of great evil. But we have also seen that cities can be places of refuge or worship of God when God's people are at work in those cities. In most cities, there will be both great evil and great good happening at once. And we have seen that God calls us to love the cities that we find ourselves in. We must not be like Jonah who preached only out of duty, but rather we must preach with a heart of love for our cities. We must pray for our cities, look for the good in our cities, engage in the life of our cities, serve our cities, and bring development to our cities so that they prosper and so that we prosper. We must not fall into the sins we see around us in our cities, but keep our Christian identities and preach the gospel without fear. And as we do so, we play a role in the overall movement of God's redemptive plan, which moves from a garden to a city. All of this gives us the theological foundation that we need in order to do urban ministry. Urban ministry is about loving the people of our cities in our words and our deeds as part of God's redemptive plan.

1. **What would it look like specifically for your church to seek the peace and prosperity of your city (or the city nearest you)?**
2. **If your church suddenly disappeared from your city, would anyone notice? Would anyone say, "How is our community going to survive without this church?"[16]**

Urban Ministry: Opportunities and Challenges (20 minutes)

Urban churches and their pastors face particular challenges in the city that they would not face in rural areas. These challenges can be physical, emotional, and spiritual. But there are advantages to living in the city as well. And urban churches have unique opportunities for ministry and partnership that many rural churches do not.

Discuss the questions below as a large group and write their responses on the flip chart so that you have one list of opportunities and one list of challenges.

1. **What are some specific challenges that urban churches and leaders face in ministry because of being in the city?**
2. **What are some of the unique ministry opportunities and benefits that urban churches and leaders experience because of being in the city?**

After the participants have answered, you can list any of the points below they did not mention, but don't repeat what was already explained.

Challenges

1. **Material poverty**. Cities in Africa have many materially poor people living in slums and many are without meaningful work. People come from the rural areas into the cities looking for a better life, but some of them end up in worse living conditions in the city. Many church planters and urban pastors find it difficult to lead churches in the city because there are so many materially poor people asking for help, and often the church members are materially poor themselves. Some church leaders will be overwhelmed by the needs of so many people and frustrated at their inability to fix all the problems that they see. Churches often feel unequipped to know how to help orphans, homeless people, refugees, prostitutes and other types of people they are faced with in the city.

2. City land is much **more expensive** and generally the cost of living is higher in cities. This affects both the church property, and the housing costs for church leaders.

3. **Diversity**. The city is home to various types of people, with different languages and cultures, and different economic and educational levels. This requires church leaders in urban churches to be more educated than rural pastors in order to communicate effectively to well-educated church members. Church leaders will also have to be knowledgeable about different cultures so as to reach people of different cultures. Church services may need to be interpreted into multiple languages. Church unity can be difficult with so many different types of people in the church. It is hard for churches to adapt to being multi-ethnic and multi-cultural.

4. City residents are often **more mobile** than people living in rural areas. Some church members cannot be at church every week. People who serve in important positions at church may suddenly move to another city, leaving the pastor with the responsibility of replacing that person.

5. **Competition**. There is more competition between churches in the sense that people have so many different churches to choose from and the choice may depend on what the church offers.

6. Living in cities, a person is more likely to experience **discrimination, crime, and violence**.

7. Many cities are **loud, crowded, dirty, and stressful.** Some people find this exciting. But for many people it can be overwhelming, frustrating, and uncomfortable. If you move to a city for ministry you might never feel truly "at home" there.

8. In the city there are more **conflicts** between the church and the government. Sometimes the church speaks out against injustices done by the government and this brings tension between the church and the state. This can result in suspension of church activities or the arrest of church leaders.[17]

9. **Distractions**. Cities are full of new sights and opportunities for entertainment. It is easy for people to become distracted and materialistic with less interest in spiritual matters. A church event which might attract hundreds of people in a rural area, might attract very few people in the city as people are busy and have many more options for how to spend their time.

10. In cities there tends to be more **conflict between people of different religions**, especially between Christians and Muslims.

Opportunities:

1. **Large population.** The city provides the church with the opportunity to reach out to a large population of people, many of whom are in walking distance.

2. **Sharing space**. A city church building may be shared with other groups also in need of space, making the building multi-purpose. This might give the church an opportunity to save money or an opportunity to interact and witness to other groups. In some cases, the church can even let another group use the building for free or for a low-cost in order to help them and as a way to build relationships with other groups of people.

3. The city is full of **skilled and resourceful people**. Urban churches can utilise these people to reach out to the poor and also to serve the church through their unique skills, social networks, and their financial giving.

4. **Partnership**. There are many opportunities for urban churches to partner with other churches and faith-based institutions which widen the church's ability to offer services to support materially poor people. Additionally, churches can work together to hold joint worship services and outreach events to make a bigger impact.

5. **Infrastructure**. There is usually better infrastructure and services in the cities including better roads, plumbing, healthcare, schools, and telecommunications.

6. In cities, **people tend to be more willing to change**, as opposed to rural areas where people hold more closely to traditions. This means people might be more open to hearing about the Christian faith, and more willing to change behaviour so that they can grow and develop in their four fundamental relationships.

7. Doing ministry in a city has a **multiplier effect**. If you reach a few people in a city with the gospel, you will indirectly reach the surrounding rural areas as these city people travel to their original homes in rural areas and bring the gospel with them.

8. Cities are full of **strategic people** that the church needs to reach. This includes the youth who often make up the majority of the urban population, cultural leaders in charge of companies and the media, and unreached people groups who have not had many chances to hear the gospel.

9. **Unique ministries**. The human suffering due to poverty, crime, and immorality in cities provides the church with unique opportunities to share the gospel in word and in deed. The list of potential ministries of an urban church are almost endless. In rural areas, the options are much more limited. In the city, there are many types of holistic ministries to choose from, where you have an opportunity to preach the gospel and at the same time help people with their physical needs. These opportunities include prison ministry, hospital ministry, helping unemployed people find work, children's Bible school programs, sports ministry, community service projects, and hosting concerts. It can mean reaching out to various types of people including prostitutes, homeless people, street children, refugees, security personnel, tourists, university students from other countries, and those addicted to drugs or alcohol.

Facing the Challenges and Seizing the Opportunities

For some of us, working in the city sounds terrifying, uncomfortable and difficult. This is a common feeling, but we must overcome it with God's help. We need to look to Christ as our example. Jesus gave up his glory in Heaven to become a human being. He walked among us, spoke our languages, wore our clothes, and ate our food. He was even homeless throughout the time of his ministry. In order to save us, he became like us. He had to become human in order to take the punishment for human beings. Jesus was ridiculed, betrayed, beaten and crucified for our salvation. As we take part in God's mission of redemption in this world, we must also be willing to adapt and become like the people we are trying to reach. We need to humble ourselves, deny ourselves, and be willing to sacrifice. Are we willing to live in the cities they live in? Are we willing to learn their languages, eat their food, breathe the same pollution they breathe, face the same dangers of crime, and deal with the same traffic jams? This is also what the apostle Paul did. Read **1 Corinthians 9:19-23**. We need leaders who are willing to sacrifice their comfort in order to bring transformation to cities in Africa.

Many church planters prefer to start new churches in rural areas. And many churches in rural areas easily get comfortable and forget about the people who need to be reached in cities. If we do not live with materially poor people in the cities, how will we get to know them and build relationships? We cannot solve the problems of the city from far away. We cannot simply send gifts. We must relate with the materially poor and live with or among them if we want to see real transformation. We need to encourage more church planters to move to the cities. And for those of us who are urban church leaders, we should focus on the strategic opportunities for ministry in cities and participate in identifying solutions to city problems instead of complaining about them. Just as we encourage materially poor people to focus on their assets rather than their problems, we, as urban churches, should do the same thing. We can put our trust in our gracious God who will be with us to help us every step of the way.

Orphans and Vulnerable Children (30 minutes)

There are over 52 million orphans in Africa as of 2017.[18] Many of them are in our cities. Some are homeless, some beg to drivers stuck in traffic jams, and some are stealing in order to survive. Living in the cities in this way has exposed these orphans and vulnerable children (also known as OVCs) to many risks. One of the issues that will confront almost every urban church is the dilemma of trying to figure out how to care for orphans and street children who live in their city, and particularly those who spend time in the neighbourhood of the church.

Ask the participants the questions below and take note of their answers on a flip chart.

1. **Briefly explain the risks faced by orphans and vulnerable children in the city?**
2. **What is the best way for local churches to support orphans and vulnerable children in the city?**

After the participants have answered, you can share any points in the following notes that were not already shared by the participants.

Risks Faced by OVCs

- Health risks because of lack of food and shelter, and inability to access medical services. This can result in malnutrition, stunted growth, or disease.
- Exploitation and abuse including child labour and trafficking, child sexual harassment/ prostitution, and early marriages or pregnancies.
- Lack of parental care, guidance, and teaching.
- Lack of access to quality education or no education at all in many cases.
- Psychological challenges like stigmatisation, trauma, fear, and low self-esteem, as well as other emotional problems and disorders.

How We Can Support OVCs

- The local church should be like a family for orphans and for street children who don't have families or are away from them. They should feel cared for and loved by church members.
- Church members should be patient and forgiving when dealing with misbehaving street children. They should talk to authorities when necessary but discipline and deal with the children in love rather than anger.
- Churches should reach out to OVCs by helping them with both their spiritual and physical needs. Church members should preach the gospel to them and help them to grow in their four fundamental relationships.
- Church leaders should try to find out where the family members or relatives of street children and orphans live. When possible, church leaders should try to reunite OVCs with their family or relatives in the hope that they can resume living with them. Sometimes church leaders will need to work with charitable organisations and civil servants to accomplish this difficult work.
- Churches can work through official government channels to connect children to families who are willing to adopt them. Ideally, some families of the church will also adopt children, treating them as their very own, even though not related by blood.
- Churches can give OVCs educational support. This might mean paying for school fees and other scholastic materials. It could also mean starting mission schools hosted by local churches that offer subsidized or free education to OVCs.
- Churches can offer some health support. Churches could provide access to medical care to OVCs by paying for their medical bills or forming partnerships with health facilities to enable OVCs free access to medical care. Some churches may be able to start their own clinics that can help OVCs. Care must be taken not to simply hand out medication to children who may go and sell it to others.
- Churches can offer psychological support. Churches can build relationships with specific children and offer them counselling services.
- Churches can engage in advocacy. Churches can speak to government officials as well as organisations to ask for better OVC policies, better funding and care, and integration of OVC support in government programs.

Orphanages

Let's take a few minutes to discuss orphanages as one way in which we can care for vulnerable children. In recent years, there has been a lot of criticism against orphanages. Some people are criticizing orphanages for the abuses which happen at many of them, and others are criticizing orphanages because they say that there are better ways to care for orphans. Some countries in Africa are working to reduce the number of orphanages in their countries and care for orphans in other ways. For example, Rwanda has pledged to be the first African country which has no orphanages.[19] Since 2012, Rwanda has closed 25 of 39 orphanages.[20] They are working to place orphans within families of their relatives or in foster families. Let's examine some of the reasons people are in favour of orphanages, and the reasons people are against orphanages as the best way to care for orphans.

Arguments Against Orphanages

1. Some argue that orphanages are a foreign idea that does not fit in well with African cultures and family systems. Traditionally, in many African cultures, relatives would take in and care for orphans if their parents died. The child is considered to have many mothers and fathers and many homes to live in within their community.[21] Then these orphan children grow up with family structures and remain a part of their clan. Orphanages instead remove children from their relatives and clan, and if adopted by foreigners, these children can be lost to the community forever. Over time, orphanages can cause communities to neglect their responsibilities to care for their orphans and become dependent on outsiders to raise these children.

2. Orphanages require much more money to raise each child compared to the cost of families taking in orphans to raise along with the rest of their children.

3. Some people argue that orphanages bring division and conflict in the community because the orphans may be raised at a different standard of living compared to the surrounding community. Orphanages that are understaffed and underfunded may neglect the children and not care for them well. Other orphanages that are well-funded may give the orphans a far better standard of living than children in the community. This can result in the community feeling envious. It is also not uncommon for healthy parents to drop their children at orphanages because they want a better life for their children or they want their children to get the free education that the orphanages provide. In these cases, orphanages are dividing families rather than building them up. Instead of building more orphanages, we need to spend our resources and time caring for parents so that they have better jobs and are better able to take care of their children. Working for community development will help children a lot more than building orphanages will.

4. Growing up in an orphanage can be very problematic for a child's development.[22] Children can grow up with various psychological problems due to neglect, physical abuse, or sexual abuse. It is estimated that institutionalised children are six times more likely to be exposed to violence than children in a family setting.[23] On average, children growing up in orphanages have an IQ of 20 points lower than those in foster care, and are far less likely to find employment as young adults. When children eventually leave, they are 10 times more likely to enter prostitution and 40 times more likely to gain a criminal record.[24] Many children in orphanages suffer from attachment disorders as they often cannot form long-term relationships with caregiving adults. This is due to

regular turnover of the orphanage staff, as well as the fact that many orphanages operate by using national or foreign volunteers who may only serve for a couple weeks or months at a time.

5. Some people claim that governments may become dependent on orphanages funded by churches and NGOs and neglect the hard work of reuniting missing children to their families or finding homes and safe places for children on the streets.

6. Some orphanages and adoption agencies make children more vulnerable to human trafficking. Traffickers can emotionally manipulate the lonely children and coerce them to leave the facility. Some ill-managed facilities even intentionally cooperate with traffickers. Some orphanages "facilitate child trafficking rings by using false promises to recruit children and exploit them to profit from donations."[25]

Arguments in Favour of Orphanages

1. Most people agree that it should be the relatives to care for orphans, but the reality is that this is not always happening. Street children are already separated from their home communities. Some street children and orphans are being ignored and neglected by their relatives. In other cases, children are living on the street in the city because they ran away from violence or sexual abuse in their homes. Other orphans don't have traceable families. Orphanages fill the gap for children in these situations.[26]

2. Some people agree that many orphanages provide a better standard of living than children receive in the rest of the community, but they argue that orphans deserve our special attention. In many places, the Bible mentions the need to give special care to orphans. Orphans have had enough suffering and difficulties already, and their future life as an adult will remain difficult with no support from parents. We should do as much as we possibly can for them while they are in the orphanage.

3. Christian orphanages give orphans and street children a chance to hear the gospel and experience the love of Christ. Many orphans are coming from communities where people do not know Jesus.[27]

4. Orphanages offer protection, care, shelter, education, and food to vulnerable children who might have no other place in society to go.

5. Orphanages save the lives of many children who would have otherwise been aborted or killed after birth. It is very common throughout Africa for newly born babies to be dropped off at orphanages by desperate mothers who feel they don't have the ability to care for these children, or they are ashamed of having a child out of wedlock.

6. Orphanages as institutions help to facilitate the process of adoption so that orphans can be placed within loving families.

What do you think? Should we be working to close orphanages and care for orphans in alternative ways? Or are orphanages a necessary and effective way to care for orphans?

This is a complicated debate and you should refrain yourself from giving a final and "right" answer to the question. Share your own opinion freely but allow people to agree to disagree.

Acknowledge that there is truth on both sides, in both perspectives. The goal is to get people to engage the ideas and think through the issues carefully. Emphasize the need to learn from one another. We should all be quick to listen and slow to speak, and slow to make judgements. In the end, we should celebrate when people are trying to care for and love orphans, even if they do not do it in the same way that we would choose to do it.

The Role of the Urban Church in Fighting Poverty (5 minutes)

We have looked at what the Bible teaches about working for the good of cities, we have looked at opportunities and challenges in urban ministry, and discussed how to care for orphans and street children. Now, let's summarise briefly what urban churches can do to fight poverty in their communities, taking into account what we have learned in previous lessons.

- Preach the gospel in word and deed. The church is the centre of transformation in any society. Jesus brings transformation to people's lives and people's relationships that no program can achieve and no money can buy. Teach people a biblical worldview. Disciple them and walk with them as they grow in Christ.
- Work for reconciliation. Help people to grow in their relationships with God, self, others, and the rest of creation.
- Help people to discover their assets and skills and use them to do meaningful work to support themselves and their families.
- Give generously to people in need in your community through your church's benevolence ministry.
- Work to overcome and change broken systems in your city. Advocate and lobby for justice on behalf of those who are oppressed. The church should be a voice for the voiceless. Hold leaders to account in order for people in your neighbourhood to receive good governance and quality service delivery.
- Form partnerships with other nearby churches and organisations and work together to address poverty and challenges in the community. For example, churches can work together with government officials or organisations to construct a school or a medical centre.
- Plant new churches in other areas of the city, especially materially poor neighbourhoods which other churches may be avoiding. Avoid competing with other churches for members, but prioritise preaching to those who do not yet know Jesus.
- Urban churches should lead by example. They should be role models of transparency and integrity in the community. They should lead the way in loving and embracing people of other cultures and backgrounds.
- Seek the good of your city and your neighbourhood. Clean up the rubbish and plant trees in your neighbourhood. Repair holes in the roads nearby. Volunteer to help in the schools and clinics. Look for ways to serve people in your community. Even small acts of service can make a big difference and give people hope.

Urban Churches Making an Impact (10 minutes)

Can you mention a specific urban church in your country that is making a positive impact in its city? Explain what the church is doing and why you think it is successfully making an impact.

You should appreciate the participants for their answers and then tell them you have some additional examples for them.

1. There was a church of about 20 people in Kagishu, a slum community in Nairobi, Kenya. Meshack, a young man from the church, attended a Christian conference about development, and went back home to challenge his pastor that their church should be doing more holistic ministry in their community. The pastor wondered how they could meet the needs of others when his church members were already so poor. There were children in the community who were not able to afford going to school. So the pastor's wife and Meshack started teaching children without pay and later opened a school that started with 30 students. Within only one year the school enrolment grew to 313 students, and six staff members. Because the community saw how the church cared for people in need, the church grew and doubled in its membership. Today the school has about 450 students with 20 paid staff, and three additional primary schools and a secondary school have been started.[28]

2. God Bless Nigeria Church, in Lagos, Nigeria, has been intentionally trying to reach out to commercial sex workers. The church leaders go out to the streets and invite the young women to the church. The church established a 42-bed residential house called Genesis House to help the women stay away from the sex markets. In some cases, the church helps these former sex workers to pay off the men who managed them and even the hotels where they had rented rooms. The recovering prostitutes are mentored and given training in various skills. Pastor Akinnola reports that about 40 percent of the women who pass through the program avoid prostitution on a long-term basis. Some have gotten married. Others have used their new skills to pursue hair-dressing, catering, tailoring and other legitimate professions.[29]

Take-Home Activities for Lesson 17

The facilitator should provide detailed guidelines and clear instructions on how to go about the take-home activities. All participants should try to do both of the activities below.

1. Lead a Bible study with your family or a small group from church to study what the Bible teaches about cities. Study the passages together that are discussed in this lesson. Additionally, try to find other relevant Bible passages that also relate to cities. Use a concordance to help you. Seek to learn more about how God wants Christians to view and interact with cities.

2. Research the neighbourhood near your urban church. Talk to residents of the area and find out what they believe to be the opportunities, assets, challenges, and needs of the community. Either with a few other volunteer members from church or together with the official church leadership, make an action plan for serving your urban neighbourhood. Begin with something small. It could be as simple as starting a weekly football game and Bible study with children, planting trees, re-painting houses and signs that have deteriorated, starting weekly hospital visits to encourage doctors and patients, or talking to a government official about needed repairs in the neighbourhood. Try to make at least one positive and specific change in your community.

Small Group Discussion (30 minutes)

Read out loud the questions that they will be answering and make sure they understand them.

Divide them up into groups of 5 people (anywhere from 3-6 people per group). They can be the same groups as before, or you can put them into new groups. They will not be presenting their answers to anyone.

If you have organised the whole workshop to take longer than what has been outlined, then feel free to give the participants a longer time for discussion.

Remember to move around and listen in with the groups as they discuss. Be available to answer their questions. You can give guidance or input if necessary during their discussions, but they have heard you talk a lot, so try to let them do the talking now.

Remind them periodically about how much time remains for their discussion.

Showing Hospitality

In addition to reaching out in love to our urban communities, we should also make sure that our churches are attractive places where people will feel welcome. Our churches should be places where people can visit and experience the love of Christ and hear the good news of the gospel. They should have the opportunity to see God's people worshipping the living God, so that they become interested to learn more. But how can we make sure our churches are friendly and hospitable so that people will feel welcomed and loved? We will discuss this in our groups. As you come up with answers, only suggest ideas that your church realistically has the time and money to be able to do.

Divide the participants into small groups as you normally do at the end of each lesson. But inform them this time that they will need to write down their answers. They will be presenting their answers to the large group after the small group discussion. They will discuss for 20 minutes, and then the last 10 minutes will be used for sharing their answers with the other groups.

What can we do to make our urban churches more hospitable places for:

1. **Materially poor people?**
2. **People from other races and ethnic groups?**
3. **People with physical or psychological disabilities?**
4. **First time visitors?**

If there is still time remaining after each group has presented their answers, you can offer a few of these ideas below that have not been mentioned already. Choose to share the ones that you find most helpful for your group and context.

1. Materially poor people?

- Offer everyone a cup of a tea after each Sunday service, or have a meal once a month after the church service with the whole church.
- Don't save certain seats only for rich and influential church members, but give the good seats to materially poor people or those who visit who are not dressed well.
- Church members should be involved in caring for the needs of the community throughout the week and building relationships with materially poor people. Then when people come on Sunday to church they will already have relationships with some of your members.
- We need to make space for suffering in our worship. Sing lament songs and pray about challenges that people are going through. Don't speak as if the Christian life is easy. For materially poor Christians life has many difficulties.

- During the offering, tell visitors that giving is optional and they should not feel pressured, but at the same time encourage church members to tithe and give generously as a part of worship. Don't applaud church members who give a lot of money and shame people who give small amounts. People should be encouraged to give according to their ability. The amount is not important compared to a person's attitude in giving. What is easy to give for one person may be a sacrifice for someone else.

2. **People from other races and ethnic groups?**

- The church should intentionally make sure that the leaders of the church and the various church ministries are not all from the same ethnic group.
- Church services can be done with translation into another language. Alternatively, the church can run two different worship services, each in a different language.
- When the ushers or pastors identify a visitor who does not speak the language the service is in, the church can provide a church member who knows their language to sit next to that person, and whisper periodic translations.
- Worship leaders can intentionally plan to sing songs from various regions, languages, and cultures. Worship leaders can use a variety of music styles.

3. **People with physical or psychological disabilities?**

- A wheelchair ramp could be installed at the church entrance instead of only having stairs. Latrines could also be adjusted so that those with wheelchairs can still use them.
- Large print Bibles can be made available to borrow during the service for those who have problems with their eyesight.
- You could pay for one church member to be trained in sign language. This person can stand up front and translate what is spoken throughout the service into sign language for those attending who are deaf.
- Pastors should teach their church members to be accepting of people with psychological disabilities who might make more noise and distractions in the service compared to other people. These people should be appreciated for the unique people that they are. Church members should take time to build friendships with people who have disabilities.
- Look for ways to allow people with disabilities to still serve in various ways in the church.
- For parents in the church who have children with special needs, take time to help them out. This might mean giving them assistance caring for the child on Sunday morning, or it might mean staying with the child for an afternoon during the week so that the parents can have time to go out and do other things.

4. **First time visitors?**

- The church can have people set aside who greet people as they come to church. These people should look for visitors and guide them about where to park their vehicle or bicycle, and show them where to go.

- Instead of only greeting visitors during the worship service, individual church members should be encouraged to shake the hand of a visitor before and after the service and try to get to know them. If someone comes to a church for the first time and no one talks to them, they might never come back.

- There should be a sign for the church on the main road or near the church that specifically explains that visitors are welcome. Putting directions and the times of the service on the sign is also helpful. For churches who are able, this information is good to have on a website.

- Worship services should begin on time and end on time, so that visitors are able to make their commitments and plan well. You don't want visitors leaving while feeling frustrated and annoyed because the service went too long.

- The worship leader should guide the congregation through the various parts of the worship service, explaining what is being done and why. Non-Christians should not feel lost and confused, but should understand what is happening in the service.

- Churches should allow worship that is passionate and emotional, but also everything should be done in an orderly and organised way so it doesn't feel chaotic to visitors. See 1 Corinthians 14:39-40.

- In the sermon, the pastor should not use "Christianese." This means they should not use hard to understand Christian words without explaining them, such as "saved" or "sanctification" or "spiritual gifts." Preachers should always preach imagining that they are preaching to some non-Christian visitors.

- Cell groups from the church should be intentional about inviting new people to join their small groups.

- Churches can give short classes to new members to explain the history and beliefs of the church, and discuss the expectations and responsibilities of church members.

- Churches should provide a way for guests to give feedback about their experiences at the church, perhaps through a small card that they can drop in the offering basket.

Helping Without Hurting in Africa

Facilitator Manual

Lesson 18: Mission Trips Within Africa

Lesson 18: Mission Trips Within Africa[1]

In this section, you will find:

- A guide for planning and implementing fruitful short-term missions trips.
- Benefits and disadvantages of short-term missions.

Lesson Objectives:

- To learn how churches can plan fruitful mission trips while avoiding common mistakes.

Time Length: 1.5 hours

Notes to the Facilitator

- Prepare in advance the paper handouts that you will give to each one of the participants for the group activity about culture. Alternatively, if doing the activity as only a drama with one other volunteer, make sure you find and prepare this person beforehand.
- Ensure that long notes, quotations, and group questions are prepared in advance and written on flip chart paper.
- Unless otherwise noted, all Scripture passages in **bold** should be read out loud by a participant for the whole group.
- When the participants read the selected Bible passages throughout the lesson, make brief summaries of what each Bible passage is about and what it means.
- At the end of the lesson, explain the take home activities clearly to participants.
- If there is time at the end of the lesson, consider asking participants questions to review the key points made during the lesson.

Opening Survey (10 minutes)

Romans 10:14-15 – "(14) How, then, can they call on the one they have not believed in? And how can they believe in the one of whom they have not heard? And how can they hear without someone preaching to them? (15) And how can they preach unless they are sent? As it is written, 'How beautiful are the feet of those who bring good news!'"

Many of our churches have a strong passion for mission and evangelism. We want to tell people of all nations about Jesus so that they can also come to know him, experience forgiveness and transformation, and receive eternal life. We preach the gospel to people in our own communities, and sometimes we send out missionaries to other countries.

In this lesson, we are going to be discussing mission trips. What is a mission trip? Specifically, we are looking at mission trips as outreaches undertaken by local churches or groups of Christians to neighbouring communities or to more distant locations. These volunteer trips are taken to preach the Word of God or to give some assistance to materially poor people. In this lesson, we are focusing on churches in Africa going on mission trips to other African communities and countries, even though some churches in Africa send missionaries to countries outside of Africa. There are also many churches from other continents who send groups of Christians on mission trips to the African continent. But this will be discussed in our next lesson where we shall talk about foreign mission trips to countries within Africa.

How long is a mission trip? While many churches send out long-term missionaries to stay in one location for years, in this lesson we are going to focus our discussion on trips that are one week to one month in length. We can refer to these trips as "short-term mission trips". But for short we can call them "STMs".

This curriculum, *Helping without Hurting in Africa*, is not primarily focused on evangelism methods and church planting. But it is important to talk about short-term mission trips because many STMs are planned in order to help materially poor people. This is a good thing. The church needs to proclaim the good news of the Kingdom of God in words and in actions. We need to tell people how they can know Jesus personally and also find ways to love and serve people in their daily lives. We should work with them towards reconciliation in their relationships and a reduction in their material poverty. As our churches engage in STMs and try to help materially poor people, we must plan these trips wisely and we will be discussing common mistakes that churches make concerning STMs.

To begin this lesson, I'm going to take a quick survey to see what our experiences have been regarding STMs.

Ask the participants the questions in the survey below. You can have them all raise their hands so you can count their responses. Record on the flip chart the number of people who raise their hand for each question, and you can record all the different materials that were given out on mission trips.

Group Survey

1. **How many of you have ever gone on a STM to another community or region?**
2. **How many of you did evangelism on your trip? How many of you tried to serve or help materially poor people on your trip?**
3. **How many of you gave out resources or money on your trip?**
4. **What specifically did you give to people?**
5. **How many of you consulted the people, communities, or region before you went?**

Summarise their answers, and point out any trends or patterns that you see in their responses.

Benefits of STMs (10 minutes)

Before we look at the challenges and common mistakes of STMs, let's first look at the benefits of these trips. When planned well, STMs can bring about many positive changes in the lives of the host community and also in the lives of the participants going on the trip.

Encourage the participants to use specific examples in their answers. List their answers on a flip chart so that people can take them down as notes. Instruct the participants to consider the benefits for both the participants going on the trip and also the benefits for the people in the host community.

What are the possible benefits or fruits of short-term mission trips?

Briefly touch on the points below only if they have not already discussed them as a group. When you as the facilitator contribute any of the points below, list those on the flip chart as well.

1. STMs provide an opportunity to proclaim the gospel in word and deed. Members of the host community may have an opportunity to hear the gospel for the first time and put their trust in Jesus as their Saviour and King.

2. STMs may create an opportunity for church expansion and church planting.

3. STMs allow for new relationships to form between people of different regions and cultures. This provides opportunities for friendship, mutual encouragement, sharing of ideas, and praying for one another. Over time, this can result in a more official relationship and partnership between two local churches from different regions.

4. Short term mission trips can be an effective way to respond to communities who need relief after disasters. In such cases, the long-term missionaries and aid workers may need extra help from volunteers. For example, volunteers may be able to help carry out food distribution, needs assessments, caring for those who are sick, or cleaning up an area after a disaster.

5. STMs provide opportunities for service and giving. Participants of STMs can experience the blessing of sharing their time and resources with those in need and materially poor people of the host community can experience a reduction in material poverty and improved relationships.

6. Participants of STMs will gain new experiences that may change them and their character. They may learn how to look at the world and their lives in a new way after talking to people of other cultures. Participants of STMs might feel new gratitude for the material possessions God has blessed them with and they may become more generous to materially poor people. Hopefully they will return from STMs with a greater desire to form relationships with materially people in their home community.

7. Participants of STMs can improve in their understanding of the ministry of long-term missionaries. Hopefully this will make them more passionate and generous in their financial support, encouragement, and prayer for long-term missionaries.

8. Participants of STMs may sense God calling them to long-term missions through their experiences on STMs. Additionally, going on an STM may help someone who already feels called to long-term missions to determine which people and location God is calling them to serve.

Challenges and Mistakes in STMs (30 minutes)

Ask the questions below and take note of answers on a flip chart. Encourage the participants to use specific examples from their own STMs in their answers. The first question deals with issues that make STMs difficult or less effective, whereas the second question looks at specific mistakes that can be made on STMs.

1. What are some challenges or weaknesses of STMs?

Explain the points below to the participants if they have not been mentioned already or if they do not seem to be clear to the participants.

1. **Language barriers**. Often the host community speaks a different language than the STM team. This requires planning ahead to find a translator.

2. **Cultural barriers.** Often the host community is culturally very different, which can be hard for the STM team to fully understand.

3. **Short time for relationships**. Poverty is rooted in broken relationships. But it is extremely difficult to build healthy and lasting relationships with the people of the host community within such a short time frame. By the very nature of a short trip, the natural tendency will be to focus more on quick projects than on people.

4. **Inflexibility and disappointments**. STMs require a lot of preparation and planning. When participants of the team arrive to their target location, they have a very clear picture of what they want to accomplish. It can be extremely difficult for the participants to be flexible and adapt to the real situation that they learn about after talking to the people in the host community. The participants may end up going home being disappointed that they did not accomplish what they had in mind to do.

5. **Short time for development.** Within a short time period, it is unlikely that there will be great improvement in community development. In 1-2 weeks, it is difficult to do holistic ministry, taking into account all four fundamental relationships and trying to find ways to overcome broken systems. This leads many STMs to focus on giving handouts instead, which can be done quickly but does not usually result in a big reduction of material poverty or in improved relationships.

6. **Focus on needs**. In a short amount of time, it will be difficult to help people discover their assets and skills and also work with them to develop those assets and skills. Instead, STMs may tend to focus on the needs of the people and what they lack.

7. **High financial cost**. STMs are sometimes expensive for the host community because of the hospitality that they will show to a short-term team. STMs are also expensive for the participants in terms of travel. Most of the time, the money could be used more effectively to support long-term missionaries and development organisations that are trying to help materially poor people. Most of us like to do hands-on ministry with the poor because it makes us feel good about ourselves, but we must deny our own desires, and try to help people in the most effective ways. Sometimes this might mean saying "no" to planning a STM.

8. **Difficult follow-up**. Because of the distance between where the participants come from and the host community, it can be very difficult to follow-up, both in terms of the discipleship of new converts, and in encouraging and assisting in any projects that were started together.

9. **Big man effect.** Many STMs create an environment in which the "big man effect" can cause problems. If a person with material wealth or high position visits a materially poor community, they have power to influence people without even trying. The person might make a simple comment without thinking about it. For example, he or she could say to a community, "I wish you had a school closer to your homes." And because the community views this person as a "big man" (or as a "big woman") who might want to donate money to an educational project like this, the people may go forward trying to fund-raise to build a new school even if it is not what they really think they need.

2. What mistakes have you made on a STM that caused harm either to people in the host community or to the STM participants?

Explain the points below to the participants if they have not been mentioned already or if they do not seem to be clear to the participants. Participants may tell stories as part of their answers. If they do, try to summarise the mistake that was made in each answer, and see if you can match it to one of the points below.

1. **Lack of proper planning for the STM**. This may include failure to determine the financial and human resources needed for the trip, the time frame for the trip, the ministry plan, etc. We can make many mistakes by not learning about what other STMs and NGOs have been doing in a community. We should remember the story from West Africa about the many different groups trying to help with water filters which resulted in the communities being harmed.

2. **Lack of clarity on the purpose of the STM**. This may bring confusion to both the mission team and the host community.

3. **Lack of involvement**. We should not make the mistake of planning trips and projects without the involvement of the host community. Remember that for real development to take place there needs to be community participation and ownership of the entire process of development.

4. **Paternalism**. We should not make the mistake of doing work "for" the host community rather than working "with" the host community. This results in labour paternalism. For

example, a team might build a new house for a local pastor or a materially poor family, without the local church or community taking part in the construction.

5. **God-complexes**. We should avoid building up our god-complexes through STMs. We don't want to act as if there is a big difference between "us" and "them". As participants of STMs we can easily feel we are the saviours of the materially poor people we are trying to help. We might go with an "I know it all" attitude. We might want to do things our way without regarding the suggestions and opinions of the host communities. This may frustrate the host communities and make them feel inferior.

6. **Creating dependency**. Many STMs focus on giving handouts to people, or operate with a relief approach even if rehabilitation or development is actually what is needed. If we make the mistake of giving relief when it is not needed, this can create dependency and shame. In certain cases, giving too many handouts can also undermine the local economy. Giving relief on a STM is very good if relief is what is needed, but we must take care to understand the situation well and diagnose the true causes of poverty in each situation. Furthermore, there may be many STMs from different churches and organisations to this same community. When each of these STMs gives hand-outs, they can all add up to one big dependency-creating situation.

7. **Ignoring the circles of priority**. Remember that as we try to help materially poor people and communities, we should take care not to get in the way of others who have the privilege and responsibility of helping. Our helping causes harm when we destroy the opportunities for other closer people to help with love, generosity, and stewardship. Don't try to take the place of families, local churches, local governments, or communities who may be able to help.

8. **Not listening**. We must make sure we do not make the mistake of spending all of our time preaching and lecturing on a trip. We must spend time with people, build relationships, work together, and eat together. Above all, we must listen to the people and respect their opinions and be willing to learn from them. Failing to listen will build up our god-complexes and make the host community feel inferior.

9. **Ignoring local leadership**. We should not simply enter a new community and do whatever we want to do. We need to take the time to meet the local leaders and submit to their authority. We should work with them, not against them. The local church in a community is the primary manifestation of Christ in that community. We must do all that we can to make sure we build up that local body, not undermine it.

10. **Taking photos without permission**. We must be careful with photography. Often on STMs, we take photos in a way that makes people feel like animals in a game park. We should get permission to take people's photos (whether of individuals or groups in a church or workshop) and again get permission to share people's photos on social media. It is offensive to treat people as objects for the purpose of showing what material poverty looks like to people back in our home churches. Remember that they are people made in the image of God. Take special care in taking photos of people you don't know, and take special care not to take photos of children unless you get permission from their parents.

11. **Broken promises**. On short-term trips, people feel strong emotions. It is easy to fall into the mistake of making false promises. We may promise to visit them again. We may promise to send Bibles or financial support. But we should not make promises we cannot keep. In the short term, people might feel good when they hear the hopeful promises we

make, but in the long term, it will completely destroy trust and the relationships if we don't fulfil the promises we make.

12. **Bribing**. On a STM, it is possible to give out gifts in a way that makes it look like people are becoming Christians only in order to receive the gifts. We must be careful that our gifts are not bribes given to entice people to become Christians. A good approach is to help all people in a community, rather than only helping those that convert to the Christian faith.

13. **Misunderstanding culture**. This is a mistake that is most often done unintentionally. But both the host community and the STM participants may be offended because of cultural differences. These differences may cause confusion, misunderstanding, or even conflict on a trip.

Cross-Cultural Group Activity (25 minutes)

This group activity is intended to help people think through the complications of short-term mission trips when interacting with people of another region and culture. After the activity, the participants should better understand the need for preparing well for a short-term mission trip, should understand the need for flexibility and adaptation on a short-term mission trip, and better understand some ways it is possible to offend on a short-term mission trip.

The way you carry out this activity in your training group should be determined by your context. We recommend that you have all participants take part if they are comfortable doing so, and if you have enough time and space for the activity. If you are worried that some people will be too uncomfortable or nervous to take part in the activity, or if you are short on time, you can simply find one participant to take part in the activity with you as the facilitator. In such a case, you as the facilitator will take the part of either a member of the host community or a visiting short-term missionary. Then your volunteer participant will be the other. If it's you and only one volunteer, you can prepare it as a drama.

Divide the participants in half. One half will act as the missionary group, the other half as the host community. The activity will be an acting out of the short-term missionaries visiting the host community. The main activity will be greeting each other and introducing themselves to each other. Tell the participants to act just like they normally would, except for only a few cultural changes which you will instruct them about. Guide them that giving gifts can be done using any objects that you have available. For example, they could give a pencil or Bible, (and they can get it back after the activity is over). Instruct people to act offended if they would actually be offended according to their culture (which you will instruct them about).

After giving these general instructions to everyone, put the two groups in separate rooms if possible so they cannot overhear the other group discuss. One group could stay inside and one group could go outside. Hand out the instructions you've prepared on small pieces of paper to the participants in each group.

For the short-term missionaries, give them these written instructions:

1. Your culture is very informal and you speak quickly. You get impatient with too many rituals.

2. You are generous. Be sure to bring a small gift for each person you are meeting for the first time. This is how you intend to show the love of Christ. You are very excited about being able to share with materially poor people.

For the host community, give them these written instructions:

1. You are very formal and respectful and greet visitors by very slowly bowing. You don't shake hands, and aren't familiar with that style of greeting. You speak very slowly and carefully.

2. You believe a good host will give a gift to visitors. And it would be shameful for a host to receive a gift from a first-time visitor.

Let the participants of each group practise together so that they learn their new "culture" well. Have them practise greeting one another within their own group according to their new "culture". Then bring the two groups together. Each participant should find a person of the other group to meet with so that everyone has a partner. In some cases, it might be preferable for groups of four to join up, two missionaries, and two people of the host community. After people have matched up, they should act out meeting each other for the first time. They should greet, give their names, get to know each other, and give a gift, if appropriate. The focus is mainly on the greeting, so this interaction should take 5 minutes or less.

Hopefully the participants will all realise that there are differences between the different cultures, and they should have found greeting and visiting with the other group difficult. Gather everyone back to their seats and then ask these questions.

1. Did the missionaries do anything that confused or offended the host community?

2. Did the host community do anything that confused or offended the missionaries?

3. When you realised your cultural differences, were you able to adapt to the situation?

4. How did you handle the issue of gift giving?

5. Read 1 Corinthians 9:19-23. How might this passage help us to think about cultural differences while on STMs?

Planning Fruitful STMs (15 minutes)

We will now conclude this lesson with some additional advice for how to plan fruitful short-term mission trips. Here are some final principles to reflect on:

1. Learn as much as you can about the culture, social norms, language, and environment of the place you intend to visit. Learn about the dress codes of the host community, as well as the ways that they greet, and what expectations they might have of visitors. Do not allow church members to go on the trip unless they demonstrate a commitment to learn and spend time in preparation.

2. Make sure your STM has a clear and specific purpose. Don't plan a trip just because it sounds like an interesting thing to do or just because you desire to help people. As we've learned in these lessons, a desire to help is not enough. We must help wisely. Think through the purpose of the trip very carefully first and make sure that it is well understood and owned by all team members.

3. Remember to proclaim the good news of the Kingdom of God. Minister to people holistically by working for reconciliation in their relationships with God, self, others, and the creation.

4. A representative of your church should try to visit the area first on their own. He or she can learn about the community and the situation and find out whether the host community would welcome a team from your church. This person can plan together with the community about what your team will do on the visit. Allow the host community and/or host church to take charge in the decision-making process. This will build confidence and self-esteem and promote ownership of any activity your team will do together with the community.

5. After carefully planning your trip, if you realise that it is too expensive, or that the risks outweigh the possible benefits, then be willing to say "no" to the idea of the STM, and use the money to support long-term missionaries in that region, or invest more in helping materially poor people in your own community.

6. Remember that your STM should bring glory to God. It is not a chance to make yourselves look good, or to build up the reputation of your church, or to glorify an evangelist or pastor.

7. Prayer is very important for the success of any mission trip because through prayer God gives guidance on the direction to take and also wisdom on how to do it. Prayer for your STM will also help you to confront and repent of any god-complexes you may have before leaving on the trip.

8. Focus on long-term development. Although building relationships takes a long time, it's critical in order to work for long-term development with another community. You cannot expect much development to take place in a week. So focus on supporting churches and ministries that are already there. They are the ones who are able to develop long-term relationships and to engage in the long-term development process that is at the heart of poverty alleviation. Your STM may be the beginning of many visits to support local ministries, and it may create later opportunities for people from the host community to visit your church and region as well.

9. As much as possible try to help people discover their assets, skills, and opportunities. Focus on encouraging and building people up.

10. Be flexible and willing to adjust. You need to be prepared for the possibility that things may not go according to plan. There will be surprises and you need to be ready to embrace them. For example, you might have planned to preach and then share a meal together afterwards, but if the host community requests that you eat together first before preaching, then you should accommodate their request to allow for harmony and a good relationship.

11. Request participants on the STM to invest their own resources on the trip. This will ensure that people are not going on the trip simply for something interesting to do. They should feel a sense of ownership for the trip.

12. Think carefully about who should lead the STM. It is preferable that STM leaders are already engaged in missions and are people who love and know materially poor people. If possible, the leaders should have learned the principles in this curriculum, or other similar training materials.

13. Be a learner. It is important to realise that you do not know everything. You also have things you can learn. You should appreciate the fact that the host communities or the materially poor people you intend to reach out to understand their situation better than you do. You should be slow to speak, quick to listen, and ask a lot of good questions.

14. Be careful about how you talk about materially poor people when speaking to your local church about the trip and when speaking to people in the host community. We don't want to always refer to the people we will visit as "the poor". Their material poverty should not define their whole identity. There is more to them than their poverty. Remember that they are people made in the image of God. Remember God is already at work in their community through his Holy Spirit.

15. Utilise the various gifts of your team members. Be creative in planning the trip. Each person has different ways that they can teach, serve, or encourage. Read **1 Peter 4:10**.

16. Generally, it is a good policy to avoid bringing resources to hand out unless the people are in need of relief because of a crisis. Emphasize fellowship, encouraging, and teaching rather than giving handouts. If you develop a partnership with the local church or community, it may eventually be helpful to complement local resources by bringing in outside resources. But those outside resources should be used to match local contributions not to undermine them. Never do for people what they can do for themselves.

17. When visiting the host community, look for ways to work together and partner with local churches, local development organisations, and other leaders in the government and community.

18. After the trip, take time to review the experience with the whole team:

- Find out what each team member learned about their own brokenness in their relationships with God, self, others, or creation.
- What did they learn from the people? What positive things did they observe in the local people's relationships with God, self, others, and creation?
- How do you think you strengthened the churches and ministries that are there for the long term?
- Are there any ways that you made things more difficult for the churches and ministries that are there for the long term?
- Discuss whether the trip has made you more generous, more willing to support missionaries, or more willing to make friendships with materially poor people in your area.

- In order for these changes to become a reality, you must act on them not just talk about them. So write down action steps that you will take to change as a local church or as individuals.
- Discuss whether a future trip might be helpful to continue the relationship with the host community over the long term.
- Most importantly, don't forget to ask the host community members what they really thought about the trip, and whether it was helpful to them. Try to go beyond their polite thank-yous and try to figure out the host community's long-term ability to pursue lasting change.
- Make a commitment to keep praying together for the host community. Rejoice in the privilege of taking part in God's mission to preach good news.

After you finish teaching the points above, ask the participants if anyone has any further advice about STMs that they would like to share or if anyone has any questions. To finish the lesson, you can pray as a group. Consider repenting about mistakes made on past STMs, and ask God to help you plan STMs more carefully in the future.

Take-Home Activities for Lesson 18

The facilitator should provide detailed guidelines and clear instructions on how to go about the take-home activities. All participants should try to do both of the activities below.

1. Think about the long-term missionaries your church has sent to other communities or countries. Contact them and see how they are doing and find out if they need any more encouragement or support of any kind. Ask them if it would be helpful to their ministry and beneficial to the community for the church to send a short-term team to visit them or if there is another way that you could be of more support.

2. Next time your church plans a STM, study the principles in this lesson with the STM leadership and planning team. Use the guidelines you have learnt in this lesson to prepare your STM wisely.

Helping Without Hurting in Africa

Facilitator Manual

Lesson 19: Foreigners, Missionaries, and Sponsors

Lesson 19: Foreigners, Missionaries, and Sponsors

In this section, you will find:

- Insights into cultural differences between foreigners and nationals that can cause conflict and tension in ministry.

Lesson Objectives:

- To learn how to have healthy working relationships between Africans and foreigners working in Africa.

Time Length: 2 hours

Notes to the Facilitator

- Ensure that long notes, quotations, and group questions are prepared in advance and written on the flip chart.
- Unless otherwise noted, all Scripture passages in **bold** should be read out loud by a participant for the whole group.
- When the participants read the selected Bible passages throughout the lesson, make brief summaries of what each Bible passage is about and what it means.
- At the end of the lesson, explain the take-home activities clearly to participants.
- If there is time at the end of the lesson, consider asking participants questions to review the key points made during the lesson.

Opening Large Group Discussion (20 minutes)

People in Africa work with many foreigners on a regular basis. We will categorise them into four groupings to make things easier for discussion:

- The first group are foreigners living in Africa who are Christian missionaries from different countries like the United States, South Korea, Brazil, Germany, the United Kingdom, and many others. Some of these foreign Christian missionaries spend most of their lives in Africa, while others may only come for a week-long visit.
- The second group are foreigners working for humanitarian and development organisations here in Africa. Some of these are Christian organisations and some are not.

- The third group are foreigners living in Africa who represent foreign governments, or who are working for private companies from other countries.
- The fourth and last group are the foreigners we call partners who are not living in Africa at all, but who we may regularly communicate with. We can refer to these people as partners, sponsors, or donors. They consist of both Christians and non-Christians, and they are trying to support communities and churches in Africa by giving material or financial donations. They may do this by forming relationships with pastors and churches, sponsoring children, providing scholarships for education, or by supporting NGOs and charities in Africa.

This lesson is a very sensitive one as we will talk openly and honestly about frustrations and tensions that arise between foreigners and the people of Africa. As we discuss together, try to be honest and open, but be slow to judge others. Let's be patient with one another and listen to each other well. Some of our conversations may be uncomfortable, but if we speak in love, they can be very fruitful and meaningful conversations. We need God's Word to guide our attitude. Let's read together **1 Corinthians 13:1-3** and **Ephesians 4:2** and **Ephesians 4:29**. We need to speak the truth in love, with humility and patience.

Ask participants to discuss the questions below in groups of three or four people. If possible, have them just turn and talk to the people sitting next to them, rather than moving around the room. If any foreigners are present in the training, tell them to join any group of three. They should simply listen to the answers that the participants from Africa give during this opening discussion. Give them 10-15 minutes to discuss together.

Walk around and listen to the groups as they discuss. If you hear any common experiences or themes, take note of them on the flip chart and present them to the whole group after they are finished discussing.

In groups of three or four, each person should briefly discuss their experiences of working with foreigners from any of these four categories.

1. **Describe the best relationship you have had with a foreigner.**
2. **Describe a difficult relationship you have had with a foreigner.**
3. **If you have worked together with a foreigner, who took the leadership role and made most of the decisions?**
4. **Do you know a foreigner who you consider to be a true friend? Explain.**

After the discussion, you can take one minute to comment on common experiences you heard from the discussions. Then ask this next question only if you have several foreigners taking part in your training group. Otherwise you can skip it.

One of the questions was about leadership and decision making. Now I'd like to ask you a sensitive question. Please answer carefully and with love. Without giving names or trying to make anyone feel bad, let's analyse our training group. As you went through the lessons of this curriculum, who has usually been taking charge in small group discussions and activities? Foreigners or Africans and why?

Give them time to ponder this question and after they have answered, then ask the next question.

"What can we learn from this? Is there anything foreigners can do differently next time, or is there anything we as Africans can do differently next time?"

After a brief discussion, continue with the following conclusion to the opening discussion.

Many foreign governments, companies, organisations, missionaries, and sponsors have greatly contributed to the gradual development and improvement of lives in Africa. This has happened through evangelism, teaching, financial aid, training, job creation, infrastructure development, and other gifts and services. However, foreigners have also caused harm in the process, even if it's sometimes done unintentionally. In fact, the very mistakes that we have mentioned and repented of as we went through these lessons together are often made by foreigners when they try to support or work with African communities. Sometimes their methods and attitudes have caused harm both to our communities and to the foreigners themselves. This could help to explain why there is still so much poverty in Africa despite the vast resources in Africa and the large volumes of foreign aid that is regularly sent here. Thankfully, some foreigners have been transformed in their mind-sets, changed their approach and repented for the mistakes that they have made in the past. Some of them are trying to help in a better and more kingdom-focused way, thanks in part to books like *When Helping Hurts*, on which this curriculum is based.

In this lesson, we will discuss how we can best work together with foreigners in Africa, so that together we can truly help materially poor people in our countries without causing harm. For development to take place, we must build stable and meaningful relationships of mutual respect. In this lesson, we will learn about typical problems that may come up in these relationships due to cultural differences, mind-sets or complications involving money. We need to help each other overcome the tensions that arise at times between us as Africans and the foreigners working in Africa. We will learn how to have more honest and fruitful relationships.

Cultural Misunderstandings and Conflicts (20 minutes)

It is sometimes very difficult to embrace and begin working in a place with a different culture. Many people have "culture shock" when they move to different regions or continents. This applies to foreigners when they move to African countries and try to adjust to the cultural differences, and also to Africans when they move to other countries outside Africa. The difficulty of adjusting to different cultures can cause discomfort, irritation, a negative attitude towards the host country, and in some cases even reinforce a foreigner's god-complex. The result can be a breakdown of the relationship as we try to work together with foreigners. In some cases, foreigners may even end up harming a community they are trying to help.

Foreigners need to be willing to adjust to our cultures as they work here, but we also need to be patient with them and teach them gently. It takes a long time to learn and adjust. And as Christians, we know that all cultures are imperfect and fall short of the glory of God. We ourselves should also be willing to adapt in order to work together peacefully and effectively with foreigners. Every relationship requires sacrifice and service in order to flourish. And remember that there is much we can learn from different cultures around the world.

As we talk about misunderstandings and conflicts over culture in our relationships with foreigners, remember that cultures are very diverse and complex. We have hundreds of different cultures in Africa. And while there are certain issues that almost all foreigners will struggle to adapt to in Africa, there will be great differences between Chinese, Indian, and French foreigners in Africa. Some aspects of culture might be easy for one foreigner to adapt to but extremely difficult for another foreigner, depending on their country of origin. And we must also not forget that people are all unique. We can't judge what a whole foreign country is like by the actions of one foreigner, in the same way that people cannot judge the African continent as a whole based on the actions of a few Africans.

As we discuss the next question, the goal is that we will all grow in our understanding of cultural conflicts so that we can be sensitive to the culture shocks we and others face, and be able to help foreigners and ourselves adjust so that we can work together well.

In the large group, ask the participants the question below and encourage them to give examples that support their answers. You can record their answers on the flip chart.

What are some common cultural misunderstandings and conflicts between foreigners and Africans that bring frustration into our relationships or cause problems in our attempts to help poor people together?

The facilitator can summarise the key points below if they have not already been mentioned by the participants. But it is better for the answers to come from the participants for learning purposes and better understanding. Allow them to speak first, and then add the ideas from the notes below that they did not mention. As you give the points below, remember that there is variety among African cultures. For example, some African cultures prefer a direct communication style while others use an indirect communication style.

1. **Different views of time**. Some foreigners think of time as a limited resource that needs to be used wisely and not wasted, while in Africa, we tend to think of time in a more

expansive way and prioritise relationships and spending time with people. Some foreigners say, "Time is money!" Foreigners might be in a hurry to accomplish activities at the expense of taking time to build relationships. This can frustrate Africans who value relationships and may feel that they are being rushed, and also frustrate foreigners who feel like the work is not getting done in an efficient and timely manner. Foreigners may be looked at as inflexible, impatient, and disrespectful, and Africans may be looked at as not serious, time-wasters, or inconsiderate of other people's time.

2. **Different views of the individual and group**. African cultures tend to focus on an individual's identity as part of various groups such as family, clan, and tribe, while some foreign cultures have more of an emphasis on an individual having a personal identity apart from groups. Some foreign cultures prioritise freedom of the individual, making personal choices, and pursuing individual advancement, while African cultures tend to prioritise making decisions that will benefit the family or whole group. Some foreign cultures put less emphasis on loyalty to the group compared to African cultures. However, this is gradually changing as we see some people in Africa becoming more individualistic.

3. **Differences in language**. In most cases, it is difficult to communicate or understand each other because of our differences in language and expression. The difficulty and the time taken for one to learn a foreign language may also cause some discomfort and irritation or tension that can affect the relationship. Sometimes foreigners may have an unfair expectation that it is the task of the Africans they work with to learn the language of the foreigner. And when communication is done through a translator, it is easy for misunderstandings to occur, because every translation involves interpretation.

4. **Different views of authority**. Some foreign cultures are more open and less hierarchical compared to African cultures, which tend to be more hierarchical. Hierarchical cultures place great importance on respecting the authority of specific leaders such as bishops, chiefs, kings, managers, and elders. In less hierarchical cultures, people feel more freedom to do things their way without consulting others and are more likely to publicly challenge the opinions of leaders. This cultural difference can create a lot of tension if not well understood. For example, there can be tension when a foreigner openly challenges an African leader, or when a foreigner expects Africans to openly challenge or be willing to disagree with their leaders.

5. **Different communication styles**. Some foreign cultures are more direct in their communication style. Some African cultures tend to be more indirect, especially if the matter to be discussed is regarded as sensitive and could affect the relationship. People will speak carefully in an ambiguous way, without saying directly what they mean. This cultural difference can sometimes result in serious communication gaps between Africans and some foreigners. A foreigner might perceive Africans to be secretive and not open to sharing how they feel, while Africans may feel that foreigners are impolite and offensive when they speak directly.

6. **Different views on moral issues**. When foreigners and Africans have different views on moral issues it can cause serious conflict among them. For example, they could have different views about the way a visitor or foreigner is supposed to conduct him/herself in the community, different dress codes, or different beliefs and practices about other issues like drinking alcohol, smoking, tattoos, piercings, and activities done for entertainment, etc.

7. **Food choices**. The difference in food choices and preferences can also result in discomfort or conflict. Some Africans may be uncomfortable with what the foreigners choose to eat or offended when foreigners don't eat the local food given to them during visits. Similarly, foreigners may also be uncomfortable with what Africans choose to eat.

8. **Visits**. Some Africans may be offended when foreigners are too busy to make time for home visits and fellowship meals. Foreigners may feel frustrated when they receive too many invitations and they do not have the ability to accept them all. They may also be frustrated about spending so much time talking instead of doing work together.

9. **Gender**. Foreigners and Africans may be mutually frustrated or offended by different views on gender, and particularly the roles of women in the family, church, and society. This can include something as simple as where men and women sit in churches and homes.

10. **Hospitality**. Africans are known for their hospitality and in this, they may want to show special care for their foreign guests by preparing special meals and sometimes special chairs for the guests as a welcome gesture. However, foreign guests may feel uncomfortable when they are given a lot of attention and treated as special during the visit. They may also get uncomfortable when many people they don't know come to greet them and continue staring at them. This can cause hurt feelings on both sides.

11. **Different views of material poverty**. Sometimes foreigners and Africans have different views about what it means to be materially poor. In some countries, a person might be considered materially poor if he or she cannot afford to buy their own vehicle, while in other countries, a person might be considered materially poor if he or she does not have enough food to eat or if he or she does not own a single pair of shoes. These types of differences in how material poverty is viewed can sometimes cause confusion when foreigners and Africans are trying to work together.

Case Study on Cultural Misunderstandings

A foreign missionary was leading a workshop for national church leaders involved in Bible translation. The missionary did not realise that, in this particular culture, the oldest man is always the first to speak, then the next oldest speaks, then the next oldest, and so on until finally, the youngest person can speak. The missionary proposed a discussion question to the whole group. Everyone was silent. The missionary asked the question again. The group was still silent. The missionary did not realise that the oldest man was unsure of the meaning of the question, and no one else dared to speak. The missionary didn't know what was going on, so she stopped using the participatory approach with this group and just presented the information herself.[1]

1. What do we learn from this story?

2. What could the church leaders have done to help the missionary?

Conflicts Over Money (20 minutes)

In some ways, we covered this topic already in detail in Lesson 13 – "African Culture and Money". If you can remember the characteristics of African cultures that we discussed in that lesson, those are the very same characteristics which foreigners can find difficult to understand and adapt to.

What aspects of our culture's use of money can you remember from that lesson that would be hard for foreigners to adapt to?

Allow the participants to answer this question, and you can try to summarise their answers, if helpful. You may continue by explaining the issues below if they are not well captured by the participants.

Probably the most important characteristic to remember from that lesson is that the nations in Africa have relational cultures that encourage people to support their friends in need by giving either financial or material resources, and failure to adhere to this cultural value may harm relationships. This practice ensures mutual interdependence and care in the relationship. This can be very hard for some foreigners to understand when they come from cultures in which friendship is not necessarily attached to any financial or material support. For some foreigners, friendship is only about spending time together or having someone to go to for advice. When Africans and foreigners speak together about being friends, it is important to discuss what each party means by "friendship". This can prevent misunderstandings and offences on both sides.

Here are some specific examples of conflict between Africans and foreigners because of different views of friendship and money:

1. Some Africans may feel disappointed when foreign friends do not give them any financial or material support. A true friend in Africa is viewed as one who helps the other in times of need. Some Africans might look at the rich lifestyles of foreigners with their pets and expensive vehicles and assume that they are very rich, creating a feeling that foreigners are selfish and only care about themselves while the people living around them are in painful material poverty.

2. Foreigners may be frustrated when they have many African friends, but they do not know which friends truly care about them, and which friends are just looking for a financial donor.

3. Africans can be offended when a foreign visitor or friend turns down a gift. This can make some of them feel inferior or assume that the foreigner is proud. The foreigner may want to refuse the gift because they see that the person giving the gift is in more need of it and they don't want to burden materially poor people. This mistake may come from a compassionate heart, but it is very harmful as it robs Africans of the dignity, blessing, and joy of being able to give to others.

4. Foreigners may try to give generously to help their African friends and neighbours, but sometimes they are limited financially and therefore cannot help everyone. This may cause them a great amount of stress as they try to decide who to help and in what way.

5. Africans are often frustrated by foreigners who don't admit when they have needs or when they need help. Africans want to care for their friends who are foreigners, but it is hard to know how to help if foreigners try to live independently, act proud, and don't admit that they also need help sometimes.

6. Some foreigners have sacrificed to come to Africa and do not have a lot of money. Some may even be unpaid volunteers. They can be frustrated when Africans assume they are rich just because of their country of origin. Sometimes Africans do not understand their sacrifice and may think foreigners are looking for employment opportunities in Africa that they could not get at home.

Before you continue, see if anyone would like to make a comment or a reflection about the examples that you gave.

What are some other common conflicts between Africans and foreigners that are about money or finance? As you answer, try to offer a helpful solution to prevent or resolve that conflict.

As you did with the section on cultural conflict, allow the participants to answer the questions and only mention the points below if they were not already mentioned by the participants. If you explain the points below to the group, make sure to allow for questions or comments on each point before moving to a new point.

- There may be conflict over record-keeping and accounting in the use of money and resources. Some foreigners may prioritise strict accounting and record-keeping practices that promote openness and transparency, and may be unwilling to adapt to the current situation and demands of the host country. Furthermore, many foreign or international organisations often presume that their local partners should look like them or do things their way without understanding the harm they may be causing in the process. For example, foreigners may force local organisations to adhere to their foreign structures and accounting systems which may have a financial cost, taking away money that could go to programs trying to help materially poor people. Foreigners may be frustrated by what they see as a lack of clear financial structures and transparency in some African financial dealings. They are frustrated by corruption, lack of proper record-keeping, failure to account for funds, and diversion of funds to a few individuals instead of the targeted communities. Sometimes Africans and foreigners may share the same values like transparency, accountability and integrity but conflicts can arise at the level of commitment (walk the talk) or the lack of political will.

- Foreigners may be frustrated by Africans in shops and markets charging them higher prices for goods or services just because they are foreigners. To the foreigners, this feels like corruption or racism. To Africans, it may feel like a normal part of their bartering system.

- Many foreigners living in Africa, or even overseas donors, may want to make all the important decisions about how money and resources will be used when working together with Africans. Sometimes they try to work with very little participation from the host community or local leaders. This can build up the god-complexes of the foreigners and offend African partners who will feel disrespected. It can also cause projects to be unsuccessful because foreigners are not willing to listen to the ideas of Africans who know the situation best. Additionally, if foreigners do everything for the host country, the local people will not own the project and it will not have sustainability.

If you have enough time, you could ask these questions relating to the point above on decision making. ***Does this explain why some projects fail and why some are not sustainable? Have any of you experienced this while working with foreigners in Africa? Please share.***

- Many foreign missionaries, organisations, and governments may focus more on donor compliance while Africans may focus more on actual impact on the ground. Some foreigners put a lot of emphasis on policy and procedure, while Africans want to be more flexible, making sure that the outcomes are achieved.

- The lack of a clear purpose is another factor that has many times affected the relationships between Africans and foreign governments, organisations, missionaries, and donors. Some foreign organisations come with an unclear agenda, while others have agendas that conflict with the cultural values of the African countries in which they are working. Can anyone share an example where you have seen this?

- Some African churches and organisations may want to contribute financially to projects and ministries when in partnership with foreigners. Sometimes foreigners will tell them not to give because they can cover all the costs themselves. This is a big insult to Africans and can make them feel offended, ashamed, inferior, or angry. As we have learned in this curriculum, it's important for all people to own the project together and use their assets to contribute what they can. Africans should own the process of development in their own countries, and foreigners should consider them as equal partners in fundraising for ministries and projects.

Speaking about the Conflicts

It is important that we don't quickly brush aside the frustrations that Africans and foreigners feel in their partnerships and relationships over culture and money. These issues may seem small but over time they can lead to the total breakdown of relationships between Africans and foreigners. When these issues begin to cause frustration, we are often tempted to ignore them for the sake of "keeping the peace". We act patient and don't speak up until we become so annoyed that our bitterness boils over. This boiling over can result in complete destruction of a relationship, shouting at one another, or resigning from a position.

Instead of ignoring the issue, we must keep on striving to speak the truth in love. Instead of avoiding uncomfortable and awkward conversations, we must talk openly about our real feelings so that our relationships can become healthier, less frustrating, and more fruitful.

Let's reflect on **Romans 12:18** and **Matthew 18:15-17** together.

How do these commands guide us in how to handle conflicts between Africans and foreigners, especially foreigners who are Christians?

As we have important conversations with foreigners, we should also be ready to change, repent of our own mistakes, and be willing to forgive as God forgave us in Christ. We should be patient with one another as God is patient with us. Generally, it is helpful to assume the other person has good motives for their behaviour and might only be following the norms of their culture. We need to continually communicate, discuss, and learn how to relate well together.

Building Healthy Relationships (10 minutes)

Ask the participants the question below and encourage them to include examples in their answers. You can take brief notes of their responses on a flip chart.

Briefly share what actions we can take to build healthy and fruitful relationships between Africans and foreigners.

The facilitator can summarise by mentioning the points that have not been brought out by the participants and also clarify the points that may not be clear to the participants.

- We need to learn about other cultures. Foreigners should learn about their host community and country and try to adapt to the culture there. For example, they should try to learn some of the language, greet according to the style in that country, and dress appropriately according to the specific African culture of that area. Africans should try to learn about the cultures of their visiting foreigners so that they can communicate well and work well with them. Both foreigners and Africans should learn to appreciate some of each other's cultural differences. Look for aspects of the other person's culture that are beautiful, praiseworthy, and honouring to God.

- We need to recognise that the presence of cultural differences does not necessarily imply that one culture is right and the other is wrong on a particular issue. There are many issues in which there simply is no right or wrong. Maybe we could look at some of the differences as casting light on different aspects of God's character. For example, God creates both individuals and communities and calls both of them "good". So if we only recognise one of these, we miss out on the other aspect of God's beautiful creation and become imbalanced.

- As much as possible, Africans and foreigners should view each other as equal partners as we all try to help African communities to grow in their four foundational relationships with God, self, others, and the creation. Both Africans and foreigners need to remember that we are all created in the image of God, gifted with different skills and abilities.

We also need to appreciate our God-given individual talents and embrace learning from each other. We should treat each other with mutual respect and as equal ministry partners. This includes listening to each other's views and opinions, and allowing the host community and local leadership to make decisions relating to their situation. Decision making power should not be based on who has the most money.

- Foreigners should be encouraged to learn about the conditions, people, culture, and environment before they travel to an African country. This will better prepare them in every aspect and reduce culture shock. Likewise, Africans also need to learn about foreigners who are coming to work with them, and try to understand their culture. This will help to reduce conflict.
- We learned in this curriculum that people have many different definitions of poverty. It is important for both foreigners and Africans to discuss what they mean by "poverty" and what they believe the causes of poverty are. Foreigners should be willing to learn from Africans about poverty in Africa and the true causes of poverty. Unfortunately, many foreigners do not see poverty as a breakdown of the four foundational relationships, and they only see poverty as a lack of money or material things. We who have gone through this training should be ready to teach them that there are various types of poverty and that only holistic approaches will be effective.
- We all need flexibility in cross-cultural relationships. We all need to be prepared for the possibility that things may not go according to plan and we need to embrace changes that come. Foreigners may have to adjust their plans to accommodate Africans's ways of doing things, and Africans may have to adjust their plans to accommodate the foreigners's needs as well.
- Ensure that there are clear communication channels and timely information flow to promote a clear understanding of what is expected from all parties: foreign donors, foreign workers in Africa, African leaders, church members, and community members. We need to be open and transparent in our working relationships to foster development. Communicate and clarify what you mean multiple times in order to avoid misunderstandings. Discuss issues openly with genuine hearts and gentleness. This will build trust among the different parties and the commitment to work together.
- We need to hold each other accountable. We should all be accountable to the communities we are trying to help, accountable to African leaders, and accountable to foreign donors and organisations. Africans need to be held accountable for any foreign funding they receive, and also hold foreign governments, development organisations, missionaries and sponsors accountable. Africans should be willing to speak up and correct foreigners who are making mistakes and causing harm in Africa. Sometimes Africans keep quiet out of fear of losing funding, but we must have the courage to speak up. Additionally, we need to hold our leaders accountable. For too long Africa has allowed corrupt leaders to negotiate unfair deals with foreign countries and corruption has taken centre stage between Africans and foreign agencies at the expense of the people. It is time for the African people to rise up and hold African leadership and foreign agencies accountable. May God give us courage and love to do this well. You can read more about accountability in the "Further Reflection" section at the end of this lesson.

Closing Prayer

Before you explain the take-home activities and send people to small groups for discussion, take some time to pray together. Repent for mistakes that Africans and foreigners have made in their relationships together. Ask God to give everyone wisdom, patience, honesty, and love for one another as they together try to help African communities. You can pray or ask someone else to pray.

Take-Home Activities for Lesson 19

The take-home activities will include assignments or activities that the participants should carry out in their communities, churches, or place of work, applying the lessons they have learned. The facilitator should provide detailed guidelines and clear instructions on how to go about the take-home activities.

1. **For Africans who know foreigners** – Invite a foreign friend or colleague to visit you at your home for a meal. Take time to discuss your different cultures so that you can learn from one another. Tell your foreign friend some of the things you have learned about in this lesson. Ask your friend what you can do differently in the relationship to adapt to your friend's culture in order that you have a more fruitful relationship together. If the friend is willing, pray together after this conversation.

2. **For Africans who do not know any foreigners** – Think about if there has ever been any foreign missionary or organisation who has worked in your community. If you think you have received any personal benefit from the work of the missionary or the organisation in your community, then take a step to show gratitude for their work. You could approach the missionary or organisation in person to thank them for the work they have done, or you could write a personal letter to thank them for what they have done and send it to them by post or through email.

3. **For foreigners** – Invite an African friend or colleague to your home for a meal. If you are only in Africa for a short visit, you can arrange to meet together at a different location. Take time to discuss your different cultures so that you can learn from one another. Tell your friend some of the things you have learned about in this lesson. Ask your African friend to be honest with you and tell you things you can change to better adapt to the local culture and community so that you can have healthier and more fruitful relationships. Ask if there is anything that you are doing that is seen as offensive or frustrating to your friend or other local people. If the friend is willing, pray together after this conversation.

Small Group Discussion (50 minutes)

During this small group discussion time, try to make the groups diverse. If you have a few foreigners in your training group, make sure that they are divided up into various groups rather than being in one group by themselves. Ideally, there would be a mix of foreigners and Africans in every small group so that people can learn from each other's perspectives on these hard issues.

Remind participants to be sensitive, patient, gentle, and loving in these discussions about relationships and culture which can sometimes be uncomfortable. Encourage them to be slow to speak and quick to listen.

Read out loud the questions that they will be answering and make sure they understand them.

Divide them up into groups of 5 people (anywhere from 3-6 people per group). They can be the same groups as before, or you can put them into new groups.

If you have organised the whole workshop to take longer than what has been outlined, then feel free to give the participants a longer time for discussion.

Remember to move around and listen in with the groups as they discuss. Be available to answer their questions. You can give guidance or input if necessary during their discussions, but they have heard you talk a lot, so try to let them do the talking now.

Remind them periodically about how much time remains for their discussion.

1. **What were you most surprised to learn about in this lesson?**
2. **Is there anything in this lesson that you disagreed with, or that you found hard to understand? Let your fellow group members explain for you any topics that were difficult for you to fully understand.**
3. **Have you ever asked a foreigner to give you money or material resources? Why or why not? If you are a foreigner, have you ever asked Africans to give you money or material resources? Why or why not?**
4. **Has a foreigner ever helped you by teaching you something new about God, or new practical knowledge or skills? Were they also willing to learn things from you? If you are a foreigner, what have you learned from Africans?**
5. **What harm have you seen foreigners cause in Africa?**
6. **Would you rather have a foreign missionary come to live in your community for a few years or have a different foreign church group come every few months for only a week at a time? Why?**
7. **What can foreigners do differently to improve their relationships with you as Africans?**
8. **What can Africans do differently to improve their relationships with you as foreigners?**

Further Reflection

Read this section at home for further learning.

As we engage with each of the four categories of foreigners that were mentioned at the beginning of this lesson, there are some principles to consider that will help us as we interact with each group.

A. Short-term and Long-term Missionaries

These foreigners are brothers and sisters in Christ. They are in Africa to preach the gospel and to help us in our fight against poverty. When interacting with these foreign missionaries, remember to follow the Bible's teachings about how to relate to brothers and sisters. We should work with them as part of the same team, the body of Christ. When they make mistakes or fall into sin, we should confront them gently and try to restore them.

Some principles to reflect on:

1. Don't judge all foreign missionaries by your personal experience with one missionary. Foreign missionaries come from countries all over the world. They are extremely diverse not only in terms of culture but also in terms of doctrinal beliefs, church practices, and lifestyle practices. And be careful not to judge what people are like from a particular country based on what one missionary is like. A foreign missionary from Canada is probably very different in many important ways from the average Canadian.

2. Many foreign missionaries are trying to help in Africa. They care about the problems here and want to see change happen. But they may come with god-complexes, or limited understandings of the true nature and causes of poverty. Many of them end up hurting in Africa while trying to help. As Africans, we must be ready to gently challenge them to improve on their poverty fighting techniques, and gently challenge them to see their god-complexes and pride. Whenever possible, we should encourage them to participate in future *Helping without Hurting in Africa* trainings.

3. There are a lot of short-term missionary groups that visit Africa from other foreign countries. Most of these groups could greatly benefit from the principles we looked at in Lesson 18 – "Mission Trips Within Africa". The same principles that we learned for trips within Africa also apply to trips to Africa from foreign countries. Don't say "yes" to hosting every intern, visitor, or short-term team that wants to come from a foreign country. Make sure that such a team will plan their trip well and actually benefit your church or community. Be willing to tell them "no, you should not come", when necessary. This can be very hard, especially if saying "no" means losing out on financial aid or gifts that would come along with the trip. Remember what we have learned in this curriculum, that the solution to poverty is not as simple as giving money. If a trip is going to cause more harm than good, have the courage to say "no" or be honest with them about how they can change their plans so that the trip will be more helpful. Consider telling foreign teams that they are required to work through *Helping without Hurting in Africa* before visiting you. Or you could tell them that they need to read the American book called, *Helping Without Hurting in Short-Term Missions* before visiting.

4. Foreign missionaries come to Africa for different reasons. Some come to learn, and others come to minister, and hopefully even those who come to minister will also be willing to learn. For those missionaries that are coming to minister and work in Africa, we should encourage them to come when they are skilled and trained. It causes African communities a lot of frustration when foreign missionaries come to Africa with a desire to change the world quickly even though they do not have the training that they need. This is especially common among young foreigners who have just finished secondary school or university. They want to make a difference in the world. This desire is good, but we should encourage them to be fully equipped for the work that they want to do. Encourage foreign missionaries that if they want to teach pastors, they should be theologically trained. If they want to work with homeless people in Africa, they should have experience working with homeless people in their country of origin. If they want to come to Africa to help sick people, they should have studied medicine in their country of origin. Hold missionaries accountable to the work that they do, and insist that they be well-trained and skilled people.

5. Take time to appreciate missionaries for their ministry. They have left their original homes and families to preach the gospel or help materially poor people in Africa. They have sacrificed. And some of them have also given up materially rich lifestyles in their home countries in order to live in Africa. When you see missionaries help without hurting, thank them for their ministry.

B. Development and Humanitarian Organisations

Development organisations, humanitarian organisations, and charities are extremely diverse in their activities in Africa. Organisations distribute relief aid after disasters, dig wells, sponsor children for their education, rescue people from human trafficking, organise savings groups, counsel and treat people with HIV, teach new agricultural methods, teach on sanitation practices, etc. The list of activities is almost endless. Many organisations are doing great work that African countries and communities have benefitted from. But there are also a lot of organisations that are making the mistakes we have looked at throughout this curriculum.

Some principles to reflect on:

1. Hold organisations accountable to doing quality work with integrity in African countries and communities. When you find out that there are corrupt staff, either foreigners or Africans, make sure you report the corruption to the highest levels of the organisation, and sometimes it may be important to report that corruption to your government leaders as well.

2. Try to encourage Christian staff at development organisations to go through this curriculum, *Helping without Hurting in Africa*. This will help organisations to do more effective work in fighting poverty by being more holistic in their approach, and looking at the deeper nature and causes of poverty, as well as common mistakes that are made. Even in cases where the staff and the organisation are not Christian, you can still try to hold them accountable to helping without hurting, by sharing with them some of the principles you have learned in this curriculum and showing them what is actually happening in your community.

3. Encourage organisations to work with local communities so that the local people will take ownership of their own development. Encourage participation of the local people at every level of planning and implementation and evaluation. Encourage the organisations to be accountable not only to donors but also to local churches, community groups, and generally to all the people of the community they are working in.

4. If an organisation offers free handouts to your community in a way that you know will create dependency or other kinds of harm, be willing to tell that organisation that you don't want the free gifts, and that their approach will not help the community. Set an example by returning the free gifts you personally received back to the organisation. Don't take things just because they are free if you know that a bad approach is being used.

5. Try to influence your government's regulation of organisations in your country. It would be helpful if governments required all organisations to be compliant with certain standards of integrity in their work. You could also encourage organisations to comply with certain international standards in their operations and work. For example, one possible standard is called the Core Humanitarian Standard. The Core Humanitarian Standard (or CHS) focuses on nine quality commitments for organisations. These include making sure that organisations are involving communities in decision making, that there are ways for staff and community members to raise complaints, and that money is used responsibly as intended.[2] As you connect to different organisations working in Africa, you can also consult charity evaluators that monitor the work of charities and organisations. In the United States, a couple examples are the Evangelical Council for Financial Accountability and Charity Navigator.[3]

6. When you see organisations doing good work in your community to care for the materially poor, find ways to financially support that organisation, even if your contribution is small. Don't fall into the mind-set that all development work being done through organisations in your community should be funded by foreign donors. Raise local resources to supplement the work of these good organisations.

C. Foreign Companies and Governments

There are many foreign countries who have government officials living in Africa as well as employees of private companies. Some of the countries with the strongest presence in Africa today include China, the United States, and the European Union. But there are many other foreign countries working in African countries as well.

Foreign governments and companies often try to help African countries, but at the same time, they are also looking to benefit their own companies and governments. We should not be naïve and think that they are all in Africa only to help materially poor people. They are here to find profit for themselves as well. The relationships between foreign governments and African governments can be very complicated. In the same way, partnerships between foreign companies and African governments and African workers can also be very complicated. On the one hand, Africa has benefitted extensively from these partnerships in terms of infrastructure development, loans, aid during times of crisis or disaster, and job creation.

However, at the same time, some foreign companies and governments have caused immense harm, suffering, and instability in Africa, from colonial times up to the present day. Perhaps the most tragic part is that many Africans and many people around the world are ignorant of the abuses currently happening in Africa. A large amount of Africa's resources are being shipped out to other countries, and often, there is very little benefit to common African people.

Some points to reflect on:

1. Use grants offered by foreign companies and governments wisely. Be careful to read the agreements carefully and see what strings are attached. Make deals with foreign companies and governments that will not only benefit you personally, but your community and country as well.

2. Be careful about taking loans from foreign governments which could make your community or country a slave to unpayable debt. Consider the impact of loans on future generations or future people in your position. It's easy to think that loans are very helpful and positive when repayment is allowed to be postponed. But consider what harm you are causing to those who will come after you who will be forced to repay those loans.

3. Reduce bureaucracy, work for stability and safety, build infrastructure, and enforce rule of law in order to make your country a favourable environment for foreign companies who want to invest in your country.

4. Remember to care for staff of foreign governments and companies as people. They are all different. Some are Christians and some aren't. Some of them are trying to make a very positive difference in Africa and some are not. Get to know them as individuals and build friendships with them. Help them to settle in well to the communities that they live in as it can sometimes be lonely living in a foreign country. Invite them to your churches.

5. Hold accountable African leaders who are making deals with foreign governments and countries in exchange for personal profit or even bribes. Many times, these leaders personally benefit while their country is looted by these foreign governments and companies. These evil practices must stop. We must not ignore what is happening. Additionally, we need to be willing to report corrupt foreign officials and hold them to account. Nobody should be above the law. Sometimes it may be advantageous to request the help of foreign missionaries in holding foreign leaders to account. During colonial times, there were many foreign Christian missionaries who stood up against their own governments to oppose slavery and protect the land rights of Africans.

A few examples of what is happening today in Africa involving foreign governments and companies:

"Nigeria in West Africa has pumped more than 400 billion dollars's worth of oil since it was discovered there in the 1950s – enough to cancel all of Sub-Saharan Africa's debt. However, more than 80 per cent of oil revenue has accrued to just 1 per cent of the population, while the majority of the population have got poorer, leading to a violent rebellion in the oil-rich Niger Delta."[4] The Niger Delta "is the poorest region of the country and there is only 1 secondary school per 14,000 people."[5]

"Around 70 per cent of Gabon's timber exports are sent illegally to China, while the figure for Equatorial Guinea is thought to be 90 per cent."[6]

"During the 2000s, up to US$300 million a year in tuna, shrimp and lobster were being stolen by foreign trawlers in Somali waters each year.... The plundering of Somali territorial waters by foreign fishing fleets gave rise to an armed response by local fisherpeople. This 'piracy of the rich' was what sparked the 'piracy of the poor' in response."[7]

D. Sponsors, Donors, and Partners Living Outside of Africa

The money being spent in Africa by foreign organisations and missionaries mostly comes from donations given by ordinary people in foreign countries. People sacrifice money that they could have spent on themselves. They choose to give so that they can see the gospel spread in Africa, or they give to help materially poor African communities. These are foreigners we might never meet in person, but they have a huge impact on our lives in Africa, in positive ways but sometimes also in negative ways.

Some points to reflect on:

1. Stop using the term donors, because it reinforces god-complexes and feelings of inferiority by classifying everyone into either a giver or a receiver. It is better to refer to people as ministry partners or financial resource partners.[8]

2. When possible, communicate to these financial resource partners and thank them for their sacrificial giving. You can do this through email or social media or phone calls, but this can also be done by communicating to the missionaries or organisation's staff workers who are on the ground in Africa. Remember that there is poverty in every country of the world. Every dollar or shilling given to Africa is money that could have been spent on fighting poverty in the foreigner's home country. Sometimes it is hearing a simple "thank you" that will encourage people to continue to give generously.

3. Hold financial resource partners accountable. It is common for those who are giving money to dictate what will be done through organisations and missionaries. They have a plan and an agenda and sometimes this gets forced on African communities and churches. Be willing to speak up to these partners directly, or indirectly through development workers and missionaries. Push for the involvement of the local community in every aspect of any project or ministry plan. Remind financial resource partners that they do not fully know what things are like on the ground, and therefore it is very important for foreign partners and African community and church members to listen to each other well and learn from each other. Encourage them to learn about African culture and to consider African solutions to African problems.

4. Communicate clearly and regularly to avoid misunderstanding. Share accurate and unexaggerated stories with foreign partners. Always tell the truth. It is tempting to make a situation sound terrible so as to make people feel pity and give more. It is also tempting to exaggerate success stories so as to make people give more. This is lying, pure and simple. We must be people who tell the truth. Remember what we learned in

Lesson 11 about corruption. When we tell the truth, we and foreign partners can work together to overcome new challenges so that ministries and projects can be successful.

5. Communicate your expectations clearly to foreign partners, and ask them to also communicate their expectations clearly to you.

6. Try to remember that your particular church or ministry is one of only thousands of ministries that God is using to advance his kingdom in Africa. Other ministries are not in competition with us. They are part of our family in the body of Christ. If God has called a foreign partner to be involved in X activity, and your ministry does Y activity, then help the foreign partner to connect to another organisation near you that engages in X activity rather than trying to make your ministry sound like it is really about X.[9]

7. Encourage foreign partners to come and visit your country regularly. This will help them to learn about African life and culture and to learn more about the ministries that are happening in your communities. This is also important in order to build stronger relationships with these foreign partners. Foreign partners need to be reminded that fighting poverty is about reconciling relationships, not just giving money. Visits bring the foreign partners face to face with the people they are trying to help. And these visits are also important for accountability. There are corrupt organisations in Africa who are receiving donor money and lying about their programs. We should always encourage foreign partners to visit so that they can see what is actually happening, and in turn so that they will support the organisations that are honest and doing good work.

Helping Without Hurting in Africa

Facilitator Manual

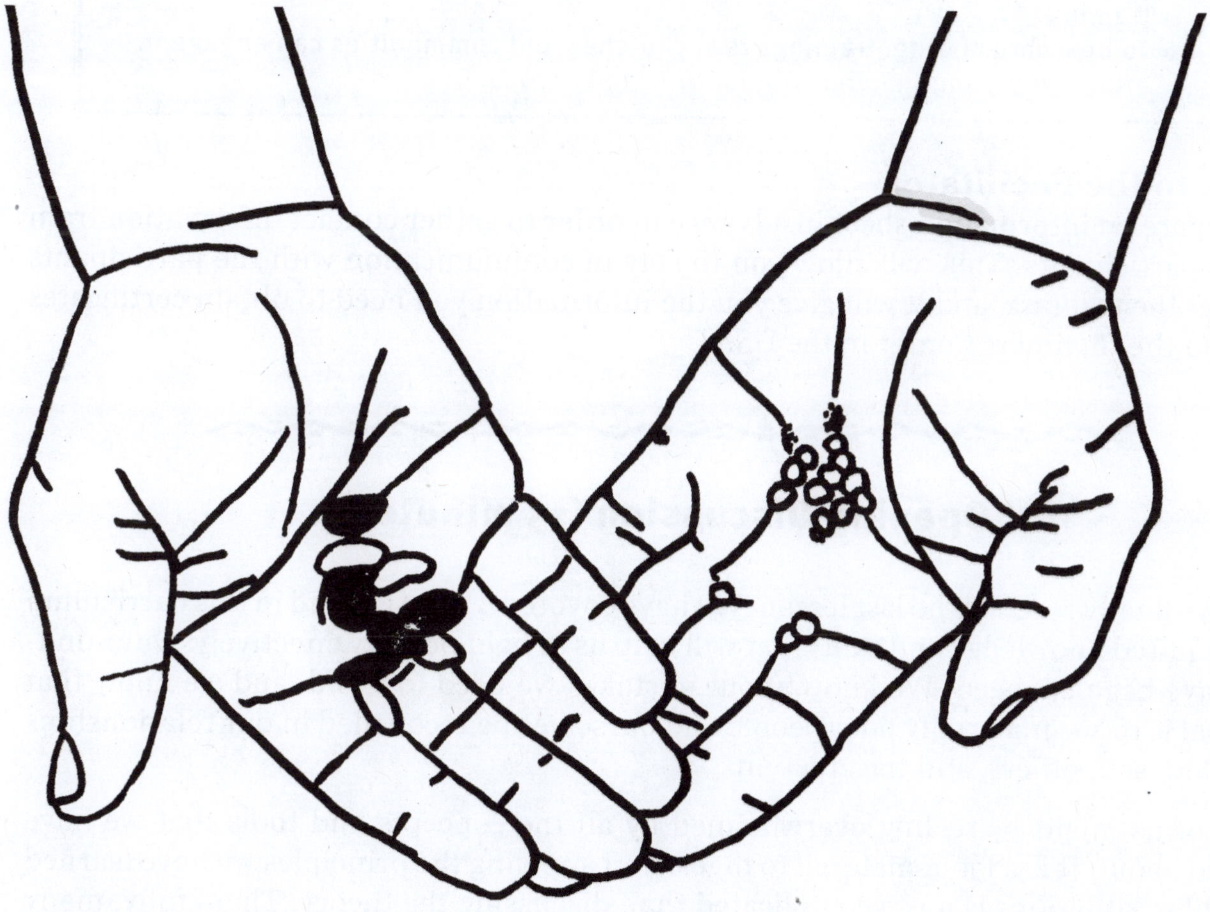

Lesson 20: Seed Projects and Further Resources

Lesson 20: Seed Projects and Further Resources

Time Length: 1 hour

In this section, you will find:

- An action planning template for church or ministry seed projects.
- A list of books and further resources for a deeper look at fighting poverty after this training.

Lesson Objectives:

- To draw an action plan and put into practise what we learned from this training.
- To be aware of other trainings that churches and communities can engage in after completing *Helping Without Hurting in Africa*.

Notes to the Facilitator

- Prepare an information sheet in advance in order to gather contact information from the participants. This will allow you to stay in communication with the participants after the training, and it will give you the information you need to obtain certificates from the Chalmers Center in the USA.

Opening Discussion (15 minutes)

We have finally reached the last lesson. We have covered a lot of ground in this curriculum and acquired knowledge and skills that will help us to fight poverty effectively. Our mind-sets have been changed. We know about mistakes we need to avoid, and we know that our goal is to see materially poor people and ourselves be reconciled in our relationships with God, self, others, and the creation.

Some of us might be feeling overwhelmed by all the concepts and tools that we have learned about. It is a lot of material to digest and applying the principles we have learned to real life situations is more complicated than discussing the theory. Thankfully, many of the ideas in these twenty lessons can be simplified to a few basic principles that can help us in our day to day lives. If you are unsure of what to do in a particular situation as you try to help a materially poor person, focus on these basic but important principles:

1. God has called us to have compassion on materially poor people. As God has loved us and been generous to us, we should also love materially poor people and give generously of our time and resources.

2. When you want to help materially poor people, consider if your action will move both you and the other people closer to being in right relationship with God, self, others, and the creation.

3. As much as possible, work *with* materially poor people, not *for* them. Don't do for people what they can do for themselves.

4. Encourage people to use their assets and skills to work hard to support themselves and their families and to share with others who are in need.

5. Pray continually and seek God's guidance as you go out to try to help the poor. Don't try to do it alone. Depend on the Lord to empower you through his Holy Spirit.

Even with these helpful principles, poverty is still a very complicated issue. There will be times when we make mistakes as we try to help poor people. When we fail, (and we all fail sometimes), we need to repent, thank God for his grace, learn from our mistakes, and then keep on trying to help people. The Bible shows us that God regularly uses imperfect people to carry out his plan in this world, and that includes us.

Because poverty is complicated, there will also be times when we disagree with each other about the best approaches. Let's learn how to disagree in a loving way, always assuming the best about each other, and being patient with one another. We need to leave this training not with pride, but with humility. We should not become judgemental people who are always criticising others who are trying their best to care for poor people. Let's be attentive to recognise the good that we see people doing and thank them for how they are spending themselves on behalf of the poor. At the same time, we can also challenge people when we see areas that they can improve, but we should do so carefully, gently, and with love.

And the most important thing is to begin with looking at ourselves. We should not remain the same; we should leave here changed. We should be people who are even more filled with love and generosity than we were before, and we should be people who are going to work hard and thoughtfully in order to truly help materially poor people without hurting them.

Don't leave from here feeling paralysed with fear, worried that you will make so many mistakes. Fear will prevent you from moving on and starting something new to fight poverty. Transformation of people is God's work, not ours, and it's our privilege to be used by God to bring reconciliation. God is the author of change.[1] We only need to be faithful citizens of God's kingdom; we can leave the transformation up to God. Our job is to do what God has called us to do. God does not leave us alone in this work. He empowers us to preach good news to the poor. We can go out with courage knowing that God is with us. Read **2 Timothy 1:7**.

In this last lesson, it is now time to prayerfully draw a plan of action for how you and your church will apply what you've learned. What will you do next to help materially poor people and fight poverty so that you can begin to see some changes in your life, family, church, community, and your nation as a whole?

Have faith in our living God that he can work through you today, this week, and this year. You can see real change in your community. We echo the words of Obiageli Ezekwesili, the Nigerian co-founder of Transparency International,[2] "There's absolutely nothing that the God I believe in cannot do!" God is going to use you to bring transformation in people's lives. We know that things will not be perfect until Jesus returns, but in the meantime, Jesus will continue to carry out his work of reconciliation, and he will use you to do it!

Ask the participants the question below and encourage them to reflect on the lessons they have learned when giving their responses. Take note of their responses on the flip chart.

Now that we have finished this training, give specific examples of possible next steps you can take as an individual to follow up on what you have learned and to help materially poor people.

After they finish answering, you can suggest a couple next steps:

1. Reflect on your God-given gifts, skills, knowledge, and resources. It is important to remember that transformation starts with you. Begin by looking at what you can do to bring change to yourself, your family, your church, and your community using the resources and abilities that God has given to you.

2. Consider doing a resource map or asset map with your family or your community as we discussed in Lesson 15.

3. Try to carry out any take-home activities that you have not already completed.

4. Be intentional about spending more time building strong relationships with materially poor people in your family, church, and community.

5. Begin to preach and teach in your local church what you have learned in this curriculum.

6. Give even more generously than you did before, but use wisdom and creativity in your giving, following what you have learned in this curriculum. Here are some ideas:

- Support your local church by giving more generously financially or materially.
- Rarely give things to people for free unless it's a personal gift to a friend. Instead, offer items at a reduced rate. Then people will feel ownership of what they purchase from you, and you will know if they truly value what you are offering to give to them. Additionally, you will be able to save money and help even more people. For example, instead of distributing water filters to a whole community for free, charge people at least 10% of the actual price of the filters.
- Invest in the development of other people by helping them pay for education.
- When giving a gift to someone or to an organisation, consider making it a matching or proportionate gift. For example, you could say that your church will contribute one shilling towards a project in another community for every one shilling raised locally in that community.
- Help people start new businesses through a one-time investment gift, or by giving them a loan.
- Give financial gifts to local organisations that are doing good development work in your community.

Seed Projects (10 minutes)

In addition to the next steps you can take as an individual, it's good to consider what steps your local church can take to begin fighting poverty in your community. We have learned about the complicated nature of poverty in this curriculum and thought about many different things we can do to help without hurting. But it can be overwhelming trying to decide where to start after receiving so much information! It is wise to start with something small and simple. Starting with a small activity will enable you to practise applying what you have learned before you move on to more complex projects and initiatives. Starting small and simple will also make your first initiative more likely to succeed. When people of your church see the transformation that results from the small activity, they will be encouraged and inspired to do more to continue trying to help materially poor people.

When we speak of small initiatives that local churches or communities can do, we call these **seed projects**. Seed projects are small practical actions that local churches or communities can carry out in their local area to fight poverty. These actions should demonstrate God's love and help materially poor people.[3] Seed projects are like a seed planted in the ground. The goal is that the small seed grows up and bears large fruit. A seed project is a small beginning of your church's ministry to help the poor and fight poverty in your community. As your church or community engages in the seed project, your members will be able to gain experience in putting into practise the principles you and they have learned throughout this curriculum. They will continue to learn from any mistakes that they make and they will be encouraged to continue showing love to materially poor people in the future.

Seed projects should be done as a way to preach and show the good news of the Kingdom of God, but not used as a bribe or tool to manipulate people into joining the church.[4] Seed projects should be done using local financial and material resources. And churches should always try to work alongside other community members in their seed projects so that there is community participation. Although seed projects are simple, they should be planned thoughtfully and prayerfully so that they are done following the principles we have learned in this training.

Here are some possible examples of seed projects for local churches or communities:

- Planting trees throughout the neighborhood.
- Starting a ministry at the church to provide emergency safety, food, and accommodation to women when they need to flee from domestic violence.
- Inviting a few beggars from the neighborhood for a fellowship meal with some of the church members, learning about their situation, and discussing ways to work together.
- Spending one day cleaning the local health centre together and praying for the sick patients.
- Starting a community savings and loans group.

What are other possible seed projects that local churches or communities could do?

Allow the participants to come up with more seed projects on their own and then you can list these additional ideas below if they have not already been mentioned by the participants.

- Planning for skilled church members to teach job training skills to interested church members and other people in the community.
- Cleaning the neighborhood streets of rubbish.
- Speaking to a political leader about a broken system that is oppressing materially poor people in your community.
- Digging a new well for your community, with the participation of other community members.
- Volunteering in a local school to tutor children who need extra help in their studies.
- Having church members donate blood to the local hospital.
- Saving money as a church in a relief fund, so that the next time there is a fire or flood in the community, and people need urgent help, your church will be able to respond.
- Visiting the homes of elderly people in the community to encourage them and to see if they need any assistance in repairing their homes or help in their gardens.
- Hosting a day of football and Bible study for street children and church children together.
- Employing homeless people to work part-time at your church on a regular basis doing maintenance and cleaning.
- Conducting a community awareness day on health and sanitation issues.

These seed projects may seem small, but they can make a big impact. Hear the words of Desmond Tutu, former Archbishop in South Africa: "Do your little bit of good where you are; it's those little bits of good put together that overwhelm the world."[5] As a local church or community, begin by doing something small in obedience to God's commands about how we should care for the poor, and then praise God for any change that he brings.

Action Planning (10 minutes)

As people, we make decisions to do something new or to change our behaviour almost every day. For example, we may have the good intention of finding time to visit a certain materially poor church member.[6]

What happens to many of our good intentions?

We often have good intentions but then we fail to follow through on our decisions. We might get too busy. Or we may simply forget about the decision that we made. Or a couple of weeks go by and we might lose interest, or motivation, or we might start to feel lazy.

Good intentions are not sufficient to bring about real change. It is important to turn good intentions into what we call "action plans". An action plan is a document that highlights the steps that must be taken in order to achieve a specific goal.

When you make an action plan, you pray and ask God to guide you, you think carefully to make a wise plan, you write down that plan, and then you go home and make sure to carry out all the steps of your plan. An action plan can make the key difference between good intentions that produce no fruit, and real lasting change. Many times when we talk about action plans we tend to think it is for big projects or for organisations to use when asking for funds. We need to correct this false mind-set because each one of us needs an action plan to enable us to achieve the change we want to see.

A simple action plan can consist of two parts: one goal and several activities.[7]

1. The **goal** is what you want to see happen, or the positive change that you want to see.

2. The **activities** are things that we need to do in order to see that change happen.

It is important that every activity includes the **person responsible** for the action and the **time frame** in which the activity must be completed.

Examples of Goals

1. Three unemployed people in my church will find daily work that will allow them to support themselves and their families by March 28th.
2. Four trees will be planted at my church by June 5th.
3. My community will have a new well for obtaining clean drinking water by August 1st.

Examples of Activities

(These three example activities could all fit with goal #3 above.)

1. On Sunday the 10th, I will host a meeting for other church leaders and community leaders in our area to discuss about our idea for making a new well. If they agree, we will elect committee members who can lead this project.
2. On Thursday, the 14th, the elected committee will speak to our local government officials and see if they can permit us to build a well or participate in the project with us.
3. On a Sunday next month, each of the local churches involved in this well project will have a fundraiser within their congregation. The pastor of each church is responsible to see that this is done.

It is helpful to make sure that action plans are specific, both the goal and the activities. Write down what needs to be done, when it needs to be done, by whom it needs to be done, and what resources are needed to do it. To make your action plan succeed, try to make sure that you set deadlines and then follow through on the timeline that you make. Communicate well to everyone who will participate in the action plan. Make sure it's well understood by everyone that reads it. Ask for feedback and make adjustments to the plan based on the advice that other people give to you. Make sure that your plan is reasonable and attainable. You can also consider putting people or a system in place to monitor the progress of your activities and evaluate whether the goal was achieved.

Action plans can be for a short or a long period of time, depending on the context and the urgency. An action plan can be done on an individual or family level, or a church or community level, or a regional or national level.

Has anyone ever done an action plan for yourself as an individual, or with your family? If yes, please share about your experience and the benefits of your plan.

We should all consider making action plans for ourselves and our families. Change begins with us. We must lead by example. Let's work on changing our own behaviour before we begin to challenge others. The same thing is true for our local churches. Often we complain about the government or organisations when we see the problems of poverty in our community. Let's not wait for others to solve our problems. Let's do something through our local churches and communities and trust that God will use us to bring change.

Activity – Make an Action Plan (20 minutes)

If you have time and if you think your group needs the extra help, you could write an example of an action plan on the flip chart to show them. Write an example goal in about 1 or 2 sentences. Then you can write between 3 and 5 steps or activities that could be done to try to achieve that goal.

My Action Plan:

Goal:____

Activity 1:____

Activity 2:____

Activity 3:____

Activity 4:____

Activity 5:____

Right now we are each going to begin to work on an action plan. If you are here at this training as an individual, you could make an action plan for what you will begin to do as an individual or together with your family to put into practise what you've learned, or to help a specific materially poor person. If you are here at this training with other members of your church, you could begin to create an action plan for a seed project as part of your church's ministry. Consider the different kinds of seed projects that we have discussed, and think about what God might be calling your church or local organisation to do as a first step in showing God's love and fighting poverty in your community. What you write today can be a rough draft that you will then discuss further with your other church members or community members.

The participants can spread out as individuals or small groups into different places around the room or outside. As they work on their action plans, move around and give advice and answer questions. Encourage the participants to help one another, especially after they have finished writing their own action plan.

After people have written at least a rough draft of their action plan, take some time as a large group to hear what kinds of plans people have made. Ask for a few volunteers who can share about their action plans for seed projects. If you have enough time, you can have every participant share at least a one sentence goal with the group.

Resources, Trainings, and Books (5 minutes)

Ask participants to answer the question and take note of their responses on the flip chart.

What other resources, trainings, and books can you recommend to the group as helpful next steps after completing this training? What tools or programs would help local churches and communities as they try to fight poverty and see development?

There are many tools we can use to bring development and change in our lives, in our churches, and our communities as you can see from this list generated from our discussion. Here are some other ideas for further action from the authors which you can read and analyse at home.

Training in Microfinance Ministries

Microfinance enables low-income households to access financial services such as savings, loans, and insurance. Poor households use these services to meet a wide range of economic needs, including consumption smoothing, business investments, household investments, life-cycle needs, and emergencies. When combined with evangelism and discipleship activities, microfinance can be a powerful tool for holistic ministry, addressing people's economic, social, and spiritual needs.

Unfortunately, poorly designed microfinance initiatives can do considerable harm: burying poor people in debt, undermining the testimony of the church or ministry, and bringing dishonour to the name of Christ. In particular, it is extremely risky for churches and small ministries to operate microloan programs, as their cultures are not conducive to enforcing loan repayment. An alternative that has proved highly successful is for churches and small ministries to promote savings and credit associations in which poor people save and lend their own money to one another.

- Before trying to launch a microfinance ministry, read the following book written by the Chalmers Center:
- Brian Fikkert and Russel Mask, *From Dependence to Dignity: How to Alleviate Poverty Through Church-Centered Microfinance* (Grand Rapids, Michigan: Zondervan, 2015).
- For help in promoting church-centred savings and credit associations, the Chalmers Center's *Restore: Savings* curriculum can be downloaded from the Chalmers Center's website at https://chalmers.org/restore-savings/
- The Chalmers Center's *Business, Home, and Health* curricula can be used to provide additional training in the context of microfinance ministries. Download from the Chalmers Center's website at https://chalmers.org/bhh/

Trainings to Mobilise Churches and Communities

- **Restore: Innovation** – A process for training churches to be ambassadors of reconciliation. Church members are guided through a repeatable process of designing and implementing initiatives to share Christ's love in their communities. Available at www.chalmers.org.
- **Timothy Leadership Training** – Practical ministry training created by Raise Up Global Ministries to equip church leaders to make action plans for church and community transformation. https://www.raiseupglobal.org/leadership/tlt
- **Truth-Centered Transformation** – A program of Reconciled World designed to equip churches to apply God's truth to their lives, reach out and serve their communities, and learn basic life skills. https://tctprogram.org/
- **Church and Community Mobilization Process** – A comprehensive manual produced by Tearfund that equips churches to mobilise their communities to pursue asset-based community development. https://learn.tearfund.org/~/media/files/tilz/churches/ccm/2019-tearfund-ccmp-facilitators-manual-en.pdf
- **Shalom Manual: A Manual for Christian Workers** - A one-week workshop using participatory adult education principles to teach Christian leaders how to engage in transformation of their communities. Contact Mary Crickmore at info@worldrenew.net
- **Community Health Evangelism** – A program of Medical Ambassadors International that seamlessly integrates discipleship and church planting with disease prevention and community-based development. https://www.chenetwork.org/
- **Vision Conferences** - These events by Disciple Nations Alliance provide an opportunity to unite the local body of Christ around a biblical vision for church-based social transformation and to receive practical training and tools for immediate application. https://www.disciplenations.org/resources/vision-conference-2/

Trainings in Business

- **Kingdom Business: Christ-Centered Business Education** – A resource produced by Surprised by Hope that covers the basics of starting a business https://programs.surprisedbyhope.org/
- **Business, Home, and Health** – A series of courses by the Chalmers Center to equip microenterprises and the low-income households in which they are embedded. https://chalmers.org/bhh/

Books for Personal Study

1. *When Helping Hurts* by Steve Corbett and Brian Fikkert (Moody, 2012)
2. *The Challenge for Africa* by Wangari Maathai (Pantheon Books, 2009)
3. *Prosperity? Seeking the True Gospel* by Michael Otieno Maura, Conrad Mbewe, and Ken Mbugua (Africa Christian Textbooks- Registered Trustees, 2015)
4. *Walking with the Poor* by Bryant Myers (Orbis Books, 1999)
5. *Dead Aid* by Dambisa Moyo and Niall Ferguson (Farrar, Straus, and Giroux, 2009)
6. *African Friends and Money Matters* by David E. Maranz (SIL International)
7. *The New Scramble for Africa* by Pádraig Carmody (Polity, 2016)
8. *Against all Hope: Hope for Africa* by Darrow L. Miller with Scott Allen (Disciple Nations Alliance, 2005)

Take-Home Activities for Lesson 20

The take-home activities will include assignments or activities that the participants should carry out in their communities, churches, or place of work, applying the lessons they have learned. The facilitator should provide detailed guidelines and clear instructions on how to go about the take-home activities. Everyone should do each of these activities:

1. Continue to finalise your action plan in discussion with your family, church, and community. Once the action plan is finished, be diligent in carrying out the activities you planned. Be sure to pray for your plan regularly.

2. Decide with church leaders and community leaders about what other curricula or programs might be helpful for your church or community (such as those discussed in this lesson), and make a plan for how you will get access to those resources.

Feedback, Testimonies, Evaluation, and Prayer (30 Minutes)

This is an optional section that should take you around 30 minutes to complete. You can divide the 30 minutes up between the three activities however you would like.

Be sure to remind the participants that they will receive a certificate if they have completed all the lessons in *Helping Without Hurting in Africa*. As the facilitator, it is your responsibility to carefully record the names of all participants who have completed all twenty lessons. You will then be able to email the Chalmers Center in the USA to request the certificates. Submit names and request certificates at this email address: HWHAfrica@chalmers.org. If possible, try to get the following information for each participant:

- Name
- Phone number
- City of residence
- Name of church or organisation
- Job title or ministry position
- Email address

The certificates will be emailed back to you, the facilitator, as a digital file. You can then print the certificates locally and award them to the participants. The Chalmers Center will also send an email of congratulations to all the participants who have an email address. The email will make the participants aware of the various resources available on the Chalmers Center's website.

I hope that all of you will go home and put into practise the take-home activities in your churches and communities. I will be praying that God empowers you to do those activities! Remember also to review the lessons again when at home, and take time to read the "Further Reflection" sections that we did not cover.

Some of you may be thinking of others who need this training. Please talk to me after we close, if you have any interest in facilitating your own group. I can give you more instruction about how to do this, and also help you to locate a Facilitator Manual. Not everyone will have the time or ability to facilitate this training, but I hope that many of you will consider doing so! The authors of this curriculum would love to see many pastors and development workers facilitating this training for other church leaders and community leaders in their region and for the leaders of their own churches.

Testimonies

We have completed the curriculum and now it's time for testimonies. Anyone is welcome to share with the group how this training has changed your life and how it will benefit you going back home. You are also encouraged to share how you plan to use what you have learned in your family, church, and community, and if you plan to teach these principles to other people. If you would like to write a testimony and give it to me, that is also very helpful to me, the authors, and the Chalmers Center which will be issuing your certificates. Just write on the testimony page and give it to me later, or you can use any piece of paper. You are also free to email me.

Encourage participants to be concise in their testimonies so that more people have time to speak.

Evaluation

We shall now spend a few minutes hearing feedback from you so that this curriculum can continue to be improved. You can share what you thought was good in the training, what you think needs to be improved, and also share about how I the facilitator can improve. Remember what we discussed about criticism earlier. Please speak in love, but know that I and the authors value your advice as we seek to serve Christ more faithfully and make this a very effective curriculum.

There is an optional evaluation page in your manual that you can write your evaluation on. You can complete it after we close today, tear out that page, and give it to me. Or you can use any other piece of paper.

Evaluation Questions

1. **Is there anything we have discussed that you are confused about? Is there anything I can help you understand better?**
2. **What lessons or activities did you appreciate the most?**
3. **What changes will you make in your ministry based on what you have learned?**
4. **What can be improved in this training or in my facilitation?**
5. **Would you recommend this training to a friend? Why or why not?**

Consider giving the participants your contact information so they can call you later with follow-up questions and ideas. If you have time, stay around after the training finishes so that you can answer individual questions that people have for you.

Please consider emailing the Chalmers Center a summary of what participants said during this feedback, testimonies, and evaluation session at HWHAfrica@chalmers.org. You can also scan and email the written testimonies and evaluations, or type up a few of the helpful testimonies and evaluations to send to the Chalmers Center. If you have a camera or smartphone, please consider sending photos of the group (with their permission), or even a video testimony from one of the participants.

Prayer

Thank you for sacrificing your time to complete this training. You have put in a lot of work so that you are better equipped to care for materially poor people in our churches and communities. Now go out with the Lord's blessing, knowing that he is with you, and that he will equip you to do his work by the power of the Holy Spirit. As we close and go out to face a world in which there is poverty and suffering, hear these words of comfort from Isaiah 41:10 – The Lord says, "So do not fear, for I am with you; do not be dismayed, for I am your God. I will strengthen you and help you; I will uphold you with my righteous right hand."

Be sure to close the course with prayer in a way that is appropriate for your group. Pray for the action plans and the take-home activities that the participants will go home and do. You want the participants to go with courage, trusting in God that he will help them to put into practise what they have learned. You want them to go home with generous hearts full of love and compassion for materially poor people. Commit them and their action plans to our powerful and merciful God who is willing to use even people like us for his work in this world!

Concluding Note

Dear facilitator,

We the authors, Jonny and Anthony, and the staff at the Chalmers Center, wish to thank you for your service in teaching this material to African leaders. We rely on your sacrifice and devotion in order for this teaching to spread. We praise God for the ways he has used you!

Acknowledgements

I would like to thank the Almighty God for giving me the ability, wisdom, and the opportunity to write this curriculum. I am grateful and deeply humbled by the professionalism and teamwork displayed by the co-authors and extend my word of thanks to the people that encouraged me, shared their experiences, and tirelessly engaged in discussions that helped me develop the content in this curriculum.

My special thanks go to Brian Fikkert and Steve Corbett who started the journey by sharing their experiences and knowledge through writing a book titled *When Helping Hurts*, a book that has challenged, inspired, and equipped not only the church but many other institutions in caring for the poor in a way that uplifts them. It was through this book that the idea of writing a training curriculum (*Helping without Hurting in Africa)* was birthed. Brian, I am very grateful for the support, encouragement, knowledge, and guidance you gave us in writing this curriculum.

Anthony, it was great meeting and writing this curriculum with you. Thank you for your patience and for sharing your knowledge on western culture and society. Your theological knowledge and ability to relate biblical principles to the lessons in the curriculum was amazing.

In addition, I would like to extend my special word of thanks to the people, church leaders, pastors, development organisations and institutions that shared their stories, experience, and knowledge that enriched the content in this curriculum. We learnt a lot from you.

I also want to appreciate my friends and colleagues in the development profession, both in Africa and out of Africa, for sharing their development expertise and the informational materials used in the lessons.

Special thanks go to the Chalmers Center for giving me the opportunity to work with you on this resourceful project. Justin Lonas, Lisa Brown, and all staff at the Chalmers Center-thank you for the editorial and technical support.

Finally, I would not have managed to write this book without the selfless support, encouragement and professional discussions with my dear wife Jenninah Kabiswa and lovely children, Emmanuel Kabiswa, Elizabeth Kabiswa and Divine Kabiswa. Thank you for your unique and challenging perspectives.

Jonny Horton Kabiswa Kyazze, Author

I am immensely grateful to the Lord for giving me the privilege of helping to write this curriculum. I am thankful for the many wise and generous people who have supported me and my fellow authors with their advice, ideas, and stories. We could not have done this work alone!

Let me begin by thanking Steve Corbett and Brian Fikkert who forever changed my life through their book, *When Helping Hurts*. Steve and Brian, thank you for your mission to equip the church to care for materially poor people in a loving, wise, and effective way. Brian, thank you for your many personal encouragements to me. I appreciate you as my teacher and my friend.

Jonny, it has been a pleasure to write this curriculum with you. You have a wealth of wisdom to share. And you have been very patient with me as we have written together. You always corrected me gently. Thank you for all you have taught me about African culture and society. I am grateful for your family and the love you have always shown to me.

Edward Etanu, my dear friend. I can never repay the gift you have given to me. We spent days together discussing the content for every lesson in this curriculum. You encouraged me greatly. I have learned so much from you over the years, and you have guided me every step of the way as I have lived in Uganda. Your friendship is a priceless gift.

I would like to thank all of my East African friends who have taught me about poverty and development in Africa and who have encouraged me in this project, especially Engolu Tom and Okwalinga Emmanuel. I am also grateful for all the foreign missionaries and East Africans who attended the early forms of this training. I learned so much from interacting and discussing with all of you, and your feedback helped to improve this curriculum in countless ways.

I wish to give special thanks to the following people for sharing with us your ideas and stories for this project: Mary Crickmore, Okello Gideon, Barb Harbert, Anna Ho, Nick and Tessa Laing, Leslie Mosher, Joshua Ramatlali, Renita Reed, Mike Ribbens, Opila Robert, Lawrence Temfwe, Dennis Tongoi, Chris and Terry Shindu, Samuel and Brenda Soumaila Souleymane, Steve Sywulka, Naji Umran, and Jim and Josephine Zylstra.

Raymond Mutava, Jenninah Kabiswa, Barbara Kayanja, Mary Dykstra, and Andrew Rienstra, my World Renew supervisors, thank you for your encouragement and for allowing me to integrate this project into my work. Additionally, I am grateful to all of my World Renew colleagues in East Africa who have taught me and encouraged me.

I am deeply grateful for all of my supporting churches and individuals in North America who expressed such great interest in this curriculum and faithfully prayed for me year after year. I am extremely grateful for my family and my wife's family, for their perseverance in walking with me through the long years of writing this curriculum. They have prayed for me without ceasing.

I really appreciate Lisa Brown, Justin Lonas, and the rest of the staff at the Chalmers Center. You have put in so many hours of editing and technical work behind the scenes. It truly has been a pleasure to work with all of you. Thank you for your patience with me and my perfectionist tendencies! Thank you for the grace you've shown to me in every email and meeting.

Eric Ranck and Nathaniel Veltman, you both spent many hours proofreading these lessons. Thank you for that service and sacrifice. Thank you also for so many thoughtful discussions about these topics. I've learned so much from both of you.

Lee, my brother, thank you for your steadfast affirmations, encouragements, and prayers. You are my mentor and my hero. Your attention to biblical accuracy and theological nuance while proofreading was extremely valuable.

Sara, my dear wife, you are my partner in life and ministry. Without you, I would never have been able to complete this project. We have had thousands of conversations about these topics and many tough conversations about how to wisely help specific people in our lives. I am thankful that you keep me humble, grounded in reality, and you are willing to correct me when I need it. You have spent innumerable hours proofreading all of these lessons. You have sacrificed so much of your time to serve me, to give me more time to work on this project. Most of all, I thank you for your love and encouragement.

Anthony Sytsma, Author

Notes

Line drawings at the beginning of Lessons 1, 3, 4, 6, 7, 8, 10, 11, 12, 13, 14, 15, 16, 18, 19, and 20 were drawn by Lisa Brown from photographs. The line drawings for "About this Training" and Lessons 2, 5, 9, and 17 were drawn by Justin Lonas from photographs.

Photo credits:

Lessons 1, 7, 8, 10- Tabitha Kapic, Chalmers Center

Lessons 3, 11, and 12- Adobe stock photos

Lesson 4- Musa Tukurah, World Renew

Lessons 5, 9, 14, 16, and 17-Anthony Sytsma

Lesson 6- Chris Shiundu

Lessons 13 and 18- Sean Hawkey, World Renew

Lesson 15- Juvencio Mataria, World Renew

Lessons 19 and 20- Liz Bacon, World Renew

About This Training

1. Adapted from this quotation by Michael Fairbanks: "Having a heart for the poor is easy. Having a mind for the poor is the challenge." Chad Jordan, *Rethink Missions,* (Grand Rapids, Mich.: PovertyCure, 2015), 14.
2. Wangari Maathai, *The Challenge for Africa,* (New York: Pantheon Books, 2009). Kindle, ed., Loc. 248-53.
3. Ibid., Loc. 289-94.
4. Quoted in John Battersby, "Mandela", *Christian Science Monitor* 92 (10 February, 2000), accessed online: https://www.csmonitor.com/2000/0210/p15s1.html.

Lesson 1: Introduction

1. Jordan, *Rethink Missions*, 14.
2. Battersby, "Mandela", *Christian Science Monitor*.
3. Kathleen Beegle, Luc Christaensen, Andrew Dabalen, and Isis Gaddis, *Poverty in a Rising Africa* (Washington D.C., World Bank, 2016), xi, accessed online: http://www.worldbank.org/en/region/afr/publication/poverty-rising-africa-poverty-report.
4. "Recent Economic and Social Developments in Africa", *Economic Report on Africa 2016* (New York, United Nations, 2016), 3, accessed online: http://www.uneca.org/sites/default/files/PublicationFiles/era2016_chap1_en-rev6may.pdf.
5. Beegle, et al., *Poverty in a Rising Africa*, 88.
6. Ibid., 11.
7. Dambisa Moyo, *Dead Aid: Why Aid is Not Working and How There Is a Better Way for Africa* (New York, Farrar, Straus, and Giroux, 2009), Kindle ed., Loc. 240-241.
8. Amy Frykholm, "Ending Extreme Poverty", *Christian Century*, (8 June, 2016), 133, accessed online: https://www.christiancentury.org/article/2016-05/ending-extreme-poverty?CID=POV_TT_worldbank_EN_EXT.
9. Moyo, *Dead Aid*, Kindle ed., Loc. 248-50.

10. *Economic Report on Africa 2016*, 26.

11. Beegle, et al, *Poverty in a Rising Africa*, 136.

12. Ibid., 92.

13. https://borgenproject.org/10-quick-facts-about-poverty-in-africa/.

14. Beegle, et al, *Poverty in a Rising Africa*, 12.

15. Paul Collier, *The Bottom Billion: Why the Poorest Countries Are Failing and What Can Be Done about It* (Oxford University Press, 2007), Kindle ed., Loc. 1700-1701.

Lesson 2: Why Did Jesus Come to Earth?

1. Kevin DeYoung, *What is the Mission of the Church?: Making Sense of Social Justice, Shalom, and the Great Commission*, (Crossway Books, 2011), Kindle ed., Loc. 1781-82.

2. Timothy J. Keller, *Ministries of Mercy: The Call of Jericho Road*, 2nd Ed. (Phillipsburg, N.J., P&R Publishing, 1997), 52-53.

3. Desmond Tutu, *God Has a Dream: A Vision of Hope for Our Time,* (New York, Doubleday, 2004), vii-viii.

4. Matthew Michael, *Christian Theology and African Traditions,* (Eugene, Ore., Resource Publications, 2013), Kindle ed., Loc. 5809-10.

5. From "The Kingdom in Action: A Case Study on Financial Education and Community Savings from Central Burundi, Cuba Parish, Gitega Diocese, Bugenyezi Commune", Five Talents. Used by permission.

6. Shared with the Chalmers Center by Richard Lister. A story from Nigeria of Tearfund's Church and Community Transformation program.

7. Scott Allen, Darrow L. Miller, and the African working group of Samaritan Strategy Africa, *Against All Hope: Hope for Africa,* (Phoenix, Ariz., Disciple Nations Alliance, 2005), 49, accessed online: http://www.disciplenations.org/media/Against-All-Hope-Hope-for-Africa_ENGLISH.pdf.

Lesson 3: What is Poverty?

1. World Bank, *Hear Our Voices: The Poor on Poverty*, DVD (New York: Global Vision, 2000).

2. As quoted in Deepa Narayan with Raj Patel, Kai Schafft, Anne Rademacher, Sarach Kock-Schulte, *Voices of the Poor: Can Anyone Hear Us?* (New York: Oxford Univ. Press for the World Bank, 2000), 65.

3. Ibid., 37.

4. Ibid., 70.

5. Ibid., 38.

6. Ibid., 39.

7. Ibid., 43.

8. Ibid.

9. This section is adapted from Steve Corbett and Brian Fikkert, *When Helping Hurts,* 2e (Chicago: Moody Publishers, 2012), 52-54.

10. Corbett and Fikkert, *When Helping Hurts*, 75.

11. Adapted from a story in Corbett and Fikkert, *When Helping Hurts*, 60.

Lesson 4: Broken Relationships in Africa

1. Ellie Kemp, ed., "Africa Report on Internal Displacement", (Oslo, Norwegian Refugee Council, 2016), 5, accessed online: http://www.internal-displacement.org/assets/publications/2016/2016-Africa-Report/20161209-IDMC-Africa-report-web-en.pdf.
2. Ibid.
3. Quoted in Joe McCarthy, "It's Time for a Woman to Lead the UN: Here Are 5 Candidates", (Global Citizen, 24 August, 2015), accessed online: https://www.globalcitizen.org/en/content/its-time-for-a-woman-to-lead-the-un-here-are-5-can/.
4. Quoted in Shirley A. Jones, ed., *Simply Living: The Spirit of the Indigenous People* (Novato, Calif., New World Library, 1999).
5. Luc Christensen, "Domestic Violence and Poverty in Africa: When the Husband's Beating Stick is Like Butter", (World Bank, Africa Can End Poverty blog, 18 January, 2016), accessed online: http://blogs.worldbank.org/africacan/domestic-violence-and-poverty-in-africa-when-the-husbands-beating-stick-is-like-butter.
6. "Child Labour in Africa", (International Labour Office, 2002), accessed online: http://www.ilo.org/wcmsp5/groups/public/---ed_norm/---declaration/documents/publication/wcms_decl_fs_37_en.pdf.
7. Mathaai, *The Challenge for Africa*, Loc. 3482-93.
8. John-Paul Iwuoha, "Africa's Addiction to Charcoal—Everything You Need to Know about This Billion-Dollar Business!", (Smallstarter, 15 September, 2013), accessed online: http://www.smallstarter.com/browse-ideas/how-to-start-a-charcoal-business-in-africa/.
9. "Deforestation 'Faster in Africa'", (BBC News, 26 May, 2009), accessed online: http://news.bbc.co.uk/2/hi/africa/8066871.stm.
10. Steve Nix, "The African Rainforest", (ThinkCo., 5 June 2017), accessed online: https://www.thoughtco.com/african-rainforest-1341794.
11. Bryant L. Myers, *Walking with the Poor: Principles and Practices of Transformational Development,* (Maryknoll, N.Y.: Orbis Books, 1999), 129.
12. Ibid., 127.
13. Renita Reed, "Development Malpractice in Ghana", (Reeds in the Wind blog, 24 April, 2017), accessed online: http://reedsinthewind.blogspot.com/2017/04/development-malpractice-in-ghana.html. Permission pending.

Lesson 5: Fighting Poverty through Reconciliation

1. "2016's Shocking Homelessness Statistics", Social Solutions Blog, accessed online: http://www.socialsolutions.com/blog/2016-homelessness-statistics/.
2. Desmond Tutu, *God Has a Dream: A Vision of Hope for Our Time* (New York, Doubleday, 2004), 49-50.
3. Wangari Maathai, *The Challenge for Africa,* Loc. 3975-79.
4. Taylor Smith, "Together Doing More: Breaking Barriers to End Hunger", (The Banner, October 2017), 23-24, accessed online: https://s3.amazonaws.com/prod.assets.thebanner/36907%20Banner_2017oct._final%20low%20res.pdf.

Lesson 6: Relief, Rehabilitation, and Development

1. Story shared in personal correspondence, used by permission.
2. Personal conversation with Jim Zylstra.
3. Robert D. Lupton, *Toxic Charity: How the Church Hurts Those They Help and How to Reverse It,* (San Francisco, Harper One, 2011), Kindle ed., Loc. 1438-43.
4. Mary Crickmore, "Shalom: A Manual for Christian Workers", (self-published, 2011), 69.
5. Personal Correspondence from Edward Etanu.
6. Story told by Simon Nizaramakena in the book: Scott Allen, Darrow L. Miller, and the African working group of Samaritan Strategy Africa, *Against All Hope: Hope for Africa,* (Phoenix, Ariz., Disciple Nations Alliance, 2005), 52, accessed online: http://www.disciplenations.org/media/Against-All-Hope-Hope-for-Africa_ENGLISH.pdf.

Lesson 7: Asset-Based Community Development

1. Paraphrased from Scott D. Allen and Darrow L. Miller, *The Forest in the Seed: A Biblical Perspective on Resources and Development*, (Phoenix, Ariz., the Disciple Nations Alliance, 2006), 55-56. Used by permission.
2. Summarised from Gideon Heugh, "God's Great Love", (London, Tearfund, 2017), accessed online: https://www.tearfund.org/2017/02/gods_great_love/. Used by permission.
3. Samuel and Brenda Soumalia Souleymane, personal correspondence. Used by permission.
4. Traditional. Quoted in "Called to Transformation: An Asset-Based Approach to Engaging Church and Community", (New York, Episcopal Relief, 2015), accessed online: http://calledtotransformation.org/team-building/called-to-facilitation/.
5. Tokunboh Adeyemo, ed., *Africa Bible Commentary,* (Nairobi, Grand Rapids, WordAlive/Zondervan, 2010), 25.
6. See K. A. Matthews, *Genesis 1-11:26,* Vol. 1A, (Nashville, B&H Publishers, 1996), 423.
7. Accessed online: http://reedsinthewind.blogspot.com/2018/08/when-life-gives-you-lemons.html.
8. Summarised from David Kangangi, "Entrepreneurial Spirit Activated", (World Renew, December 2017), accessed online: https://worldrenew.net/our-stories/team/entrepreneurial-spirit-activated.

Lesson 8: Opening Exercise Evaluation

- No citations.

Lesson 9: Working for God's Glory

1. Definition from Cambridge dictionary, access online: http://dictionary.cambridge.org/dictionary/english/work.
2. Jan-Emmanuel De Neve and George Ward, "Does Work Make You Happy? Evidence from the World Happiness Report", (Harvard Business Review, 20 March, 2017), accessed online: https://hbr.org/2017/03/does-work-make-you-happy-evidence-from-the-world-happiness-report.
3. Jeff Robison, "The Luther Family and the Reformation of Marriage." (the Gospel Coalition, 27 October, 2015), accessed online: https://www.thegospelcoalition.org/reviews/katharina-and-martin-luther-radical-marriage/.

4. Kenman L. Wong and Scott B. Rae, *From Business for the Common Good: A Christian Vision for the Marketplace*, Christian Worldview Integration Series, (Intervarsity Press, 2011), Loc. 1285-89.

5. Summarised from "Daring to be Daniel", (Reeds in the Wind, 16 May, 2016), accessed online: http://reedsinthewind.blogspot.com/2016/05/daring-to-be-daniel.html.

6. For the rest of the points of the manifesto go here - https://www.lausanne.org/content/wealth-creation-manifesto.

7. "Africa Statistics Flash", African Centre for Statistics of the Economic Commission for Africa, (United Nations Economic Commission for Africa, June 2017) accessed online: https://www.uneca.org/sites/default/files/uploaded-documents/ACS/africa_stat_flash_june_2017_en.pdf.

8. Video: "George Ayittey on Foreign Aid vs. African Entrepreneurship," (Poverty Cure, 21 March, 2011), accessed online: http://povertycure.org/learn/media/george-ayittey-foreign-aid-vs-african-entrepreneurship.

9. Quoted in "Education at the Sonrise School in Rwanda- Training Job Makers," accessed online: http://www.povertycure.org/learn/issues/human-person/education.

10. Chad Jordan, *Rethink Missions*, (Poverty Cure, Grand Rapids, Michigan, 2015), 29.

11. Kenman L. Wong and Scott B. Rae, *From Business for the Common Good*, Loc. 1589.

12. "Africa's Dream: Ghana's Herman Chinery Hesse," (BBC, 6 September, 2011), accessed online: http://www.bbc.com/news/world-africa-14793780.

13. "Wealth Creation: A Godly Gift and Command", (Transformational SME, 23 August, 2016), accessed online: http://www.transformationalsme.org/tag/business-is-a-noble-vocation/.

14. A Quote from John Wesley, (Good Reads), accessed online: https://www.goodreads.com/quotes/113423-earn-all-you-can-give-all-you-can-save-all.

15. Tim Keller, sermon, "Treasure Vs. Money" 1999, on Matthew 6:19-34: access online: https://gospelinlife.com/downloads/treasure-vs-money-5088/.

16. Shortened and edited from original, and used with permission from Leslie Mosher, from curriculum – *Entrepreneurship: Christ Centered Business Education*, Session 1: "Preparing your Spirit and Mind", 14.

17. Summarised and partially quoted from Jim Zylstra, "Vocational Skills Training Changed my Life", (World Renew, 11 May, 2017) accessed online: http://worldrenew.net/our-stories/team/vocational-skills-training-changed-my-life.

18. Scott Allen, Darrow L. Miller, and the African working group of Samaritan Strategy Africa, *Against All Hope: Hope for Africa*, (Phoenix, Ariz., Disciple Nations Alliance, 2005), 51, accessed online: http://www.disciplenations.org/media/Against-All-Hope-Hope-for-Africa_ENGLISH.pdf.

19. "Insights: The Need to Invest in Africa's Emerging Economies", (the Foresight Initiative 1 December, 2014) accessed online: http://theforesightinitiative.org/thejournal/2014/12/1/insights-the-need-to-invest-in-emerging-african-economies.

20. "Business as Mission," Lausanne Occasional Paper No. 59, (Lausanne Committee for World Evangelization, Pattaya, Thailand 2004) access online: https://www.lausanne.org/docs/2004forum/LOP59_IG30.pdf.

Lesson 10: Worldview Transformation

1. Lisa Kemmerer, *Animals and World Religions*. (Oxford University Press, 2011), pp. 100–101, 110.

2. Personal Correspondence from Joshua Ramatlali.

3. Edited from Anna Ho, Executive director of Reconciled World, "Truth-Centered Transformation" Presentation, used with permission.

4. ibid.

5. Many ideas in this section come from Gayle Van Rheenen, "Animism, Secularism and Theism: Developing a Tripartite Model for Understanding World Cultures," (IJFM, October 1993) accessed online: http://www.ijfm.org/PDFs_IJFM/10_4_PDFs/04_Van_Rheenen.pdf.

6. From notes taken during a presentation on worldview by Dennis Tongoi.

7. Scott Allen, Darrow L. Miller, and the African working group of Samaritan Strategy Africa, *Against All Hope: Hope for Africa* (Phoenix, Ariz., Disciple Nations Alliance, 2005), 43, accessed online: http://www.disciplenations.org/media/Against-All-Hope-Hope-for-Africa_ENGLISH.pdf.

8. https://www.brainyquote.com/quotes/authors/k/kofi_annan.html.

9. Van Rheenen, "Animism...", Page 1 (pg.169).

10. ibid. 2.

11. From notes taken during a presentation on worldview by Dennis Tongoi.

Lesson 11: Broken Systems

1. "Can Africa Afford Free Education?", *Global Education Monitoring Report*, (World Education Blog, 27 January, 2017) accessed online: https://gemreportunesco.wordpress.com/2016/01/27/can-africa-afford-free-education/.

2. Many of these ideas taken from "State of education in Africa report 2015", (The Africa-America Institute, New York, NY 2015) accessed online: http://www.aaionline.org/wp-content/uploads/2015/09/AAI-SOE-report-2015-final.pdf.

3. Ibid.

4. https://www.vocabulary.com/dictionary/bureaucracy.

5. Dambisa Moyo, *Dead Aid: Why Aid is Not Working and How There Is a Better Way for Africa* (New York, Farrar, Straus, and Giroux, 2009), Kindle ed., Location 1706-9.

6. Ibid., Loc 1717-20.

7. Daniel J. Cantor, Juliet B. Schor, *Tunnel Vision: Labor, the World Economy, and Central America*, (South End Press, 1987), p. 21.

8. Carmody Pádraig, *The New Scramble for Africa*, 2nd ed., (Polity; 24 October, 2016) Highlight Loc. 3069-72.

9. Ibid., Highlight Loc. 1450-53.

10. Shah, Anup, "Structural Adjustment—a Major Cause of Poverty", (Global Issues, July, 2007).

11. Stephanie Hanson, "Corruption in Sub-Saharan Africa", Transparency International (Council on Foreign Relations, 6 August, 2009) accessed online: https://www.cfr.org/backgrounder/corruption-sub-saharan-africa.

12. Moreau, A. S., Netland, H., & Engen, C. *Evangelical Dictionary of World Missions*, (Baker Reference Library, Grand Rapids, MI; 2000), 233.

13. Kenman L. Wong and Scott B. Rae, *Business for the Common Good: A Christian Vision for the*

Marketplace, Christian Worldview Integration Series, (Intervarsity Press, 2011), Kindle Loc. 2991-96.

14. https://www.lausanne.org/networks/issues/integrity-and-anti-corruption.

15. Robert Longley, "The End of South Africa's Apartheid", (Thought Co. May 2018) access online: https://www.thoughtco.com/when-did-apartheid-end-43456.

16. Tanya Glaser, "Summary of 'Truth and Reconciliation Commission; South Africa'", (Beyond Intractability, retrieved 3 March 2020) access online: https://www.beyondintractability.org/artsum/reconciliation-truth.

17. "How Nelson Mandela Tried to Heal the Wounds of Apartheid" (CBS December 2013), access online: https://www.cbsnews.com/news/how-mandela-tried-to-heal-the-wounds-of-apartheid/.

18. Many of the ideas in this section come from: "Aid vs. Trade," (EIIFF) accessed online: http://www.eiiff.com/aid/trade.html.

19. Paul Collier, *The Bottom Billion: Why the Poorest Countries Are Failing and What Can Be Done about It* (Oxford University Press, 2007), Kindle ed., Loc. 1716.

20. Quoted by Dambisa Moyo, *Dead Aid: Why Aid is Not Working and How There Is a Better Way for Africa* (New York, Farrar, Straus, and Giroux, 2009), Kindle ed., Loc 2489-91.

21. From an interview with Kofi Annan by *The Globalist*, (6 February, 2001), access online: https://www.theglobalist.com/kofi-annan-on-global-futures/.

22. Paul Collier, *The Bottom Billion*, Kindle ed., Loc. 2502-13.

23. Wangari Maathai, *The Challenge for Africa* (New York: Pantheon Books, 2009). Kindle, ed., Loc. 1826-45.

24. Renita Reed, personal correspondence and access online: http://reedsinthewind.blogspot.com/2016_05_30_archive.html.

25. Personal Correspondence from Tessa Laing.

26. Mary Crickmore, "Shalom: A Manual for Christian Workers", (self-published, 2011), 15.

Lesson 12: The Prosperity Gospel

1. https://www.lausanne.org/content/ctc/ctcommitment.

2. Some of the points are borrowed from: Michael Otieno Maura, Conrad Mbewe, Ken Mbugua, John Piper, Wayne Grudem, *Prosperity? Seeking the True Gospel*, (Africa Christian Textbooks Registered Trustees, Kenya, 2015) Published in partnership with the Gospel Coalition, 3.

3. ibid, 15.

4. For more on this topic see Kelly Kapic, *Embodied Hope*, (Downer's Grove, Illinois, IVP Academic June 6, 2017).

5. Michael Otieno Maura, et al. *Prosperity? Seeking the True Gospel*, 27.

6. ibid, 5-6.

7. Kwabena Asamoah-Gyadu, "The Prosperity Gospel and its Challenge to Mission in our Time", (Lausanne Movement, July 2014), access online: https://www.lausanne.org/content/lga/2014-07/the-prosperity-gospel-and-its-challenge-to-mission-in-our-time.

8. J. Lee Grady, "Five Ways Prosperity Gospel is Hurting Africa", (Charisma Magazine, January

2013), access online: https://www.charismamag.com/blogs/fire-in-my-bones/19113-5-ways-the-prosperity-gospel-is-hurting-africa.

9. Michael Otieno Maura, et al., *Prosperity? Seeking the True Gospel*, 29-31.
10. Joe Carter, "What You Should Know about the Prosperity Gospel", (The Gospel Coalition, May, 2017), access online: https://www.thegospelcoalition.org/article/what-you-should-know-about-the-prosperity-gospel.
11. Köstenberger, A. J. *John: Series Baker Exegetical Commentary on the New Testament* (Grand Rapids, MI: Baker Academic, 2004)., 433–434.
12. The Africa Chapter of the Lausanne Theology Working Group's "Statement on the Prosperity Gospel", access online: https://www.lausanne.org/content/a-statement-on-the-prosperity-gospel.
13. See Brian Fikkert and Kelly Kapic, *Becoming Whole*, (Chicago, Illinois, Moody, 2019).

Lesson 13: African Culture and Money

1. David Maranz, *African Friends and Money Matters*, (SIL International, Dallas Texas, 2015), 1.
2. Ibid. 25.
3. Ibid. 25.
4. Story from Chad Jordan, *Rethink Missions*, (Poverty Cure, Grand Rapids, Michigan, 2015), 16.
5. Stephen Dovers and Colin Butler, "Population and Environment: A Global Challenge", (Australian Academy of Science), access online: https://www.science.org.au/curious/earth-environment/population-environment.
6. "Causes and Consequences of Overpopulation", (Acciona), access online: https://www.activesustainability.com/sustainable-development/causes-consequences-overpopulation/.
7. Dovers and Butler, "Population and Environment".
8. Ibid.
9. Vandenbroucke, Guillaume, "The Link between Fertility and Income", Federal Reserve Bank of St Louis (13 December, 2016, USA), access online: https://www.stlouisfed.org/on-the-economy/2016/december/link-fertility-income.
10. Burton, James, "30 Countries With The Youngest Populations In The World," (WorldAtlas, April 2017) access online: https://www.worldatlas.com/articles/the-youngest-populations-in-the-world.html.
11. Statistics from: https://www.nichd.nih.gov/health/topics/infertility/conditioninfo/common.

Lesson 14: What Causes Change in Someone's Life?

1. Activity taken from https://change.walkme.com/7-fun-and-engaging-change-management-exercises/.
2. Samuel and Brenda Soumalia Souleymane, personal correspondence. Used with permission.
3. Mary Crickmore, "Shalom: A Manual for Christian Workers", (self-published, 2011), 22.

Lesson 15: Participation of the Community

1. For more ideas on how communities and organisations can hold each other accountable and have healthy partnerships, read about the Core Humanitarian Standard - https://corehumanitarianstandard.org/the-standard.
2. Mary Crickmore, "Shalom: A Manual for Christian Workers", (self-published, 2011), 54.
3. ibid., 55.
4. If you are in need of a good savings curriculum, see this free resource available from the Chalmers Center, called *Restore: Savings*. https://chalmers.org/restore-savings/.

Lesson 16: Church Benevolence Ministry

1. Many ideas in this segment are drawn from Steve Corbett and Brian Fikkert with Katie Casselberry, *Helping Without Hurting in Church Benevolence,* (Chicago: Moody Publishers, 2015), 52-53, 57. Used by permission of Moody Publishers.
2. Brian Fikkert and Russel Mask, *From Dependence to Dignity*, (Zondervan, Grand Rapids Michigan, 2015).
3. Edited from *Helping without Hurting in Church Benevolence,* 53.
4. ibid. 57.
5. This form has been adapted with permission from the Chalmers Center website: https://chalmers.org/wp-content/uploads/2018/09/HWH_Benev_Tool_2_Intake_Form.pdf.
6. These questions are adapted *HWH in CB* from 52-53.
7. This form has been adapted from the Chalmers Center website, accessed here: https://chalmers.org/wp-content/uploads/2018/09/HWH_Benev_Tool_3_Action_Plan.pdf.

Lesson 17: Urban Ministry: Opportunities and Challenges

1. City, (2019), In Vocabulary.com, access online: https://www.vocabulary.com/dictionary/city.
2. Marian Starkey, "African Urbanization", (Population Connection, January 28, 2015), access online: https://www.populationconnection.org/article/african-urbanization/.
3. See *World Urbanization Prospects: the 2014 Revision* (United Nations, New York, 2014), 1, access online: https://esa.un.org/unpd/wup/publications/files/wup2014-highlights.pdf.
4. Mariama Sow, "Foresight Africa 2016: Urbanization in the African Context", (Brookings Institution, Washington DC, 30 December 2015), access online: https://www.brookings.edu/blog/africa-in-focus/2015/12/30/foresight-africa-2016-urbanization-in-the-african-context/.
5. Somik Vinay Lall, J. Vernon Henderson, Anthony J. Venables, *African Cities: Opening Doors to the World*, (the World Bank, Washington DC, 2017), 38, access online: http://documents.worldbank.org/curated/en/854221490781543956/122290272_201711346052345/additional/113851-PUB-PUBLIC-PUBDATE-2-9-2017.pdf.
6. Ibid.,48.
7. Ibid., 140.
8. Ibid., 88.
9. "Unemployment Threatens World Cities; Jobs are Needed to Check Growth in Urban Poverty",

(International Labour Office, 29 May, 1996), access online: https://www.ilo.org/global/about-the-ilo/newsroom/news/WCMS_008055/lang--en/index.htm.

10. Timothy Keller, *Center Church: Doing Balanced, Gospel-Centered Ministry in Your City*, (Zondervan, Grand Rapids, Michigan, 4 September, 2012), Loc. 3858-62.

11. Ibid., Loc. 3865-67.

12. Ibid., Loc. 3899-3905.

13. Ibid., Loc. 3938-43.

14. Ibid., Loc. 4796-4800.

15. Ibid., Loc. 4197-4202.

16. Timothy Keller, Twitter Post, 9 January 2014, 7:31AM, Access online: https://twitter.com/dailykeller/status/421257802854592512?lang=en.

17. Timothy Keller, *Center Church*, Loc. 4453-4505.

18. *On Orphans*, (UNICEF, 16 June, 2017), access online: https://www.unicef.org/media/media_45279.html.

19. Jack Graham, "Rwanda Wants to Become Africa's First Orphanage-free Country-Here's How", (Apolitical, 24 May, 2018) access online: https://apolitical.co/solution_article/rwanda-wants-to-become-africas-first-orphanage-free-country-heres-how/?fbclid=IwAR1Y9s5BPpsv7kkOxHP_YYZ7uu8kO45hjXSqDg4cOB9GopW-VZEISKnTNqQ.

20. Ibid.

21. Conrad Mbewe, "Orphans, Adoption and the African Extended Family", (The Gospel Coalition, 31 December, 2018) accesss online: https://africa.thegospelcoalition.org/article/orphans-adoption-african-extended-family/.

22. For summaries of the research, see the following:

    Save the Children Policy Brief, Institutional Care: the Last Resort, (May 2014) access online: http://www.thinkchildsafe.org/thinkbeforedonating/wp-content/uploads/Institutional-Care-The-Last-Resort-Save-The-Children.pdf

    Faith to Action Initiative, Children, Orphanges, and Families, (2014), access online: http://www.faithtoaction.org/wp-content/uploads/2014/03/Summary-of-Research4.pdf

23. Camaleo, "Orphanages Need to be Closed and Here is Why", (17 July, 2017), access online: http://camaleoproject.org/en/orphanages-need-to-be-closed-here-is-why/.

24. Jack Graham, "Rwanda Wants...".

25. US Department of State fact sheet: "Child Institutionalization and Human Trafficking", (28 June, 2018), access online: https://www.state.gov/child-institutionalization-and-human-trafficking/#:~:targetText=Orphanages%20have%20also%20kept%20children,sympathy%20and%20money%20from%20donors.&targetText=These%20orphanages%20facilitate%20child%20trafficking,them%20to%20profit%20from%20donations.

26. In this light, some are trying to develop best practices for orphanages. See Philip Darke and Keith McFarland, *In Pursuit of Orphan Excellence*, (Credo House Publishers, Grand Rapids, Michigan, 2014).

27. Conrad Mbewe, "Orphans, Adoption...".

28. Scott Allen, Darrow L. Miller, and the African working group of Samaritan Strategy Africa,

Against All Hope: Hope for Africa, (Phoenix, Ariz., Disciple Nations Alliance, 2005), 50, accessed online: http://www.disciplenations.org/media/Against-All-Hope-Hope-for-Africa_ENGLISH.pdf.

29. Danny McCain, "Addressing Urban Problems Through Kingdom Theology: The 'Apostles in the Market Place' Model in Lagos, Nigeria", (Africa Journal of Evangelical Theology 32.1 page 61-80, 2013), 68, View in PDF format pdf [Reproduced by permission of the current copyright holder]: https://www.biblicalstudies.org.uk/pdf/ajet/32-1_061.pdf.

Lesson 18: Mission Trips Within Africa

1. Many of the concepts in this chapter are based on ideas from Brian Fikkert and Steve Corbett, *Helping Without Hurting in Short-Term Missions*, (Moody Publishers, Chicago, IL, 2014).

Lesson 19: Foreigners, Missionaries, and Sponsors

1. Mary Crickmore, "Shalom: A Manual for Christian Workers", (self-published, 2011), 45-46.
2. For more information on CHS go to https://corehumanitarianstandard.org/the-standard.
3. For more information on the ECFA go to https://www.ecfa.org/. For more information on Charity Navigator go to https://www.charitynavigator.org/.
4. Carmody Pádraig, *The New Scramble for Africa*, 2nd ed., (Polity; 24 October, 2016) Highlight Loc. 3069-72.
5. Ibid., Highlight Loc. 3077-81.
6. Ibid., Highlight Loc. 4412-13.
7. Ibid., Highlight Loc. 4535-39.
8. Brian Fikkert and Kelly Kapic. *A Field guide to Becoming Whole*, Moody (Chicago: Moody Publishers, 2019), 86.
9. Ibid., 87.

Lesson 20: Seed Projects and Further Resources

1. Steve Corbett and Brian Fikkert with Katie Casselberry, *Helping Without Hurting in Church Benevolence,* (Chicago: Moody Publishers, 2015), 147.
2. Quote taken from a speech given by Obiageli Ezekwesili at the Time 100 Gala, 21 April 2015. Speech can be heard here: https://praisephilly.com/2669383/bring-back-our-girls-founder-obiageli-ezekwesili-gives-emotional-speech-at-time-100-gala/
3. Adapted from *If Jesus Were Mayor* by Bob Moffitt (2006, Monarch Books), chapter 13: "Seed Project Planning", page 1, Adaptation by Disciple Nation and can be found here: http://www.disciplenations.org/media/Seed-Projects-Overview-and-Planning-Guide.pdf
4. Ibid., page 1.
5. Desmond Tutu, Quote re-published by the Desmond Tutu Peace Foundation (7 October, 2015), Access online: http://www.tutufoundationusa.org/2015/10/07/10-pieces-of-wisdom-from-desmond-tutu-on-his-birthday/
6. Timothy Leadership Training, Caring for God's People 6e, (Timothy Leadership Training Institute, 2016), 13.
7. ibid., 13.

Notes

Notes

Notes

Notes

Notes

Notes

OASIS INTERNATIONAL

Satisfying Africa's Thirst for God's Word

Our mission is to grow discipleship through publishing African voices.
Go to oasisinternationalpublishing.com to learn more.

HIGHLY FAVOURED: OUR POWERFUL GOD'S COVENANT WITH YOU
Stuart J. Foster
The God of the Bible is not unreliable or inaccessible like the spiritual beings in African traditional religions. He chooses to have a covenant relationship with his people and we do not have to earn God's favour.

AFRICANS AND AFRICA IN THE BIBLE
Tim Welch
This book shows the presence and the participation of Africans in the biblical text, helping demonstrate that Christianity is not a "white man's religion" and that Christianity has deep roots in African soil.

AFRICAN CHRISTIAN THEOLOGY REVISITED
Richard J. Gehman
For all African Christians, *African Christian Theology Revisited* is a powerful plea to think through your faith in African contexts under the authority of the Word of God.

PARENTING WITH PURPOSE & AFRICAN WISDOM
Gladys K. Mwiti
This practical guide for Christians is a relevant, thoughtful presentation on the characteristics of parenting that delivers results.

ANSWERS FOR YOUR MARRIAGE
Bruce and Carol Britten
Offers practical insights to marriage issues and facts on sex, pregnancy, family planning, child-raising, money issues, adultery, HIV, and sex-related diseases. If your marriage is in despair, look to this book for some answers for your marriage.

LEARNING TO LEAD
Richard J. Gehman
With its discussion questions and practical applications, this book will guide you to obtaining character and skills, and help you become an effective Christian leader. It was written from the living experience of African leaders, and it has been shaped by 36 years of training church leaders in Kenya.

HABITS OF HIGHLY EFFECTIVE CHRISTIANS
Ron Meyers
In today's world of rushed deadlines and hurried lives, it's easy to forget that the Bible holds principles that provide a proper foundation for living. Learn about 17 habits that can help you lead a more fulfilling, healthy life both professionally and personally. Challenge how you think about the way we live in the 21st century.

BIBLICAL CHRISTIANITY IN MODERN AFRICA
Wilbur O'Donovan
Biblical Christianity in Modern Africa describes the major issues facing the church in Africa and offers suggestions on how these problems can be overcome.

OASIS INTERNATIONAL PUBLISHING

oasisinternationalpublishing.com | oasisinternational.com

AFRICA STUDY BIBLE
OASIS
AFRICA STUDY BIBLE
NLT